Unfairly
Structured
Cities

To the spirit that was Mandala

Unfairly Structured Cities

BLAIR BADCOCK

Basil Blackwell

First published 1984
Basil Blackwell Publisher Limited
108 Cowley Road, Oxford OX4 1JF, England

British Library Cataloguing in Publication Data

Badcock, Blair
  Unfairly structured cities.
  1. Cities and towns
  I. Title
  307'.3   GF125
    ISBN 0-631-13395-X
    ISBN 0-631-13396-8 Pbk

Typesetting by Oxford Verbatim Limited
Printed in Great Britain by
TJ Press Ltd., Padstow

Contents

Preface

Unfairly structured cities is not for beginners. It is designed for use in urban studies programmes by third or fourth year tertiary students. While the text's object – urban space – commends its use in geography courses in particular, I anticipate that it will also have broad appeal to students reading urban and regional planning, urban sociology, and maybe even politics or economics; indeed, the contents are trans-disciplinary. As the title suggests, I have endeavoured to *fuse* an account of the processes that structure cities with questions of justice in relation to resource allocation within cities. Although this suggests an explicitly urban focus, readers will encounter a perspective broad enough to embrace the more general societal processes that impinge upon both the development of advanced capitalist cities, and living conditions within them. To be more specific, British, US and Australian cities form the core of the analysis. Through the drawing of comparisons it should be possible to demonstrate the particularity of urban outcomes; that is, the patterns and processes obtained under conditions which are, often mistakenly, assumed to be identical because of the obvious resemblance of the capitalist social formations that have evolved in the United Kingdom, the United States and Australia.

Now that some sort of steady-state has been regained after what amounts to a theoretical metamorphosis in urban and regional studies, the time is ripe for a recasting of the materials available for urban courses. Naturally a text such as this must represent a departure from the standard approach of the generation of urban texts that it seeks to replace. One of my principal aims is to evaluate many of the recent 'markers' in urban theory, and provide a bridge between them and the huge library of materials in urban and regional studies. The text by design is critical and deliberately provocative in places, expressive of the author's personal values, and conscious of the pertinence of policy. Those concerned about the epistemology will find that after the critique of positivist urban theory in Part I, the rest of the analysis is couched in a form which is implicitly compatible with a realist conception of science.

Because of the ambitious scope of the text a number of sacrifices have been made. Firstly, at times I have had to assume considerable background knowledge on the part of readers approaching the material from outside my own discipline. I have tried to overcome this drawback by directing such readers to additional references in the literature. Also, because some of the territory will be unfamiliar and some of the theory pretty dense at times, the book is well signposted and 'written down' for easier assimilation. Secondly, some topics and issues are omitted altogether – the growth of the urban system, urban development during the interwar years, the busing programme in US cities – while others may not be treated in enough depth for students with specialized interests. Urban sociologists, for example, will find the allusions to class insufficiently well developed for their needs. Thirdly, I do not always manage to deal systematically or evenhandedly with processes or phenomena in each section of the discussion. Sometimes, I prefer to look selectively, instead, at the exemplary case or development in order to highlight the differences in the British, American and Australian urban experience. I firmly believe that these concessions are worth making because a comparative approach does yield important theoretical and substantive insights that tend to be glossed over or missed altogether in single-society case studies.

As to the substance of the book, Part I presents a critique of the two main positivist frameworks: the modelling of residential location, and the view of the city as a resource distributing mechanism. Part II is given over to the rudiments of a political economy of urban space, in which capital is represented as the architect of spatial structures. Part III endeavours to determine in what sense and to what degree the use of urban space and social provision within capitalist cities are subsidiary sources of inequity and redistribution. The concluding part reports the demise of 'spatial' policy, not necessarily as a casualty of the state's disengagement from urban programmes, and canvasses a range of alternative approaches to redistribution (including the socialist vision as it is taking shape in Communist cities, and versions of the social democratic model in Western Europe).

A venture such as this leaves one indebted to a host of people. Firstly, thanks are due to John Davey for the sure editorial direction and judgement he has given the project from the start. Peter Williams not only read large parts of the manuscript when he was under pressure, but he also acted as a sounding-board throughout. His generosity is greatly appreciated. Peter Saunders, Andrew Parkin, and Mike Berry also brought their particular expertise to bear upon those segments of the text that encroach on their discipline. Although I have benefited from the shared thoughts of all these people the usual disclaimers apply. The real toilers, of course, are the typists – Joanna Gagliardi, Jeanette Brooker, Branka King – and cartographers – Chris Crothers, Debbie Oakley, Max Foale – who prepared the manuscript for publication. More generally I am grateful to my colleagues in the department at Adelaide for their forbearance during the writing of this text; not to mention the Honours and third year students who have participated in the courses that it is based upon. Lastly, and closer to home, I have been supported by Carole and the boys who, amongst other things, went without their summer holidays in 1982–83.

Acknowledgements

The publisher and author would like to thank the following for permission to reproduce these materials:

(Figure 1.2) Macmillan Publishing Co. Inc., for figure 7.14, pp. 128–9, in Berry, B. J. L., and Kasarda, J. D.: *Contemporary urban ecology*; (figure 1.4) Macmillan Press Ltd., for figure 8.6, p. 126, in Evans, A. W.: *The economics of residential location*; (figure 3.1) Methuen and Co. Ltd., for figures 3.1a–e, pp. 53–8, in Dear, M., and Scott, A. J. (eds): *Urbanization and urban planning in capitalist societies*; (figure 3.2) Edward Arnold (Publishers) Ltd., for figure 5.3, p. 109, in Harvey, D. W.: The urban process under capitalism: a framework for analysis, *International Journal of Urban and Regional Research*, **2**, 1; (figure 6.4, table 6.7) Australian Institute of Urban Studies and Dr H. L. Kendig, for figure 8.1, p. 136, and table 2.2, p. 20, in Kendig, H.: *Buying and renting: household moves in Adelaide*; (figure 6.5) Longman Cheshire Pty. Ltd., for figures 4.1–3, pp. 77–9, in Logan, M. I., Maher, C. A., McKay, J., and Humphreys, J. S.: *Urban and regional Australia: analysis and policy issues*; (figure 11.1) Frederick A. Praeger Inc., Publishers, for the diagram on p. 12 in Taubman, W.: *Governing Soviet cities*; (figure 11.2) Pergamon Press Ltd., for figure 3.1, p. 118, in Jeffrey, N., and Caldwell, M., Planning and urbanism in China, *Progress in Planning*, **8**, Part 2; (table 4.1) the MIT Press, for data from tables 4.1 and 4.3, pp. 146–8 in Pred, A.: *The spatial dynamics of US urban-industrial growth, 1800–1914*; (table 4.2) Routledge and Kegan Paul Ltd., for table 17.4, p. 424, in Dyos, H. J., and Wolff, M. (eds): *The Victorian city – images and realities*; (table 4.4) Routledge and Kegan Paul Ltd., for the data tabulated on p. 290, in Kellett, J. R.: *The impact of railways on Victorian cities*; (table 4.5) Oxford University Press, for data selected from p. 176, in Stedman Jones, G.: *Outcast London*; (table 5.5) Sage Publications Inc. and Professor W. W. Rostow, for table 3, p. 93, in Perry, D. C., and Watkins, A. J. (eds): *The Rise of the sunbelt cities*, vol. 14, Urban Affairs Annual Reviews; (table 6.3) Allen Lane Publishers, for table 5.27, p. 226, in Townsend, P.: *Poverty in the United Kingdom*; (table 7.8) Dr R. King, for table 4.4, p. 50, in King, R.: *Interest rates, energy and house prices: some aspects of the Melbourne housing market, 1966–80*; (table 8.4) Harper and Row Publishers Inc., for table 8.2,

p. 233, in Lineberry, R. L., and Sharkansky, I.: *Urban politics and public policy*; (table 8.6) Oxford University Press, for table 3.5, p. 40, in Johnston, R. J.: *Political, electoral and spatial systems*; (table 8.7) Sage Publications Inc. and Professor R. L. Lineberry, for table 5.1, p. 107, in Lineberry, R. L.: *Equality and urban policy*; (table 9.1) Centre for Urban Policy Research, for the exhibit on p. 364, in Sternlieb, G., and Hughes, J. W. (eds): *America's housing: prospects and problems*; (table 10.1) P. N. Troy, for table 2, p. 140, in Troy, P. N.: *A fair price. The Land Commission Program, 1972–77*, (table 11.2) Macmillan Press Ltd., for table 8.9, p. 227, in Schapiro, L., and Godson, J. (eds): *The Soviet worker*.

Part I
Putting Space in its Place

This part of *Unfairly structured cities* is given over to a critical evaluation of what one might describe as the mainstream fare in urban spatial theory. In order to set the later work in perspective it is necessary to appreciate that while several of the approaches reviewed may appear to be in competition, they share a common bond to the extent that they are all grounded in a positivist epistemology. Chapter 1 begins, therefore, by briefly outlining the implications for urban analysis of adopting this particular conception of science in preference to realism or conventionalism (see Keat and Urry, 1975). The rest of the chapter is given over to a critique of ecological and neoclassical theories of the city. One difficulty with some of the pioneering work in urban ecology is that it tended to degenerate into a crude determinism wherein spatial structures were believed to determine patterns of social organization. Likewise, it is partly because the modelling of spatial relations, regularities and properties becomes an end in itself in so much neoclassical urban analysis that its critics argue that the approach is impoverished.

In chapter 2 the conception of the city as a resource distributing mechanism is examined. The concept reflects the realignment in thinking that took place within the social sciences with the rediscovery of poverty in US and British cities during the mid-1960s, and with a revival of interest in questions of social justice. Because the ideal of *distributive justice* is woven into the text, chapter 2 contains an evaluation (which is a little more discursive than usual) of the prevalent ideas about social justice, equality and equity, and universality and selectivity in redistribution. This is followed by a review of the three main liberal conceptualizations of the mechanisms that determine 'who gets what where?' in advanced capitalistic cities: Smith's 'welfare' approach; Harvey's model of the redistribution of real income by the urban property system; and Pahl's 'managerialist' framework.

Chapter 2 also serves a related purpose, to inter the notion that somehow space, in itself, is an original or even independent source of inequality. It is apparent that space is inert until it is transformed by social processes, and that the most damaging and persistent inequalities are structural. Space functions, at best, to reinforce or mediate structurally determined inequalities. Nonetheless, socially transformed space should not be condemned to total passivity: 'social practices are spatially patterned, and . . . these patterns substantially affect these very social practices' (Urry, 1981: 456).

1

Positivist Explanations of
Residential Differentiation

Positivism reigns . . . positive?

This book was conceived, in the healthiest sense, as a reaction to the mainstream fare in geography. Naturally, disaffection does not take place in a vacuum. Reaction to and disaffection from what . . .? In a nutshell, the epistemology, the method, and the value assumptions inherent to logical positivism in geography.

So what is this positivism? During the 1950s several small cells of workers in US universities developed the beginnings of the approach and tools that presaged a fundamental change in the way geographers viewed and analyzed the world about them. The approach that these geographers and their adherents adopted and propagated is the scientific method known as logical positivism. Whether this development elevated geography to the status of a science is a matter of judgement. The characterizing feature of this approach can be regarded as spatial analysis. Nevertheless, positivism came to dominate human geography along with the other social sciences during the 1950s and 1960s.

Positive versus realist science

The following encapsulation of the key features of the positivist and realist conceptions of science is taken from a short article by John Urry (1981) who, himself, has further refined the material presented jointly with Russell Keat (Keat and Urry, 1975). They draw mainly on Hempel (1965) and Popper (1959) for the positivist philosophy of science and Harré (1970) for the realist view of explanation. For the positivist, science is the means by which observers attempt to gain predictive and explanatory knowledge of the world around them. The positivist proceeds by constructing theories, or highly generalized statements (laws) which express the regular relationships between separate, discrete events arising in the natural world. Positivism provides a particular approach to explaining and predicting events:

To explain something is to show that it is an instance of these regularities or laws; and predictions consist of the deducing of empirical consequences from such laws. Empirical testing of laws through observation and experimentation is the only sure basis of knowledge. It is not the purpose of science to get behind these empirically demonstrable regular relationships to give us knowledge of mechanisms or essences which might somehow necessitate these phenomena. According to the positivist there are no necessary or logical connections in nature. There are only regularities, successions of separate events or phenomena which can be represented within the universal laws of science. Logical relations consist in deducing empirical consequences from the laws and antecedent conditions. (Urry, 1981: 459)

Positivist precepts and methods were widely adopted in human geography throughout the sixties, some would say in a bid for scientific respectability:

hypotheses were tested, paradigms traded, models proposed, theories suggested, explanations offered, systems simulated, and laws sorely sought after. This search for order was directed more by available techniques than by a set of coherent objectives; reality was ransacked in search of theory. (Smith, 1979: 356)

Although somewhat jaundiced, this assessment of Smith's nonetheless conveys the sense of great intellectual excitement and discovery that characterized human geography during the 1960s. With the benefit of hindsight it is possible to say that much of this energy was misguided, since once one accepts that space is formed by societal processes rather than *intrinsically* spatial processes, a general science of spatial relations is negated.

The realist is committed to an ontology which seeks to discover the structures or mechanisms that lie behind the separate and discrete empirical events or phenomena under observation. Realist science is based on the premise that these structures or mechanisms are not always readily apparent in events or phenomena (spatial distributions); and that, accordingly, there are two orders of reality: 'That of persistently enduring real structures, and that of certain events and phenomena to which the former contingently give rise, if they, are placed in an appropriate spatial relationship (Urry, 1981: 461). The realist, therefore, advocates that science should concern itself with the constitution of these structures or mechanisms, with describing how they are formed, their powers, and how they respond to changes. For the realist, 'a scientific theory is a description of structures and mechanisms which causally generate the

observable phenomena, a description which enables us to explain them'
(Keat and Urry, 1975: 5).

Finding fault with positivism

Logical positivism dominated human geography for the best part of two
decades, from its premature championing by Schaefer (1953), to its final,
symbolic enclosure with the publication of *An introduction to scientific
reasoning in geography* (Amedeo and Golledge, 1975). By the beginning of
the 1970s positivism in social science was being assailed on all sides
(Andreski, 1972; Marcuse, 1964). It is the shortcomings of urban 'spatial'
models in an explanatory capacity that has led many geographers to
discard them. Johnston (1980: 404), for example, is critical of King and
Golledge (1978) for conferring the status of *theory* or *law* upon the
empirical regularity known as the rank-size rule, when, in fact, 'this rule
contains no explanatory power whatsoever.' That spatial analysis was in
danger of suffocation and atrophy was being recognized from 'within' by
the seventies. Several of the most trenchant critics of spatial analysis had
actually been instrumental in developing its methods and concepts.
Significantly, no sooner had David Harvey completed the definitive statement on the epistemology and methodology of logical positivism in
geography (Harvey, 1969a), than he was circulating drafts of a paper in
which he condemns the recycling of 'inhouse' generalizations: 'marginal
returns are apparently setting in as yet another piece of factorial ecology,
yet another attempt to measure distance decay effect, yet another attempt
to identify the range of a good, serve to tell us less and less about anything
of great relevance' (Harvey, 1971: 9). Leslie King, who wrote the text
Statistical analysis in geography (King, 1969), expressed an opinion in 1976
that: 'Much current formal theoretical work in economic and urban geography appears to be heading in the wrong direction' (King, 1976: 308);
while Ron Johnston, who has been nothing less than prodigious in the
cause of spatial analysis, recently decried the 'explanatory sterility of both
spatial science and behavioural geography' (Johnston, 1980: 411).

This sense of disillusion with the fruits of positivism in human geography also carried over into urban and regional studies (Massey, 1978:
Massey *et al.*, 1976; Sayer, 1976 and 1979): much of the theory about the
city was caught in a spatial 'vortex'. Objections have been raised, as shown
below, on methodological, epistemological and ideological grounds. Out
of all this questioning has come a new-found vitality in urban and regional
studies. Many of these new ways of looking at the same phenomena are
incorporated in the discussion that follows. This revitalization in urban
and regional research has its basis in the healthy tension created amongst
the various proposals for a superior theory of city-forming processes.
There is no doubt that our understanding of the city has been resuscitated

by this fermenting of ideas and perspectives. This has lent force to Hugh Stretton's (1978a: 15) belief that, 'every social science *ought* to harbour rival theories and methods'.

In moving towards a realist version of the structuring of space within cities it is necessary to be alert to these competing interpretations. It is only now, with the dust beginning to settle, that we can really indulge in this exercise in reconstruction with a fair measure of confidence. It might be argued that a particular intellectual framework offers the most convincing means of integrating the statements about cities (i.e. a 'structure'), but that need not dictate, in a formalistic and rigid way, all elements of the analysis. Similarly, with this comes the recognition that the deployment of a particular concept or tool does not necessarily imply complete acceptance of the methodology with which it is most closely associated. Quite simply, depending upon the objective situation, one frame of reference may be preferred to another.

In 'putting space in its place', the text progresses initially from a consideration of how the ecological and neo-classical theories of the city were dominated by an obsession with spatial properties, to the conception of the city as a resource-allocating mechanism. The notion of 'capital as the architect of spatial structures' is then introduced. It is this view of the city as a socially produced form, resulting from interplay between the state, capital and space, that dominates throughout the text.

The city and spatially conventional 'wisdom'

Pioneers' bequest

The corpus of theory dealing with cities under capitalism includes an inheritance from the two differing perspectives that evolved during the pre-positivist phase of enquiry. One view of the city is the work of the Chicago school of human ecologists; the other is due to an American land economist, Homer Hoyt. Because their original suggestions about the organization of space within cities are intertwined with so much of the subsequent theoretical elaboration that has taken place it is necessary to précis their view of the city.

The group of human ecologists that came together at the University of Chicago in the 1920s were concerned with '. . . the spatial aspects of the symbiotic relations of human beings and human institutions' (McKenzie, note 2 in Hauser and Schnore, 1965: 390). This was the perspective that they brought to bear on the city of Chicago which served as their laboratory. In the work of one of their group is found the earliest cohesive enunciation of the processes involved in shaping urban space. In Burgess's (1925) proposal, the spatial configuration of industrial cities developing at that time was a direct expression of a set of processes analogous to those found in nature. The germ of this idea, of course, was borrowed from Charles Darwin. His view of evolution, as the outcome of species competing to survive, had been taken up by Herbert Spencer amongst others (Hawthorn, 1976), and recast as a brand of social Darwinism. Spencer, who was the originator of the phrase 'survival of the fittest' was to see his evolutionary account of social change distorted in order to uphold social inequalities as a natural state.

Burgess intended that his explanation of the growth and residential differentiation of Chicago extend to other cities undergoing industrialization. As he saw it, the significant processes shaping the Chicago of his day could be likened to those operating within natural ecosystems. Hence, the imperative of competition for space forced the *invasion* of the most convenient parts of the city and, eventually, their *succession* by a more dominant activity or group. Where the property market was free of restrictions, areas of the city would be 'naturally selected' for occupation by the function that could maximize the use of the site, block, subregion or whatever. In due course *natural areas* would evolve that were distinguishable because of their social or ethnic homogeneity – the ghetto, the 'Gold Coast', the slum, Little Italy or Chinatown.

Obviously processes of this kind do not have a momentum of their own. The successive waves of immigrants attracted from Europe between 1880 and 1920 (Ward, 1971: 51–7) by the industrial expansion occurring in North America (Pred, 1966) were an essential prerequisite. Typically, in city after city, the newest arrivals converged on the cheapest housing close to the heart of the low-skill job market (Chicago's factory zone). Here, they could share the costs of central area rents by packing into tenement quarters and avoid fares for the journey to work. This pressure on the innermost housing space produced a response from some of the better established households which fed the zonal spread of the city: as their real income improved they were able to leave behind the most overcrowded and dilapidated housing, to afford a workingman's fare, and to seek out a more congenial neighbourhood. According to Burgess this set up a ripple effect similar to that produced by a stone dropped into a pond. His model[1] reveals a definite zonation corresponding to the occupational mobility and the ability to save, of immigrant households at different stages of adjustment. Because of the tendency for ecological processes to sort similar households, Burgess felt justified in generalizing about the residential composition of any zone at a respective distance from the city centre.

It is when we probe beneath the surface abstraction of concentric zonation that we discover the much more significant relationship between the class composition of suburbs and distance from the centre of Chicago. The relationship has been stereotyped as a gradient, with 'socio–economic status' rising as a function of distance from the centre. Indeed, the bulk of urban land-use theory assumes that this is the standard form for the

[1] I have assumed that most readers will already be familiar with the idealized diagrams of Burgess and Hoyt.

distribution of incomes within western cities (Nourse, 1968; Richardson, 1969; Mills, 1972a). For this reason much urban modelling has been directed at the derivation of functions that specify this form for the relationship (Muth, 1969: 29; Mills, 1972b: 85–8). However, some very thorough empirical work by Schnore during the sixties (1963, 1966) has shown that a strong positive relationship between indicators of socio-economic status and 'distance' only exists in the older and larger US cities. Of 184 cities investigated, at best 40 per cent complied with the hypothesis.

The spatial geometry of the city proposed by Burgess was first queried by a land economist in the 1930s. In the process of assembling some material to help the Federal Housing Administration with its decisions on mortgage insurance Hoyt became convinced that residential growth in American cities was more axial than concentric: 'rent areas in American cities tend to conform to a pattern of sectors rather than of concentric circles. The highest rent areas of a city tend to be located in one or more sectors of the city. There is a gradation of rentals downward from these high rental areas in all directions' (Hoyt, 1939: 76). These conclusions were based upon his mapping of the shifts in the location of high rent areas in six US cities between 1900 and 1936. What is more, the sectoral orientation of intra-urban residential movement invited an explanation of the underlying process. Why did fashionable areas expand outwards from the city centre along the main commuter lines and towards the enclaves occupied by business magnates and public figures, while placing as much physical distance between themselves and the industrial zones? Hoyt suggested that the answer lay in the dynamics of the property market which transfers obsolete housing from higher income groups, who vacate in order to occupy stylistically fashionable dwellings, to middle-income groups. The vacancies they create are, in turn, filled by lower-income households. With consecutive building cycles adding new housing to the edge of an expanding city, this leaves the housing vacated by the wealthier households to *filter* down to the less affluent families. Unlike Burgess's invasion and succession model, the impetus for moves through the housing stock comes from the creation of new dwellings on the city's outskirts. This provides a real incentive to the construction industry to ensure that those households that can afford to are prompted to 'up-date' their home on an occasional basis. With further refinement this mechanism came to form the basis of 'filtering theory' (Smith, 1964).[2] Hence, residential

[2] Acceptance of the validity of 'filtering theory' and a belief in the efficacy of the free market actually leads to its promotion as an element of public housing policy (Gray and Boddy, 1979). As such, the theory serves to legitimize the persistence of gross inequalities in housing provision and to maintain an allocation of resources away from the needy. In the United States, for example, public housing is both basic and insufficient, while private tenants have to content themselves with housing 'hand-me-downs' that are often unfit for habitation.

change in the city is activated on the demand-side in Burgess' model, with the competition for inner city housing coming from new arrivals. Hoyt, on the other hand, stresses supply-side mechanisms, with the production of new housing at the edge of the city being the catalyst for change.

The essential soundness of Hoyt's spatial hypothesis has been re-affirmed in a study by Richardson and his co-researchers (1974) of Edinburgh over a 66 year period (1905–71). They claim that their findings are all the more noteworthy because Edinburgh is a less than ideal candidate for testing Hoyt: it is topographically eccentric; one-quarter of the housing stock is public; the high quality Georgian period housing (the New Town) built close to the city centre remains intact; the Scottish tenurial system prevents unrestrained property development. Despite these drawbacks the study of Edinburgh confirmed that: the most expen-sive residential property was confined to one or two pie slices, which coincided with the higher ground; radial-sector price differentials were large, and the high-and-low-price sectors repelled each other; the high-price sectors were remarkably stable over long periods of time. According to Richardson (1977: 13–14), Hoyt's contribution lies in breaking away from the restrictive emphasis on accessibility which is implicit in the competition for the most central space. Secondly, although unsophisti-cated compared with the work that was to follow, Hoyt's inductive approach does offer alternative insights for understanding the residential spatial structure of western cities. In particular, he directs attention to the agglomerative tendencies of contrasting social classes or income groups and the locational interdependence of much urban activity.

It was one of Burgess's close colleagues, R. E. Park, who first con-sidered the social homogeneity of localities within cities. Like Burgess, Park was impressed by the analogy that could be drawn with the dynamics of plant communities. In a classic paper that in every sense is a forerunner of the later work on urban residential differentiation, Park (1926) observes that the processes of social selection and segregation accompanying the growth of the urban community lie behind the creation of natural social groups as well as natural social areas within cities. Park recognized that while language, culture, religion, and race provided the motivation for residential segregation, geographical barriers and physical distance along with improved mobility provided the means to practise it. Thus physical distance is relevant to social relations when it is interpreted in terms of social distance.

The city's spatial order, in this view, reflects and affects its social order; social changes can be located by accurately tracing their spoor. Park's formulation posits not only a correspondence between physical and social distance, but also the converse: the near-identity of residential proximity and social equality. (Feldman and Tilly, 1960: 874)

This connection that Park made between social distance and geographic space has since given rise to a genre that makes extensive use of dissimilarity indices in urban research to measure ethnic, religious and social segregation, the distribution of minority groups, residential propinquity, and distances between partners in marriage (see Peach, 1975).

'Zones' or 'sectors'?

For a long time the impression remained in urban studies that Burgess's concentric zone model and Hoyt's sectoral hypothesis were diametrically opposed spatial representations of the city. This impression was finally dispelled in an important piece of analysis by Anderson and Egeland (1961), who concluded that the concentric and sectoral models 'were not mutually exclusive but were in fact legitimate descriptions of two different aspects of reality' (Abu Lughod, 1969). This progress towards a resolution of the debate surrounding the spatial aspects of the Burgess-Hoyt hypotheses has been due to the development of social area analysis. While the originators of social area analysis (Shevky and Williams, 1949; Shevky and Bell, 1955) disclaimed interest in the ecological tradition '. . . their work has now laid the basis for a spatial model of the internal socio-economic pattern of cities in which the relevance and role of the traditional concepts is clear' (Berry, 1964: 158). Hence, an unintended, but significant, consequence – at least for urban and social geographers – of the efforts of the Los Angeles group of sociologists was the crystallization of previously held views about urban residential structure.

An underlying assumption of both the concentric and sectoral models was that, *a priori*, the residential differentiation within cities is unidimensional. Drawing on census tract data for Los Angeles, Shevky and Williams (1949) ascertained that each 'social area' (a census tract) within Los Angeles could be characterized in terms of social rank, urbanization and segregation scores. Their social area analysis was tapping the distinctive variation that can be found within any city's sub-area populations. Partly because of the set of census variables they selected with which to typecaste local residential populations,[3] three axes of variation emerged: the social rank 'construct' was summarizing the individuality of each social area within Los Angeles according to indices like occupation, rent

---

[3] Although Shevky and Bell (1955) claim that the determination of appropriate variables was deduced from a theory of social change, and that their analysis reflects the end result of *increasing societal scale*, there is no logical connection between their broad theory of society and the social differentiation of urban space. The explanation for the social patterns derived from social area analysis lies elsewhere.

and education; 'urbanization' served to highlight inter-area differences in household membership, tenure, participation of females in the workforce, and fertility levels; 'segregation' combined information about the ethnic and national composition of 'social areas'. It follows that each 'social area' within Los Angeles, or any other city using this method, can be scored on each of the three axes of variation in turn. From this it is an easy step to mapping the social mosaic of the city with the distributions for each of the three, or *n*, constructs separately identified.

Social area analysis anticipated the 'mechanization' of the social sciences. Whereas Shevky and his colleagues were forced in the late forties to hand-pick a few well chosen variables in order for the analysis to proceed, the advent of computers which could rapidly process large amounts of data, together with the development of multivariate statistics, opened a Pandora's box for the new infant, spatial analysis. This facility, when matched with the urban geographer's natural interest in spatial organization, gave rise to a 'new' methodology for *describing* the social patterning of cities. It became known as *factorial ecology*. While factorial ecology builds upon social area analysis there are some notable differences: (a) it employs a factorial design, commonly principal components analysis; (b) the approach to selecting the expanded set of variables is inductive; (c) the social space diagram (see Herbert, 1967; Parkes, 1971) is replaced by maps of factor scores.

After a decade or so of over-indulgence, when the more sober assessments of factorial ecology were beginning to appear (Rees, 1971; Robson, 1973b), geographers could at least talk with some authority about the residential differentiation of cities. This was, however, limited to relatively 'low-level' science. On the one hand, there was sufficient consensus as to what represented a parsimonious *description* of North American, Australasian and British cities (Johnston, 1971; Timms, 1971) to justify Harvey's rebuke that diminishing returns had set in (Harvey, 1973: 128); while, on the other hand, factorial ecology was widely utilized as a procedure for *regionalization* within cities (Logan *et al.*, 1975) and the *classification* of urban areas in terms of their between-city differences (Berry and Smith, 1972; Moser and Scott, 1961).

Factorial ecology is little more than a reasonably sophisticated statistical method for pattern identification. When the findings from the numerous analyses of North American cities (see Berry, 1971) are compared, the overwhelming tendency is for the distribution of the 'social class/status' scores to be *sectoral*, while the mapping of the urbanization construct – 'family or household status' – is *zonal*. Thus, those same spatial properties emphasized by Hoyt and Burgess respectively emerge as complementary elements of residential structure. That 'socio-economic status' is predominantly sectoral, and 'family status' predominantly zonal, is confirmed in a set of more formal tests for a range of cities using analysis of variance (Anderson and Egeland, 1961; Johnston, 1970; Murdie, 1969; Sweetser, 1969; Rees, 1970).

The quest for spatial generalization culminated in a descriptive schema, or model, which presents an integrated view of the city as seen through the eyes of North American factorial ecologists:

> If the concentric and axial schemes are overlaid on any city, the resulting cells will contain neighbourhoods remarkably uniform in the social and economic characteristics. Around any concentric band communities will vary in their income and other characteristics, but will have much the same density, ownership, and family patterns. Along each axis communities will have relatively uniform economic characteristics, and each axis will vary outwards in the same way according to family structure. Thus, a system of polar co-ordinates originating at the central business district is adequate to describe most of the socio-economic characteristics of city neighbourhoods (Berry, 1965: 116).

While some workers were obviously intoxicated by a method that could apparently reduce the social structure of the city to such a simple geometry, others were sounding a note of warning. At least two people studying English cities (Herbert, 1967; Robson, 1969) were beginning to appreciate the complicating effects of 'remnant' housing stock from nineteenth-century development, and the 'distortion' created by public housing provision on a large scale: 'The appearance of such large areas of local authority housing has made nonsense of the rings or sectors of the classical ecological theory. Indeed, the game of hunt-the Chicago-model seems to be exhausted as far as the analysis of modern developments in British urban areas is concerned' (Robson, 1969: 132).

Apart from that, comparative analysis revealed that the distribution of socio-economic status and income in western cities does not comply unerringly with the Burgess-Hoyt prediction of an upward gradient from the city centre. In North America and Australia, particularly, the home and car ownership that was restricted to higher-income households during the 1920s and 1930s has been extended to households across the class spectrum. The scale of postwar suburbanization, especially in Australia, was such that the prime residential areas in many cities were often out-flanked by fringe subdivision. The typical response of the wealthy involved consolidating their residential dominance of the well-endowed suburbs adjacent to or midway between the centre and fringe of Australian cities (Johnston, 1966; 1969). These differences in the configuration of class and income within US, Australian and West European cities left such a strong impression upon Ivan Szelenyi when he was based in Australia that he sought to represent them schematically (figure 1.1).

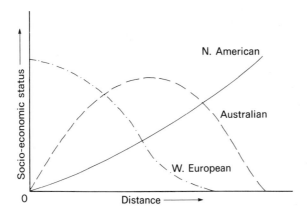

Figure 1.1 Income curves showing residential location of different socio-economic groups relative to distance from the city centre
Source: Szelenyi, 1978: 16

Theoretical embellishments of residential differentiation

Although the spatial conformation of residential phenomena within cities remained a source of intrigue for some considerable time, it must be said in retrospect that it really was a 'lightweight' problematic. In treating only the measurable characteristics of households and the housing stock, factorial ecology only came to terms with one component of the broader social structure of cities. There were omissions in at least three spheres. Firstly, except for a few of the 'tailend' studies, reference to discrepancies in the allocation of institutional and service amenities was absent from factorial ecology. Yet, tangible elements of social welfare such as the provision of hospitals and schools play an important part in illuminating the life styles of, and the relationships between, social groups (Robson, 1973b: ix). Secondly, other exceedingly important aspects of social structure proved elusive because they were not amenable to measurement, nor were they always areally bounded – social networks, group affiliation, social movements. A final category of structural elements has no spatial visibility and yet is vital to a description of the social system – class relations, class consciousness, the distribution of power and authority, mechanisms for social control. It is apparent, therefore, that factorial ecology could only hope to yield a very partial description of the city as a social product.

Despite these various inadequacies of residential differentiation it never-theless served as the descriptive base towards which explanations of the city's spatial organization were directed. If nothing else, the aggregate generalizations of factorial ecology did provide valuable guidelines to the patterning of residential characteristics within cities. What was called for was an elucidation of the processes by which those patterns were produced, altered or maintained. Two alternative explanations were forthcoming, both of which were explicitly positivist. One focused upon the moving behaviour of individual households in the belief that, 'Only by tying together the aggregate patterns of social ecology and the characteristics of such residential mobility can one hope to translate the findings of factorial ecology into more meaningful understanding of the processes which underlie them' (Robson, 1973b: viii). The other approach, which draws upon the analytical insights of neo-classical economics, took the 'Chicago' stereotype of the city as its point of departure.

The behavioural link

The spatial order ascribed to the city by factorial ecology is articulated through the residential moving behaviour of individual urban households. Berry and Rees (1969) suggest in figure 1.2 that the type of community (community space) in which a family resides is related to the social status and stage in the life cycle of the family (social space) and the type and quality of housing that the family requires and can afford (housing space). Our knowledge of how a household comes to terms with the basic locational decision – where to live – is gleaned from a range of studies of residential mobility in cities (Short, 1978). There is substantial agreement that the principal determinants of such a housing choice are three in number (after Berry and Kasarda, 1977: 126–31): the purchase price or rental of the dwelling; its structural form; and its location, both within a neighbourhood and environment and relative to place of work. Within the population there are the households with the income levels, the housing requirements, the lifestyle preferences, and the locational flexibility which permit the household to respond to the vacancies in the housing stock created on the supply side. Because households tend to seek out compatible neighbours who share essentially the same views and attitudes, relatively homogeneous social areas ('communities') are created within cities. Of course, in any large city a family moving house can usually choose from any one of a number of comparable communities within the community space (this choice attenuates towards the ends of the class spectrum). Any residual indifference between similar community spaces on the part of the household is removed by the locational decision which weighs considerations such as accessibility to work against family needs. This is the decision that ultimately fixes the geographical position of the household in physical space (figure 1.2). This posited congruence between the housing space, social space, and community space occupied by households has been formally researched by Yeates (1972) for Kingston and

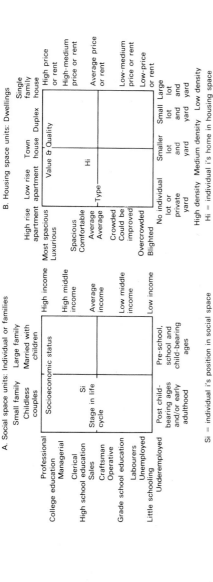
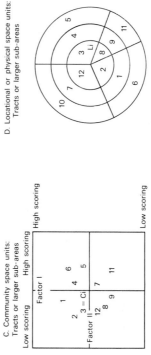

Figure 1.2 Where to live: the matching of social, housing, community and physical space

Source: Berry and Kasarda, 1977: 128–9

Winnipeg, Canada. His findings indicate that while the correspondence between house quality and social status exceeds expectations, the co-incidence of stage in the life cycle and type of home breaks down due to the intercession of various constraining factors (Yeates, 1972: 403–10).

While the brevity of this account is conceded, I believe it fairly represents the line of reasoning developed by supporters of a behavioralist interpretation of the city's social topography. As with the work before it, geographers contributed in particular to the underpinning of the spatial adjuncts of moving behaviour. The central concerns included the con-figuration of the mover's mental map and action space, and the directional bias embodied in aggregate movement behaviour (Adams, 1969; Donaldson and Johnston, 1973; Horton and Reynolds, 1971; Poulsen, 1976). The problem with this sort of analysis is that it was moving dangerously close to tautology, with the investigator seeking explanations for spatial variation in spatial behaviour or process. That is, suburbs group together households that are directed in their residential moving behaviour by a spatial template comprising the transportation network and other infrastructure.

An even more compelling reason for ultimately rejecting the behavioural attempt to link spatial structure with social process is that its emphasis on the individual as decision-maker leads to an atomistic view of social processes. And, as a corollary, this deflects attention from the structures that bound that behaviour. A careful examination of the behavioural perspective (see the review by Golledge *et al.*, 1972) will reveal that the primacy of consumer *choice* is implicit throughout. While there is a belated recognition that the action space can bias the search pattern of movers (Brown and Longbrake, 1970; Johnston, 1973; Menchik, 1972), the emphasis in all of this work is upon the opportunities presented by the housing market. This stress is best captured in the title of a national survey of 1,500 households in various metropolitan areas in the United States, *Moving behaviour and residential choice* (Highway Research Board, 1969).

The weakness of a purely demand-orientated approach is that in taking the action spaces and housing sub-markets as given it ignores the processes responsible for the *structures*, institutional and otherwise, that shape the residential environment in which decisions about moving house are made. Models of the household's locational decision-making process (Brown and Moore, 1970) play down the restrictions imposed by the supply-side, while otherwise thorough empirical enquiries of housing choice (Michelson, 1977) fail to address the issue of constraints. This is due in part to the nature of the housing 'environment' in those countries from which most of this research emanated. The assumption that choice prevails in most housing allocation is grounded in the high level of owner-occupation and the poorly developed public housing sector in both North America

and Australia. However, recent research, even in these countries, is showing how choices are governed by the income available for housing at
different phases of the family cycle (Kendig, 1981).

It is natural that an opposing view should have emerged in Britain, an
economy with a high degree of government intervention, centrally and
locally, in the provision of housing. The counter argument is that access to
housing is constrained by the state at all levels and the institutions that
mediate the allocation of housing finance (Clarke and Ginsburg, 1975;
Gray, 1975). 'To conduct research into choice, voluntariness or preference
in so constrained and competitive a market situation is merely the in-
dulgence of an ideology which promises what it cannot deliver' (Lambert
and Filkin, 1971: 332). The atomistic treatment of behaviour together with
the neglect of structural determinants, then, represent the sorts of
deficiencies that render the behavioural 'explanation' 'theoretically and
empirically barren' according to David Harvey (1969: 49).

Urban economic theory and residential location

The charge of superficiality would badly misrepresent the alternative
body of theory developed to explain the residential structure of cities. It is
distinguished by its use of the standard analytical tools and concepts
familiar to neo-classical economics. The models constructed to reproduce
residential patterns within the city only form a branch of urban land use
theory, so we cannot hope to do justice to the scope or the vitality of what
has been dubbed the 'new urban economics' (Mills and MacKinnon, 1973;
Richardson, 1977). Urban land use theory[4] along with the allied models of
residential location, serves to demonstrate just what can be accomplished
by positive science in urban research. One cannot help being impressed by
the elegance and simplicity of the basic 'trade-off' model, nor with the
relative power of the theory's predictions; for these are the criteria that set
good theory apart from bad.

Yet, having just received tacit approval, this theory of residential location will shortly be placed to one side. It will become apparent that the

[4] Foremost amongst the neo-classical models that treat urban activities in a general way are
those developed by Alonso (1964), Wingo (1961), Mills (1967, 1969) and Hoch (1969).
Alonso presents an ambitious general theory of land rent in which the organization of
urban firms and households is fixed in a market equilibrium. Wingo undertakes an
investigation of the effects of changes in the urban transport system on urban land uses, but
especially residential uses. Mills and Hoch derive the land value surface for quasi-equilibrium
states. The models hinge upon factor substitution which is determined by manipulating
adapted forms of the Cobb-Douglas production function. In Hoch's model (1969) the
substitution is between land and building space. Mills' first model (1967) looks at the
market equilibrium obtained for three industries: city transport; CBD goods; housing. In a
simplified, and therefore more successful form of the model, Mills (1969) derives the factor
combination in equilibrium for just two sectors. The two sectors, 'single-product' production and intraurban transport, compete for the predetermined urban land.

simplifying assumptions, so necessary if the models are to be solved numerically, render the idealization of the city unrealistic. What results is a *fabrication*, and a partial one at that, of the processes that really assign households to housing submarkets and residential locations within the city. According to Richardson (1977: 42), 'the conception of cities has been moulded to suit the favoured mathematical tools.' In addition, the predictions that are derived with the solving of the sets of equations tend to be too general for our purposes; for example, a negative rent or population density gradient, or the poor living closer to the city centre than the rich. Indeed, it is a moot point whether these predictions are as universally applicable as is assumed by the urban economists. 'To this extent the capacity to generate the standard predictions is a weakness, and an indication of the theory's restrictiveness or the theorist's blinkered outlook, rather than testimony to its soundness' (Richardson, 1977: 235).

It is important that any denouncement and final rejection of such an obvious contribution to the theory of the city should be well-informed. The most thorough and sustained criticisms of the structure and value of the residential location models have come from within (Mills and MacKinnon, 1973; Richardson, 1973; Wheaton, 1979); otherwise, people have taken issue with epistemological and ideological allegiance that urban land use modelling commands.

Modelling the 'trade-off' between access to the city centre and the space requirements of the household

The sub-class of models that is of primary interest shares many features in common with the more general theories of urban land use, except that they are exclusively concerned with residential activities (Muth, 1969; Evans, 1973). These models seek to deepen our understanding of how residential phenomena (densities, rent and land-values, the distribution of incomes and social class) are arranged within cities.[5] The parentage of the basic model can be traced back to von Thünen (see Hall, 1966) and the land economists working after the turn of the century (Hurd, 1903; Haig, 1926; Ratcliff, 1949). The latter were the first to appreciate the complementarity between urban rents and transport costs ('accessibility').

The structure of the model is grounded almost entirely in neoclassical

---

[5] The earliest models of urban land use (Wingo, 1961; Alonso, 1964) project a vision of space reminiscent of that presented by Burgess in his classic diagram. In equilibrium, land uses are allocated according to their ability to outbid competitors for the most convenient sites, resulting in a series of homogeneous, concentric zones oriented around the CBD (figure 1.3). Admittedly, the concentric zonation of land uses is not essential. It is just a by-product of assuming a set of well-balanced bid-price curves for the rent: distance functions; and, there is no real reason why these curves must be well behaved. In spite of this, the highly regularized representation of space has found its way into all the standard textbooks on urban land use theory (Nourse, 1968; Richardson, 1969; Mills, 1972a).

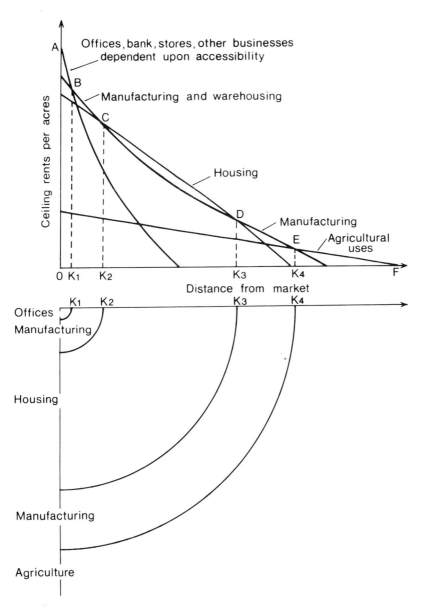

Figure 1.3 The derivation of urban land uses using bid-rent analysis
Source: after Nourse, 1968: 115–16

economics. But in order for the traditional theory of consumption and production economics to be handled in space some simplifying assumptions are essential. These are the *a priori* conditions that predispose the solution to *monocentricity*. By monocentricity we mean a single centre which is the point of origin of the rent and density gradients. Firstly, the model assumes a circular city (with the possibility of pie-slice radians taken out for topographical constraints) in which transportation is possible in all directions. (In the 'second generation' models this means that the city can be represented by a linear ray from the CBD (central business district) to the urban boundary and treated as one-dimensional space.) As a corollary, all economic activity including employment opportunities are confined to a single centre, the CBD. (These are vital requirements if the urban economist is to derive the rent and density gradients as continuous functions with differential calculus.)

Secondly, it is assumed that each household provides at least one member of the workforce. Then, in the best traditions of utility theory (see Richardson, 1977: 26–30), a household utility function is specified with the demand for residential space, income elastic. The household's utility is maximized, subject to the usual budget constraints, by trading off space consumption against commuting costs. That is, a household finds 'its optimal location relative to the centre of the city by trading off travel costs, which increase with the distance from the centre, against housing costs, which decrease with distance from the centre, and locating at the point at which total costs are minimized' (Evans, 1973: 7–8). This is the key mechanism, which distributes households, such that in equilibrium, we obtain rent, land value, and population density gradients that resemble those identified by the urban ecologists.

Thirdly, it is assumed that capital is sufficiently fluid and mobile for households to maximize satisfaction in relation to the consumption of space. This denies the durability of existing housing stock, or other physical structures, and thereby implies that households are indifferent in their locational decisions to external effects and past land use patterns.

Shortcomings of the standard 'trade-off' models

The least acceptable aspects of the 'trade-off' explanation of residential structure can be traced to the simplifying assumptions or, more fundamentally, to some of the conceptual 'Achilles heels' of micro-economic theory: the treatment of utility; indeterminacy; the elusiveness of equilibrium, even in the long run.

Perhaps the most transparent of the assumptions is that relating to monocentricity and single workplace:

all workers are assumed to received the same gross wage. CBD workers are nevertheless in equilibrium wherever they live in the suburbs because land rents just offset transportation costs. But some workers are employed in the suburbs and they are obviously better off than CBD workers living in the same neighbourhood. (Mills, 1969: 237)

Yet the inclination is still to produce solutions for the monocentric city – because it is much more difficult to obtain determinate solutions and smooth and differentiable rent and density surfaces for multi-nodal regions and suburban employment.[6] For example, both Muth (1969: 71–4) and Mills (1972a: 82–4) are able to predict the specific form (negative exponential) of the rent-distance functions and the land value and population density functions from general equilibrium models.

The derivation of the household income surface within cities represents the other major challenge to the modellers of residential location. Mills's (1972a: 71) predicted pattern of incomes is representative of the most *common* solution of the model:

if there is an arbitrarily large number of income groups, if all satisfy the conditions of the theorem, their residences will be ranked by distance from the city centre inversely to their rank by income; that is, the lowest income group will be closest in, the next lowest will be the next closest, and so on. This is a remarkably realistic result, and it mirrors closely the predominant pattern in U.S. urban areas.

It has already been noted that Schnore's (1966) investigation of the relationship between incomes and distance from the centre within large US cities contradicts Mills's concluding note of self-congratulation. Moreover, because of the considerable variation in the patterning of incomes within cities other investigators have discovered positive (Diamond, 1980a) or, at best, neutral (Ball and Kirwan, 1977; Wheaton, 1977) relationships between distance and income. Subsequent modelling, therefore, has sought to build greater flexibility into the prediction of income patterns. This is achieved by recognizing the wide dispersion of income elasticity of households about the mean in their demands for space (Evans, 1973: 120–28). In the commonest solution by Mills above, all households have income elasticities greater than one, which causes a move to a new optimal location further from the CBD with each increment in the rate of pay. In order to obtain the distribution of income depicted in

---

[6] Of course, with added ingenuity, it is possible to relax some of the simplifying assumptions and move closer to reality. There have been various attempts to incorporate subcentres in the modelling (Mills, 1972b; Papageorgiou, 1976; Papageorgiou and Casetti, 1971; Odland, 1978; Ogawa and Fujita, 1980; Romanos, 1977); but, the results are unwieldy, and lack the simplicity and sense of harmony characteristic of the vintage model.

figure 1.4 the mean income elasticity of demand for space must lie between the values of 0.5 and 1.0. This means that as well as exclusively occupying the outermost suburbs, households with the highest rates of pay may also elect to displace the lowest-income families near the city centre.

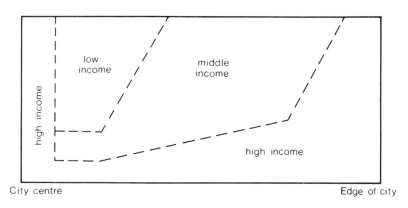

Figure   1.4 The spatial distribution of urban incomes derived by Evans
Source: Evans, 1973: 126

Notice, however, that in order to achieve a more realistic and versatile prediction we have weakened the theory by introducing indeterminancy. The respective locations of income groups can no longer be deduced *a priori* but are now contingent upon the relative values assigned externally to the main parameters (Richardson, 1977: 106). Take the example of low-income groups on the periphery, which is the dominant Australian pattern. Mills (1972a: 86–7) finds that such a result can be accommodated only by violating two of the initial conditions of his model: if higher-income workers place a *relatively* higher value on travel-time in relation to the wage rate than do low-income workers; and, if the marginal disutility of commuting increases with the amount of commuting undertaken by the household. Thus, it might be speculated that because of the rather more uniform shares of residential space in Australian cities, and because the state governments have failed to provide central city commuters with the highway networks and complementary systems of high speed transit that funnel suburban commuters in to the core areas of US cities (Stegman, 1969: 27–8), there is a diminished incentive for higher-income households to 'trade-off' access to the CBD for living space.

The second objection to the 'trade-off' model of residential location revolves around the use made of utility theory.[7] When pressed, economists will concede that the problems that arise from trying to base an

---

[7] Although some of the criticisms relating to utility and spatial choice have been recently countered by Golledge (1981: 1335–6), the technical difficulties surrounding the incorporation of disaggregated utility functions into the 'trade-off' models remain.

operational model upon utility theory are insuperable. The assumed voluntariness of all transactions in the housing market is especially open to criticism:

> Housing is a necessity, and it is indivisible (an infringement of the assumption needed to derive continuous indifference curves and budget lines). A low-income household may have virtually no choice at all as far as the housing market is concerned. Low incomes and indispensable housing needs on the demand side, a possible scarcity of low-cost housing and strong market power exerted by slum landlords on the supply side – this combination may force the poor households to take any housing it can get at high rents. The compulsion may absorb a very high proportion of the household's low income, leaving an inadequate residual for allocation among alternative priority spending claims. (Richardson, 1977: 30)

Because of the heavy reliance of the 'trade-off' model upon utility theory, with its pretensions of relatively free consumer choice, it cannot escape the gibe from some quarters that it is an 'ideological sham' (see Richardson, 1977; also Sheppard, 1980).

The other simplifying assumption that rests rather uneasily with reality is that which ascribes mobility to capital. It is this assumption which provides the convenience of 'an instantaneous market clearing process' (Harvey, 1973). Housing, though, is an especially durable form of capital; once built, it yields returns to the owner which provide an opportunity cost against subsequent construction for a very long time. Likewise, once they have their plot, property owners can be notoriously hard to budge if they wish to be obstinate. Consequently, the efficiency of the perfectly competitive market, where prices and consumers are immediately responsive to shifts in supply and demand, is checked in innumerable ways in the housing sector. For example: a lot of property is rented on a long-term lease, so that rents progressively fall behind market rates; concessional rents and rates are extended to some organizations so that they continue to occupy sites that would otherwise be unprofitable; some residents are tied to areas for reasons of nostalgia or inertia even though a transfer to a new site would increase utility or welfare. As Richardson (1977: 39) points out, imperfections like these are supposed to be ironed out by the time the long-run equilibrium is attained. But this amounts to wishful thinking on the part of the urban economist, since it is most doubtful that a long-run equilibrium is attainable. Again, an approach to the locational assignment of residential activities based on competitive equilibrium is just a technical convenience. Because the treatment is static it leaves a formidable list of questions unanswered about: locational interdependencies; the role of expectations in relation to future changes in rents; lags, rigidities, and inertia on both the supply and demand sides; institutional effects. In summarizing, it is noteworthy that the criticisms that we have dwelt upon were levelled from within the fraternity of urban land use modellers. So, understandably, they are couched mainly in terms which are consistent with the methods and biases of the modellers. But it is necessary to set to one side, for the time being, a whole litany of complaints which often go very much deeper in attacking the very basis of the theory and asserting that the neoclassical toolbag is irrelevant.

Neoclassical location theory 'under fire'

It is perhaps useful to air some of the more fundamental misgivings about the employment of neoclassical economics in general, for it is this reaction within the humanities and social sciences that was the catalyst that spawned the alternative approaches to be discussed later. Remember that residential location theory is only an extension of the neoclassical method, and that the criticisms directed at it merely serve to represent a series of critical reactions to other forms of positive social science. Thus, the reliance upon neoclassical economics in developing location theory during the fifties and sixties have been attacked as mechanistic, ideological, and devoid of ethical content. Each of these complaints will be dealt with briefly as a prelude to considering the 'welfare approach' to the city as a resource-allocating mechanism.

Mechanistic

The social sciences harbour groups of scholars that take exception to the way in which man is treated by positivist science. In geography the differing positions are represented by the behaviouralists and the humanists. If behavioural geography is one expression of the aversion to treating man mechanistically (i.e. as a rational decision-maker operating in an abstracted environment), then humanistic geography is a revolt against the technical and epistemological apparatus which strips people of their essential humanness, and impedes an appreciation of the richness of human existence, and the individuality of human beings. The philosophical wellhead and inspiration of the humanists is phenomenology, which takes the everyday world with its inevitable mesh of fact and value as its central concern (Levy, 1977). The problem of constructing an acceptable alternative to positivist social science has been tackled by Schultz (1970), who sets out to avoid what many consider to be an artificial dichotomy between 'object' and 'subject'. However, it is easy to lose sight of the point of phenomenology in the 'elaborate intellectual scaffolding' erected by Schultz: 'its main contribution to the restructuring of social and political theory is the way it forces us to examine critically the taken-for-grantedness of the social and political worlds' (Bernstein, 1976: 252). Put another way, phenomenologists seek to bring knowledge into closer harmony with lived experience:

> Challenging many of the premises and procedures of positive science, they have posed a radical critique of reductionism, rationality, and the separation of 'subjects' and 'objects'. With existentialists, they herald the liberation plea of lived experience, appealing for more concrete descriptions of space and time, and their meanings in everday human living. (Buttimer, 1976: 278)

According to Buttimer and Seamon (1980), the interplay between the subject's cognitive processes and the objective reality of spatial structures can only emerge if the researcher is prepared to share the meaning and experience of *place* and *space* in their everyday guise. Rowles's (1978) exploration of the geographical experience of older people represents one of the first examples of experiential fieldwork. It amounts to an intensely personal and sensitive involvement with five elderly pensioners living on Winchester Street, a downtown neighbourhood of an eastern seaboard city in the USA. Although this work is in its infancy, and the methodology developed thus far must be provisional, it is subject to two basic flaws that weaken its utility.

Firstly, how can procedures which take fieldwork well beyond the accepted conventions of participant observation be verified? Is it really conceivable that two phenomenologists would bring forward the same set of observations about the object under investigation, or even know when they had (Mercer and Powell, 1972)? Secondly, undeniable depth provided by experiential insight is gained at the expense of breadth. How representative are Rowles's five pensioners? Even if the researcher has formed well-measured judgements, there is no basis for generalizing the findings to the point where they can be used in explanation (Johnston, 1980: 406). Whatever the merits of a more humanized conception of space or the humanist's encounter with the decision-maker, the conclusion that immersion in the daily lives of a handful of human beings provides a pretty shaky foundation for theory-building, or the framing of social policy, cannot be avoided.[8]

---

[8] What we probably have to settle for is sensitive involvement with individuals or groups within the context of a more formal research design. One thinks of the findings that have emerged following the participation of the Lamberts, Bob Blackaby, and Chris Paris in neighbourhood based action in Birmingham (Lambert *et al.*, 1978; Paris and Blackaby, 1979). Similarly, an appreciation of the life-style, 'sense of place', and mundane problems of the boarding and lodging population was an essential ingredient in a recent study of the impact of housing displacement in inner Adelaide (Badcock and Urlich-Cloher, 1980).

Ideological

One of the principal accusations levelled at positivist frameworks like neoclassical economics is that they are powerful ideological instruments. Although avowedly value-free, there is no doubt that neoclassical economics has functioned to nurture and legitimize market capitalism. With the very superstructure of capitalism underpinned intellectually in economics textbooks, its perpetuation is assured. According to the radical critique (Gray, 1975; Slater, 1975), these emphases mask and hide the deeper processes of class exploitation; as within the land and housing markets of capitalist cities, for instance. This implies deliberate intent on the part of economists and other social scientists, when a more charitable view would allow that most researchers during these years were un-wittingly engaged in the promulgation of capitalist ideology, and by default in the preservation of the status quo. Indeed, it is symptomatic of the pervasiveness of logical positivism during the sixties that none other than Richard Peet, the high priest of radicalism in geography, was himself making fairly effective use of the neoclassical toolbag (Peet, 1969).

Avoidance of ethical questions

One of the characterizing features of positivist economics and location theory was that they imposed a frame of reference for analysis and research that appeared to exclude an awareness of social conditions and issues.[9] The posture typically adopted by orthodox economics is unequivocal: 'The economist is not concerned with the ethics of want' (Braddock and Archbold, 1970: 50); nor, it might be added, of allocation. It is the dominance of this ethos which enabled Evans (1973: 29), for example, to accept without comment the necessity of the following limiting assump-tion in developing his theory of residential location: 'Full employment is assumed to prevail both in the city and in the economy as a whole. There are no vacant jobs or any unemployed resources.' What a Utopian state! (To be fair to Evans, he has obviously recanted, since unemployment and poverty both form major topics in his subsequent writing (Evans, 1980).)

Although Roger Lee (1976: 11) has subsequently pointed out that the maldistribution and inequities that now offend were implicit in the pre-dictions of most location theory, it never occurred to the majority of analysts to question the essential fairness of the allocations they were

[9] There were, of course, a number of great minds that stood outside their disciplinary establishment; Gunnar Myrdal comes to mind in the field of economics. In human geography, during the sixties, a few academics managed to elude the vortex of spatial analysis. In even rarer instances, this was marked by an uncommon social awareness. At Victoria University, Wellington, for example, Keith Buchanan had gathered around him a likeminded group – McGee, Armstrong, Franklin, and Watters – who throughout the sixties were working in socialist or Third World settings.

modelling. Gould freely admits that most human geographers were anaesthetized to questions of equity: 'I honestly do not think geographers ever consciously thought about such matters. I certainly did not, and I do not recall any seminar, article, or book which did' (Gould, 1979: 146). Of course, Gould was in good company. In 1971, Joan Robinson, an eminent Cambridge economist, was warning her established colleagues of the dangers of neglecting 'the great problems which everyone feels to be urgent and menacing'. On the fundamental question of income distribution, she continued, 'we have nothing to say on the subject which above all others occupies the minds of people which economics is supposed to enlighten' (Robinson, 1972: 8).

To a younger generation of researchers caught up in the social turmoil of the sixties this was quite unacceptable. They set about devising a more relevant, policy-directed human geography (Smith, 1974; Peet, 1977b). Plainly, they were not alone in this, for like other social scientists they were 'creatures of their time'. One of the products of this change in direction was the conceptualization of the city as a resource-allocating mechanism. This idea is discussed in the next chapter.

2

The City as a Resource
Distributing Mechanism

This chapter outlines how social research was sensitized anew during the 1960s to the plight of the less fortunate in otherwise well-off capitalist societies and the realignments that this inspired in the field of urban studies. There was a rediscovery of poverty in the forgotten corners of large cities. This in turn rekindled a general debate, especially in Britain, about the performance of the welfare state and a reassessment of the criteria for distributive justice. Because so many of the concerns aired by social philosophers and administrators were subsequently taken up by social scientists engaged in policy-oriented research, it is necessary to review the debate on social justice, and define some of the key terms and criteria which will be used throughout this text – equity, equality, egalitarianism, universality and selectivity.

As social analysis and policy reorientated itself, workers on both sides of the Atlantic began to ask themselves how they might tackle the new research agenda. Attention switched to the palpable differences between individuals, neighbourhoods and regions; how they arose, and the reforms proposed to eliminate them. The efforts of one group have since been characterized as 'liberal formulations', while another broke entirely new ground by seeking comprehension through versions of Marxian analysis. Both these developments have led to a far more critical treatment of space in urban and regional studies, such that many of the earlier claims have now been discredited or moderated. With tongue in cheek one could say that 'space has been put in its place.' To appreciate fully the reasons for this we have to take one or two detours through the literature of social administration.

Rediscovering poverty

In the post-war flush of sustained growth and general prosperity it was accepted that poverty was on the decline and inequalities were in the process of being levelled. The Beveridge Report and a series of reforms introduced by the Attlee Labour government between 1945 and 1951 ushered in Britain's welfare state. With undertakings like a national health system, better provision for child allowances, old age pensions, and unemployment benefits, the expectation was that nobody need ever again face the poverty and hardship that had scarred Britain during the 1930s. Similarly, Fanklin D. Roosevelt's New Deal legislation was designed to eliminate the mass impoverishment and misery created in the United States by the Great Depression. Unemployment relief, the Wagner Act, farm subsidies and social security payments were supposed to guarantee minimum living standards to all members of society. Hence, through the 1950s, according to Michael Harrington (1962: 9), America's anxieties were products of abundance:

> There was introspection about Madison Avenue and tail fins; there was discussion of the emotional suffering taking place in the suburbs. For all this, there was an implicit assumption that the basic grinding economic problems had been solved in the United States.

This was buttressed ideologically by the belief that economic growth, *per se*, was capable of promoting all but the incapacitated from the ranks of the poor. All the while, the social scientists busied themselves with value-free, non-judgemental activity. Policy-orientated research, which was very much the exception, was mainly the province of the infant discipline, social administration.[1]

It was not until the sixties that poverty and inequality were reinstated as persistent features of societies dominated by capitalist mechanisms. The rediscovery of poverty in Britain, the United States and other nations marked a fundamental shift in the way in which such societies conceived of themselves (Banting, 1979: 1). This came partly with the realization that the market penetration of consumer durables like radios and television, refrigerators and washing machines, and cars had left an impression of shared affluence which was superficial. But other factors played a part: there was a mass migration of America's poorest families from the rural south to the cities of the north during the 1950s, where they were more conspicuous and overloaded the labour market. Once investigators turned to penetrate the false front of mass consumption they found that, despite a 50 per cent rise in average living standards, poverty had not been eradicated and that the shares of income and wealth had grown less equal. Surveys in the US revealed that one child in four and 30 per cent of the elderly were living below the poverty line in 1966.

[1] Many of the key advisors to the various Labour governments that constructed the British welfare system were student protegés of Richard Titmuss, who occupied the first Chair in Social Administration at the LSE (names like Pinker, Donnison, Townsend, Abel-Smith, and Young come to mind).

A reawakening to the degree of 'hidden' poverty followed the publicity given to studies like *The poor and the poorest* (Abel-Smith and Townsend, 1965) in Britain, and *The other America* (Harrington, 1962) and *The poorhouse state: the American way of life on public assistance* (Elman, 1966). It was evidence like this which convinced Titmuss (1976: 141) that economic progress need not naturally lead to social progress without distributive intervention by the state. This was a clear rebuff to those commentators who argued that national gains in the command over resources would be evenly and proportionately distributed among all spending units. Indeed, subsequent national surveys of poverty in Britain (Townsend, 1979) and Australia (Commission of Inquiry into Poverty, 1975) have emphasized the intractibility of 'hard core' poverty and wrung the belated admission that it is an inevitable condition of capitalist societies.

Americans only came to realize how deep-seated and potentially destructive the poverty in their midst was with the eruption of violence within the black ghettoes towards the end of the 1960s. Starting as isolated brushfires in 1964, this expression of racial tension and social discontent reached a climax in the summer of 1967–68, when 125 people were killed and sizeable areas of 200 cities were devastated. Perhaps, we might add, this was not necessarily because of the failure of the Johnson Administration's 'War on Poverty', but in spite of it.

These events, which were among the most dramatic of a series of social upheavals that occurred during the 1960s (Reich, 1972), had a profound effect on the direction of the social sciences and the nature of social policy. Firstly, they helped to arrest the self-indulgent tendencies within disciplines like sociology, economics, psychology, and geography which had lost their social conscience (Andreski, 1972). Secondly, they challenged people to rethink and debate again the very principles and goals that shape western societies. Social justice assumed prominence as the 'fashionable idea of the 1970s' (Goldsmith, 1980: 146). In particular, Rawls's *A theory of justice* (1971) rekindled interest in the nature of equality – an interest that had been dormant since Tawney had placed the capstone on the debate about equality that had raged 30 years earlier (Tawney, 1952). The full implications of this are seen most clearly, for example, in the redefining of poverty:

> Poverty is seen by at least some social scientists, such as the late Richard Titmuss in Britain and Lee Rainwater in the United States, as inequalities in the command of resources, and especially those inequalities that derive from the dynamic and evolving life-style, rights and opportunities available to the average members of society . . . the new principles are evolving around issues of equity in the distribution of public resources: who pays and who benefits and who is excluded from established policies? Does the distribution of public largess

multiply privileges or redistribute advantages? . . . The social policies that emerge from this perspective reject minimum subsistence as a relevant goal of public intervention and also the concept of poverty as a failure to achieve subsistence standards, defined in absolute terms. When poverty is viewed as exclusion from membership in society, public policies become necessary which will attempt to alter the distribution of resources. (Rein, 1976: 123)

Criteria for distributive justice

Martin Rein is worth quoting at length, because as well as representing a vastly different perspective on poverty to those it supersedes, this statement embodies most of the normative principles linked with that elusive ideal of a just society: social justice, equality and equity, universality and selectivity. As such they have provided the underlying rationale for the forms of intervention in market economies that are the hallmark of the welfare state. But, more to the point so far as this chapter is concerned, these precepts have now been absorbed into the mainstream of urban theory and policy. Consequently, it is necessary to be acquainted with them if any sense is to be made of the conceptualization of the city as a resource distributing mechanism. While the refinement of these precepts is most closely identified with workers in the field of social administration (Pinker, Runciman, and Titmuss in Britain), their antecedants include the moral philosophy of Locke and Rousseau, and some of the shared convictions of Fabian Socialists like William Morris, the Webbs and R. H. Tawney.

Social justice

The most majestic enunciation of the nature of social justice is to be found in *A theory of justice* (Rawls, 1971). Importantly, Rawls's idea of social justice is not to be confused with the usual interest in equitable allocation, or distribution *per se*. A major purpose of Rawls's scheme is to model, in the abstract, a basic structure of society, arranged in such a way as to satisfy the principles of justice. It is a conception of social justice that provides in the first instance 'a standard whereby the distributive aspects of the basic structure of society are to be assessed' (Rawls, 1971: 9).

Rawls begins by asserting the primacy of justice, which for him is inviolate. He 'insists that justice is the first claim on institutions. It is their fundamental virtue, just as validity is the fundamental virtue of arguments' (Ryan, 1981: 228). But here he parts company with recent moral philosophy, which likens justice to 'desert', or worthiness of recompense, either favourable or punitive. This concept carries with it overtones of entitlement and merit (Rachells, 1978) which Rawls rejects.[2] 'Notoriously, Rawls argues that the notion of justice is most closely linked to that of fairness' (Beauchamp, 1980: 133). It places the claim for equality in society above all other claims save that of liberty.

One of the requirements of lasting social co-operation among people is some unassailable concord about what is to count as just and unjust. Rawls assumes that each person in society has a clear set of preferences (they want more social goods rather than less, they wish to safeguard their liberties), and that in furthering their own interests they will make rational choices. However, a necessary prior condition in building up a model of a just basic structure is that none of the members of society should be undeservedly or preferentially placed in the choice of principles. If information about their class position or social status, their physical or intellectual endowment, is withheld from the members of this society (Rawls's 'veil of ignorance'), then each person would be obliged to agree intuitively to fair dealings and equal shares.[3]

Rawls is now in a position to argue that under these circumstances (where individuals act rationally, are mutually disinterested and enjoy symmetrical relations with one another),[4] the affairs of this hypothetical society would be ordered by appeal to two 'principles of justice for institutions'. Formally expressed (Rawls, 1971: 302), the first principle states that 'Each person is to have an equal right to the most extensive system of equal basic liberties compatible with a similar system of liberty for all.' The second principle requires social and economic inequalities to be arranged, subject to two conditions: firstly, so that the arrangement is to the greatest benefit of the least advantaged members of society . . . (his difference principle); secondly, so that they are attached to offices and positions open to all under conditions of fair equality of opportunity. Rawls assigns priorities to these principles. The right to equality in basic liberties takes precedence over all other virtues, followed respectively by equality of opportunity for advancement, and positive discrimination in favour of the disadvantaged to ensure equity.

Underlying these principles are two vital convictions about social justice. Firstly, the difference principle reflects Rawls's firm view that

[2] Even though *A theory of justice* is scrupulously argued, as moral philosophy it is founded on a *conviction* about justice.

[3] Sir Isaiah Berlin (in Atkinson, 1972: 79) arrives at a similar judgement: 'If I have a cake and there are ten persons among whom I wish to divide it, then if I give exactly one tenth to each, this will not, at any rate automatically, call for justification, whereas if I depart from this principle of equal division I am expected to produce a special reason.' This shifts the burden of proof to the opponents of equal shares.

[4] A number of criticisms have been levelled at the 'veil of ignorance', some carping, some more serious: 'social goods' are not differentiated in Rawls's scheme; the making of decisions does not allow for equal probabilities, but assumes that there is only one correct strategy in all cases.

because inequalities of birth, historical circumstance, and natural endowment are undeserved, society should reduce inequalities by redressing their unequal situation (i.e. by positively discriminating in their favour). For this reason, Rawls is pre-eminently an *egalitarian* in his conception of social justice: 'The idea is to redress the bias of contingencies in the direction of equality' (Rawls, 1971: 100–1).

Secondly, it is important to Rawls that this principle of *fair* equality of opportunity is not mistaken for the conception of equality that 'leads to a callous meritocratic society' (Rawls, 1971: 100). He denounces the liberal commitment to equal opportunity, which assures everyone of an equal position at the starting gate, but has the race going to the swiftest and the prize to the most deserving (Schaar, 1980: 166). Although the implementation of equal opportunity has seen birth, patronage and tradition replaced as the sole determinants of access to place and privilege, it has really just substituted more insidious forms of inequality for the stark injustices of the past.

The meritocratic society accepts the principle of 'careers open to talent' (Young, 1958). So long as everyone has equal access to the institutions that equip people to assume the positions of authority and prestige, so the argument goes, justice is said to be done. Have not the incumbents of those positions earned them by meritorious performance? Like it or not, the liberal version of equal opportunity still distributes wealth and income according to the 'natural' distribution of abilities and talents (Rawls, 1971: 73–7).[5] Hence, an advocacy of equality of opportunity amounts to support for the perpetuation of the status quo. And the status is nothing to *quo* about as Marx's maxim makes clear: 'to treat unequals equally is to give privilege to the strong'. So for Rawls, equal opportunity must go beyond the liberal principle of equal opportunity. There is not much doubt that his basic sympathy lies with the more egalitarian claim that a fairer measure of social justice is equality of expectations, or even equality of results (or outcomes).

Naturally, a theory as provocative as Rawls's is not without its detractors. Critics on the left dislike its 'bourgeois' overtones of self-interest, while others feel that, for all its talk of protecting individuals, *A theory of justice* is really collectivist (Ryan, 1981: 230). This polarity finds expression in the material principles that actually determine the allocation of benefits and burdens in most societies. In egalitarian societies the commitment is to equal access and equal distribution of goods and services; socialist societies give priority to need, subject to the size of the

---

[5] This is why Rawls's scheme requires social institutions to nullify, so far as possible, undeserved advantages, and compensate the disadvantaged. His suggestions include the spending of greater resources on the early education of the less intelligent than the more intelligent (p. 100), and the setting of a minimum social wage that will maximize the long-term expectations of the worst-off in society (p. 285).

social product; libertarian societies reward contribution and merit in a free market framework; whilst utilitarian societies pursue a mixed strategy so that public and private utility are maximized. I hasten to add that this typology implies a pure model of society when most societies combine several of these elements of distributive justice; moreover, outside the confines of academic and political discourse, the moral absolutes implicit in them – 'individualism' *v.* 'collectivism', 'egoism' *v.* 'altruism' – are rarely found in such uncompromising forms (Pinker, 1979: 7).

Equality and equity

Although John Rawls regards equality and equity as the *means* by which a socially just society is attained, in practice they assume the status of social objectives. The distinction between the two terms allows for the fact that equality (equal distributions) and equity (fair shares) need not necessarily coincide; that is, unless people have identical needs, policies need not be both equitable and equal. Rather, because varying individual and community needs are the norm, social policy is faced all the time with the task of accurately measuring the degree of inequality in society and deciding what kind of redistribution is necessary to produce equity (Goldsmith, 1980: 148).

Yet, with the expectation that any society should accomplish equal provision, let alone equal outcomes, we have obviously entered the realm of the pipe-dream. For Tawney (1952: 47), 'The important thing is not that it should be completely attained but that it should be sincerely sought.' Indeed, part of the purpose of this book is to show that certain indirect and frequently concealed mechanisms operating within cities have the capacity to counteract redistributive measures, no matter how well designed they might be. Therefore, apart from the other market mechanisms that frustrate social policy, it is a reduction of inequality that is sought both on moral grounds and for pragmatic reasons. The challenge is to design policies to redistribute real income and wealth, discriminate positively in favour of the underprivileged, and promote equality of opportunity such that the inter-personal differentials are steadily reduced. How far the quest for equality and equity is actively pursued is obviously a matter that each society decides essentially according to the ethical disposition of a majority of the voting population.

One of the restrictions imposed by a bipartite system of government is the reality that, in Donald Horne's words, 'Winner takes all' (Horne, 1981). But beyond that restraint Runciman (1966) has cautioned that once the existing disparities had been removed fair shares would have to be defended by a continuous transfer of wealth from the high to the low paid (and permanently unemployed) workers. Indeed, evidence shows that while reformist governments have occasionally brought about a perceptible narrowing of inequality with progressive incomes policy and social measures, the process of redistribution in most of the capitalist societies has been halting, if not stationary. In Britain, for example, most of the narrowing of incomes took place between 1938 and 1949. The bitter irony is that shares of wealth apparently widened under Callaghan's Labour government in the mid-seventies (figure 2.1). Consequently the Left in Britain has grown increasingly disillusioned with the welfare state under Labour as well as under the Conservatives. Radical British political theorists like Anderson and Blackburn (1965) and Miliband (1972), venture that it is time to confront and limit the social power of capital which they see as the major source of inequity in the distribution of wealth and income.

Universality and selectivity in redistribution

Planned redistribution by governments – what Titmuss calls the 'social

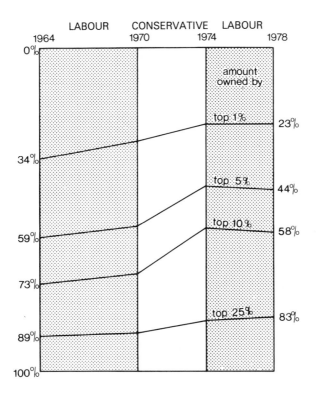

Figure 2.1 Distribution of personal wealth in the United Kingdom, 1964–78
Source: constructed by Kellner, 1980. Based on data from the Royal Commission on the Distribution of Income and Wealth, 1978, and *Social Trends*, 1981

market' – has grown out of a recognition that the way the 'economic market' in capitalist societies distributes welfare is largely unacceptable.

In the liberal view this intervention is a human reaction to the tendency of the market to allocate resources in the best interests of capital rather than human need (in Edward Heath's words 'the unacceptable face of capitalism'); whereas, a Marxist writer like Gough (1979), construes the welfare state as *both* functional to the needs of capitalist development *and* as the spoils of battle of the working class. In any case, the welfare state performs two sets of functions. It provides social services like social security, health, education, job retraining, and housing, and it regulates private sector activities (individuals and corporate bodies) that have the ability to upset living conditions in the community. Government regulation includes taxation policy and a wide range of legislation from Factory Acts and building by-laws to consumer protection and pollution control.

Welfare can be redistributed in the form of cash payments or 'in kind'. The revenue needed for cash payments or other kinds of income support for the young, elderly, ill or unemployed comes mostly from the taxation of company and personal income. The extent to which the whole system of taxation redistributes income from the rich to the poor is a measure of its 'progressiveness' as opposed to its 'regressiveness'. Redistribution in kind, on the other hand, involves the provision of free or subsidized services. According to Neutze (1978a: 38–9), economists tend to favour redistribution of cash because it leaves the recipients free to make their own decisions about how to spend the income supplement and thereby maximize their welfare; and it helps to contain administrative overheads. Alternatively, redistribution in kind ensures that the 'social wage' is spent in an approved way; that is, the purpose for which the allocation was meant is fulfilled. Understandably tension can and does arise over the best mixture of cash and 'kind' in redistribution: tax-payers expect value for taxes paid, while other parties try to defend the interests and preferences of the beneficiaries.

On another axis choices have to be made between 'universality' and 'selectivity' in redistribution. As the terms suggest, universality argues for the provision of a service or benefit to all, so long as everyone contributes to its cost; while selectivity argues for the restriction of the benefit or service to those who meet specific criteria relating to needs. Britain's National Health Service is perhaps the most often cited example of a service provided on a universal basis, whereas most applicants for public housing assistance are means-tested and may have to meet other eligibility criteria in Britain, Australia and the United States. While accepting that resources are scarce and often need to be rationed, some social administrators argue quite passionately that the state should avoid selective provision. In the opinion of Richard Titmuss (1976), the process of selection is unavoidably punitive, discriminatory, and erodes the self-respect of the poor; while means-tested allowances tend to 'foster both the sense of personal failure and the stigma of a public burden'. Because 'the fundamental objective of all such tests is to keep people out . . .' the poor are regarded as supplicants rather than as beneficiaries or consumers.

Titmuss suggests that selective provision is especially unjust when the item in question represents outright compensation for a disservice caused by society. It might simply serve to restore the *status quo ante*: for many of the victims of technological change the service may not be an increment to welfare at all. The service probably does no more than redress a previous grievance, and as such represents: 'partial compensation for disservices, for social costs and social insecurities which are the product of a rapidly changing industrial-urban society. They are part of the price we pay to some people for bearing part of the cost of other people's progress' (Titmuss, 1976: 133).

Titmuss associates the stigma of selective services with the denial of access. Accordingly, redress can be achieved through positive discrimination which 'implies direction of resources without stigma towards a particular group' (Reisman, 1977: 54). The virtue of this is that services assume the status of 'social rights' and reach the deprived as residents of priority social areas or other such impersonal groupings. Provision on a territorial or group basis avoids the creation of 'separate, apartheid-like structures' (Titmuss, 1968: 114) for the dependent, and concentrates resources on those groups/areas in the community perpetually at risk. For a time during the 1960s and early 1970s area-specific positive discrimination was favoured by successive British governments as a major element of planned redistribution (Edwards and Batley, 1978). When the discussion of urban policy evaluates the Urban Aid Programme it will be necessary to remember these arguments in support of priority areas, for they tend to be overlooked by most critics of spatially directed redistribution (Eyles, 1979).

Lastly, according to Pinker (1979: 40) we should not lose sight of the fact that 'insofar as social policy is concerned with redistribution it also functions as an agent of discrimination which always seems to favour some at the expense of others'. He adds: 'The key differences between societies lie in . . . the degree to which one set of discriminatory criteria is imposed to the exclusion of others. The question for all practical purposes is not whether discrimination occurs, but who practises discrimination and upon whom, on whose behalf and at whose expense?' (Pinker, 1979: 40).

Liberal formulations

These are the precepts which find their way into the liberal formulations that set out to present new ways of looking at cities. It is this explicit concern with the fairness of resource allocation, with discrepancies in access, and with the efficacy of social intervention that sets these contributions apart from those of the urban ecologists or the location theorists of chapter 1.

There are three frameworks sharing this concern that deserve attention. Firstly, the quest for greater social relevance in geography received considerable impetus from the work of David Smith, who married the distributional focus of welfare economics with some of the postulates of spatial theory. The extension of this approach to social problems in the city was self-evident, though ultimately not as convincing as either of its companion frameworks. The second of these liberal formulations has been much more successful in advancing urban theory. In the first part of *Social justice and the city* (1973), David Harvey draws attention to how *space* complicates resource allocation within cities and interferes with the distribution of real urban income. His propositions owe much to Rawls's work and to other thinkers who have written on social policy. It becomes apparent, however, that this is very much an interim statement from Harvey, as he makes a decidedly more radical substitution in the second half of his book (his socialist formulations).

The 'liberal' Harvey has much in common with the nascent Raymond Pahl, who trained as a geographer at Cambridge but is now a prominent British sociologist. In 1975 he recommended that the allocative machinery of the urban system should command our attention: 'I now see an important area of study concerned with space as both a cause and also a reflection, both of patterns of *allocation* of given services and facilities, and also of patterns of *access* to these same services and facilities' (Pahl, 1975: 9). The part of Pahl's work, though, that genuinely advanced the 'state of the art' is known as 'urban managerialism'. In a paper published in 1977 he reaffirms an earlier conviction that it is the urban manager who, steering resource allocation at the local government level, largely determines who will benefit and lose from public provision. Pahl contends that whatever the social system, the managerialist perspective, firmly grounded in the Weberian concepts of status, power and control, offers the most promising avenue for urban research.

(Social) consciousness-raising and the spatial vortex

One thing that these three frameworks have in common, which tends to set them apart from much of the work with which they were contemporaneous, is their judicious treatment of space. Even allowing for the transitional nature of socially oriented research, too much 'explanatory power' was indiscriminately ascribed to spatial form, location, distance effects and so on. It was natural enough that geographers should react to the social turbulence about them by focusing on the spatial manifestations of social problems (see Albaum and Davies, 1973; National Academy of Sciences, Committee on Geography, 1973); but in turning to the problems in the cities, American geographers in particular adhered to the familiar concepts and modelling skills that had been acquired in the previous decade or so. The literature is now replete with spatial optimization procedures, with applications ranging from the assignment of medical services (de Vise, 1973; Erikson, 1970; Schneider and Symons, 1971; Shannon and Dever, 1974) and mental facilities (Dear, 1977; Smith, 1976) to equitable solutions for the reorganization of school catchments (Shepard and Jenkins, 1972).

At the heart of much of this modelling of optimal location and accessibility to community resources is the assumption that urban poverty and disadvantage can be alleviated by improving the spatial distribution of opportunities within cities. The danger is that a preoccupation with what are commonly subsidiary effects, such as access to job opportunities, can obscure the much more fundamental causes of inequality. Indeed, this is the lesson that emerges from Bederman and Adam's (1974) investigation of the contribution of job inaccessibility in Atlanta to inner-city underemployment. The authors took 37 sample tracts in Atlanta and established that a significant positive relationship ($r = 0.55$) existed between the percentage underemployed and the average accessibility score. According to the canons of location theory this is a counter-intuitive result, since it implies that the closer the jobs the higher the rate of underemployment within Atlanta census tracts. However, on further inspection Bederman and Adams found that 'structural' effects were much more closely associated with tract unemployment rates. Atlanta's critically underemployed are mainly black female heads of families, and no matter where they live in the metropolitan area they have neither the skills to qualify them for the new jobs being created, nor the opportunity to acquire marketable skills (Bederman and Adams, 1974: 386). That is, *the inequality of job access transcends the disadvantage of physical access.*

The 'welfare approach': where does who get what and how?

In endeavouring to develop a welfare theory of spatial allocation both Chisholm (1971) and Smith (1977) turned to welfare economics for their explanatory cues. Welfare economics extends the study of resource allocation within the market economy beyond the determination of the technical optimum, where the criterion is the maximization of welfare within a society as a whole, to a consideration of how welfare *ought* to be allocated amongst competing demands. All the time the welfare economist guards against making value judgements on the distribution of welfare by sticking to an assessment of efficiency.

The pursuit of a socially optimal allocation begins with Pareto's criterion, which states that a transfer of resources is an improvement, from the point of view of community welfare, if it leaves an individual (or group) better off, in that person's estimation, and nobody worse off. Paretian optimality flounders for the following reason: it can be satisfied without altering a pre-existing distribution that could, for example, increase the wealth of the rich without materially affecting the poor one way or the other. In this sense, Paretian optimality is inadvertently conservative: it is 'a powerful sanction in favour of preserving the particular inequalities of the *status quo*' (Wallace, 1978: 94). Later formulations range from Kaldor's compensation principle, which regards a transfer as a social advance if the gains to the beneficiaries are valued at a higher level than the losses to the losers, to the General Theory of the Second Best (Lipsey and Lancaster, 1956). The compensation principle comes closer to a usable criterion because it assesses benefits and costs according to ability to pay; all the same, the preferences of the rich are weighted more heavily than those of the poor (Neutze, 1978a: 48–9). Not only can they afford to pay more for gains, they demand greater compensation for losses.

To give him his due, Smith (1977) does eventually concede the futility of persisting with a Paretian criterion for distributing welfare; or, for that matter, the other conceptual refinements of welfare economics. Inevitably, all these developments founder on the principle that subjective value judgements are inadmissable; hence, they lack prescriptive power. Rather than persisting with this approach Smith opts for an explicit ethical preference (equality becomes the norm) and a simple yardstick against which to measure variations in the factor endowments of spatial units like urban districts (the Lorenz curve). With these constructs Smith (1977 131–57) attempts to attach some operational meaning to the concept of spatial injustice, and move towards a judgement about the equity (fairness) of alternative spatial arrangements of society.

David Smith will be remembered more for his substantive contribution than for his attempt to adapt the theory of welfare economics in the cause of spatial analysis. He led the way in the use of social indicators in social area analysis, which for too long had drawn on the restricted set of demographic and housing statistics available in national censuses. The relevance of territorial social indicators to policy formulation and the monitoring of the delivery system goes without saying. The task of developing a set of urban social indicators assumed a high priority on both sides of the Atlantic as the anti-poverty programmes expanded through the 1960s. In the United States, the Department of Health Education and Welfare devoted a lot of time to establishing a set of social indicators with which to monitor the effectiveness of the anti-poverty programmes.

Social indicators research quickly took on the proportions of a growth industry within the social sciences (see Hill and McRae, 1978; New South Wales Planning and Environment Commission, 1978; OECD, 1977; Vinson and Homel, 1976, for a few samples). In time the original brief broadened out to include studies of the spatial variation of quality of life or 'social well-being', and the isolation of deprived areas. Smith's work (1973) fell into the category of the former, while British researchers have been more concerned to isolate pockets of severe deprivation within British cities. Much of this latter work formed an essential prelude to the designation of residential areas deserving of urban aid (see chapter 10) or supplementation under the Rate Support Grant (see chapter 8).

Notwithstanding his efforts, Smith's proposal represents more of a theoretical retreat than an advance (Wallace, 1978: 94). The welfare approach, which also suffers from spatial introspection, is definitely weak spatial theory if one is looking for predictions about specific patterns of resource allocation, or an explanation of spatial unevenness. Smith himself has recently come to accept this. In appreciating that the measurement and detection of inequalities between and within cities cannot be an end in itself, he advises that there is a role for the geographer 'as analyst of spatial pattern and process, but only within the broader, multi-disciplinary perspective of contemporary political economy' (Smith, 1979: 266).

Redistribution of real income in an urban system

'I . . . regard the city as a gigantic resource system, most of which is man-made' (Harvey, 1973: 68). David Harvey was one of the first scholars thoroughly to think through the capacity of the urban system to *thwart* the redistributive objectives of social policy. His contention is that planned redistribution is negated to varying degrees by distributional effects that are a product of the way in which cities are structured (and not just spatially) in capitalist societies.[6] Although some of the distributional effects that Harvey refers to are due to imperfections and failures of the market, the source of other forms of redistribution may be less apparent. It is this obscurity that led Harvey to term these the 'hidden mechanisms' of redistribution (Harvey, 1973: 52). Although these mechanisms are poorly understood, few would disagree with Harvey that they consistently operate, especially in larger cities, to increase inequalities rather than to reduce them. What is more, because they tend to be unevenly con-

---

[6] This happens because the urban system has an ability to generate 'fringe benefits/losses' independently of any intentional redistribution of income. If we think of a rip at sea we have something akin to the process Harvey has in mind: while the surface appearance is of a high volume of water surging shorewards, beneath the surface there is a similarly impressive undercurrent.

centrated regionally within cities, these distributive effects are typically discriminatory and can be potent unequalizers.

Additional import derives from Harvey's awareness that many of these distributional effects upon the real income of different groups within the city can be traced to allocational decisions (public and private) dealing with transport networks, industrial zoning, location of public facilities, location of households and so on. . . . Insofar as the city is continuously being restructured, redistributive effects are always in the pipeline; yet, they are seldom envisaged and mostly unintended by the agents responsible for resource allocation.

The importance taken on in Harvey's analysis by these concealed mechanisms for redistribution rests on a more expansive concept of income than that which applied in the past. For this Harvey draws on Titmuss who argues that an equitable definition of income must embrace 'all receipts which increase an individual's command over the use of a society's scarce resources' (Titmuss, 1962: 34). Hence, income is more than just the 'market value' of rights exercised in consumption (in loose terms, 'purchasing power'); it must also take account of changes in the real value of property. Nor is it just those changes in capital value that follow decisions taken by an owner to invest or disinvest; it must also include the *unearned* (or social) *increment* to the value of property. Apart from this, the capacity to exercise rights in consumption (the realization of purchasing power) cannot be determined independently of accessibility to, and the price of these resources. Availability and cost depend upon the nature of a resource and its management. Consequently, an individual's income as defined by Titmuss can change in a number of ways:

> The individual can earn more (less), he can receive positive (negative) benefits from a change in the value of his property, he can simply have more (less) resources made available to him at a lower (higher) price, or he can have any combination of these gains and losses over a particular period. (Harvey, 1973: 53–4)

Thus the task that Harvey sets himself is to establish 'how changes in the spatial form of a city and changes in the social processes operating within the city bring about changes in an individual's income' (Harvey, 1973: 54). He argues that income flowing to individuals and households in the form of wages and salaries, progressive taxes, welfare payments and so on, is susceptible to redistribution in the following ways: (a) through the uneven imposition of greater accessibility costs, where employment opportunities and the availability of housing fail to keep in balance; (b) as a result of changes in the availability and price of resources; (c) as a result of the relative shifts in the value of property rights. Although these are represented analytically as separate effects the redistribution that takes place in an urban system is often far more complicated and may have compound causes. It is Harvey's main ideas which are the present concern, bearing in mind that the greater part of chapter 7 is a discussion of the redistribution of income by urban land and housing markets.

Command over resources, which is a good general definition of real income, is partially a function of locational accessibility and proximity. The journey to work, movement to community centres, and the delivery of welfare services to the point of consumption, all incur a cost which comprises the price of overcoming distance and the valuation of time. These costs are never constant since every time the spatial form of the city is modified (by building new housing, extending the transport network, relocating employment centres, schools, etc.), the price of accessibility for any urban household changes. And every alteration to the cost of accessibility entails a redistribution of real income among households, depending on precisely where they live in the city. Ultimately, the magnitude and incidence of such redistribution rests with: (a) the responsiveness of the urban system to changing technology, and shifting patterns of investment and demand within the wider economy; (b) the equity of service provision; and (c) the size of the city (Harvey, 1973: 54).

The resources that enhance our quality of life are by no means ubiquitous, nor are they uniformly distributed within cities. On the one hand, households pay rates and taxes for the delivery of services like schools and hospitals, sanitation, policing and fire prevention within their local areas; on the other, they pay a premium in property prices to congregate near well-endowed community centres and in socially desirable neighbourhoods. The most important allocational decisions affecting the location of these public goods within cities – collectively provided services – are made by government bodies. Needless to say the exercise of these powers can effect a profound redistribution of real income amongst urban households, particularly where they are discriminatory in a locational sense. And yet it is only relatively recently that policy analysts (Davies, 1968; Hirsch, 1977) have come to appreciate that 'Government, and especially local government, had grown to such an extent that the life chances of individual citizens could be altered by the precise way in which public spending decisions impacted on urban space' (Cameron, 1980: 6). Suffice it to say that, in the North American and Australian urban context where intervention has been subservient to market forces (capital) and efficiency – rather than equity-oriented – public policy appears to be characteristically regressive in its distributional impact. This is discussed further in Part III.

Harvey's third concern is with the fluctuations in property values that result from the investment decisions of neighbouring property owners. Because the property owner has little effective control over developments on adjacent sites or in nearby areas, and because there is seldom any way that the market mechanism can anticipate them, these are known as external effects, or externalities. They can be positive or negative, and may go wholly or partially unpriced. The disposal of water or airborn wastes are the classic examples of external effects which until recently have gone unpriced and unregulated.

Externality effects within the urban economy have now been sufficiently well studied to be able to state that the larger the city the more intricate and potentially affective they become. It is through the property system that the potential of externalities to affect a redistribution of real income within cities is realized. Apart from the more obvious externalities discussed in chapter 7 – air pollution, the location of 'threatening' facilities such as homes for the mentally insane etc. – property also redistributes real income in other ways not foreseen by Harvey at the time. While Neutze (1978b) and Archer (1974) in Australia, and Clawson (1971) in the US have probably done most to draw attention to this, a quote from Stretton provides a resumé of some of the transfers that can arise from imperfections in the markets for land and housing (ahead of a fuller treatment in Part III):

> Most big capitalist societies allow land to be a double unequalizer. As economic growth stimulates demand for accessible urban land, its price increases faster than the price of labour or anything else, so its unequal ownership further unequalizes wealth and income. There are the direct transfers via rents and prices to inheritors and investors in land, and indirect transfers from those who don't own land and houses to those who do. There is often some further unequalizing among investors. Those who lose (especially in periods of inflation) are the institutions which lend on mortgage at fixed interest for long terms. Those are chiefly savings banks, building societies, life assurers and superannuation funds, and governments – i.e., institutions which chiefly lend the small savings and taxes to large numbers of people with low or middling incomes. Rich investors don't lend on land, they do better by buying and selling it, often with money borrowed from savers poorer than themselves. (Stretton, 1976: 217)

Hence, some areas and submarkets outperform others to the income advantage of their participants. That this happens is due, more often than not, to the political power exercised, and the successes achieved in bargaining for public goods, by coalitions of residents organized on a territorial basis (see chapter 9).

Management of the urban system

The person most consistently associated with the remaining conceptualization of the city as a resource-allocating mechanism is Raymond Pahl. Lacking the power of fully fledged theory, his framework for the analysis of urban society nonetheless supplies valuable insights into 'Who gets the scarce resources and facilities? Who decides how to distribute or allocate these resources? [and] who decides who decides?' (Pahl, 1975: 185). While his first utterance on the city as a resource-allocating mechanism appeared in 1969, the 'definitive' Pahl is not offered up for inspection until 1977; along the way he fortifies and moderates the original edifice in light of the challenge mounted by his radical critics – see the reviews by Leonard (1982) and Williams (1982).

If Pahl's original set of propositions are outlined it is then possible to decide in what respects his updated version represents an improvement on what has been called 'early managerialism'. Pahl (1975) affirms that the city is a socio-spatial system in which access to scarce urban resources is fundamentally constrained at the local level: firstly by limitations upon physical mobility (expressed in time/cost distance);[7] and, secondly, according to the distribution of power within society. By this Pahl meant that the workings of the socio-spatial system were controlled by members of the local government bureaucracy called 'urban managers'. Because the responsibility for designing the rules and procedures governing access and allocation was seen to lie with the 'urban managers', and because 'social gatekeepers' like housing managers and social workers were in a position to control urban resources and regulate life chances, Pahl concluded that they were the 'independent variables' in the socio-spatial system.

A number of comments need to be recorded about Pahl's agenda for studying the city. First, it reflects the general awakening to the role of institutional constraints in urban development and the housing assignment process. Secondly, it incorporates the basic message conveyed in Davies's enquiry into *Social needs and resources in local services* (1968): local authorities differ quite radically in terms of the resources they have at their command, the ways in which they are allocated, and the quality of the service they provide. Davies confirmed that where one lives in British cities can materially affect one's life chances (Pahl, 1975: 204).

The Weberian inheritance

Pahl owes an intellectual debt to Rex and Moore (1967) who, with their concept of housing classes, provided a link in a chain of reasoning that extends back to Max Weber. In Weber's *Theory of social and economic*

---

[7] Pahl bases his case on the evidence indicating that, in Britain at least, the physical mobility of the population has been greatly overstated. A Political and Economic Planning study, for instance, revealed that even in the seventies 'less than one third of the adult population have the optional use of a car' (Hillman *et al.*, 1973). For many urban households the time/money costs of 'bridging' space represent a real impost.

organization (Parsons, 1968) class situation is ascribed to the individual's position in the market as a consumer. The significance of this stems from Weber's proposition that life chances are mediated mainly through the market rather than in the sphere of production. For him, life chances are 'the kind of control or lack of it which the individual has over goods or services and existing possibilities of their exploitation for the attainment of receipts within a given economic order' (Parsons, 1968: 424). This sets Weber apart from Marx with absolutely no room for compromise between their protagonists: Marx grounds the class structure in the relations of production, whereas Weberian theory emphasizes distribution and the associated phenomenon of the market. Further, the broad types of classes that Weber distinguishes makes it fairly clear that he saw no need to specify class solely in terms of wage-labour or ownership of capital: (a) 'property', based on the life chances embedded in ownership of property; (b) 'acquisition', linked with the exploitation of non-property resources such as skills and qualifications; (c) 'social', allowing the plurality that arises from mobility. The type of social statification obtained and the patterning of life chances derive from the distribution of power in society, which lies in the political, social and economic spheres. Plainly the quest for power and control is potentially divisive and likely to give rise to tension, and even conflict, between groups in society.

These are the rudiments of Weberian theory adapted by Rex and Moore (1967) in bringing forward a plausible account of the social processes that they observed in their study of Sparkbrook, a racially intruded working class neighbourhood of Birmingham, England. Thus, a class struggle over the uses of houses becomes for them 'the central process of the city as a social unit . . .' (Rex and Moore, 1967: 273). The concept of 'housing classes' need not detain us at this point of the discussion, except to say that it has been recast by Pahl (1975), scrutinized from various angles (Bell, 1977; Bell and Newby, 1976; Couper and Brindley, 1975; Haddon, 1970; Saunders, 1978: 66–142), and superseded as an explanation of urban change and conflict (Harloe, 1975; Lambert *et al.*, 1978; Political Economy of Housing Workshop, 1975). The fundamental problem with the concept of 'housing classes' is that it 'focused on conflict *between* these classes in the city rather than considering the origins of the situation in which different groups were forced to enter into competition with one another' (Harloe, 1977: 4).

As has been noted, the recasting of Weberian theory by Rex and Moore represents a direct challenge to the Marxist position which holds that the determination of life chances is monopolized by the labour market. Their suggestion that the process of housing allocation was capable of generating 'structures of inequality distinct from the field of employment was a major step forward at the time' (Pahl, 1975: 247). This relation was further generalized by Pahl in the 1969 paper – he postulated a set of spatial inequalities quite apart from the inequalities that derive from place in the workforce. Implicit in this is the suggestion that consumption, especially access to collectively provided services, must be taken just as seriously as the sphere of production as a source of inequality.

Pahl under seige: 1 How much, and what powers do urban managers wield?

The propositions originally assembled by Pahl under the aegis of 'urban managerialism' contained a fair measure of supposition; if for no other reason, they were bound to attract careful scrutiny. Of those studies that evinced an interest in 'managerialism' (see the review by Williams, 1978), the early ones were mainly preoccupied with gatekeeping functions and evidence of malpractice and incompetence within local bureaucracies (Davis, 1972; Dennis, 1970, 1972). However, these narrow concerns were soon to be broadened as the need arose to explain the outcome of resource allocation in terms other than the internally established policies and priorities of local government.

This shift in emphasis is stamped upon the monograph by Lambert and his co-workers (Lambert *et al.*, 1978). The group found it increasingly difficult to comprehend the processes of urban change and housing allocation within the inner neighbourhoods of Birmingham. For example, familiarity with the management structure and policies of the City of Birmingham yielded only a partial account of Birmingham's housing situation during the sixties and seventies. Repeatedly their enquiries compelled them to ask why the housing programme, which was designed to rehouse Birmingham's most vulnerable housing classes, had halted; or why the housing queue was growing longer. They became convinced, along with other researchers operating in a similar vein,[8] that many of the developments taking place in the local built environment were quite literally 'beyond the control' of local authorities and their managers. On the broadest of levels they put the responsibility for these developments down to central government and various fractions of capital. Obviously findings like these pose a real challenge to Pahl's oft-repeated (1975; 1977; 1979) claims about the independence of 'urban managers'.

Pahl has drawn fire from several Marxian writers who object to the ideological nature of 'urban managerialism'; but, more importantly, they cannot conceive of a framework which, at first glance, appears oblivious to material forces in society (Harloe, 1977). One does not have to side with a Marxist critique to appreciate that any suggestion that 'urban managers'

---

[8] Here I am referring to 'action-research' which typically finds the researcher actively involved with the local groups and areas he/she is studying. Perhaps the best known British example is the Community Development Project (Edwards and Batley, 1978). An Australian equivalent is the Centre for Urban Research and Action, which is based in Fitzroy, Melbourne.

are not subject to various constraints is vacuous. Yet those that would paint Pahl into that sort of a corner apparently misunderstand him. As Saunders (1979: 181) points out, Pahl is well aware from his own work on corporatism that central government imposes real limits on local power through monetary and fiscal measures. Certainly the consensus from recent studies of local–central government relations leans to the opinion that 'the operations of the local state are severely constrained by the central state' (Dear and Clark, 1981: 1280).[9]

Pahl's response to evidence of strictures has been to concede the overriding constraint of central government funding or capitalist enterprise: 'I would not now want to emphasize locality-based constraints quite so strongly. I am more impressed by the way broader flows of investment and other matters at a national and international level do much to make our cities what they are' (Pahl, 1975: 6.) At the same time he continues to profess that 'urban managers' exert a *separate* distributional impact, over and above these more pervasive effects, which can have significant repercussions for local residents: 'States may attempt to centralize in the interests of equality and efficiency, but discretion must still remain at all levels' (Pahl, 1979: 43). Indeed, one is reminded by the examination of state housing policy in Australia (Badcock, 1982) that even though the states receive proportional shares of housing funds under the Commonwealth–States Housing Agreement, their financial commitment to welfare housing is sufficiently varied for it to have an important bearing on housing access according to where one lives in Australia.[10] The point being that 'however narrow the limits managers might well have sufficient choice and discretion to materially affect the outcome of a particular situation.' (Williams, 1978: 238–9).

Appropriately, it is Pahl who has helped to clear this log-jam by bringing forward a reasonably parsimonious typology which appears to account for most of the alternatives in relation to resource control and allocation within cities. He specifies the following four 'ideal types' (Pahl, 1975: 270–271):

1 *The 'pure' managerialist mode.* The assumption is that control of access to local resources rests solely with the professional officers concerned; hence, allocation will presumably be in the interests of those professionals, and the conflict internecine.

2 *The statist model.* The overall direction of resource allocation is

[9] This is not the place fully to air the idea of 'the state' (see chapter 3), except to say that current usage of the term usually employs a degenerate form of the Marxian theoretical category, i.e. that set of institutions which serves to reproduce the interests of capital. Thus, Cockburn (1977: 51–2) sees the central state mainly concerned with the sphere of capitalist *production*, with the local state primarily involved in capitalist *reproduction*.

[10] For example, compared with a national per capita average of $A16, Victoria, New South Wales, and South Australia allocated $A6,, $A13, and $A47 respectively to public housing in 1979–80.

dictated by central government, leaving local professionals or managers with very little room for manoeuvre. Deakin and Ungerson (1977: 14–15) comment that allocation invariably depends upon how the central government sees its interests or ideology best served. This shifts the locus of conflict to the national scene where politicians of different brands, and public servants, contest for scarce resources.

3 *The control-by-capitalists model*. The implication is that at both the federal and local level, 'the state' is the handmaiden of capital. Its prime function is to preside over the accumulation of capital and ensure that the resources are allocated to serve that end. For example, 'the state' comes to the party by providing the costly non-productive urban infrastructure that is so essential to the reproduction of a docile, well-trained and healthy labourforce. Typically, at the local level, the vested interests of private capital see to it that profit remains the chief criterion for deciding the 'best' use of resources.

4 *The pluralist model*. This view of 'Who gets what?' in a given spatial context envisages 'a permanent tension between national bureaucracies, committed to obtaining and distributing larger resources (following partly their own internal logic of growth), and the interests of private capital manifested through the economic pressures of 'the City', private industry, and the political party representing the dominant class' (Pahl, 1975: 271). Here, conflict is part of the model itself with public and private sector institutions bidding for a greater share of federal funds. The flow of resources to the regional or local tier of government normally generates further conflict amongst a range of prospective consumers of public goods. It might be inferred that such a system is inherently unstable since the claims made by different pressure groups for public assistance will always be subject to intermittent review.

Pahl under seige: 2 Can inequality have a spatial component?

Two kinds of criticism are levelled at Pahl's treatment of space. The first is predicated on the conviction that space need not be organized unequally. Behind this lies the notion that uneven development is peculiar to capitalism (Peet, 1980) and that a strict adherence to socialist criteria of need would eliminate territorial injustice. After assessing this claim, Pahl decides that 'territorial injustice is inevitable and that the realization of socialist objectives within modern big cities is impossible' (Pahl, 1977: 51–2). This is more than a simple expression of faith: there is a growing acceptance that, notwithstanding the most disinterested allocation, the very nature of big cities acts to prevent an entirely egalitarian distribution in space. Moreover, evidence is surfacing that would seem to indicate that, despite an ideological commitment to equal provision, the distribution of collective goods and services in socialist cities is not especially even.

Although some of the reasons for this are singled out in chapter 11, the relevant point for the time being is that equal shares and equal access have rarely been achieved in their most uncompromising forms.

The other criticism also comes from some of the more doctrinaire Marxists who deny the existence of significant sources of inequality – one of these being space – outside that of the labour market. Unmoved, Pahl continues to argue for the existence of spatial inequalities that do not necessarily coincide with the traditional lines of class inequality: whereas the wage-fixing process sees to it that the earnings of workers with the same skills and/or qualifications are broadly comparable, the real conditions of life may vary to such an extent between areas that a worker may be motivated either to move to a better area (change his accessibility) or to improve his/her own area's system of allocation so it is more favourable (Pahl, 1975: 9).

The assertion of the primacy of spatial sources of inequality was in the ascendency in the early 1970s in Australia. This was linked in Prime Minister Whitlam's 1972 policy speech with an allusion to the inherently regressive nature of the planning and development of Australian cities:

> Whatever benefits employees may secure through negotiation or arbitration will be immediately eroded by the costs of living in their cities; no amount of wealth redistribution through higher wages or lower taxes can really offset the inequalities imposed by the physical nature of the cities. Increasingly, a citizen's real standard of living, the health of himself and his family, his children's opportunities for education and self-improvement, his access to employment opportunities, his ability to enjoy the nation's resources for recreation and culture, his ability to participate in the decisions and actions of the community are determined not by his income, not by the hours he works, but by where he lives.

Apart from the inverted causality – by and large income determines where households live – this came as a heresy to those socialists for whom the structural basis of inequality is unassailable (Catley and McFarlane, 1974: 11).

The restrictiveness of the classical Marxist interpretation of inequality has been admitted by the French structuralist, Manuel Castells (1977a). Part of his thesis draws attention to the range of inequalities generated by state agencies with the responsibility of distributing collective goods and services. In fact this places Castells – on this point at least – much closer to Pahl than a lot of neo-Marxists would care to admit: 'the State becomes, through its arrangement of space, the real manager of everyday life' (Castells, 1977b: 64). For him, inequalities in distribution can be just as pressing as inequalities fixed by the relation to the means of production.[11] According to Castells (1978: 15), 'it seems that the traditional inequality in terms of incomes, which is inherent in capitalism, is expressed in new social cleavages related to accessibility and use of certain collective resources.'

Putting space in its place

For those commentators who occupy the middle ground, most of these unresolved matters can only be settled with empirical soundings. It is worth repeating that theory is of little value if it fails to illuminate 'real world' phenomena and processes in a convincing way. Therefore, in addressing important issues such as the relative autonomy exercised by respective sectors of the economy, the nature of territorial inequality and where the ultimate responsibility lies for the shaping of space, theoreticians are obliged eventually to consult the evidence. On this hinges an acceptance or rejection of much current theory about cities. But first we must be clear as to how 'space' should be regarded. In effect that means how, and to what extent, should space as an explicatory factor be incorporated in our account of unfairly structured cities? A number of suggestions have been made that can help us with our deliberations.

Throughout the discussion of the three 'liberal formulations' some of the irresolution surrounding the use (some say 'manipulation') of space by society has been apparent. What is the relationship between space and society? How does their interaction affect the structure of cities? Is there something innate to space, in terms of its properties and qualities, that contributes to its own structuring and transformation? Likewise, the function of space in the generation of inequality remains vexatious. Can space have an independent effect upon inequality? In Troy's words, 'Is there something inherent in the nature of spatial organization and the process of urban development which itself leads to some pattern of inequality and/or inequity? (Troy, 1981: 19.) Pahl suggested that until capitalism gives way to 'socialism' in an advanced industrial society the issue will remain unresolved: 'In these circumstances it would then be clear that urban processes are not *all* created by economic processes: the relative autonomy of spatial forms and their effect on distributive systems would be made more explicit' (Pahl, 1975: 10). In the absence of the type of social

[11] On a superficial level commonsense suggests that inequality will owe far more to the labour market in a society with a minimally developed welfare system; conversely, the more elaborate and comprehensive state provision becomes the greater the scope for either the amelioration or the exacerbation of any inherently structural inequality.

transformation[12] envisaged by Pahl can we even conceive of a non-capitalist arrangement of space not deformed by uneven development and free from territorial inequality?

Attributions to the functional significance of space in the creation of inequality range from unadulterated forms of spatial causality to one Marxist judgement that would anaesthetize space altogether. These obviously stand as the extremities of opinion; but, even in the case of the more moderate views, the tendency has been to state the problem diametrically. Thus in Harvey's work on urbanism the key question is whether the organization of space has '*a separate structure* with its own laws of inner transformation and construction'.[13] Or is it the 'expression of a set of relations embedded in some broader structure (such as the social relations of production)'? Even 'the most spatially sensitive Marxists seem impelled to establish eternal 'primacy' of the (non-spatial) social determinants (Soja, 1980: 208). For example, Slater asserts that space is nothing more than the material debris formed by social processes, and therefore spatial theory must be condemned to vacuity. It follows that geography has nothing to add to the insights yielded by dialectical materialism (Peet and Slater, 1980: 543–4).

'*Space' can be reflexive*

It is apparent that if we are to begin to comprehend the organization of space (and if we decide to restrict our spatial domain to the city then that is entirely arbitrary), then we have to investigate the social processes that shape space. Because social processes are *registered* or etched in space the city can be considered as a 'projection of society on space' (Castells, 1977a: 115). But while this constitutes an indispensable starting point it is an incomplete conceptualization of space as it stands. What is missing is an acceptance that 'spatial structures are also implicated in social structures and that each has to be theorized with the other' (Gregory, 1978: 112).

Soja (1980: 211) agrees that the most profitable way of studying the structuring of space is in terms of a 'socio-spatial dialectic' in which the social relations of production – for the Marxist – are both space-forming and space-contingent. In his opinion the endless argument among Marxists and various bystanders about pre-eminence and which *causes* which is time-wasting. Because the way in which society and space can combine varies according to the local situation, the creditability of a rigid

---

[12] Apparently Pahl has in mind a social transformation far more thoroughgoing than that witnessed in Sweden, and Czechoslovakia following the Second World War, if not the change in France in 1981. Perhaps some, and some parts of, post-Revolution Chinese cities approximate a socialist model of the city.

[13] The French Marxist geographer, Lefebvre, advocates an interpretation of space along these lines.

structural analysis is suspect from the start. At this level of abstraction it is sufficient to accept that reciprocity exists between social structure and spatial form without needing to be specific about the magnitude of the respective causal weights attached to them. As Gregory (1978: 120) would have it, 'spatial structure is not, therefore, merely the arena in which class conflicts express themselves but also the domain within which and, in part, through which class relations are constituted. . . .' Urry (1981: 456), for instance, is prepared to admit that 'With respect to the spatial, sociology (apart from its urban specialism) has tended to pay insufficient and ineffective attention to the fact that social practices are spatially patterned and that those patterns substantially affect these very social practices.' Giddens (1979), Joyce (1980) and Urry (1981) have all recently shown how the organization of space under capitalist conditions has clearly affected social relations. Of course, acceptance of the existence of a reflexive relationship between society and space also bears the hallmarks of a realist approach to explanation.

To extend this idea: as well as simultaneous interplay, the socio–spatial dialectic implies a series of chain reactions. Not only is the city fused with the wider society, but as a social artifact it, in turn, is capable of calling forth a response from social agents and forces (the capital market, governments etc.) which are obliged to take account of space. Social intervention then instigates another round of spatial restructuring which leads eventually to a new spatial realization, and so on. There is, however, one important proviso. How the market or other social instruments and practices refashion the city, or affect the lives of its inhabitants, rests *largely* with the economic structure or base. It prescribes the response, or sets the degrees of freedom within which development or action can take place consistent with local interpretations or appropriate to local conditions. Hence, when I propose in the next chapter, that capital is the principal architect of spatial structures I am respecting the prescriptive tendencies of capitalism, without insisting upon the inviolable determinancy of the economic structure as Marxist dogma is prone to do.

It may be possible to crystallize this general proposition about the relation between society and space by returning to the nature of inequality. The relative location of those disadvantaged families living on fringe housing estates in Australian cities is not the root cause of their inequality. That derives from their position in the labour market, which in turn limits where they will be located by the housing market. Poor households that find themselves badly located with respect to supportive community services and transportation are put in that position invariably because of their situation in the labour market. In this instance the most damaging and persistent inequalities are structural, whereas space functions, at best, to reinforce or mediate these structurally determined inequalities. We should constantly be aware that, while the city is plainly a projection of society in space, it can be shown that under certain conditions socially formed space can act to refract social processes, compound inequalities, and redistribute real income. Space is a complicating factor that cannot be excluded from a discussion of the nature of cities or, for that matter, of the derivation of inequality.

Part II
Capital as the Architect of Spatial Structures

In the next three chapters some steps are taken towards the framing of a political economy of urban space. So far, it has been argued, as part of a general concern with who gets what in capitalist societies, that the outcome of resource allocation is etched or registered in urban space and, therefore, that an inquisitiveness about spatial organization must assuredly lead to a questioning of the mechanisms and processes that produce spatial inequalities and uneven urban outcomes. Spatial organization, looked at in this way, provides a mirror that can be held up against society, allowing society to see itself in its own reflection, presumably more clearly. For this reason I will continue with a spatially oriented account of cities under advanced capitalism: 'the spatial outcomes of a system founded in the capitalist ethic, provide manifest evidence of unfairness and inequality; a spatial analysis has, therefore, a part to play (Williamson and Byrne, 1979: 198). Part II presents a historically grounded analysis of the processes and mechanisms that help to account for the spatial realizations, the urban outcomes, and the inequalities that constitute present-day capitalist cities in Britain, the United States and Australia. This paves the way for part III which delves more deeply into the sources of inequality and redistribution within such cities.

In part I four main approaches to fathoming the spatial organization of cities were evaluated – urban ecology, neoclassical location theory, welfare-directed spatial analysis, and urban managerialism. Part II is given over entirely to assembling the rudiments of a political economy of urban space. The revival of interest in political economy, which has Marxism as its driving force, coincided with the disillusion with positivist science that swept the social sciences during the 1970s, and the economic turbulence that has plagued the capitalist economies since the mid-1970s. The certitude of neoclassical economics, for example, is crumbling as many of the advanced capitalist economies lurch from crisis to crisis.

Although this is not a Marxist analysis one is bound to say that in urban studies these days the Marxist depiction of society, predicated upon capitalist relations of production, receives very serious consideration. As

Heilbroner (1980: 167) remarks towards the end of his superb extemporization of Marx's analysis of the capitalist system, 'Marx is certainly not infallible. . . . He is better thought of as *unavoidable.*' The analysis and materials laid out before the reader in part II are informed by, and represent a critical response to, the very rich vein of ideas originally mined by a group of urban sociologists affiliated with the Centre de Sociologie Urbaine in Paris, together with one or two American pioneers. Chapter 3 attempts to compress the central features of capitalism as viewed by Marx and shows how elements of Marx's theory have been reworked by urbanists seeking to construct better theories about cities in capitalist societies. While Marx has very little to say about urban space as such, it will be seen that: the capitalist city has been variously represented as the best arrangement of space for maximizing production, and for speeding accumulation and the transfer of surplus value; the urban land market can be theorized in terms that are reasonably consistent with Marx's concepts of rent and property relations; in suburbanization Marxist scholars have sought a characteristically capitalist response to the postwar crisis in 'underconsumption'; much urban-based conflict has been conceived as a transposition of the class struggle from the factory to urban neighbourhoods. And although relations between capital and the state were nowhere near as complicated in Marx's day, his writings have nevertheless served as a wellspring for pondering the role of the state in urban change.

The intention in chapter 4 and 5 is to decide how far the structuralist analysis is an aid to understanding, and where it is unworkable and factually wide of the mark. A historical perspective is the key to this: the logical coherence of the strict Althusserian approach that we encounter in the early work of Castells and Harvey, for example, can be shattered simply by comparing the urban outcomes obtained under conditions which are, often wrongly, assumed to be identical because of the superficial resemblance of the social formations characterizing the United Kingdom, the United States and Australia. Our version of capital, unlike the structuralists', is not hegemonic: there are limits to the capacity of capital to reproduce itself, and these lie in the power of the state to supervise and regulate capital, and with the realization that 'the accumulation process itself undermines its own bases, generating conflict and crises' (Edel, 1981: 32). This tends to happen when the rate of profit declines, with crises in 'realization', and when subservient property 'fractions' successfully resist or block the capital-creating programmes of the state or business corporations (see chapter 9). But it is not possible to be specific in advance about the underlying process or its spatial expression: 'the specific outcomes are not logically deducible from the existence of the capitalist mode of production or from the tendency to accumulation' (Edel, 1981: 41). As Enzo Mingione pointed out when he visited Australia in 1982, 'not everything has been immediately or obviously functional to capital.' The strategy for Part II is to present the essentially undiluted Marxist theory in chapter 3, and then hold it up for closer inspection against the historically constituted urban processes and structures that have formed under early (chapter 4) and advanced (chapter 5) capitalism.

3

The Rudiments of a Political Economy of Urban Space

Introduction

The first part of this chapter provides an introduction to the main features of capitalism as observed and theorized by Karl Marx and Frederick Engels under nineteenth-century conditions. I will allude to the Hegelian incubator in which Marx's ideas were hatched, describe the capitalist mode of production (CMP), admit to the centrality of class relations, and interrogate the accumulation process as the power-house of capitalism. Then the various approaches to the role of the state in the CMP will be outlined, in recognition of the interpenetration of the state and capital in the more advanced stages of capitalism, and the application of Marx's method in urban research will be discussed.

Perhaps the first thing to appreciate is that there is not a single Marxist analysis – there is Marx's theory, which in itself underwent considerable revision as Marx matured, and now, with the revival of interest in political economy, there is a very broad spectrum of what passes for Marxian analysis. 'There are many Marxisms, and the issues that separate them are both complex and controversial' (Duncan and Ley, 1982: 54). Probably most of the broadsides within Marxism have been fired between the supporters of a theoretical treatment of political economy and those more enamoured with an historiographic approach. The difference between the two Marxisms is hinted at in the opposing descriptors, scientific *v.* critical (Gouldner, 1980) and structuralism *v.* humanism (Thompson, 1978). It is enough to say that until very recently Marxist urban theory, with the exception of the contributions from Edel (1977), Gordon (1977) and Mingione (1981), has been dominated by a structuralist reading of political economy. As Mingione's work reveals, what is appropriate is neither separate historical *v.* dialectical materialism, but both, grounded in case studies of the experience of capitalist societies (Mingione, 1981: 20). Throughout Part II it will become apparent that the reaction to Marxist theory which set in at the beginning of the 1980s had as its main target the uncritical theoretical foreclosure that is the hallmark of structuralist

Marxism. In their reflections on developments in the field Harloe and Lebas (1981: xi) comment that 'One sees now a greater variety and subtlety of Marxist perspectives which appear to dominate without, however, monopolizing the field' as Althusserian structuralism did.

Marx's method

Dialectical materialism and the Hegelian incubator

The Marxist system of thought rests upon the twin pillars of the Hegelian dialectic and the materialist conception of history. Marx, who as a student was strongly influenced by the German philosopher Hegel, espouses a view of history that is dialectical in the sense that every idea or force is said to breed its opposite. Out of this opposition comes a gradual synthesis, to be followed again, in time, by contradiction and antithesis. Marx's vision was for an inexorable transformation of societies until they reached the socially perfect state of communism. Marxism is also materialist because it is grounded 'on the terrain of social and physical environment' (Heilbroner, 1980: 141) rather than in the world of ideas. According to Marx every society is built on an economic base, out of which develops a system of government and laws, religions and philosophical precepts (these are the superstructural elements of society). In a later elaboration (*Anti Dühring*), Engels explains (a) that the system of production and exchange developed by differing societies at each point in history determines how those societies will be divided into classes and estates; and (b) that it is change in the mode of production and exchange that is the real catalyst of social change and political revolution, and not simply human aspirations, or ideals of emancipation and liberation. The main theoretical task before Marx was the structural characterization of various modes of production including primitive communism, the ancient, Asiatic, feudal, capitalist and so on. And since constant change in the economic base means that no mode of production will ever exist in a pure form, Marx settled for typing a society's formation according to the mode dominant at the time, so, for example, nineteenth-century Britain is the classical instance of capitalism. Marx's method is described as a two-stage process: the first stage involves the elucidation of the internal structure of each mode of production; the second, the analysis of the ways in which different modes of production are co-present within a given society (Keat and Urry, 1975: 97). Dialectical materialism, therefore, is 'a method that seeks to identify the transformation rules through which society is restructured' (Harvey, 1973: 290).

Although the Marx of *Das kapital* was to make an emphatic break with Hegel's idealist notion of *Geist*, or world spirit, he retained other elements of the philosophy which shaped his intellectual development as a university student in Germany. For while Marx substitutes 'labouring productive man' for Hegel's spirit as the main agent of history (Rex, 1981: 65), he keeps the teleological perspective on history and continues to subscribe to a holistic philosophy of internal relations (Ollman, 1971: 37). Marx's teleologism, or belief that events are somehow shaped by the underlying purpose or design that is served by them, is resuscitated much later on by Althusser with his insistence on the theoretical sufficiency of a system defined and solely governed by the relations between its own inner parts (cf. mathematics whose truth, instead of relying on external referents is internal to its logic). It is the ontology of internal relations which is invoked by Harvey (1973: 288–96) in his attempt to theorize the dynamics of urbanism. Capitalism possesses an inner logic – the inner laws of transformation – which is sufficient, in itself, to 'shape the parts so that each part *functions* to preserve the existence and general structure of the whole' (my emphasis). The trouble with this is that it seems to require a shutting out of human action and non-economic agencies (Duncan and Ley, 1982: 38–40). Amongst Marxist geographers, Harvey, Walker, Clark, Dear, Cox, and Peet in particular, 'have been preoccupied with theoretical structuralisms of such forbidding abstraction that they leave scant space for human agency' (Gregory, 1982: 256). As with most epistemological standoffs the difference is more one of degrees. Gregory's notion of the 'boundedness of human activity' gets much closer to a commonsensical view of structural constraints: 'if men make history they do not do so entirely under conditions of their own choosing – hence the significance of boundedness, which ensures that the production of social life coincides with the reproduction of social structures' (Gregory, 1978: 71).

The capitalist mode of production (CMP)

This section draws heavily upon Edel's (1981) very readable and incisive description of the capitalist mode of production. But firstly, what is a 'mode of production'? In the formal language of Hindess and Hirst (1978) it is a structure that articulates forces and relations of production. These driving forces include both the technical methods by which production is carried out, and the social relationships between classes defined by their role in directing and carrying out production. The meaning of 'mode of production' is best conveyed by grouping actual economies and societies, or 'social formations', according to whether one class works for another, how labour is co-ordinated, and how the ruling class extracts the surplus produced by the workers:

> Thus, in feudalism, individual peasants or artisans do the work, deciding individually or in small groups what and how to produce.

Their product is, in part, taken from them in various forms of rent, including tithes, feudal dues and the like. . . . In primitive communism no class exists to capture a surplus produced by others. But no large-scale coordination or planning exists to allow much surplus to be created for workers themselves. In an advanced communist mode of production, the workers in a large society would coordinate and plan production above their subsistence needs, and direct the investment of the surplus themselves.

Under capitalism, wage-labour, coordination by capitalist managers and by market relations between enterprises, and the appearance of the surplus in the form of profit are the characteristic features. (Edel, 1981: 21–2)

Before the discussion is narrowed to the CMP note should be taken of two important claims that Marx made for the structure of any type of society. Firstly, each element of a mode of production is causally inter-related with the rest and 'is also a condition of functioning of those elements' (Keat and Urry, 1975: 102); that is, Marx clearly subscribes to a functionalist account of 'social formations'. Secondly, the social relations of production dominate all other elements in the mode. In capitalism it is the social relations of capital and labour which are foremost. Hence, above all else, capital in the Marxist scheme takes its meaning from its *relation* with the other elements in the CMP and is not merely an item of wealth (conventionally 'capital goods'). 'Fundamentally it is the ability to command labour and to accumulate more wealth through the ownership of wealth' (Edel, 1981: 22).

In his outline of the general or defining characteristics of capitalism that have been identified by the Marxist tradition of analysis, Edel (1981) separates the necessary elements of the CMP (the domination of the economy by a ruling class through the control of capital; the presence of a proletariat, which depends upon wage labour for its livelihood; the extraction of surplus value in the process of production; the existence of a market in which commodities can be exchanged) from those additional elements which he suggests contribute to the variations found between capitalist societies. These variable characteristics within the capitalist mode include: the institutions developed to cater for land/property ownership; the family and social institutions that see to it that the bourgeoisie and the proletariat reproduce the labour power necessary for capitalism's survival; differing approaches to the role of the state and organizing government; varying degrees of unification and class consciousness in each of the two contending classes. We need to be fully aware that here Edel is making an important break with structuralists like Poulantzas, Castells, Harvey and Peet. One of the reasons for selecting three urban societies that are expected to exhibit the common elements of advanced capitalism is to describe precisely their systemic deviations and locate variable urban outcomes.

Social relations of production

An unambiguous definition of the Marxian category 'class' is really only available as an abstraction, in which case it is defined in terms of a functional position relative to the mode of production, i.e. the proletariat is functionally dependent as labour-power upon the owners of capital – the bourgeoisie. While the bourgeoisie control and monopolize the means of production (capital, materials and land), workers only have their labour-power to contribute to the production process which they bring into being by transforming naturally occurring raw materials into a commodity. They infuse the raw materials with the value of their labour-power, which is the source of *surplus value*.[1] The relationship is palpably exploitative because the owners of the means of production appropriate the surplus value created by the working class, which has little option but to sell its labour-power to capitalists.

Although the underlying pattern of social relations is given by the structure of productive relationships within the CMP, this is not sufficient for genuine class formation according to Marx. 'A class for Marx only properly exists when it assumes a directly *political* character' (Keat and Urry, 1975: 108), remembering that class conflict and struggle traditionally takes place around the means of production:

> The economic conditions have in the first place transformed the mass of the people of a country into wage-workers. The domination of capital has created for this mass of people a common situation with common interests. Thus the mass is already a class, as opposed to capital, but not yet for itself. In the struggle, of which we have only noted some phases, this mass unites, it is constituted as a class for itself. The interests which it defends are the interests of its class. But the struggle between class and class is a political struggle. (Marx quoted in Rex, 1981: 47–8)

[1] Surplus value arises from the conjunction of two processes: firstly, the competition for jobs amongst individual workers acts to keep the price of labour power (wages) close to the social minimum, which is just enough to allow the working class to subsist and reproduce itself; secondly, assuming that the value of production must exceed labour costs, workers' wages are set at the social minimum irrespective of their productivity. Because the productivity of a worker depends, in part, upon the technical capacity of the machinery he/she is operating, an efficient manufacturer can be expected to end up with products worth a good deal more than the original costs. This is what Marx terms surplus value. It is the source of the capitalist's profits, rent for the use of land, taxes, and the interest repayments on borrowed money. (Marx also regards these other forms of revenue as shares in the total surplus value created by labour even though they are not payments for actual work done. See Edel, 1981: footnote 6, 42.)

A sensible analysis of classes, therefore, is obliged not only to show how they are defined in terms of their relation to the means of production, but also to show how they are structured by ideological disposition, by patterns of political action, by institutions of power and property, and by the policies of the state.

Marx is frequently ridiculed for reducing social relations to the class dichotomy; for example, patricians and plebians in ancient society, lords and vassals in feudal society, factory owners and factory operatives in industrializing England. In his later work, Marx readily admitted that his typification of capitalist society was idealized and that in England 'the stratification of classes does not appear in its pure form'. He continued, 'Middle and intermediate strata even here obliterate lines of demarcation everywhere (although incomparably less in rural districts than in the cities)' (Marx, 1967: **3**: 885). Moreover, in his own social history of Louis Bonaparte's France, Marx identified half a dozen class interests. Marx is not perturbed by these discrepant social 'classes' because they can still be explained in terms of the basic structure of productive relations within society. Transitional classes are left over from previous historically dominant modes, or are antecedent (merchant capitalists within feudalism). There are sectors of the major classes, such as the corporate managers or the so-called lumpenproletariat. Intermediate classes such as the petit bourgeoisie or the 'new middle class' within capitalism are also accommodated in Marx's expanded typology. Finally, slaves in the ancient mode or the peasantry in medieval Europe are accorded the status of quasi-classes (Keat and Urry, 1975: 108).

Despite the strength of some of the more insistent Marxist claims for class solidarity, Edel argues that the extent of class unity among the owners of capital, and within the working class, can be expected to vary between capitalist societies. For one thing, although the common interests of capitalists in the preservation of capitalism are well known, competition always sets individual capitalists up against each other. 'Fractions of capital' – groups with interests in different industries or kinds of investment – may favour different policies. In some countries differences between domestic and foreign capitals are a source of disagreement (Edel, 1981: 28). Alternatively, the solidarity of the working classes can be strained by inter-union rivalries and divided by racial, religious and regional tensions. These days powerful trade unions too often reveal a callous disregard for those 'marginalized' members of the working class, the 'non-working poor'. This perspective which Edel, and others like him (Byrne, 1982; Mingione, 1981), are developing will bear importantly on later references to captive cities, and the case for diverse urban outcomes.

Accumulation: the powerhouse of capitalism

Edel (1981: 29) defines capital accumulation in the Marxist sense,[2] as 'an increase in the generalised wealth controlled by capital'. Basically, it is the competitive environment in which capitalists operate that impels them to accumulate 'one accumulates or one gets accumulated' (Heilbroner, 1980: 153). This is an allusion to the conditions found in the topsy-turvy world of takeover, liquidation, increasing concentration, monopolization of the market, the undercutting of competitors, and on occasions, industrial espionage. More down to earth is the requirement for the owners and managers of capital not only to pay attractive dividends and interest, but to maximize the rate of return on borrowed money, to meet workers' demands for an expanding share of the surplus value (benefits, workers' compensation, superannuation), to fulfil their social obligations (taxes, rates, surcharges) out of profits, and to maintain a programme of re-investment (R & D, replacement of equipment and plant, training workers). Because of these pressures and commitments (capital's requirements), accumulation is an imperative of the capitalist system. If capital fails to reproduce itself, stagnation and atrophy follow: capitalism is not equipped to cope with zero, and certainly not negative, economic growth.

Although reinvestment of profits and public policies that are supportive of continued growth are the normal tendencies of state capitalism there is no guarantee 'that growth will be either continuous or tranquil under capitalism' (Edel, 1981: 32). The 'healthy' competition that breeds growth also leads to: the bankruptcy of small manufacturers, businesses, and owner-operators; the deskilling of labour and structural unemployment; greater social polarity and tension; more unequal regions and urban neighbourhoods. Marx also contends that even when the capitalist economy is growing and some of the material benefits of growth percolate down to the working class the system of class domination remains intact, producing the usual winners and losers in disproportionate numbers.

Marx's analysis of capital accumulation concludes that the process contains the seeds of its own destruction, that it is inherently crisis-prone. As competing capitalists substitute labour-saving machinery to counteract rises in the real wage rate, their rate of profit falls. With this rise in the organic composition of capital the ratio of living labour – the source of surplus value – to total output shrinks. Profits are trimmed, consumption dwindles as the purchasing power of the unemployed is withdrawn from the market for goods, producers panic and begin to dump their goods on the market, and smaller firms go under. At the same time the workers thrown out of work (Marx's *Industrial Reserve Army*) are prepared to

---

[2] Notice in passing the broad similarity between the two paradigms: where political economists refer to 'accumulation' and 'the logic of capital', the neoclassicists speak of 'profit maximization' and 'the invisible guiding hand of the market'.

undersell themselves in the labour-market to regain employment. (Neo-classical economists make a similar connection between capital intensification, labour replacement and structural unemployment.) Thus, after a time, surplus value is restored:

> The forward march is taken up again. But it leads to the same catastrophic conclusion: competition for workers; higher wages; labour-displacing machinery; a smaller base for surplus value; still more frenzied competition; collapse. And each collapse is worse than the preceding one. In the periods of crisis, the bigger firms absorb the smaller ones, and when the industrial monsters eventually go down, the wreckage is far greater than when the little enterprises buckle. (Heilbroner, 1980: 157–8).

These are prescient words, for 1982 saw the collapse of the Penn Square bank and Braniff airlines in the US, and the failure of the West German electronics giant, AEG-Telefunken.

The Marxist development of theory to account for the periodic crises that disturb economic growth under capitalism[3] makes use of a 'device' called a contradiction.[4] Indeed Marxist theory anticipates that the accumulation process will be periodically interrupted by contradictions of its own making; but that with resolution, stability can be restored to the system moving capitalism onto a higher plane. The most fundamental contradiction embodied in the accumulation process is the tendency in the long run to change the division of labour in society (see chapters 4 and 5) which, of course, is bound to undermine the social formation that is doing the accumulating. Marx appreciated the likelihood that under competitive capitalism, production was bound to become more and more centralized and concentrated (making for a 'socialization' of production), while the appropriation of property would tend to 'privatization'. Otherwise, Marxists have tendered a number of suggestions[5] for the onset of economic downturn and imminent crisis (there is no agreement about the order of importance): as labour struggles/bargains for a greater share of the surplus value in prosperous times, profits are squeezed; a 'crisis' of underconsumption can be brought on by a collapse in demand (Baran and

---

[3] The 'bourgeois' analysis of economic crisis homes in on symptoms like inflation, over-expansion of credit, slow growth in productivity, historically high energy costs, dis-equilibrium in the international monetary system.

[4] Duncan and Ley (1982: 42) explain that unlike their functionalist counterparts, who ultimately have great difficulty in demonstrating that everything is functional within the system under examination, Marxists have no such trouble with those elements that are dysfunctional to the stability of the capitalist system, i.e. 'contradictions' are actually functional to the extent that they move history onto a higher plane.

[5] An excellent synopsis of the Marxist discussion of 'crisis' can be found in O'Connor (1981a).

Sweezy 1966), or structural unemployment; public spending on 'unproductive' social investment may eventually induce 'fiscal' and reproduction crises (O'Connor, 1974); 'disproportionality' effects may follow if investment in the 'capital and producer goods' industries outpaces that in allied industries; profit margins can be eroded if the ratio of equipment to labour used in production moves too far out of kilter (Edel, 1981: 32–35). Chapters 4 and 5 examine several Marxist hypotheses relating to aspects of urban development and restructuring that are built around these contradictory tendencies in accumulation.

The role of the state[6]

Liberal (or *laissez-faire*) capitalism characterized the mid-nineteenth century environment in which Marx and Engels worked. By definition, 'the role of the state was minor and almost of negligible importance' (Offe, 1975: 127–8). Consequently, neither Marx nor Engels ever bothered to enlarge on the unrefined and fairly fatalistic judgement contained in the *Communist manifesto* (Marx and Engels, 1967 edn: 44): 'The executive of the modern state is but a committee for managing the common affairs of the whole bourgeoisie.' But with the rise of the welfare state (Gough, 1979) and the development of budget management procedures and macroeconomic instruments by central governments, an analysis of the state's role and the class position of the bureaucracy has become a necessary part of the neo-Marxist interpretation. Hence, as the title of Cleaver's book *Reading capital politically* (1979) suggests, the political and ideological elements of the superstructure are no longer overshadowed by a preoccupation with the economic base in Marxist analyses of the capitalist mode of production; indeed, one of the most invigorating debates in contemporary Marxism revolves around the role of the state (Gold *et al.*, 1975; Holloway and Picciotto, 1978; Jessop, 1977). If we put to one side the 'Hegelian-Marxist' concern, which dwells upon the diversionary nature of the state and is therefore difficult to operationalize (see Clark and Dear, 1981), it is possible to identify the nucleii of five distinctly Marxist

---

[6] What is the state? The Concise Oxford dictionary says that the state is an 'organized political community under one government, commonwealth, nation . . .'. The same dictionary distinguishes between state capitalism ('policy of State control of use of capital') and state socialism ('policy of State control of industries and services in order to benefit all equally'). Marxists would view this as incomplete without some acknowledgement of the authority-relation, state *power*, which finds expression in the content of state policy. This translation of power into policy requires state apparatus including a rule-making legislature, an administrative arm of government, a judiciary, and law enforcement and defence capabilities.

conceptions of the state:[7] (a) instrumentalist; (b) structuralist; (c) relatively autonomous; (d) the state as reactive-aversion strategist; (e) state derivationist, incorporating the 'capital logic' and 'materialist' versions. Since the issue of state intervention in urban transformation will surface again and again in this book, it will help to establish, at the very least, the key differences between each of these perspectives (though they are not always readily apparent). At the same time it must be said that the debate is ongoing and some of the participants (Miliband and Poulantzas) have shifted their ground more than once while others like Offe cannot be easily 'pigeon-holed'. But before launching into this, it is necessary to clarify the main tasks performed by governments in capitalist states like Britain, the US, and Australia.

Forms of state intervention

Although it is difficult to get most conservative commentators to admit to the ideological purposes served by state intervention (see Gough 1979), there is very little disagreement between them and radicals about the degree of involvement of the state today in the areas of production, consumption and social control. O'Connor (1974: 119–34) distinguishes between social capital expenditures and the social expenses of production. Social capital expenditures subsume the investments undertaken by governments to maintain private production at current rates of profit (social investment) and to maintain the distribution system (social consumption). Social investment covers expenditures in physical capital (like roads, utilities and the preparation of sites for industry and commerce through planned urban renewal) and human capital (state education, hospitals and clinics, sponsorship of research and development). State spending on social consumption divides into public goods and services, notably housing, and social insurance payments to the unemployed and sick, which helps to reduce the call on private capital. Functions that are commonly handed over to the public sector because their rate of profit is unattractive to private capital include: police, fire and health services; most education; some transport and communications; provision of parks and reserves, water, gas, electricity and sewerage (though private utility companies still operate profitably in the US and Canada). Szelenyi (1981a) has coined the term 'unproductive urban infrastructure' to describe this feature of state provision. On the assumption that social investment serves private capital ahead of society as a whole, O'Connor goes on to show how the socialization of unprofitable activities such as urban infrastructure

[7] This leaves out the broadly Weberian, managerialist perspective, which was discussed in the previous chapter, and the representational approach which in simple terms depicts the state as an impartial umpire, standing above and beyond the reach of the interest groups in the urban arena (see Dahl, 1963; Birch, 1964).

eventually generates a fiscal crisis in the state itself, since the revenue collected from social investment provision falls well short of the original appropriations.

Social expenses, in the form of policing and the judiciary, are deemed necessary to maintain social cohesion and control: 'These expenditures include the costs of politically containing the proletariat at home and abroad, the costs of keeping small-scale, local and regional capital at home, safely within the ruling corporate liberal consensus, and the costs of maintaining the comprador ruling classes abroad' (O'Connor, 1974: 131). This is the *legitimation* function of the state, which neo-Marxist scholars argue has become increasingly problematic with the build-up of surplus productive capacity and a pool of unemployed labour under conditions of advanced monopoly capitalism (Habermas, 1976). It can be appreciated that the need for legitimation contributes further to the growing fiscal crisis of the state by enlarging the drain on the 'welfare vote'. And because this unproductive social expenditure is committed at the expense of social investment in productive capacity the state is faced with a fundamental conflict of interests.

The state as capital's instrument

How is the role of the state to be theorized? It was Miliband (1969) who revived serious debate on the state with *The state in capitalist society* in the late 1960s. He set out to debunk the representational view (Dahl, 1963) which 'systematically underestimates the preponderate, self-interested political influence of members of the capitalist class' (Skocpol, 1980: 160). While Dahl was realist enough to appreciate that political resources and power are unequally distributed, he was not prepared to go as far as agreeing to any consistent class bias on the part of the state in its dealings with lobbyists and other pressure groups. Miliband (1969), on the other hand, saw the state as an autonomous set of institutions which is effectively 'captured' by the ruling class and used as an instrument to serve capital's ends (Figure 3.1a). His checklist for research would include the nature of the high-level linkages between business leaders and the policy-makers. The co-option of corporate managers by US presidents represents one of the mechanisms by which business keeps its finger on the government pulse. In conducting interviews for a book called *Reagan's ruling class* (Brownstein and Easton, 1983), Ralph Nader, the consumer advocate, said he found administration officials intent on producing 'a Government of General Motors, by Dupont, for Exxon':

> Reagan has turned over control of the US Government to a group of officials with a remarkably similar and limited set of experiences and allegiances that are remote from the realities of life for most

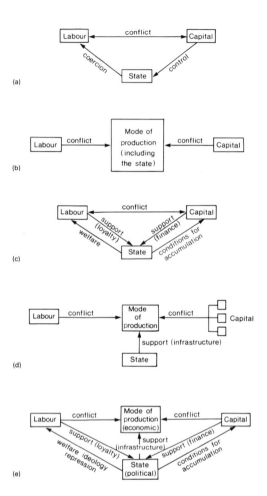

Figure 3.1 Alternative models of the capitalist state
(a) Instrumentalist
(b) Structuralist
(c) Input – output
(d) Capital logic
(e) Materialist
Source: Clark and Dear, 1981: 53, 56–8

Americans. Almost 30 of the top officials in the Administration are millionaires and many are multi-millionaires who view Government as an instrument for the powerful and wealthy, unaccountable to the public. It is a Government cadre of extraordinarily broad wealth, narrow vision and little compassion. (reported in the *Age*, 1982: 8)

Although the impression of the state as the handmaiden of capital may seem preposterous to some, consider the reported reaction of Edwin S. Crooks Jnr, stockbroker, following a week of unprecedented trading on the US stock market late in August, 1982: 'You shouldn't sell American business short. We can change the management of the country every four years if necessary. Business runs this country. As it should' (Wynhausen, 1982: 12).

Structuralism

Poulantzas (1976a) and his urban 'kinsmen', Castells and Lokjine, argue that it is incorrect to conceive of the state as a separate entity that is capable of making an independent response to economic forces. In such a criticism, therefore, the title of Poulantzas's riposte, *The capitalist state* (1976a), takes on a heightened significance when it is juxtaposed against *The state in capitalist society* (Miliband, 1969). The ruling class and the state bureaucracy become one and the same thing within the structural-relational account of the state, wherein the functions of the state are broadly determined by the structure of society itself, rather than the people who occupy positions of power (Gold *et al.*, 1975, 1: 36). From what can be deduced from Poulantzas's early work – *Political Power and social classes* (Poulantzas, 1973) is not immediately about the state – the state is collapsed into class relations, and all government planning and state intervention is directed at the reproduction of the capitalist relations of production. State capitalism, therefore, is embedded in the very structure of society – the social formation (figure 3.1b). It is not until his later exchanges with Miliband that Poulantzas (1976a and b) admits that aspects of *Political power and social classes* suffered from 'structural deformation' that concealed the main emphasis of his arguments about the state (McEachern, 1980: 27).

The 'relatively autonomous' state

Poulantzas's corrected specification of the capitalist state shifts attention to the state as 'the condensate of a *relation of power* between struggling classes' (Poulantzas, 1976b: 74). Further, Poulantzas introduces the concept of 'relative autonomy': 'the capitalist state, while predominantly representing the interests of the hegemonic class or fraction (itself variable), enjoys a relative autonomy with respect to that class and fraction as well as to the other classes and fractions of the power bloc' (Poulantzas, 1976b: 97–8). While the state is bound to attend to the long-run interests of monopoly capital, when it comes to the implementation of policy, there is no need for a consistent class bias. The problem with 'relative autonomy' is that while the main elements required for an analysis of the state are present – classes, fractions, organization and power – they are theorized in such an open-ended way that almost every conceivable situation is covered, rendering it immune from falsification (Saunders, 1979: 184). The nature, limits and determinants of the state's relative autonomy is left unspecified (Block, 1977: 9).

System equilibration: the intercession of the state and crisis resolution

To another collection of Marxists, dominated by the Frankfurt school of critical theorists (see Van den Berg, 1980) and joined by O'Connor, the state's authority relations are 'complex, semi-autonomous, and not re-ducible to an expression of the interests of the capitalist class' (McLellan, 1979: 327). The prime task for them is the interrogation of the reactive-avoidance strategies designed by the state to avoid crises of the economy, of rationality, of legitimacy and of motivation (Habermas, 1976), and to defuse class conflict. Crises arise, as we have seen, because the pursuit of profit – the organizational principle of capitalism – ultimately renders the CMP irrational and contradictory. Inter- and, indeed, intra-class tensions and animosity are precipitated by the failure of the market place to recog-nize legitimate needs. Australians witnessed a very real expression of this sort of confrontation on 26 October 1982, when 200 miners and steel-workers from Wollongong stormed the Commonwealth Parliament to protest about the withdrawal of one of the most basic rights, the right to work. Hence, state intervention and the rise of 'organized' capitalism are explained as the result of continuous adaptations necessary to protect the system against its own inherently self-destructive tendencies. Offe gives the basic representation of power relations (figure 3.1c): crises in ration-ality are the end product of the state's administrative decisions (output) whereas legitimation crises occur when the state fails to maintain mass support (input). For the first time, a clear assertion is made that the owners and managers of capital will not always gain from state policies and that intra-class fractions may be at odds. It is quite clear, to take an example of the former situation, that the Fraser government's *retrospective* legislation to retrieve $540 million of evaded taxes from 4,600 registered companies in Australia is bitterly resented by the business community. In the case of the latter situation one only needs to refer to the conflict of interests between depositors and borrowers in times of high interest rates, or the impact of concentration in retailing upon 'family' firms. Aungles and Szelenyi (1979) take these possibilities one step further by pointing out

that: 'under given circumstances the interests of the State . . . can structurally coincide with the 'interests of labour'. Therefore the hegemony of
capital above the state apparatuses is not absolute and unconditional and, if
the political preconditions are given, it can be challenged.' The conflict
between the state and monopoly capital that they allude to arose when
Broken Hill Proprietary, Australia's biggest heavy industry conglomerate, decided to close the shipyard in its own 'company town' of
Whyalla, South Australia (Aungles and Szelenyi, 1979). Elsewhere
Szelenyi (1981a: 565) asserts that 'Under the conditions of the present
stag-flationary crisis, it is becoming more and more obvious that the State
is not merely an instrument of capital or the dominant class and that the
structural conflicts emerge between the State and capital.'

Roweis (1981: 169) has summarized Offe's model of state action thus: in
contrast to the 'direct politics' characteristic of early capitalism, state
agencies now adapt as the need arises to act as a buffer between the
combating classes or fractions of capital, to handle otherwise volatile
political situations, to contrive 'workable' political 'truces', deals or com-
promises before it is too late, and to contain and temper the outcomes of
the class struggle.

'Deriving' the state: 'capital logic' or 'materialist'?

The state derivationist approach to the role of the state has crystallized
around the debate taking place initially amongst West German Marxists
(see Holloway and Picciotti, 1978) as to which is the most appropriate
method for establishing, or 'deriving', the capitalist form of the state. This
comprises two main lines of argument: the capital-logic derivation and the
historical materialist derivation. What these both have in common is the
recognition of the need to place the state outside the CMP (figures 3.1d
and e), where it can more effectively monitor and control capital through
its institutions, with the *general* objective of nurturing conditions conducive to accumulation. Of necessity the state is separate from, and no more
answerable to, one class or fraction than another, so long as the capitalist
economy maintains a full head of steam. Block's (1977) thesis is that even if
'the ruling class does not rule', and a worker-dominated government
comes to power within a capitalist system, it will have to maintain the
momentum of accumulation unless it can transform the economic base
completely. A conscious, politically directive, ruling class is no longer
necessary to account for government policy: 'Instead, capitalist rationality
emerges out of a three-sided relationship among capitalists, workers and
state managers' (Block, 1977: 27). How else can Reagan's humiliating
retreat on taxes be explained? Having been elected on the promise of
sweeping tax cuts he was forced by economic pressures to fly in the face of
his staunchest conservative supporters and increase taxes by $US98.3

billion during the period 1982–84. With mid-term elections imminent it was the only way the Reagan government could simultaneously maintain its commitment to greatly expanded spending on defence, avoid a welfare 'backlash' in the states with the highest level of unemployment, and peg back the massive deficit[8] which is a precondition for economic recovery.

According to McEachern (1980: 35) it is Hirsch, who does not accept all of the conclusions of the capital-logic position, that comes closest to linking empirical research with theoretical arguments, and the development of the state with the requirements of capital *plus* the struggles of various political groups (see Holloway and Picciotto, 1978). With a materialist perspective comes the recognition that capital fractions and classes constantly interact with the state, and that since this is an ongoing process 'the form of the State can be expected to alter as conditions of capital accumulation change' (Clark and Dear, 1981: 59). Wolfe (1977) has shown how government institutions and the forms of state intervention have continued to readjust and adapt to the evolving social formation in the United States. Six 'temporary forms' of the American state apparatus are delimited: the accumulative, harmonious, expansionist, franchise, dual and transnational state.

'Materialists' argue that it is the latest and most sophisticated phase of monopoly capitalism that has required the state to really hone its tools for crisis-management. The nation state no longer merely *reacts* to socio-economic crises, but endeavours to *execute* economic restructuring within its regions and cities under conditions which it cannot fundamentally influence because of capital's relative freedom to pursue value creation at the world market level (Hirsch, 1981: 594). At the same time the state must busy itself intercepting and compensating for the social consequences of these developments and dampen down the resulting conflicts. 'It is essential that the "crises of the cities", and connected forms of social conflict, be seen in this total context' (Hirsch, 1981: 594). Obviously this debate on the role of the state is unfinished. It can be said, now, that: 'the analyses of Jaochim Hirsch and Claus Offe seem more sensitive than much of the early French work to the political nature of relations within the state, to the contradictions inherent in its bureaucracies and the actions of its personnel, and to the problems faced by the state in its role as employer and producer' (Harloe and Lebas, 1981: xvi).

Urban research and the Marxist method

Even though an analysis of the meaning of the 'urban revolution' for capitalist relations of production really lay outside Marx's theoretical field

---

[8] The Office of Management and Budget estimates that the Federal budget deficit which was to have been eliminated by 1984 will reach $A196,100 million in that financial year.

(Lojkine, 1976) his *method* is so suggestive of theoretical payoffs that it has given a tremendous fillip to urban and regional studies during the last decade (Lebas, 1982). While many problems remain with the application of the Marxist method to urban and regional change, it has forced a broadening of the scope of urban and regional research and appears to be taking work into the orbit of more convincing philosophies of science (Duncan, 1981: 231).

In the space of a hectic decade – the 1970s – several scholars proferred Marxist versions of urban process and structure. Manuel Castells's *The Urban Question* (1977a), though subsequently repudiated in large part by the author, will always occupy a position of central importance in the development of urban studies. In it Castells follows a cathartic critique of post-war urban sociology with a reconstruction of urban process that is heavily imbued with Althusserian structuralism. Although only one of a group of Marxists writing in French[9] that addressed the relationship between the urban 'problematic' and state monopoly capitalism in their work – Lojkine, Olives, Lamarche, Preteceille, Topalov – it was Castells who left the greatest impression upon a receptive audience of British sociologists reared on a diet of empiricism (see Pickvance, 1976). Thus a very stilted form of Marxism was absorbed into the bloodstream of British urban sociology and social geography during the mid-1970s. Castells (1978: 12) has since conceded that 'the theoretical coding has been too rapid, too formal, too abstract, the reality analysed was more complex than the models used.' He now advises that 'the recognition of a new historical perspective is more important than a formalist theoretical orientation.' The harvest from this shift in orientation is laid out in *City, class and power* (Castells, 1978). Likewise, David Harvey, who stated quite openly that he was feeling his way forward with his socialist formulations in *Social justice and the city* (Harvey, 1973), admits with hindsight that he also wandered down a few theoretical cul-de-sacs and blind alleys. With his more recent work he has gone to the heart of a political economy of urbanization,[10] by linking finance capital through circulation processes with the 'classical' sources of surplus value (Harvey, 1978).

This is by way of explanation for the decision to pick the eyes out of Marxist urban analysis. Though much of the early work of Castells and Harvey was seminal, it has since been superseded. Apart from making passing judgements on some of their revised work, I will concentrate on a form of urban political economy that has won the broadest acceptance (Proctor, 1982).

[9] Castells and Olives are of Spanish extraction; Lamarche is a French Canadian.
[10] Although that description does not seem to fit *The limits to capital* (Harvey, 1982) in which Harvey laboriously attempts to recast the three volumes of Marx's *Das kapital*.

Capital as the architect of urban spatial structure

The basis of Marxist urban theory is predicated upon the following condition:

> If the city is considered to start with as a market where labour, power, capital and products are exchanged, it must be equally accepted that the geographical configuration of this market is not the result of chance; it is governed by the laws of capital circulation . . . the urban question is first and foremost the product of the capitalist mode of production which requires a spatial organization which facilitates the circulation of capital, commodities, information etc. (Lamarche, 1976: 86)

Cities in advanced capitalist societies are conceived of as a particular built form that is compatible to a greater or lesser degree with the process of accumulation. As well as concentrating the means of production, exemplified by the nineteenth-century factory town, cities also developed the urban infrastructure which facilitates the geographical transfer of surplus value (alternatively referred to as the circulation of capital).[11] Hence by connecting producers with their markets, transportation and communications networks play a vital part in sustaining the development of the CMP.

According to the labour theory of value only capital engaged in the production sphere is capable of being expanded through productive labour. Capital engaged in circulation is capital wasted because it is unavailable for production, the sole source of surplus value and accumulation. This accounts for the commitment of private and social investment to reducing transfer costs and circulation time – the whole chain reaction of transport and storage, retail distribution and marketing. 'The city thus appeared as a direct effect of the need to reduce indirect costs of production, and costs of circulation and consumption in order to speed up the rate of rotation of capital' (Lojkine, 1976: 127). Above all else the Marxists stress that the city is a medium for the circulation of capital.

The functional specialization of circulation has led to the gradual emergence of individual kinds of capital ('fractions of capital'). Lamarche (1976: 88) recognizes four in all:

1   Industrial capital, which controls the process of production.

[11] For Marx the distinction between production and circulation turned on whether the activity was productive or unproductive under the terms of the labour theory of value. The conversion of capital into a commodity form was productive, whilst circulation refers to the various transactions whereby money is exchanged (a) for labour-power and raw materials prior to the production process, and (b) for the commodity produced (this is the act/state of *realization*).

2 Commercial capital which has given rise to a category of capitalist intermediaries – merchants – that have taken over almost entirely the task of exchange (it also ensures that the producers recover the value of their goods more quickly even though stock might sit around in warehouses and shops for some time before being purchased).

3 Financial capital which, while creating neither value nor a product, allows for a reduction in the amount of operating capital that a manufacturer would otherwise require to meet periodic payments and purchases (this classical separation invariably breaks down under monopoly capitalism with the interpenetration of the banking and industrial sectors).

4 Property capital, whose primary role is to plan the spatial organization of activities within cities and thereby reduce the indirect costs of production.

Property capital has a 'planning' role which derives from the way it selects sites, and an 'equipping' role in the types of building it develops on them (Pickvance, 1976: 12). It is chiefly with urban planning in mind that Lamarche (1976: 102) suggests 'the more property capital extends its control over urban space the more it is able to create and dictate the conditions for its own profitability.' According to Lamarche (1976: 95) property developers obtain their profits from the letting of floor-space as well as extracting them from the surplus value created by labour in the building and construction industry.

Harvey (1978) has taken this framework one step further with the proposal that capital flows through a series of linked paths, or circuits, within the urban economy.[12] Capital (surplus value) created in the production process has to go somewhere besides back into the firm. When there is no incentive to invest in the primary circuit (production) the surplus value is channelled via the capital market into the secondary circuit (figure 3.2). In the process of constructing the built environment capital is fixed in place and extra value created. The tertiary circuit of capital comprises the investment in science and technology that ultimately leads to advances in productive capacity, together with the social expenditure undertaken by the state as part-contribution to the reproduction of labour-power. The relation between these three circuits is what really interests Harvey. How is investment in the built environment and the other circuits linked? Under what conditions, and in which directions, does capital circulate? What institutions channel investment? To what extent is urban investment simply a by-product of programmes created to stabilize a faltering economy?

[12] In his 1974 paper Harvey is much more attracted to the increasing dominance of finance capital over industrial capital. Here, though, the source of surplus value is restored to its proper place in classical Marxist thought.

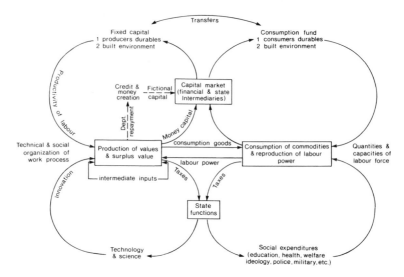

Figure   3.2   The structure of relations between the primary, secondary and tertiary circuits of capital
Source: Harvey, 1978: 109

Probably one of the best examples in Marxist urban praxis of the linking of the three circuits is the 'underconsumptionist' theory of suburbaniza-tion. The·idea that postwar suburbanization arose out a realization crisis of underconsumption was first floated by the Americans Baran and Sweezy (1966: 300–05), in their classic study of *Monopoly capital.* It is also an integral part of O'Connor's (1973) account of the fiscal crisis of the state. These three attribute the growth of public expenditure after the Second World War to the production surpluses of monopoly capital: all the labour and capital absorbing activities associated with postwar suburbanization and promoted by governments at all levels in the United States, according to this thesis, were designed to keep the American economy on the boil. Chapter 5 shows how Walker (1981), one of David Harvey's protégés, has explored the development of the American suburb by charting the circula-tion of capital in space through time.

Obstacles to the attainment of optimum conditions for accumulation within cities

The structure of no big city can ever, or will ever, meet with an optimum arrangement for the reproduction of capital. Inertia and lags, shortages of social investment capital, and class resistance to unacceptable redevelop-ment, all see to it that the restructuring of cities is an imperfect process. In part the progressive intervention of the state in the urban development processes is directed at the elimination of spatial inefficiencies, congestion costs and structural rigidities within large cities. According to Lojkine (1976: 128) the following three contradictory tendencies detract from the 'rational, socialized, planning of urban development':

1   It is apparent that the fiscal requirements for urban expenditure authorized by the state have run well ahead of the private sector's capacity to pay. Yet, if congestion costs and sources of capital inefficiency are not ameliorated, the rate of profit of urban industries will continue to fall.
2   In an effort to reduce their indirect costs of production, firms continue to be attracted to the largest and best equipped cities which exacerbates the degree of congestion and pollution within them.
3   Lojkine sees in the private ownership of land (a remnant from the pre-capitalist formation?) an improbable obstacle to the state's long-term goal of monopolistic accumulation. In addition, the private appropriation of urban ground rent is the primary cause of social segregation within cities.

The collective means of consumption

Although the updated and revised Castells (1978) is in full agreement with these previous writers about the determining role of long-term structural tendencies in the system of production – the concentration and centralization of capital and its constant battle against the tendency towards a lower rate of profit, the socialization of the productive forces, the development of the class struggle – he still chooses to view the contemporary organization of urban space under advanced capitalism as an 'expression of the process of collective treatment of the daily consumption patterns of households' (Castells, 1978: 16). More specifically, he means the massive intervention of the state in the organization of collective consumption (which shifts the onus for reproducing labour-power from the private sector to the state). Consumption is assigned this degree of importance in Castells' scheme because: (a) mass consumption is necessary if industry is to maintain levels of production close to capacity; (b) the state has come to assume progressively more responsibility for the provision of collective means of consumption and the reproduction of labour-power; (c) competition and conflict surrounding the allocation of the collective means of consumption has increased as an object of the class struggle (thus complementing the traditional class struggle around the means of production).

Castells (1978: 24–33) argues that the emphasis on collective consumption is necessary if we are to explain the qualitative differences between the big metropolitan areas characteristic of advanced monopoly capitalism and those cities developed in an era of competitive capitalism. He calls this new urban system Monopolville (Monopoly City), which has a depressingly routinized pattern of daily life due to the uniform, collective treatment of households by the state. Indeed, such is the responsibility of governments under monopoly capitalism for the provision of urban goods and services, urban planning and policy, that 'the state becomes through its arrangement of space the real manager of everyday life' (Castells, 1977b: 64). And, not without cause, this heightened involvement of the state in urban development and city life engendered a new form of urban politics and community mobilization based on struggles concerning the nature and terms of its intervention. Castells (1977a) introduced the term 'urban social movement' to describe the urban-based class struggle. His response to the criticism that this confined the study of class struggle in capitalist societies to 'the rather peripheral activities of urban social movements' (Harloe, 1981a: 7) has been to stress that for many people urban protest involves taking a position in the consumption system equivalent to that occupied in the productive system (Castells, 1978: 34–6). But where this is not the case, the formation of cross-class alliances around consumption issues, or urban social movements, should be regarded as 'a major element of the social dynamic' (Castells, 1978: 36) in so far as they help to unify anti-capitalist interests.

A part from the concerted attack on his exceedingly formalistic model of the urban system in advanced capitalist societies, the other main criticisms have related to his: exaggeration of the importance of urban planning and social movements in urban change; habit of generalizing from the restricted experience of France in urban and regional development; neglect of the role of the state in sometimes defusing conflict and fragmenting the bases for class action; inability to see beyond the functionality of state intervention for monopoly capital (Harloe 1981a: 5–7).

Urban ground rent and residential differentiation

Much of David Harvey's early disaffection with the application of neoclassical economics to space sprang from the way it treated the urban land market. The complaint was that the conventional analysis only recognized *one* of Marx's three main categories of rent; that is, a *differential* rent which is regarded as a simple surplus determined solely by the productivity of the land in question. This means, in effect, that land use determines rent and the land owner is only a passive beneficiary in the outcome (Bruegel, 1975). Marxists are wholly united in their opposition to the neoclassical presentation but they seem incapable of reaching agreement on what exactly should replace it: 'the task of developing an alternative Marxist theory of urban rent has proved difficult and many inconsistencies remain to be cleared up. One is forced to conclude that rent theory is at present in an unsatisfactory and transitional state' (Bassett and Short, 1980: 202). Because of this irresolution a swath will be quite ruthlessly cut through the disputed ground. Most attention will be paid to Harvey's reformulation of rent theory around the key concepts of class–monopoly rent and absolute space which, despite its several difficulties, does at least approach residential differentiation in a way of which Marx would probably have approved.

According to Harvey (1973: 171), the utility-maximizing models of Alonso, Muth and Mills are formulated in a *relational* space which discounts the monopolistic qualities of space. Rent is more than just an allocative device for assigning the best use of land: 'Rent is a transfer payment realized through the monopoly power over land conferred by the institutions of private property' (Harvey, 1973: 240). And when the effect of monopoly rights vested in a system of private ownership are properly recognized, then a 'sequential space packing process' makes much more sense than an instantaneous market-clearing process as an analogue for the urban property market.[13] Because the private ownership of property is an integral part of the capitalist system Harvey claims there is a need to trace the ramifications of socially created scarcities in the land market for the spatial organization of cities. He suggests, somewhat controversially, that this socially derived power to dominate the use of particular sites or tracts of land within cities is analogous to the processes which give rise to absolute and monopoly rents, the two Marxists categories left out of the neoclassical analyses.

Having admitted that Marx's inquisition of the meaning of rent was voluminous (see Harvey, 1982: 349–70), an attempt has been made to reduce his concepts to the bare bones. Marx's approach to rent derives directly from his labour theory of value; accordingly, Marx takes the view that in general rent is 'filched' from a lessee of land since a landowner, in effect, is intercepting part of the surplus value that would normally flow to the producer or the agricultural worker. Four different forms of rent are identified: two types of differential rent (DR-1 and DR-2), absolute rent, and monopoly rent. Differential rent is taken first because, despite the emphasis that Harvey places upon monopoly and absolute rents, it seems to be most immediately relevant to the situation applying in the land markets of capitalist cities (Edel, 1976). In the case of DR-1 all other rent levels in the rural land market are set against production costs on the most marginal land[14] defined in terms of fertility and location; therefore, owners of better land can appropriate higher rents from their tenants because of the combination of higher yields and/or lower production costs. DR-2 'simply expresses the effects of differential applications of capital to land of equal fertility' (Harvey, 1982: 354).

[13] Bruegel holds that Harvey's 'sequential packing model' of urban development in which 'the poor reach the city last and, finding all the "seats" filled are forced into the worst housing at the highest densities', is empirically inaccurate except perhaps for a few north-eastern cities in the US, and theoretically wrongheaded because it eschews the class struggle as a base cause of housing conditions (Bruegel, 1975: 38).

[14] In the Ricardian version the rent for the most marginal land under production was zero.

It is difficult to know quite what to make of Marx's concept of absolute rent. He conceives of a situation whereby landowners, who collude to hold some of the more fertile land out of cultivation, can force up general rent levels. This action will yield a rental income to landlords possessing even the most marginal land and raise rent levels by that increment within the regional market. At the same time landlords must be sufficiently united to block loans to individual farmers wishing to purchase labour-saving machinery, so that the surplus value is maintained at an artificially high level and profits kept unequal within the system as a whole. These are the conditions that allow for the appropriation of surplus profits in the form of absolute rent. But once mechanization of agriculture is under way and rates of profit move into line across particular sectors of agriculture, the absolute rent disappears. Despite the efforts of both Harvey (1974) and Lamarche (1976) to resuscitate the category of absolute rent and apply it in their urban work,[15] it appears to be largely irrelevant outside the very specific circumstances envisaged by Marx (Edel, 1976; Bruegel, 1975; Scott, 1976).

Monopoly rent on the other hand is something of an aberration which can only arise where the capitalist has a monopoly in production. Because of the uniqueness of a site it is possible that a producer's revenue will exceed ordinary profit levels within the industry and that the landlord will impose a surcharge in the form of a monopoly rent. Marx cites the production of the most highly regarded wines as a case in point, and the natural advantage enjoyed by manufacturers who command waterfall sites. Landowners are in a position to appropriate the extraordinary profits accruing to producers by converting them into ground-rents without in any way diminishing the 'normal' profit of the firm (Harvey, 1982: 336). (If this were really so then one must ask why manufacturers and producers went to all the trouble in the first place!) Harvey contends that these qualities are magnified in the urban land market. Because activity takes place in absolute, as well as in relative and relational space (Harvey, 1973: 184), location in the most accessible, convenient or the best endowed localities confers a form of monopoly right on the owners. In addition, as cities were built-up erratically over a long time span opportunities arose for the first merchants and pioneer families to acquire and then monopolize the most desirable space. In most cities the continuation of monopoly rights is guaranteed through planning and zoning legislation and the mediation of governmental and financial institutions (Harvey, 1977). When the enactment of these processes within space combines with the

---

[15] Lamarche (1976: 107–12) claims that the process whereby an urban landlord or property developer helps create social scarcity by witholding land, until such time as the development is ready to go ahead, is akin to extracting absolute rent. Unlike differential rent, which will accrue regularly to the owner, it is not until redevelopment occurs that absolute rent in the form of expanded profits can be realized.

institution of private ownership the conditions are right according to Harvey (1974) for the extraction of 'class monopoly rents'. The most overt example of the exercise of monopoly rights occurs where a monopoly payment is extracted from a developer or local authority by the property owner who holds out on the sale of a key city site.

Armed with this conceptualization of market processes Harvey is then in a position to apply his alternative theory of housing allocation and residential differentiation. This he does in a detailed case study of the inner city real estate market of Baltimore in 1970. The city of Baltimore is segmented into 13 housing submarkets which share a fairly high degree of internal homogeneity with respect to the following characteristics: median income; percentage of dwelling units owner occupied; mean value of owner occupied dwelling units; percentage of dwelling units occupied by renters; mean monthly rent; percentage of dwelling units occupied by blacks (Harvey, 1977). Harvey contends that these 'absolute spaces' are socially produced by the institutions making up the American financial superstructure – government agencies like the Federal Housing Adminis-tration (FHA), the home loan insurance corporations (Federal Savings and Loan Insurance Corporation), the agencies operating in the secondary mortgage markets (Federal National Mortgage Association, Federal Home Loan Mortgage Corporation) and the private intermediaries such as savings and loan associations, mutual savings banks, credit unions, com-mercial banks, life insurance companies, pension funds and mortgage banks. By channelling the flow of funds into the various housing sub-markets of Baltimore City, these institutions play a powerful part in the restructuring of urban neighbourhoods and in deciding their fate in the long-run.

Indeed, Harvey goes as far as asserting that the institutional and spatial structuring of Baltimore City's housing market is necessary for the generation and appropriation of 'class monopoly rents'. Class monopoly rent, which Harvey says approximates Marx's category of absolute rent, accrues to a class of owners that are only prepared to invest in a housing submarket if they are assured of a return in excess of some arbitrarily determined level. The class of professional landlords controlling the low-rent submarket of inner Baltimore is instanced: because they have a 'captive market' they are able to engineer high returns on their invest-ments by manipulating the market. In West Baltimore, a district with a preponderance of blacks, a 'class' of landlord-speculators exploited a device known as the land-installment contract. The transaction, which enables a lower-income household to occupy a dwelling to which the intermediary retains title, lent itself to abuse by unscrupulous speculator-renovators (Harvey, 1975: 144). Harvey also found extensive evidence of 'redlining' in the allocation of FHA-insured mortgages under the 221(d) (2) programme between 1970 and 1973. This was tantamount to a denial of federal housing assistance to lower-income home buyers living in the inner city neighbourhoods of Baltimore. On the other hand, the 221(d)(2) mortgage guarantee was used widely by estate agents operating in middle-income white neighbourhoods in northeast Baltimore. By introducing lower-income black households into these suburbs they were able to stimulate a high rate of turnover and capitalize on the instability they had induced.

Both Bruegel (1975) and Edel (1976) are sceptical about Harvey's use of the term absolute rent when he is talking about the structuring of sub-areas of cities (Harvey, 1974). They point out that for the use to be valid, 'it is necessary to show that the organic composition of capital is low in the construction sector and that there are barriers to the flow of investment into submarkets preventing the equalizing of the rate of profit over the system as a whole' (Bassett and Short, 1980: 201). Bruegel thinks that Harvey has overstated the strength of the submarket barriers present, for example, in his Baltimore study, whilst Edel indicates that in his opinion 'class monopoly rents' are really just monopoly rents. In true Marxist fashion Harvey has also been taken to task on the basis of his Baltimore work for focusing on the patterns of reproduction in the built environment rather than on patterns of production. The criticism is that insofar as it has drawn its empirical data from mortgage lending patterns, the theoretical insights remain obscure and the results consumption oriented (Smith, 1979: 24–5): 'Clearly, a theory that offers insights into the maintenance of residential patterns but not their production and alteration is of little help'.

Rudiments of a political economy of urban space

An implicit message along the following lines has been running right through this chapter and that is, if the generalization of social process is to square with the actuality of urban change it is necessary to break with literalism, the reification of pre-cast structures and categories, and the overly determined theory that has characterized the last decade of Marxist-informed urban analysis. Yet against that we must also set Gregory's (1982: 256) warning that 'Protocols of realism demand a theoretical effort if empirical endeavours are not to be ensnared in the errors of empiricism.'

The plan is to settle for an intentionally moderated form of political economy with which to expose the central relationships between the ongoing forms of capitalism and urbanization. One should reiterate that the city has been singled out for examination not because it is produced by specifically urban processes but out of a need to keep the assignment in chapter 4 and 5 manageable. It is suggested that much of the direction and coherence that might be wished for can be found in the following pre-suppositions:

1   Space is the arena in which elements of capital, class, and the state interact.

2   The capitalist mode of production undergoes continuous transformation, thus analytically providing a 'moving target'. Because classes are continually being redefined, while rates of urban and regional change proceed at an uneven pace, a periodization of the capitalist transformation raises more problems than it solves. An alternative approach is to recognize that certain phases of unbroken capitalist development ('long waves') may culminate with the domination of a reasonably singular mode of production in which the forms and expressions of capitalism appear with greatest clarity. That is not to say that the configuration of social relations or the arrangement of space is everywhere the same under capitalism; however, a focus on the 'climax' CMPs does represent the best opportunity for 'freezing' and dissecting the key relationships and processes.

3   There is a reasonable congruence between the dominant mode of production and the arrangement of space. With advances in the movement and circulation of materials, labour, and commodities, there has been an upward shift in the spatial register at which comparative advantage operates. Consider how the level, at which comparative advantage is critical for a core group of industries in any economy, has shifted upwards from the region, to the nation state, and finally to the global economy as the CMP has grown in sophistication and integration. So long as it is not expected that all spatial restructuring should be neatly synchronized then the course of urban and regional change can be partly understood in terms of technical refinements to comparative advantage in production.

4   At each stage the transition to a higher order of capitalist organization has been attended by immense dislocation, class resistance, and sometimes political disruption. Much state action and policy can be understood in terms of the need to counter these destabilizing tendencies in capitalism. Further, a stage has been reached where for the first time, perhaps, the ambivalence of the region is patent: it is less and less relevant to the transnational corporation as a unit of planning, yet is assuming more and more meaning as a unit of political organization amongst workers faced by economic restructuring. Also, as national markets are drawn into the web of world economic relations this is the arena in which the political and institutional rigidities of state policy are exposed, and the comparative powerlessness of national, regional and city governments in the face of global corporate strategies highlighted.

The attractions of a political economy of urban space can be listed as follows:

1   With the relations of capital as the lynch pin, the 'urban' is integrated into the broad socio-economic and political structures of society and situated in the international, the national and the regional settings of advanced capitalism. This often necessitates a search well beyond the city or region under examination for the basal causes of urban and regional change.

2   It places stress on the chronological and cumulative nature of urban development, and on the dynamic element of 'class' struggles, state intervention, crisis and political reaction.

3   This begins with an appreciation that it is in the nature of capitalism that 'uneveness in development can never be ironed out' (Mellor, 1977: xv). Some of the factors of production are pregiven and preset: the organization of the built environment and the location of raw materials and labour in space predispose capital to particular responses and patterns of investment.

4   It alerts us to the prospect that exploitation, inequality and injustice are endemic to capitalism.

5   Whether policy-makers like it or not, there are many counter-intuitive tendencies (contradictions) in the accumulation process (liberal economists treat many of these as market failures, imperfections or distortions).

4

Competitive Capitalism and Industrial Urbanization

There is no escaping from a chronology of urban development if the social processes that have produced the major cities of capitalist societies like Great Britain, the United States and Australia are to be contemplated properly. Indeed, one of the major objections to the neoclassical model of urban land uses is that, once committed, fixed capital normally remains in place for several generations and continues to condition all subsequent investment patterns – public and private – within the city. Historical antecedents are an indispensable part of a comparative analysis of urban development under capitalist conditions, for as Marx observed 'events strikingly analogous but taking place in different historical surroundings lead to totally different results' (in Duncan, 1981: 249). In chapter 4 the discussion is confined to the more important contextual aspects of urban form and process: (a) the interdependent nature of urbanization and industrialization; (b) the spatial concentration of the means of production; (c) the labour process, class formation and property relations; (d) circulation and the urban property market as a mechanism for value creation (e) the speculative provision of transport and housing in the suburbs; (f) experimentation with state intervention. It should be stressed again that these aspects of urban development will be illustrated selectively, but only on the understanding that the argument is not for a one-to-one correspondence between settings, processes, and outcomes in the three capitalist societies under examination.

Prometheus unbound: industrialization and urbanization

From the evidence compiled by Adna Weber (1899) in his classic comparative study of international urban growth one can easily be lulled into accepting the universality of an asymetrical model of causation: *namely*, industrialization begets urbanization. The concentration and centralization of fixed capital and labour that was an inescapable feature of the transition from mercantilism to industrial capitalism was to become the signature of nineteenth-century urbanization. In the space of 90 years, between 1801 and 1891, the proportion of Englishmen living in towns rose from one-quarter to three-quarters of the total population (or from 17 per cent in 1801 to 61 per cent in 1911 for cities over 20,000). Before 1800, London was the only city with more than 100,000 residents, but by 1911 44 other British cities shared that status. The population of industrial magnets like Manchester (in Disraeli's words 'the great metropolis of labour') and Birmingham in the Midlands doubled between 1801 and 1831, and repeated that rate of growth again in the ensuing 30 years. As Robson's (1973a) work on the growth patterns of cities in England and Wales in the nineteenth century has shown, the rates and magnitude of growth of urban centres at no stage were uniform. At each stage this reflected the variable factor endowments of the regions most affected and appeared as a wavelike progression through the sequence of staple industries that formed the prime movers in the heyday of industrial capitalism – textiles and clothing, mining, heavy engineering and metal manufacturers (these industrial groups increased the size of their work-force by 1.5 million, 1 million, and 1 million respectively between 1851 and 1911, Lee, 1981).

Urbanization in first gear

The standard account of the preconditions for urbanization in 'classical' capitalist formations like those of Britain, France, Sweden and Germany relates unprecedented population growth in the countryside and mechaniza-tion, rising productivity, and labour-shedding in agriculture on the one hand,[1] with impressive rates of capital formation, expanding employment opportunities in industry,[2] and cityward migration on the other (Lampard, 1973). Without the external sources of labour that the economies in the New World were able to draw upon when they were growing most rapidly, substitution in the agricultural sector and a rise in agricultural productivity sufficient to feed the urban population were necessary preconditions for industrial growth (not forgetting that because of the Irish famine many 'little Irelands' appeared in the northern industrial towns during the 1840s). Hence, the rural population of Europe's in-dustrializing economies represented a continuously replenished reservoir which industrialists could tap for factory operatives and the upper middle class for their domestics (Best, 1971).

[1] Significantly, a 60 per cent rise in agricultural productivity was posted in Europe in the last quarter of the eighteenth century as a prelude to industrialization, whilst between 1851 and 1911 630,000 jobs were lost in British agriculture.
[2] Notwithstanding the losses in agriculture, the British labour force grew by 2.66 times between 1841 and 1911 – from 6.9 million to 18.3 million – with 11.4 million jobs created in industry during the period.

Whereas in Britain industrialization was the great catalyst for urban growth, in the New World the tap-root of urbanization was mercantilism. Butlin (1964), Glynn (1970), McCarty (1970) and Pred (1966) have all drawn attention to the different primogeniture of American and Australian cities during the first phase of competitive capitalism. The mercantile 'hinge' cities were facsimiles of Bristol and Liverpool; but otherwise cities in the New World were different to the extent that industrialization followed urbanization. Even here it would be fatally easy to blur the divergent paths to full metropolitan status of cities in the youthful American and Australian economies.

The factory and industrial capitalism were not to become the corner-stones of US metropolitan growth until well into the 1860s (Pred, 1966; 143). Thereafter the multiplication of factories, product output and markets were to become virtually synonymous with city development. Pred explains that before the middle of the nineteenth century when the economy of the United States was agricultural, the industrial as well as the agrarian population was preponderantly rural. Secondary activity was largely concentrated in the textile industries scattered in the mill towns along the Fall Line in New England and at the base of the Appalachians. Otherwise, Pred's (1966: 146–52) archival research shows that manufacturing had an unimposing role in the economies of America's mercantile cities (table 4.1). In the case of New Orleans, the ratio of investment in the mercantile sectors to investment in industrial activity exceeded fifteen to one, and in both New York and Boston it was approaching six to one. In an 1810 survey of Philadelphia's 13,241 buildings only 230 were classified as manufacturing establishments. Hence, 'the dock, the wharf, the countinghouse and the warehouse' were the principal foci of the 'hinge' cities' economies, with the merchant middlemen (shipping merchants and importers) and agent middlemen (brokers, auction-eers, commissioning merchants, and factors) dominating the capital accumulation process (Pred, 1966: 148–9).

'In British economic history it is possible to talk of factories giving rise to towns; in Australia towns appear to have given rise to factories' (Glynn, 1970: 17). Certainly a high degree of urbanization had been achieved in Australia long before manufacturing became significant. In 1861, when approximately 40 per cent of Australians lived in cities or towns, manufacturing accounted for less than 4 per cent of gross domestic product. As in the American states before the middle of the nineteenth century, manufacturing activity like flour milling, tanneries and wool scouring were just as likely to be based in rural areas. After 1861, manufacturing, though small in scale, labour intensive, and technically backward, became an increasingly positive force in urbanization. In 1891 approximately 17 per cent of the Australian market was employed in manufacturing, especially in textiles and clothing, metals and machinery, building materials, and

Table 4.1 Economic indicators for major US cities, 1840

| | Population | Commercial houses in foreign trade | Commission houses | Capital invested ($000) | | | | |
				Commission houses	Retailing	Manufacturing	Construction employment
New York (Manhattan)	312,710	417	918	45,941.2	14,648.6	11,228.9	4,033
Baltimore	102,313	70	108	4,404.5	6,708.6	2,730.0	845
Philadelphia	93,665	182	35	1,944.5	15,177.6	5,387.5	713
Boston	93,383	142	89	11,676.0	4,184.2	2,770.3	524
New Orleans	102,192	8	375	16,490.0	11,018.2	1,774.2	1,001

Source: Pred (1966: tables 4.2 and 4.3), based on US Census data

food, drink and tobacco. However, unlike the US after 1860, when the richly endowed industrial heartland came to concentrate American manufacturing, industrial production in Australia maintained a predominantly port-side, labour market orientation (Linge, 1979a). Accordingly, by 1891, with allowance for the numerical differences in census definitions, 'two-thirds of the Australian population lived in cities and towns, a fraction matched by the United States only by 1920 and by Canada not until 1950' (Butlin, 1964: 6).

The cadence of accumulation: flows of capital and labour

The proposition is that the urban foundations in the New World were the direct creations not so much of industrial capital, but of circulating capital in the form of producers' goods, commodities, and interest bearing investment. In the process of joining the European centres of production with sources of raw materials and markets, the 'hinge' cities contributed to accumulation by improving both the means of circulation and the spatial integration of the imperial economies: 'the continuation of an industrial economy depended one way or another on the subordination of other economies' (Foster, 1968: 262). The development of infrastructure and growth of markets in the New World economies during the second half of the nineteenth century certainly helped to absorb the surpluses created by the British manufacturing giant. However, it would be wrong to suggest as Harvey does with his three circuits of capital (figure 3.2) that capital surplus to the needs of the British manufacturing sector simply spilled over into government stock or foreign ventures:

> In Britain, the nineteenth century was marked by a sharp division between the financial interests of the City of London, who concentrated their activities on government loans and foreign stock (including the American railways), and the industrial concerns of the Midlands and the North. Manufacturing industry was, by and large, self-financing from the personal wealth of the owners. The individual entrepreneur and his family and associates provided capital for accumulation, and local banks supplied short-term working capital. . . . The financial interests, particularly the merchant bankers, had developed in relation to agrarian and mercantile capitalism and were particularly involved in state finances and trade with the British Empire. (Scott, 1979: 89)

A demonstration of the interdependence of the economies of key industrial nations and those of Canada, Argentina, the United States and Australia is a central feature of Brinley Thomas's work (1972). Although the terms of trade operating at the level of the macro-economy have the greatest bearing upon economic growth *per se*, city growth according to Thomas is mostly shaped by the cyclical upswings and downturns of capital and migration flows. This coincided in the nineteenth century with alternating surges and lulls in the movement of capital and labour between the major source areas of Western Europe and the recently settled temperate zones. Thomas (1972: 6) found that the peak years for foreign investment by UK investors and for European emigration roughly co-incided in 1872, 1890 and 1907–08 with the troughs falling around 1861–62, 1877 and 1898. Walter Bagehot, in his classic study of banking, *Lombard Street*, wrote 'English capital runs as surely and instantly where it is most wanted and where there is most to be made of it, as water runs to find its own level' (Bagehot, 1888: 13). Roughly, when the 'promised' rate of returns was higher on overseas investment, the expansion of Britain's staple industries (coal, cotton, iron and steel) was retarded.[3] In this situation the rural proletariat might be expected to emigrate instead of migrating internally to British cities. With unemployment moving above 10 per cent towards the end of the 1870s in the UK (Best, 1971: 128), and the news of prosperous times in Australia, 500,000 immigrants were attracted to New South Wales alone during the decade straddling 1875–85 (Daly, 1982a: 155). To the extent that recession reduced the attractiveness of lending to the USA or Australia, British investors would redirect their attention to the domestic economy and to perhaps less spectacular investments like building and construction (Lewis, 1965). Hence, the effect of a redirection of the flow of British lending during the Victorian and Edwardian era was transmitted through the urban development cycle of cities in both Britain and Australia (figure 4.1). Olson (1979), for example, shows that the timing of a succession of 13 building booms in Baltimore between 1790 and 1970 is consistent with the North American pattern of long swings, and the inverse of the North European pattern.

A new surge in investment in the American or Australian mercantile

---

[3] By the end of the century the London capital market had become primarily an instrument of external finance, with as much as 80 per cent of the capital issues in the City of London going overseas in a typical year (Kirby, 1981: 14). This was to contribute in no small way to the eventual eclipsing of British industry by US and German industrial capital. The export of capital climbed from £230 million in 1855 to £4,000 million by 1914 (Scott, 1979: 160). So much of the Victorian industrial expansion was either self-financed or financed by local banks whose directors had few City connections that by the early 1900s British industry was plagued by chronic underinvestment (Rubinstein, 1977: 621). Also, 'overseas lending served to encourage structural rigidities in the economy by tying industry to a restricted range of export markets' (Kirby, 1981: 15). Beneficial though the export of 'staples' may have been before 1914, in the long-term it had the effect of retarding development in the machine tools and precision engineering sector. 'Overseas investment thus retarded industrial growth by reinforcing the overcommitment of the economy to the old-established industries' (Kirby, 1981: 16). Even though finance capital was acting rationally in favouring foreign portfolios this was clearly not in the long-term interests of industrial capital.

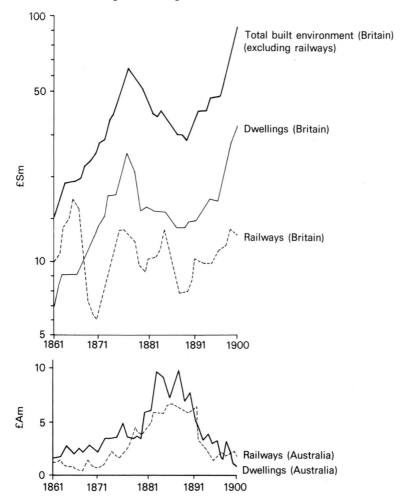

Figure 4.1 Investment in selected components of the built environment in Britain and Australia, 1860–1900
Source: Harvey, 1978: 117; and Butlin, 1964: 224

cities generally came with the expansion of the frontier or a boost in primary production (pastoral industries, goldmining, forestry). In Australia new capital formation by government climbed, albeit jerkily, from about £6.0 million in the 1860s to £35.6 million during the 1880s (with railway, road and bridge construction often accounting for three-quarters of the total in a decade). Similarly, new capital outlays in the pastoral and agricultural sectors rose from £2.3 million in the 1860s to £50.3 million in the eighties (Butlin, 1964: 132–6). In fact, the flow of

British capital into Australia in the second five years of the 1880s was such that capital imports made up almost half the gross domestic capital formation (Butlin, 1964: 135). The external benefits of this new capital formation would spill over into infrastructure, building and construction and urban services, with subsequent rounds of urban investment encouraged by immigration and growth in household formation.

> During the period 1860–1890 overseas borrowing was more important than domestic savings as a source of investment funds. Urban house-building, the construction of transport and communications facilities, grazing, and local authority works (in that order of magnitude) absorbed the major part of Australian investment. Each of these main avenues of investment, in one way or another, tended to promote urbanization, and a very large part of total investment was directly concerned with the physical extension of urban areas. (Glynn, 1970: 15)

Industrial agglomeration and the development of Victorian cities

'Coketown': the new locus of accumulation

The decades between 1780 and 1830 in Britain were marked by a progressive movement away from a system of domestic production revolving around cottage handicrafts and the assembling of piecegoods, to water-powered processing set up around the water-powered mill. That was followed by the conversion to steam of the nascent manufacturing processes in consumer goods production (cotton and woollen textiles). Thus by 1840 only 13 per cent of the Lancastrian cotton industry's energy needs were still being supplied by water-power (Rodgers, 1960). More than anything else, the conversion of industrial plant to steam encouraged industrial agglomeration: 'Steam worked most efficiently in big concentrated units, with the parts of the plant no more than a quarter of a mile from the power-centre: every spinning machine or loom had to tap power from the belts and shafts worked by the central steam engine. The more units in a given area, the more efficient was the source of power' (Mumford, 1961: 519). The same technical constraint led to power-sharing amongst the smaller operators as a cost-saving measure: as late as 1841 one-third of all Oldham's firms shared overheads in this way (Gatrell, 1977: 103).

It was the relative inefficiency of the early steam engine, coupled with the transport costs of low-grade boiler coal, that made a coalfield location obligatory at first. Thus the mercantile cities on the eastern seaboard of the United States were quickly surpassed as manufacturing centres by quite tiny places as comparative advantage adjusted to the resource base. By

1840, for example, Wheeling and Pittsburg, with 7,885 and 21,115 residents respectively, had mechanized factories and workshops with a combined power output of 3,420 horsepower or considerably more than Boston, Baltimore and Philadelphia combined (Pred, 1966: 162).

A feature of the concentration of cotton processing on the Lancashire coalfield was the rapid build-up of fixed capital in order to achieve optimum scale. Although the number of factories only grew from 900 to 1,200 between 1797 and 1834, raw materials consumed (and hence imports) rose from 30 to 300 million lbs of cotton (Chapman, 1972: 33). During the early decades textile manufacturers strove to improve their competitiveness by adopting a range of capital-saving measures, thus liberating working capital for new fixed investment in buildings, machinery and land. The transference of investment from working to fixed capital was facilitated by the following developments in production and marketing: increasing engine speeds; holding lower mill stocks; eliminating, as much as possible, the importing middle-man; using the specialist merchant houses in the continental export trade; wage-saving with the adoption of self-acting spinning mules; and, the use of child labour for piecing together broken threads, picking up waste cotton, running errands, and assisting adult machinists (Gatrell, 1977: 104). These and other developments made the cotton textile industry the most important growth sector in the early stages of the Industrial Revolution. By 1830 it accounted for 50.7 per cent of the value of total British exports and the figure was still as high as 24.1 per cent in 1913 (Kirby, 1981: 10).

The process of capital accumulation was moved into a higher gear in the late 1840s by two far-reaching developments in production and transportation technology. Firstly, the capital goods sector successfully made the change over from hand-made steam generating equipment to full machine production of plant and equipment. This was responsible for an enormous improvement in the productivity of the capital goods sector in industries like textiles and mining machinery, heavy engineering and machine tools. Industrial productivity in Britain grew at an annual rate of 1.87 per cent between the mid-1860s and 1880 (Kirby, 1981: 2). Secondly, the development in machine production and heavy engineering helped to transform related sectors like steel making, railway construction and shipbuilding. Between 1844 and 1849 the railway network in Britain trebled, signifying a dramatic expansion of capital investment in industries specializing in producers goods. Yet compared with the United States and Germany, Britain still had an economy top-heavy with the traditional 'consumer goods' industries.

Industrial capital and the 'correct' location of industry

What sort of imprint did the growth of a large-scale capital goods sector leave upon the structure of the late nineteenth-century city? In answering this the essential difference between specialized manufacturing centres like Manchester or Pittsburg, and the very mixed industrial base of Birmingham or London is acknowledged. Taking the rebuilding of Chicago after the Great Fire of 1873 as their model, Fales and Moses (1972) have laid out a set of general principles that account quite effectively for the location of much of the large-scale manufacturing found in nineteenth-century cities. They show how major materials-intensive activities like brick making, foundries, blast furnaces and meat packing were especially sensitive to the 'least-cost' locations. This is due to the significant reduction in weight that accompanies processing. Thus weight-losing industries appropriated sites either adjacent to railway yards or sidings, on the lakeside (where supplies of ice used in brewing were available on a seasonal basis at least) and along the canals. Fales and Moses decided that materials orientation was probably more decisive than market orientation in the nineteenth-century city for the following reasons:

1   Scale economies in interregional rail and barge transport helped to undercut the costs of moving freight *within* cities. The impressive economies of scale in line-haul operations meant that cartage within the city might well exceed inter-regional transport costs by up to 25–30 times per ton mile.
2   The movement of the urban workforce was more efficient than intra-urban freight. 'As a result, industry largely oriented itself to the river and the various rail terminals, and households located with reference to the horsecar lines that fed into major employment districts' (Fales and Moses, 1972: 68).

Fales and Moses also suggest that because the telegraph facilitated the rapid transmission of information between cities, but not within cities due to the limitations of the early switchboards, firms that were highly dependent on quick access to information, such as prices in regional and national markets, tendered to cluster closely to telegraph terminals. Prime examples were the banks, manufacturers' agents, the dealers on the floor of the stock exchange, their credit agencies and business services. Kellett (1969: 296) reports that the number of subscribing members of Manchester's Royal Exchange rose from about 1,500 in 1812–15 to about 7,500 by 1885.

In archetypal Manchester, the Ashton and Rockdale canals built at the turn of the eighteenth century attracted over 100 textile mills, breweries, chemical works and foundries. At Port Dundas, immediately to the north of central Glasgow, the distilleries, chemical plants and foundries – all great users of water – began to congregate along the canal system. Similarly, a two mile stretch of canal between Borderley and Aston in Birmingham packed 124 works, including soap, varnish and tar making, along its banks.

And even in the late 1860s, despite the mounting competition from the railways, Birmingham's canal system was still carrying over a million tons of coal (Kellett, 1969: 349–50). In Melbourne, right through the nineteenth century, the Yarra River was despoiled by the heavy users of water whether it was for washing and cleansing materials like wool, skin and hides, for cooling in the breweries and the soap and candle works, or for the disposal of wastes from the boiling-down works and the slaughter-houses.

Although many of the factories erected in the first half of the nineteenth century were near the rail terminals flanking the core of Victorian cities, by the 1860s the space requirements of the large-scale manufacturing firms were pressing them to relocate. Kellett (1969: 346–7) cites the extensive engineering suburbs at Gorton and Newton Heath near Manchester, Springburn near Glasgow, and Stratford in east London. In Sydney: 'The twin advantages of rail and the Parramatta River helped the spread of manufacturing along the southern bank of the river through the 1870s and 1880s. At Clyde and Granville, auctioneers proclaimed the "Birmingham of Australia" and reaped enormous profits in developing areas such as the New Glasgow Estate which gave its subdividers a 440 per cent return in 1881–82' (Daly, 1982a: 157). Similar inducements gave rise to the growth of ship-building and marine engineering downstream from the centre of Glasgow on the Clyde. 'Shipbuilding not only revolutionized the economy of Glasgow, it reorientated the city in space. . . . So it was that large-scale industry, unable to accommodate itself to the locational pattern that had arisen out of textiles and the machine shop, began a new set of Glasgow satellites' (Checkland, 1964: 47–8).

The emphasis that Fales and Moses place upon a materials orientation still leaves one very disparate group of industries unaccounted for. When it came to 'the small miscellaneous loads of the Birmingham or London manufacturer, the frequent need for trans-shipment for further processing after a short journey, the heavy terminal charges, made the railways slow and uneconomic for the local movement of goods' (Kellett, 1969: 349). Moreover, the small-scale workshops specializing in clothing, furniture, printing and publishing, precious metals and jewellery, watchmaking, precision engineering and light metals, and the repair of machinery, capitalized upon a range of externalities available by virtue of their location in the inner areas of the Victorian city. These included the facilities provided by the 'room and power' companies, a local pooling of specialist skills, and close linkages with both the suppliers and receivers of components and/or semi-finished goods. Although the individual firms were quite small and craft-based, in total they made up a highly significant portion of the industrial structure of cities like London (Hall, 1962) and New York (Pred, 1966: 196–213). They remained viable in the face of competition from the mass-produced consumer goods, partly because of the overriding advantage of proximity to the market, partly by resorting to the wholesale use of sweated labour.[4]

In fact, as Lee (1981: 449–51) reminds us, the highly integrated group of consumer-oriented and service industries have been over-shadowed by the staple economic activities in discussions of regional growth in the nineteenth century: 52.2 per cent of the six million new jobs created between 1841 and 1911 in Britain were in the service and construction industries; and of these, 20 per cent were in the 12 counties of the south-east. London concentrated the affluent classes that enjoyed conspicuous consumption and gave employment to a wide range of labour-intensive services, the domestic services, and traditional professions like law, medicine and education (Best, 1971: 73–110).

The labour process, class formation and property relations in the Victorian urban setting

The labour process and social relations of production

Perhaps the clearest expression of the social relations of production in Marx's construction of capitalism is to be found in the labour process developed in the textile mills and factories of Lancashire, *c.* 1840–60. The rise of the mill village as a unit of production marked the begin-nings of a transformation not just of the structure of industry but also of the social relations of production. It saw the first attempts to divide labour and routinize work, and set the pattern for the widespread deskilling of work. This enabled employers to hire less skilled, and therefore cheaper labour (Nardinelli, 1980). For example, with the adoption of the power loom between 1838 and 50, the scattered colonies of hand-loom weavers were steadily drawn into the mills, or faced the prospect of redundancy. Simultaneously, the perfection of the auto-matic mule paved the way for the 'prototype or optimum production' mill. Not only was the optimum mix of capital and labour approached in production, but with the introduction of the automatic mule con-siderable savings were made on the wages of skilled spinners, many of whom were displaced in the process. One firm reduced the high-wage spinning operatives from 11 per cent of its workforce in 1828 to six in 1841, effecting a 45 per cent saving on spinners' wages. One man with the help of two or three boys could now work 1,600 self-acting spindles (Gatrell, 1977: 109–13). Besides these technical effects, the organiza-

---

[4] In spite of this, in certain of the long established London trades – shipbuilding, book-binding, silk manufacturing, leather dressing and tanning, mat-making and felt hatting – nothing could ward off displacement by provincial competitors using standardized production techniques (Stedman Jones, 1971: 145).

tional requirements of the factory system saw the contract system, operated by the worker–subcontractor, gradually replaced by direct wage relations between magnates like the steel barons and cotton-lords, and their workforce (Stone, 1974). The work situation in the factory imposed discipline, punctuality, and regularity in performing tasks; remembering that between the 1780s and 1840s work was the central experience of the working classes, occupying as it did the major part of their lives (Thompson, 1981: 204).

The patriarchal factorymaster was also able to exert a fair measure of control on his workforce outside the workplace: 'Where factory paternalism was strong, as it increasingly was from the 1840s on-wards, an employer's influence extended far outside the mill into the entire institutional structure and equipment of the local community: houses, schools, church, chapel, Sunday schools, playfield, and (over them all) local government' (Thompson, 1981: 204). In the case of factory housing this could go as far as placing a foreman in the end dwelling in a row of terrace houses rented to employees and their families. Thereafter, with the rise of large firms lacking the 'intimate' employer–worker relations, one gets by the 1890s increasing independence, worker organization, militancy and class consciousness.

Nineteenth-century capitalist social relations are epitomized in John Foster's (1974) careful reconstruction of class formation, class composition and class consciousness in three towns in the north of England – Oldham, Northampton and South Shields. A picture of 'northern' urban social structure crystallizes in the vignette of Oldham.[5] By 1851 two-thirds of the borough's labour force of 40,000 was employed in the coal mining, cotton and engineering industries. A small number of families – about 70 – controlled these highly capitalized industries representing perhaps 80 per cent of the town's means of production (Foster, 1968: 341). Over three-quarters of the cotton workers were employed by 60 firms with over 100 hands; 80 per cent of the engineering workers by three dominant firms; and almost all the coalminers by one combine or the subsidiaries of cotton firms. Opportunities for upward social mobility were minimal.

Thus at mid-century there were 12,000 worker families selling their labour to 70 capitalist families. The capitalist families were very rich – annual income ranged between £3,000 and £10,000 – and most owned estates in other parts of the country. Incomes of worker *families* ranged from £50 to £100 – insufficient to keep any but the top 15 per cent of high-paid craft workers *permanently* out

[5] Foster, a social historian, takes this much further with an analysis of the evolving role of the town's bourgeoisie, the labour process, and the political struggle to avoid working class fragmentation. A summary statement is available in Foster (1968: 285–90).

of primary poverty. . . . There were regular periods of mass unemployment – sending the proportion of families in primary
poverty at *any one time* well over 40 per cent. This was the class
situation with which people had come to terms. For the first 50
years of the century their reaction was to fight it. (Foster, 1968:
284–5)

Class formation as a backdrop to residential differentiation

Relatively few of the major cities of the Victorian era displayed such
obvious social polarity as Oldham; and even Oldham had its weakly
developed middle class 'fraction' comprising shopkeepers, tradesmen,
small employers and masters. This is quite clear from scattered
studies of the occupational structure of cities like London and Paris
(Lees, 1973), Leeds (Ward, 1980), Toronto (Goheen, 1970), and
Melbourne (Barrett, 1971: 30–6). For example, around 1850 both
London and Paris were hierarchical societies with comparatively
small upper and middle classes completely outnumbered by a working
class of artisans, labourers and domestic servants (table 4.2). Although

Table 4.2 Social structure of London and Paris, 1850

Social groups		Employed population (%)	
		London	Paris
I	Capitalists, professionals, administrators, *rentiers*	4.3	10.4
II	Lower ranking professionals and administrators, patrons and small employers, shopkeepers	16.6	13.0
III–V	Working class – all levels	79.1	76.1
	Skilled labour	39.7	n.a.
	Domestic service	17.9	11.0
	Other semi-skilled labour	6.6	n.a.
	Clerks	2.0	n.a.
	Unskilled labour	10.6	n.a.
	Unclassified	2.3	n.a.

Source: Lees (1973: table 17.4), based on Census of Great Britain, 1851, 'Occupations of the People, London';
Seine, Recherches statistiques sur la ville de Paris et le département de la Seine, VI (Paris, 1860)

the size of the working class does not vary much in either city, there is
a significant difference in the top stratum of Parisian society due to the
presence of 46,000 *rentiers* or *propriétaires*. The figure for London's
men and women of independent means and house or land proprietors
was only 14,920 despite the greater size of the metropolis (Lees, 1973:
423–5).[6]

[6] In 1845–46, the population of Paris was approximately 1.2 million, London's 2.5 million.

It must be said that Marx was observant enough to realize that as structural change recalibrated the scales of occupation in mid-Victorian Britain (Best, 1971: 81–117) a categorical dissection of class would no longer do. Certain workers were better equipped than others to rise within the pyramidal structure that was Victorian society. Lack of access to education and specialized training blocked others from joining the favoured few in the ranks of the middle class or from making the 'labour aristocracy'.[7] These barriers to entry were further buttressed when the more respectable branches of the artisanal trades began to take on the character of closed shops. Therefore, newcomers like the Irish tended to be overrepresented amongst those excluded from the better paid and less precarious employment. In the bigger cities a pool of cheap labour formed – the 'residuum'[8] – whose presence represented a constant deflationary influence upon the wages of the remainder of the working class. And with the downturn of the trade cycle in the late 1880s the 'residuum' assumed a growing threat partly because it was synonymous in the minds of middle class Victorians with some of their cities' most notorious slums.

Towards the end of the nineteenth century a range of reasonably unambiguous social strata were beginning to take shape. This is reflected in the frequent contemporaneous references to class in the plural – the 'lower', 'labouring' or 'working', and 'middling' classes (Ward, 1980: 134). Although the 'residuum', or 'underclass', was quite well defined, Ward (1980: 136) indicates that there was much more fluidity between the 'residuum' and the remainder of the working class compared with 'the increasingly emphatic boundary between the working class and those whom early Victorians had described as the middling class'. By the 1870s growing numbers of managerial and clerical employees in Leeds, for example, were set on distancing themselves socially and residentially from the working class on the basis of their non-manual roles. That left those in the upper strata of the working class who had long associated with the 'middling' class

---

[7] Acknowledgement of the emerging historical reality of working class segmentation is implicit in the Marxist theory of the labour aristocracy. Hobsbawm (1968), following Lenin, sought to account for the quiescense of the British proletariat under conditions which should have sparked intense class struggle. For him the answer lay in the splitting of an upper and favoured stratum of the manual workforce, which was allegedly co-opted by the British ruling class, from the proletariat. Developments in engineering were supposed to encourage the skilled tradesmen – the 'taskmasters' and 'pacemakers' – to identify much more closely with management. In this view the labour aristocracy, therefore, was a device more or less consciously created by the British bourgeoisie to contain upsurges of working class radicalism (Foster, 1974).

[8] The 'residum' was made up of navvies; dock workers of many kinds including coal-heavers, ballastmen, stevedores, and riggers; labourers in gasworks; hodmen and helpers on building sites; carters, draymen, porters and sweepers; and domestic servants doing the menial tasks in the Victorian household (Harrison, 1979: 64–74).

with little choice but to identify their own interests exclusively with those of manual labour in general. According to Moorhouse (1978: 62), the whole of the British working class became a 'bribed one, while the old aristocrats of labour were pushed into the working class as a distinct wedge of white collar workers forced itself between this group and the higher stratum'. For Stedman Jones (1971) these changes in working class composition and circumstance in the second half of the nineteenth century were substantial enough to justify the idea of the 'remaking of the English working class'. While for Ward (1980) they hold the key to suburban movement and residential differentiation within large English provincial cities like Leeds during the last three decades of the nineteenth century. 'In the development of lower-middle class suburbs, in the identification of extreme slum conditions, and the residuum and in the retrospective recognition of a sedentary traditional working-class sub-culture, Leeds at the turn of the nineteenth century clearly displayed the dominant elements of the differentiated pattern of modern cities' (Ward, 1980: 140). Simpson and Lloyd's (1977) research on middle class housing in Britain attests to the generality of the process: Edinburgh developed its Morningside and Murrayfield; Manchester its Alderley Edge and Wilmslow; Bristol its Clifton and Redland. And beneath the social distancing and class identification lay the allocational structures of the residential property market: 'The pricing mechanism acted in the land market as a filter in the process of segregation, each gradation of price operating as a settling pool for a reasonably well-defined social group' (Rodger, 1982: 67).

Property relations and the social topography of Victorian cities

Rubinstein (1977) is to be thanked for reconstructing a picture of the concentration of Britain's *non-landed* wealth in the nineteenth century. The key information, which is drawn from the deceased estates of wealthy British males, is summarized in table 4.3. Each entrepreneur leaving an estate worth £160,000 before 1850 and £250,000 thereafter was assigned to the occupational class defined by the Standard Industrial Classification in that activity in which the greater part of the capital had been accumulated. The striking thing, considering the prominence given to industrial capital during the nineteenth century,[9] is the disproportionate showing of merchants,

---

[9] Industrial output in manufacturing, mining and building accounted for between 34.4 and 40.2 per cent of total national income during each decade, 1831–1901, while employment in manufacturing and industry moved from 43 to 48.6 per cent between 1841 and 1911. During the same period commercial occupations rose from a miniscule 1.4 per cent to 5.7 per cent (Rubinstein, 1977: 623).

Table 4.3 Occupations of major British wealth-holders in the nineteenth century (non-landed males)

		Year of death						
SIC class[a]		1809–58 (%)		1859–79 (%)		1880–99 (%)		1900–14 (%)
I	Manufacturing	16	28.6	45	34.0	88	40.6	79	31.1
	Food, drink, tobacco	1		3		37		36	
	Metals and engineering	6		19		17		24	
	Textiles	6		16		28		19	
II	Commerce and finance	31	55.4	76	57.6	89	41.0	129	50.8
III	Professional, etc.	9	16.0	7	5.3	9	4.1	10	3.9
	Total non-landed males	56		132		217		254	

[a] The classes do not sum to 100%
Source: Rubinstein (1977: tables 1 and 2, 605–06)

bankers, shipowners, merchant bankers, and stock and insurance brokers (the commercial group in table 4.3) amongst the owners of capital: despite the Industrial Revolution, the most important element in Britain's wealth structure during the nineteenth century, apart from landed wealth, was commerce and finance (Rubinstein, 1977: 606). It was this that made London more important as a centre of accumulation and investment than the northern industrial towns. If the 'millionaires' and 'half-millionaires' are taken together for the cohorts set out in table 4.3 then London was the headquarters for between 43 per cent and 64 per cent of all non-landed 'capitalists'; amongst the 'less wealthy' London's lead was even clearer (Rubinstein, 1977: 611).

Rubinstein (1977) also establishes that these same tendencies held for the middle class as a whole. From tax schedules held by the Public Record Office he estimates that Londoners accounted for more than half of Britain's middle class income in 1812. This dominance of London's middle class persisted to the end of the nineteenth century: in 1879–80, the 28 provincial towns with populations in excess of 100,000 (totalling 5.77 million) were assessed under Schedule D for £78.1 million, while the ten London boroughs, with a combined population of 3.45 million were assessed for £87.7 million. The implication being 'not merely that London possessed a larger total business income than all of the chief provincial towns combined, but that its middle class was richer *per capita* and almost certainly more numerous than that in the provincial towns' (Rubinstein, 1977: 618).

Thus far the concentration of wealth within the hands of Britain's landed aristocracy has only been hinted at. There is good cause for believing that its monopoly over rural land[10] was approached, if not always matched, in many Victorian towns and cities as estates were engulfed by subdivision. In an enquiry into urban holdings held in 1886 it was discovered that out of 261 provincial towns, 69 were largely owned by the great landlords and 34 by families from the gentry. From about 1850 onwards the large estates subdivided for urban purposes assumed growing importance as a source of revenue, particularly during the years when the agricultural estates were hit by rural recession (Thompson, 1963: 267–8). Besides the established aristocratic families, greater gentry, and squirearchy, tracts of urban land were also concentrated in the hands of the Crown, corporate bodies such as the Ecclesiastical Commissioners, Oxbridge colleges, public schools, and the great London companies. On prime land in the centre of London they ranged in size from the miniature Calthorpe estate in Gray's Inn Road (23 acres) to the 119 acre estate belonging to the Bedfords in Bloomsbury and Covent Garden, and the 500 acres owned by the Westminster family in Belgravia and Mayfair. These, in turn, were dwarfed by some of the estates in provincial towns. At its maximum size, the Ramsdens' Huddersfield estate covered 4,300 acres, while, by 1910, the Norfolks' Sheffield holdings were only slightly smaller (Cannadine, 1980: 392).

The large-scale, leasehold urban estates lent the urban property market of British cities a distinctiveness not found in either the US or Australia. Although the US and Australian cities did have their large landlords like New York's John Jacob Astor, and absent *rentiers*,[11] their urban land markets were most remarkable for the ease of entry, the countless thousands of plots and speculators, the ease of conveyancy and lack of restrictions (Cannon, 1976; Warner, 1972). By contrast, urban estate development in British cities was noted for 'The use of short-term, ninety-nine year leases; the holding of land under elaborate settlements and wills; coherent, controlled, and careful planning; a preference for high-class, residential tenants; concern for regular, secure income and long-term reversion' (Cannadine, 1980: 313). But as it stands this is an incomplete picture of property relations and ownership patterns within British urban areas. In 1914, the report of the Land Enquiry Committee concluded that substantially more than half of the urban population of England and Wales was living under ordinary freehold tenure; about one-twentieth under freehold

---

[10] The 1873 Return of Owners of Land (the 'New Doomsday Survey'), a census of land ownership designed to demonstrate the dispersion of holdings, proved precisely the opposite. Although over a million individuals had parcels of land, 7,000 families still owned 80 per cent of the United Kingdom's total land area (Thompson, 1963: 27).

[11] Australian cities were not without their absentee owners who chose to live abroad as rich *rentiers* 'at a time when their influence might have helped promote more civic consciousness and a higher standard of local administration' (Birch and MacMillan, 1962: 94–5).

subject to some form of perpetual annual payment; somewhere in the vicinity of about one-tenth under long leasehold; and rather under one-third under short leasehold (Cannadine, 1980: 319). To underline the point Cannadine (1980: 320) reminds us that late-nineteenth century Nottingham was almost all (nine-tenths) freehold, while Leeds was completely freehold.

The final significance of Cannadine's discussion (1980: 321–4) of urban development under leasehold versus freehold systems is that often the same residential structure and class shares of housing eventuated even though the underlying pattern of land ownership differed from town to town. In Birmingham (almost completely lease-hold) and Leeds (almost completely freehold) the size and location of middle class and working class housing 'was not so much influenced by the restrictions imposed by landowners or by builders, but by the amount which the inhabitants of the town could afford to spend . . .' (Cannadine, 1980: 322). Hence, the rather more sumptuous housing of Headingley, Leeds, compared with Edgbaston, Birmingham, stands as a testimony to the greater scale of the firms owned by the hardware merchants of Leeds in the late nineteenth century. In this and similar situations, therefore, the directives of capitalist land and housing markets appear to have subordinated considerations such as property law, variable estate administration and management practice, and customary rights and privileges. That is to say, a similar urban outcome can result from the play of market forces despite initial differences in institutional arrangements.

Circulation, the urban property market and value creation

Coming to terms with the structural transformation that overtook Victorian cities in the mid- and late-nineteenth century involves examining the techniques developed to affect the circulation of materials and products and the movement of labour between work-place and residence. Again, the presentation will have a bias because it is in the British cities that we can find the strongest imprint of industrial capital. Moreover, capital formation is singled out within the transportation and housing production sectors for closer inspec-tion because of their salience as structural and distributional elements: 'In an environment where so much development was small-scale and left to piece-meal speculation, the railway builders and the great estate developers . . . were the conscious moulders of Victorian cities' (Kellett, 1969: 2).

Central locations as cost-effective locations

In mercantile cities workplace and residence were either one and the same thing, or they were within comfortable walking distance of each other. A long working day and primitive urban transport militated against a lengthy journey to work. As late as 1840 most of New York's industrial workers, being handicraftsmen, had a place of work that was identical with, or within a 0.5–1.5 km walk from, home (Pred, 1966: 207). Even though the mass production techniques adopted in manufacturing in the 1830s and 1840s severed the workbench from the living room, many industrialists endeavoured to recreate the 'symbiosis' by building industrial barracks next to their factories. The hidden benefits of having factory operatives housed close to the factory were reflected in lower operating costs (if the workers' commuting costs could be eliminated and their housing costs fixed) and higher productivity (if the length of the working day could be extended). Heilbroner (1980: 155) makes mention of a Manchester factory that operated with a working week that averaged between 78½ and 84 hours in 1862.

Apart from the pecuniary benefits to industrialists and the convenience to their workers, it is also true that central accommodation was essential to the casual labour market that was a feature of many Victorian cities. At the height of the building boom in 1865 London's casual labour force was estimated to comprise at least 680,000 workers (Stedman Jones, 1971: 171). In many of the poorest-paid and casual trades workers not only had to live within walking distance, but they also had to be constantly on call. Besides, central London was the best place to hear of work and the place most accessible to all quarters of London whether it be the Drury Lane slums for the Covent Garden market, Tower Hill for the docks, or Soho for the West End tailoring trade and domestic services. Central lodgings also represented the best opportunity for wives and daughters to augment household income by taking in laundry, charring, office cleaning, flower selling or working in the sweated labour market. While certain industries continued to concentrate near the heart of Victorian cities, and working class transport did not exist, the waves of migrants moving into urban areas were bound to congregate in lodgings near the centre.

Intensification of ground-rents in the central area

The value creation that accompanied the expansion of commercial and industrial functions resulted in dramatic changes in the use of land at the centre of nineteenth-century cities. 'From the standpoint of an expanding capitalist economy, indeed, capitalism's prospects of profits, which rested on continuous turnovers, demanded the continued destruction of old urban structures, for the sake of their profitable replacement at even higher rents . . . unceasing destruction and replacement became the new rhythm of city development.' This is not a Marxist urban scholar speaking to us, but Lewis Mumford (1961: 506–07); and in 1961.

The only way working class housing could continue to compete with industrial and commercial users on the edges of the central business district was by building at densities not previously contemplated. 'In York and Leeds the courts were built in what had been the gardens of older and more spacious homes: in Nottingham and Coventry overcrowded "rookeries" were created by the shortage of building land consequent upon the refusal to enclose the common lands which hemmed in the town' (Harrison, 1979: 86). In New York, in the 1850s and 1860s, builders and developers demolished older converted dwellings to make way for the notorious dumb-bell tenement, so-called because of its shape. Encouraged by the Tenement House Law of 1879, the six- to seven-floor dumb-bell tenement usually included four apartments to the floor, with at least *one* bedroom open to the natural light. 'This kind of housing, occupied chiefly by immigrants, lay at the heart of one of the chief concerns of late nineteenth century urban reformers – the slum problem. By 1900 the number of tenements in Manhattan had increased to 42,700, and they housed 1,585,000 people, an average of 33.58 people per building' (Glaab and Brown, 1967: 162). In Sydney during the 1880s the rapid rise in land values also led to over-building by Australian standards and 'land-sweating'. Because working class terraces in the inner neighbourhoods were built speculatively and investors expected a higher yield than on shares or bonds, materials and workmanship were below par (Gerathy, 1972: 23–4).

The profits to be obtained from housing (except in cases of extreme rack-renting) paled into insignificance beside the yield of commercial and business premises. In Britain, inner area neighbourhoods which were already in decay by early Victorian times were cleared to make way for the extension of railway lines, the building of stations and goods yards, the laying of docks, the erection of huge warehouses, and for the provision of commercial and government offices. An impressive lift in land values at the centre followed: between 1861 and 1881 the rateable value of the City of London rose from £1.33 million to £3.48 million, and again by a third to £4.86 million in 1901 (Stedman Jones, 1971: 161). Thus began the depopulation of the central areas of British cities. Having attained its peak population in 1851, every ward of central Liverpool was losing households by 1871. In Birmingham four of the central wards lost population between 1851 and 1871. The

City of London's population fell from 113,387 to 51,439 between 1861 and 1881.

Displacing the urban poor

One of the constants of capitalist mechanisms within the urban land market is that the impact of value creation is unevenly born without some form of intervention, irrespective of place and time. Four main agents were primarily responsible for the demolition and displacement that took place before the late 1870s. 'First and most ostentatious of these, if not ultimately the most important, were undoubtedly the railway companies' (Stedman Jones, 1971: 161–2). 'By 1890 the principal railway companies had expended £100 million, more than one-eighth of all railway capital, on the provision of terminals, had bought thousands of acres of central land, and undertaken the direct work of urban demolition and rebuilding on a huge scale' (Kellett, 1969: 2). Kellett adds that, 'In most cities they had become the owners of up to eight or ten *per cent* of central land, and indirectly influenced the functions of up to twenty *per cent*' (table 4.4). With land costs

Table 4.4 Consumption of central area space in five Victorian cities, 1900

	Built-up area in 1840 (hectares)	Railways in central zone (hectares)	Central zone owned by railways (%)
London	5,851.4	314.2	5.37
Birmingham	582.6	30.6	5.25
Liverpool	677.3	61.1	9.02
Manchester	763.6	55.5	7.27
Glasgow	452.2	34.2	7.56

Source: Kellett (1969: 290)

generally running at about a quarter of the amount spent upon the construction of the track, and half as much again as the cost of rolling stock, engines and plant, the selection of routes and space for terminals was a critical process. And because all central city rents and land prices were at a premium the railway surveyors sought out the most undercapitalized land which invariably supported rundown, overcrowded working class accommodation. On the basis of his analysis of the Demolition Statements submitted by the railway companies to Parliament, Dyos (1955: 96) conservatively estimates that 80,000 people were displaced by the expansion of the railways in London alone between 1853 and 1901.

A second agent of displacement, at least in port and riverside localities, was dock development. Again in London, the building of the London Docks (1800–05) and St Katherine's Docks (1828) destroyed 1,300 and 1,033 dwellings respectively (Stedman Jones, 1971: 164). It is impossible to obtain a figure for the number of households displaced by the building of warehouses and the conversion of dwellings into workshops and offices in Victorian cities. Though piecemeal and small in scale, the combined effect was to dislodge a sizeable segment of the working classes especially within the zone in transition bordering the city centre – the 'twilight zone'. In Stedman Jones's opinion, 'In its arbitrary and unplanned way demolition and commercial transformation in nineteenth century London must have involved a greater displacement of population than the rebuilding of Paris under Haussmann' (Stedman Jones, 1971: 159).

From the 1830s onwards, as various cities legislated for urban improvement, slum clearance and street widening assumed growing importance as a fourth agent of housing displacement. According to Stedman Jones (1971: 167–9), London's City Corporation and the Metropolitan Board of Works both ruthlessly cleared areas considered to be hot-beds of the 'dangerous classes', the foci of cholera, crime and Chartism. It is probable that altogether street clearance accounted for the displacement of not far short of 100,000 persons between 1830 and 1880. It was not until the Metropolitan Street Improvement Act of 1877 that the Metropolitan Board of Works was required to rehouse the displaced families within the vicinity of their clearance schemes (Yelling, 1981).

Because the railway and shipping companies acquired the undercapitalized land, and medical officers advising the Metropolitan Board of Works pinpointed the unhealthiest neighbourhoods for improvement, overcrowding and rent levels by the 1880s had reached a crisis point in central London (table 4.5). It began to dawn upon local government inspectors and parliamentarians that, contrary to expectations, slum clearance was not an answer to inhuman housing conditions. Because they were so severely constrained by employment opportunities – 'A slum, in a word, represents the presence of a market for local casual labour' (Castelloe, in Wohl, 1977) – displaced workers and their families had little choice but to pile up in the nearest available housing, which was all the while being depleted. The overcrowding and poverty which went hand-in-hand were the product of structural pressures relating to the uneven nature of demand for casual labour, the need to provide cheap consumer goods in order to remain competitive, and the inevitable decline of old-established industries (Rose, 1981: 349). It was not until well into the 1880s, with the introduction of working men's fares and some suburbanization of

Table 4.5 Housing densities in Inner London districts, 1841–81

	1841	1851	1861	1871	1881
Holborn					
St. George's	8.62	9.85	10.36	11.02	11.41
Amwell	9.26	9.73	10.17	10.69	11.82
Old Street	5.88	8.04	8.71	9.02	9.16
Shoreditch					
Hoxton New Town	6.73	7.50	8.33	8.82	9.48
Hoxton Old Town	6.53	7.31	7.97	8.33	8.51
Bethnal Green					
Hackney Road	6.11	6.62	7.02	7.45	7.88
Green	6.03	6.72	7.12	7.61	7.92
Whitechapel					
Artillery and	8.05	8.88	8.97	9.72	11.28
Spitalfields	8.75	9.91	10.24	10.07	
Southwark					
Christchurch	7.50	8.49	9.03	9.20	9.63
London Road	7.25	7.54	7.85	8.23	9.53
Newington	6.11	6.49	6.65	7.05	7.65

Source: Stedman Jones (1971: 176).

industry, that the extreme pressure on central London's housing market eased. Whereas a lack of any significant industrial decentralization tied poorly paid workers to the core area, the disinclination of the railway companies to provide enough cheap and convenient working men's trains delayed the migration of even the workers with modest incomes. Thus the *Royal Commission on the housing of the working classes*, which tabled its report in 1885, cut the ground from under those who believed that sufficient physically and morally 'decent' accommodation was available for the deserving: 'even highly skilled artisans were living in overcrowded single-roomed flats and were often forced to share dwellings with the criminal poor' (Wohl, 1977: 40).

The 'eternal slum'

From the countless descriptions, ranging from Dickens' novels to systematic social surveys, and Royal Commissions conducted by government, it is possible to build up a picture of the acute distress and appalling living conditions endured by the poorest sections of the working class in 'twilight zones'. If Manchester was England's 'shock' city in the 1830s[12] then it still remained so in the 1880s. Kellett (1969: 338) provides this description of one of east Manchester's rookeries lodged in between the Lancashire and Yorkshire Railway's Oldham Road, and the Midland Railway's Ancoats, goods stations:

> Here, apart from a few shopkeepers in Ancoats District No. 1, and some clerks, mechanics and artisans in the 11th district, lived the porters, labourers, hawkers, tramps, hurdy-gurdy men and people of no definite occupation, sandwiched between the railway sidings, dye works and cotton mills, iron and boiler works, gas and sanitary installations, and works making oil and grease. The houses were of the cottage type with stone flags resting directly on a clay subsoil, unventilated, with defective drainage, a third of them occupied by more than one family. Altogether a particularly bad example of the type of no-man's land created by speculative building in the areas between railway sidings and industrial users on the other fringe of an urban central district.

Needless to say there was more variation in the quality of nineteenth-century working class housing than the popular stereotype suggests. In Leeds, for example, the rent paid by respectable working men in 1839 ranged from 2s 6d a week. At that time there were 8,331 dwellings in Leeds rented at between £5 and £10 per year, and a further 2,640 at between £10 and £20 (Harrison, 1979: 83). The cheapest of these, the ubiquitous 'back-to-back', consisted of two rooms and a cellar, built back to back, and sharing an outside toilet. Harrison (1979: 84) spells out some of rawer aspects of working-class life in such a domestic setting: the lack of indoor sanitation and consequent use of chamber pots; the absence of a water tap in the house and the difficulties of ensuring personal hygiene; the aggravation of these tribulations with an aged or sick person in the house; the elimination of through ventilation by back-to-back construction. With hindsight it is now obvious that poor housing for the working classes is one of the real costs of economic expansion. 'It is arguable that better housing would have reduced the outflow of capital which helped sustain Britain's open economy and that low standards therefore helped to channel resources into production at a rewarding rate' (Dyos, 1968b: 151). That may be so, but certainly some of the savings made at the

---

[12] By far the worst off were the 40–50,000 people living in cellars and basements in both Manchester and Liverpool at the time (Harrison, 1979: 85–6). If there was any consolation for the Victorian 'underclass' it was that they were spared the indecency of the tenement accommodation provided at the heart of most continental, and some US cities. Amongst British cities, Glasgow and Edinburgh were alone in housing families in tenement buildings up to ten floors high.

expense of the working class were used to put distance between households at different ends of the class spectrum. In this sense, 'The suburb and the slum belonged to the same declension' (Dyos, 1968b: 151).

Speculative impulse: transport and housing provision in the suburbs

The first thing to understand in relation to suburban development in the second half of the nineteenth century is that the interests of the transport operators and the land owners coincided so closely that 'traffic speculation and land speculation played into each other's hands, often in the person of the same enterpriser' (Mumford, 1961: 490). The movement to the suburbs was actively promoted, not only by the private land and railway companies but by consortia of large estate owners, developers, and speculative house builders. This structural grouping of producers was by no means the only form of housing provision in nineteenth-century Britain, Australia, or the United States; however, it did set the pace and direction of change in the housing industry. Moreover, 'Its collapse . . . at the beginning of the twentieth century was the starting point for the long, slow decline of private landlordism in Britain' (Ball, 1981a: 147).

Suburban armadas: shunting the workforce around nineteenth-century cities

Suburbanization began in a modest way in the late 1820s with the inception of horsedrawn omnibus services like the New York and Harlem Railroad. As the forerunner of fixed tract transportation it created the first significant separation of residence from workplace and higher order shopping. 'The horse-drawn railway provided the first real answer to the problem of large-scale movement of people within cities' (Glaab and Brown, 1967: 198). With their poor acceleration steam locomotives could not compete *within* the compact mid-Victorian city. In addition, the charters of railways, although generous in extending right-of-way privileges through cities (including by viaduct, 'elevated' and much later, underground), generally forbade the use of steam trains on city streets. In Warner's (1962) study of Boston's streetcar suburbs it was the horsecar that facilitated the residential development of the South End in the fifties and sixties, and of the inner parts of Dorchester and Roxbury during the seventies and eighties. An examination of 28,000 building permits for Roxbury, West Roxbury and Dorchester left no doubt that access to the suburbs was limited to the upper 40 per cent of Bostonian society. The three streetcar suburbs under Warner's microscope were clearly differentiated into three strata – the top five per cent, the upper middle class of 15 per cent, and the lower middle class of 20 to 30 per cent. In much the same way the advent of horsedrawn omnibuses in England ushered in the beginnings of a middle class exodus from the formerly fashionable neighbourhoods of Liverpool, Manchester, and Birmingham (Kellett, 1969: 355–65).

Continued dominance of the streetcar in American cities was assured with the development of the dynamo in the 1870s and the rapid electrification of the system: 'In 1890, 69.7 per cent of the total trackage in cities was operated by horses; by 1902 this figure had declined to 1.1 per cent, while electric power was used on 97 per cent of the mileage' (Glaab and Brown, 1967: 152). In addition, by 1895, 850 trolley systems operated by private companies had been installed in US cities with routes totalling 10,000 miles. During the late 1880s and early 1890s, in the case of Boston, electrification pushed the area of convenient transportation out to the edge of a six mile radius. In Sydney the tramway system served to consolidate the inner suburbs stretching in an arc from the west to south of the city centre as a working class preserve in the 1880s and 1890s (see Daly, 1982a: 156–57). Passenger journeys climbed from 440,000 in 1879, when the first steam-tram was introduced, to 39.5 million in 1885, and 65.1 million in 1891 (by which time the inner suburbs were housing 60 per cent of Sydney's population, mostly in shoddily built, rented accommodation). By comparison the impact of electrified streetcar services on English cities was slow to eventuate: in 1898, the 7.5 million residents of the largest cities generated 474 million passenger journeys on 618 miles of track (Ward, 1964: 485–6).

Urban transport and social distinctions

Because the British tramways were mostly, though not exclusively, associated with the growth of working class districts, proposals to extend the network in the 1890s were frequently vetoed by local authorities on behalf of residents. In London, middle class areas like Woodford, Stanmore, Harrow and Hillingdon opposed tramway services on the grounds that the trams were noisy and ugly; that they would increase the wear and tear on private carriages; that property would depreciate in value; and that the area would be transformed by the influx of the 'lower orders' (Pollins, 1964: 44–5). (Shades of the defence of property recounted in chapter 9.) Finally, in the 1890s when it was realized that the private operators were falling well short of their capacity to provide cheap transport for workers, the London

County Council bowed to pressure from its housing committee and started to municipalize tramway companies (Wohl, 1977: 292).

Initially the steam railways played a relatively minor part in moving workers about the city. Right from the start the fixed and recurrent costs of railway operation compared with the tramways meant that a schedule of fares was set that was bound to attract wealthier passengers moving to outlying villages and estates. During the mid-1840s the eastern railroad companies in the US began carrying regular commuters, such as merchants who lived in outlying villages but conducted their business 'downtown'. But it was not until the 1860s that suburban rail services for commuters could be regarded as a sound proposition for investors. Even in London, in the mid-1850s, 10,000 commuters at most arrived by rail according to Kellett (1969: 365); a figure completely overshadowed by the 244,000 daily foot and omnibus passengers entering the City. And although by the 1870s bustling downtown Chicago was linked with over 100 railway suburbs offering the charms of 'pure air, peacefulness, quietude and natural scenery' (Glaab and Brown, 1967: 155), their combined populations barely reached 50,000. Hence, the suburban rail passenger in the mid-1860s was still predominantly middle class or better.

It was only in the last two decades of the nineteenth century that, 'with the slow growth of cheap ticket commuter traffic, the railway companies began to make a marked impression, in London, at any rate, upon the Victorian suburbs, influencing their social composition and their direction and rates of growth' (Kellett, 1969: 18). This came about with the passing of the Cheap Trains Act, 1883, which was designed to relieve some of the overcrowding in central London by forcing the railway companies to extend the geographical coverage of workmen's fares. With the exception of some of the south-east London lines which had introduced such fares in 1864,[13] the privately owned and operated railway companies had resisted agitation to lower their fare structures. (The complaint was that workmen's trains were unprofitable and lost traffic because the working class suburbs like Edmonton-Tottenham-Walthamstow repelled middle class commuters). As it turned out only the southern railway companies and the Great Eastern Railway (GER) responded with any real energy to the provisions of the Cheap Trains Act; whereas, between them the Great Western, the London and North Western, and the Midland refused point blank to make any concessions by way of fares or services to working men. This discouraged working class housing in a great arc of virtually 90 degrees from west to north in suburban London. Conversely, the great working class concentration in north-east

[13] And even then as a *quid pro quo* for the demolition of the labouring classes' housing closer to the centre of London by the company (Pollins, 1964: 42).

London, between the Lea and the Thames, is to some extent due to the enormous number of worker's trains which the GER ran in the last quarter of the nineteenth century (Pollins, 1964: 43). Though, as Kellett (1969: 379) points out, with the genuinely cheap 2*d.* fares forming only 7 per cent of London's daily rail traffic, the magnanimity of the railway companies has been grossly overstated. Out of the 410,472 commuters from London's suburbs in 1901, only 27,569 qualified for the workmen's 2*d.* fare; 105,000 commuters paid between 9*d.* and 11*d.* daily, a rate set to attract clerical workers rather than blue collar workers; the remaining 278,500 paid the full ordinary fare. With good reason Kellett (1969: 380) concludes that the growth in commuting by rail was due to a widening of effective demand *within* the classes that could afford to meet the railway's charges, rather than a determined effort to popularize suburban travel via reduced fares.

Much the same experience has been reported for Melbourne following the petitioning of the Minister of Railways in 1882 for special working men's trains to be run at reduced fares. In 1883 there were 32 working men's services daily, in 1887 there were 59: 'Nevertheless, despite – and perhaps even because of – such innovations, social distinctions persisted between train and tram travel and since it was broadly true that lower class individuals resided in inner areas, these tended to reinforce the technical adaptation of trains to outer and trams to inner areas' (Davison, 1970: 175). With electrification there was a hardening of the arteries in both systems; that is, 'a gradual and mutually destructive interpenetration of each system upon the other's catchment areas' (Davison, 1970: 175). Electrification of the railways greatly improved the 'headway' between trains stopping at inner area stations during the 'peak', and eliminated the principal objection to underground travel (the accumulation of gas, smoke and dirt). On the other hand, the electrification of trams enabled their operators to penetrate further into the catchment areas of the railways and boost their passenger/mile returns within the system as a whole. The railway companies responded by actively promoting middle class settlement at distances of up to 20 miles from the central stations (Pollins, 1964: 45). Incentives included cheap season tickets, or in 1865 in the case of Melbourne's United Railways, a free first class ticket for the first 18 months on a house costing £300, or up to a maximum of seven years on a house costing £1,000 (Saunders, 1967: 5–6).

Estate development and house building in the Victorian suburb

The speculative nature of land development and house building in the second half of the nineteenth century repaid the originator of the inspired locational decision handsomely. That 689 private acts of parliament, authorizing the construction of 10,306 miles of railway, were passed during Britain's 'great railway mania' (1841–47) should be sufficient to suggest that the 'stakes' for landowners near the main cities were enormous. Because of the monopolistic quality of fixed-track transport, the windfall gains that followed the granting of a 'franchise' flowed to all those investors who had acquired land at rural prices. This accounts for the naked connivance between politicians and the suburban railway or streetcar promoters right through the nineteenth century, starting with the landed aristocracy owning estates near cities (Cannadine, 1980) and drawing to a close with the granting of utility franchises by municipalities in the US (Mohl and Betten, 1972).[14] The nadir was probably reached in Australia during the boom decade of the eighties when suburban rail promotion fuelled land speculation on a grand scale in Sydney and Melbourne. So extravagant were the proposals in Victoria's 1884 Railways Bill – 65 lines totalling 1,170 miles at a cost of £44 million – that it was dubbed the 'Octopus Act'. As a direct result of Melbourne's railway building mania, by 1888 the number of allotments subdivided for suburban housing in Melbourne exceeded the needs of London's population at the time (Cannon, 1976: 40).

Bouyant conditions at the beginning of the 1880s gave rise to a recklessness that was to catch up with the immature (and greedy) Australian financial institutions by 1891. Demand for housing soared following a 40 per cent jump in immigration between 1883 and 1885, while the economy was awash with risk capital since it was returning twice the prevailing British rates (Daly, 1982a: 158). During the decade, 1881–90, the Victorian government raised £30 million on the London money market, which together with private borrowing injected £60 million into the state's economy. In one year, 1888, when Victoria's population reached one million, the circulation of money in Melbourne increased by 84 per cent. Much of this money – public and private – found its way into the land market.[15] In 1880 the total investment in Melbourne land and mortgages was £5 million, in 1886

---

[14] The granting of a 50 year franchise to the Gary and Interurban Railway Company by Gary's board of trustees provided a particularly interesting case because it permitted growth to the south of the town where board members and their associates owned land, at the same time as a streetcar franchise was refused to the mighty US Steel Corporation (Mohl and Betten, 1972). This represented a resounding defeat for the corporate giant because a streetcar service would have enhanced the value of company land, permitted company control of development and land use, and the housing of workers close to the steel mills.

[15] The property boom had been supported by borrowed capital held on shaky terms and when, in 1889, the Premier Building Association of Melbourne collapsed, shock waves were sent as far as London. Property values began to fall and reduced sales affected the ability of companies to repay their loans (Daly, 1982a: 159).

nearly £12 million, and in 1890 nearly £16 million (Cannon, 1976: 24–40).

When the crash came in 1891[16] millions of pounds were stripped from the aggregate value of urban land, railway and tram services were left lying idle, and 'whole village suburbs' which had been run up with building society funds were untenanted and remained so for years afterwards (Cannon, 1976: 26). Such was the over-indulgence in building activity in Victoria in the eighties that building and construction accounted for 87 per cent of the total private investment (£53 million between 1881 and 1891).

In the Victorian land development and housing industry are found the forerunners of all the standard institutional mechanisms, policies and practices that have served the owners of capital (including domestic capital) so well ever since. That is not to say that an identical approach to the logistics and finance of house building was adopted everywhere in the United States, Australia and the United Kingdom, just as it would be incorrect to imply that building cycles always coincided with the movement of investment capital and labour within the Atlantic economy (Habakkuk, 1962). New York's dumb-bell tenements apart, nowhere in the United States or Australia were the monotonous housing estates developed by Britain's large-scale land-owners to be found. Although some financial institutions and individuals did make extensive purchases during Melbourne's land boom they tended to spread their purchases across the city (Saunders, 1967: 7). Likewise, as Barrett (1971) and Kelly (1970) have shown in case studies of representative Australian suburbs – Fitzroy and Collingwood in Melbourne, Paddington in Sydney – small-scale operators pre-dominated in land speculation and in builder and/or non-builder development. Characteristically, a speculative builder might take as long as five to six years to construct a row of seldom more than half a dozen terrace houses. Also 'The striking fact is that by the mid 1880s over 60 per cent of rental houses were owned by landlords whose property holding did not exceed four houses. . . . Again, even the

---

[16] Between July 1891 and April 1892, 21 building finance companies in Melbourne and 20 in Sydney suspended payments. English and Scottish investment in the colony completely dried up. Within a year the Federal Bank failed and twelve other banks suspended payments. When the run on the Australian banks started, their capital reserves, which stood at £25 million in 1892, were insufficient to pay creditors who had placed deposits totalling £155 million within the system (Cannon, 1976: 40). Part of the blame lay with the poorly regulated banking system and a clause of the Victorian building societies' statutes which permitted the institutions 'to buy and sell or mortgage freehold or leasehold estates'. At the height of the boom the directors used the societies' substantial deposits to compete frantically for the best real estate. Opportunists floated 'estate companies'; and land and finance companies ('land banks') were formed with minimal paid-up capital when the more conservative bankers refused to relax their lending policies. In the 1888 financial year 270 new companies were registered in Melbourne alone.

landlord owning five to ten houses rarely had them in one line – normally his houses were scattered, in small groups of two, three and four, throughout the suburb' (Kelly, 1970: 168).

A lot of what is known about the land conversion process, the structure of the housing industry, and the financing of suburban housing and social overhead capital (the provision of transport, drainage, gas and water services, schools, parks) in the nineteenth-century city is based upon an exhaustive study of Camberwell, a south London suburb, by that fine urban historian H. J. Dyos (1961; 1968c). His work has since been augmented by other studies of London suburbs, including Paddington and Kensington in the West End (Reeder, 1968), and Lambeth, Battersea and Wandsworth on the south bank of the Thames (Roebuck, 1979). So, once again London is in the limelight, without implying that its experience was universally shared. Generally, the production of suburban housing brought together five key parties in the following order: land owner, estate developer, speculative builder, building workers, and the home buyer (Ball, 1981a). Suburban conversion depended upon the owner of a rural estate – landed gentry, church, college, Corporation of London – being prepared to release land on terms which made its development for building profitable.[17] An estate developer might purchase the freehold outright, or obtain a lease which by Victorian times was never less than 60 years and could be on the well-nigh perpetual basis of 999 years; though by the last quarter of the century, the short-term or London building lease of 99 years duration was the norm in London. Mostly the owner accepted a ground-rent well short of the net income produced by the completed housing estate, on the understanding that the land plus improvements would revert to the family trust on expiration of the lease, whereupon the property could be rack-rented.[18] The developer performed the specialist task of securing much of the finance, making agreements with builders and arranging for the supply of roading, drainage, water, and sufficient other amenities to attract the right class of tenant. The builder's part was completed once an occupier (owner or tenant) had been found for his dwellings.

[17] The land to be developed was not always a greenfields site: 'There are, and always have been, within our recollection, extensive outlying districts in the suburbs of London, very strongly resembling the heterogeneous regions of squatters in a new settlement' (Smith, 1972: 364).

[18] In a description of 'How London Grows', in *Curiosities of London Life* (Smith, 1972: 370–1), the writer outlines some of the implications of the London building lease: 'eighteen months before the close of the lease, a surveyor came down upon us, in the cause of the ground-landlord, and enforced a thorough overhauling of the dwelling from the roof to the cellars, with re-painting, re-papering, carpentering, and locksmithing, the cost of which was deducted from the landlord's rent . . . by building on land rented for a limited period, a species of architecture is produced which stands at the lowest point in the scale of taste.'

Because of the prominence in the nineteenth century of master builders like Thomas Cubbitt, who almost single-handedly created Belgravia and Pimlico in the West End and London's first garden suburb (the 250 acre Clapham Park), prior to Dyos's research it was widely accepted that the large-scale enterprise was the dominant institutional form within the Victorian housing industry. It is true that by mid-century there were six general contractors at work in London each employing 1,500 men with a core of regulars on the payroll, and probably a hundred master builders employing 28,000 out of a total London building force of 38,000 workers (Dyos, 1968c: 650). Nevertheless, throughout the last quarter of the nineteenth century at least 60 per cent of all firms built fewer than six houses a year, and hardly any built more than 50.[19] An overwhelming number of these were speculative builders: Dyos estimates from the monthly returns that at least 90 per cent of house-building was conducted on speculation between the early 1870s and the late 1890s (Dyos, 1968c: 66). A range of operators got involved in speculative building: professionals and 'speculators', including ground-landlords and developers, who simply hired builders to run up 'frontage' and create the improved ground-rents against which they could borrow; the small-time tradesmen with virtually no fixed capital who managed to raise enough working capital on mortgage against the partly completed dwellings before transferring the mortgage to the homebuyer; the builders' merchants and building societies that were forced to complete houses on which they had foreclosed; the firms of jobbing builders that could retreat to their repairs and alterations when the speculative bubble burst. As always with the capitalist enterprise,

> most of the money to be made out of this process went to the men who were first on the scene, who leased or bought land before its rise, and developed or sold it on the very top of the tide. The biggest profits came from speculating in building land, not from the building operations themselves, though putting up the houses was sometimes as necessary to the realization of these gains as was the building of a suburban railway or the creation of a fashionable image for the suburb that had nothing else to commend it. (Dyos, 1968c: 645)

[19] Though by 1899 concentration in the house-building industry was becoming apparent: only 17 firms, under three per cent of the total, built 30 per cent of London's new houses (Dyos, 1968c: 678). Aspinall (1982) maintains that the degree of concentration in the London house-building industry towards the end of the nineteenth century was only really matched in the north-western counties of England.

Sources of housing finance

Although an intuitive connection is made between investment over-seas and the state of the domestic house building industry by Harvey (1978), Dyos does not believe that the supply of capital to housing in Britain ever seriously checked construction activity in London: 'there is, on the contrary, rather more evidence of *over-building* in periods of easy money than of under-building when money was tight' (Dyos, 1968c: 663). Most of the capital for the estate development that made suburban migration possible either constituted reinvestment on the part of the building firms or was drawn from the savings of the middle classes, whether in London or the provinces. Capital attracted from outside the building industry came from a limited range of sources. While the banking system had traditionally advanced money to the upper and professional classes on the security of their property, only the imprudent banks were prepared to lend directly to property developers and builders on the basis of a mortgage deed; but that did not stop a certain amount of bank money finding its way into specula-tive building via overdrafts and promissory notes.[20] Insurance com-panies appear to have been even more discriminating, with most of their housing investment restricted to the large-scale firms engaged in estate development at the upper end of the market. As it happened, housing investment by the insurance companies was dwarfed by the flow of funds to the London vestries in order to finance various drainage and other sanitation schemes, and to support the great schemes of street improvement mounted during the 1860s and 1870s. Building societies were also an important source of housing finance, especially up to the early 1870s when one in every seven or eight dwellings built in Britain was financed by these institutions (Cleary, 1965: 286–9). About this time permanent building societies over-hauled the terminating societies, which made for an improved flow of housing finance for the better paid artisans and clerks, though not the labouring classes. As well as advancing house loans to the upwardly mobile against the security of mortgages, many societies also helped to finance the building programmes of speculative builders. It was during the recession of 1868–72 that solicitors appear to have steadily replaced the building societies as the main source of working capital for London's speculative builders. Although the solicitor has gone largely unnoticed as a financial intermediary during the period, Dyos

---

[20] Many of the Australian banks contributed to their own undoing during the 1880s land boom by encouraging speculation when money was plentiful, and then calling in over-drafts when the fragility of the market was telegraphed. Once depositors caught wind of the banks' liquidity problems, those who could withdrew their savings, forcing the closure of banks with liabilities of nearly £20 million (Cannon, 1976: 31).

(1968c: 668–9) regards him/her as 'the real fulcrum for the bulk of the capital movements' affecting the housing industry not only of Victorian London but other cities as well. An exemplary case is of the South London builder who constructed over 2,500 dwellings in the Camberwell district between the early 1850s and 1907: in 1890 over 99 per cent of this operating capital, which stood at nearly £217,000, was held in the form of 270 separate mortgages negotiated through solicitors (Dyos, 1968c: 670).

The impact of experiments in state intervention upon life in nineteenth-century cities

As Duncan (1981: 236) insists, the assumption that state intervention in the mid-nineteenth century was somehow inspired by 'moral force emanating from the Idea of Reform', on the whole, is not good enough. The shaping of the first state policies and local government reforms in response to given 'social ills' did not take place *in vacuo*: it is possible to read into much of the early government action, though that is not our main purpose in describing it, instances of concessions to working class radicalism; reforms that had the added reward for industrialists of improving the quantity and quality of labour;[21] and social investment in the cities that paved the way for capital expansion. It is also true as Sutcliffe (1982: 113–14) points out that 'the most spectacular extensions of public intervention' in Britain from the late 1860s were prompted by frequent failures in the market which had the effect of undermining gains in real earnings and living conditions in the cities (urban mortality rates fell for the first time in the 1870s).

'Gas-and-water-socialism'

The early Victorian cities were still largely unpaved, unsewered, ill-lit, and inadequately supplied with clean water. It was only reluctantly that municipal councils began to assume responsibility for the provision of a minimal level of service provision and the regulation of building standards. These improvements in local government services resulted partly from the nudging by Parliament which enacted a new poor law, several railway acts and factory acts, and finally the Public Health Act

[21] And yet the class allied with industrial capital in the UK was not smart enough to forsee the foolhardiness in the long-run of its 'dismissive, almost cavalier attitude towards technical education and research with the result that by 1914 Britain had lost technical superiority in almost every staple industry' (Kirby, 1981: 7). The changes in the country's educational system necessary to produce an intermediate class of shopfloor supervisors and production and design engineers, were not instituted until well after 1890. So much for 'the reproduction of labour power' by the state.

(1848) during the 1830s and 1840s (Dyos, 1968b; Lubenow, 1971). The passage of the legislation, together with the build up of government machinery, coincided with a period (1833–48) of intense social conflict in England, which was punctuated by Chartism, the Anti-Corn Law League, the Hungry Forties and the Irish Famine. With the 1832 reorganization of local government in the 263 places which enjoyed chartered or prescriptive municipality privileges some Victorian cities began to confront the backlog of urban problems with much greater determination. Briggs (1968: 40–2) comments that even the most progressive urban corporations – Leeds, Birmingham, Liverpool – followed bursts of lavish civic spending with long spells of 'economy', 'when ratepayers' pressures were strong enough to prevent the start of large-scale building projects'. This reformism has since been referred to, rather caustically, as 'gas-and-water-socialism' (Kirk, 1980: 116). By 1870 there were 49 municipally owned gas companies in England and Wales, many of which were operating sufficiently profitably to subsidize the public works programmes of the local authorities. Further, under the Public Health Act of 1875 urban authorities obtained the power to municipalize gas companies, along with other privately operated utilities like gaslight, waterworks, tram and railway companies (Briggs, 1968: 217–30).

The attempt from the 1840s to the 1870s to improve working class housing, which took the form of street clearance, model dwellings, sanitary regulations and (in England) the schemes initiated by philanthropists like Octavia Hill, had as much to do with the perceived danger to the opulent Victorians of intolerable living conditions in the midst of their cities as it did with the social reproduction of a healthier and better housed workforce. The 'threat' appeared to middle class Victorians in two main forms. Firstly, the rookeries were seen as breeding grounds for vice, where the antisocial behaviour of the criminal class would rub off on the decent poor, and as a potential source of the sort of mass social unrest that could upset the equipoise of Victorian class structure if left to ferment.[22] Secondly, by the 1860s, informed Victorians had come to realize that insofar as the slum dwellers were at risk from infectious diseases, so too were they.

The large-scale programmes to provide acceptable drinking water, sewerage and drainage for urban Victorians were not born of uncommon benevolence or impetuous altruism. Concern for the health of the

[22] And yet the paradox is that contemporary social movements like Chartism and the Anti-Corn Law League had their strongest roots in the provinces while London was relatively isolated. Factory districts like Bolton, Stockport, Ashton, Staleybridge, and Leigh were the scene of imposing popular demonstrations in 1838. 'Chartism made a deep impression on the labouring poor and assisted their transformation into a working class' (Harrison, 1979: 188). According to Goodway (1982: 221), it was not until 1848 that 'metropolitan Chartism was most dangerous, most insurrectionary, whereas nationally the spontaneity or strength of the first phase was perhaps never repeated'.

working classes became a common concern once it was realized that infectious diseases like cholera, typhus and typhoid fever, dysentry, tuberculosis, diphtheria, scarlet fever and small pox were not transmitted by 'putrid airs' and, therefore, localized (the miasmatic and contagionist theories), but could be carried in water: 'The sewer may be looked upon, in fact, as a direct continuation of the diseased intestine', Budd, a London medical practitioner (1874) quoted in Rosen (1973: 638). Thus because typhus fever, cholera and smallpox were no respecters of persons, once the connection between the incidence of the disease and the effectiveness of sanitary prevention had been made, 'extending and perfecting sanitary requirements in the interests of the whole urban community assumed a much higher priority than that of raising living standards for the badly housed' (Dyos, 1968b: 152). Briggs (1968: 16–17) looks upon this hidden network of pipes and drains and sewers as 'one of the biggest technical and social achievements of the age'.

Responses to the 'housing problem'

Any investment going into working class housing during the nineteenth century normally shared the expectations of capital going into speculative housing for the middle classes. Rates of profit on rented working class accommodation averaged 6 to 8 per cent until the end of the nineteenth century, when new investment in working class housing ceased to be profitable because of high construction and land costs compared with feasible rents (Ball, 1981a: 155–6). Even the provision of philanthropic housing was governed by the expectation of a five per cent return. When, for example, in 1857 the Liverpool Labourers Dwelling Company yielded a dividend of 3½ per cent, and another of 4½ per cent, 'they were unhesitatingly branded as failures' (Dyos, 1968b: 153).

According to Dyos (1968b: 154) the tolerable limit to the idea of non-interference at its most extreme had been that of a building code to defeat disease, even if it cost landlords and builders something to apply it. The general housing legislation passed between 1851 and 1875 was condemned to failure because it ran ahead of public opinion, which held that there was no shortage of builders to meet the unmet demand. While local authorities were delegated extraordinarily wide powers under these acts – including the right to use their own land for the construction of lodging-houses (1851); to borrow housing funds from the Public Works Loan Board (1866–67); to meet municipal housing costs out of rates (1874); to lease land to housing associations and model housing companies for construction (1874); and to demolish insanitary housing (1875) – in practice very little advantage was taken of these opportunities to house the poor. Only a handful of towns, notably Edinburgh, Dundee, Glasgow, and Liverpool, had voluntarily sought parliamentary approval for limited schemes of demolition before the first Nuisances Removal Act in 1864. On the whole it was much easier for local authorities to treat the 'housing problem' narrowly as a sanitary issue, to strengthen orders against nuisances, and to enforce building codes in the forelorn hope that this would prevent new slums from forming. This situation did not drastically change until 1900 when the London County Council's housing policy was liberalized to allow for the acquisition of land for the construction of workingmen's housing in the outer suburbs. Within five years or so the LCC was providing seven per cent of all working class housing in London. This marked the beginning of 'an enormous stride towards large-scale municipal socialism in the field of working class housing' (Wohl, 1977: 234).

There was never the remotest likelihood that charitable societies like the Peabody Trust and the Improved Industrial Dwellings Company, or Octavia Hill with her system of firm personal management of converted houses, would make up the deficit in working class accommodation in Britain. Although the Peabody Trust was especially active in rehousing slumdwellers displaced by the Metropolitan Board of Works schemes in the 1870s and 1880s (Tarn, 1966: 24–9), examination of the Peabody tenants' earnings indicates that, in practice, only the well paid labourers or poorly paid artisans could afford the rents charged necessary to return 5 per cent (Wohl, 1977: 200–01). Despite the good intentions, philanthropic housing scarcely touched the provincial cities and even after 30 years' work in London they barely housed a number equal to six months increase in its population: by 1884, the 28 largest corporations and groups connected with semi-philanthropic model housing had housed only 32,435 people (Wohl, 1977: 200–01).

'Social investment' in nineteenth-century Australia

Arguably, one can see a social investment programme well ahead of its time in the efforts of the Australian state governments to offset the absence of a mature nineteenth-century industrial base. Indeed, the relationship between government and the private sector was sufficiently eccentric for Butlin (1959) to coin the aphorism 'colonial socialism' to describe it. At a time when the doctrine of utilitarianism denounced government intervention in economic affairs, the Australian state governments were energetically engaged in cultivating the conditions in which the private sector could prosper. Because government provision of roads, bridges, railways, telegraph and postal facilities, and schools saved the private sector, especially rural producers, from the costs of creating this non-productive, though vitally necessary social capital, the states won private approval for public foreign borrowing and capital formation on a massive scale. Except for a brief period in the 1850s, private business interests looked to and pressed Australia's state governments to assume ever increasing responsibility for accessing and accelerating the transfer of capital, labour and technology from overseas sources. Much of this public sector activity was a conscious part of a policy of 'metropolitan aggrandisement' pursued by envious colonial governments seated in the capital cities. As a result of their various interventions between 1860 and 1900 the Australian state governments: subsidized the inflow of 350,000 of the 750,000 immigrants attracted to Australia;[23] raised half of all the foreign capital flowing into the country; instigated approximately 40 per cent of total domestic capital formation, mainly in the *social investment* sector of transport and communications; owned about half of the country's total fixed capital (excluding land); and, employed about 5 per cent of the total workforce in transport and communications, water and sewerage (Butlin *et al.*, 1982: 13–18).

To put this into some sort of perspective, during the 1890s when public expenditure in Australia averaged 54 per cent of GNP, in Britain it hovered around the ten per cent mark, and in America had yet to reach that level (Encel, 1980: 319–20). Without a doubt, the level of expenditure on 'extraordinary' items like public works and social services (such as it was) went against the grain, but was justified as 'a necessary incident of the imperfect stage of development that pertains to a very young country' (*Report of the Royal Commission on the civil service of Victoria*, 1859; cited in Encel, 1980: 319). All the same, state intervention before the 1900s in Australia remained highly selective to the benefit of private capital, and to the cost of working men and women. For one thing, sewerage and sanitation remained problems in Australian cities (Barrett, 1971; Gerathy, 1972) long after urban municipalities in Britain had put their houses in order; that is, well into the 1880s. As a result of this complacency at the local level, drainage and water supply functions were transferred to a New South Wales Government Board of Water Supply and Sewerage in 1888, while Melbourne followed with the creation of the Metropolitan Board of Works in 1891. Similarly, at the time of federation (1901–02), the new Commonwealth government limited the collection of revenue to £11 million, of which most came from customs and excise duties. Of this sum, £7 million was disbursed to the states mainly to help reduce their public works debts and losses on transport and services, leaving precious little for social and welfare expenditures. As Cannon (1975: 199) remarks, the fact that the manufacturers could just about have 'bought and sold' all state governments combined is suggestive of a sweeping victory by Australia's bourgeoisie over the working classes. This glaring imbalance

---

[23] Australian governments have always viewed assisted immigration as a substitute for having to reproduce socially labour power. This policy has found the consistent support of the 'defence conscious', and private employers on the look-out for compliant construction, farm, and factory labour.

in the levels of social investment and social consumption expenditure was duplicated in the government's failure to legislate for improved conditions for workers. 'Many employers continued to regard themselves as kings in an industrial jungle, opposing interference by government, union or wages board with a system which had yielded personal fortunes' (Cannon, 1975: 290). Despite these obvious inconsistencies in state policy, a visiting French socialist summed up the forward march of the Australian working class in these terms '. . . more and more one can observe the external difference between the worker and the bourgeois diminishing except during working hours' (Métin, 1901: 270).

Endnote: the parallels are striking . . .

Some time has been spent exploring the various structural, social and spatial connotations of competitive capitalism as the dominant mode of production. Before moving forward to identify the most outstanding features of post-industrial urbanization in conjunction with monopoly capitalism it is worth pausing to reflect on the *recurrent* nature of many of the social and structural problems situated in cities, and the repetitiveness of the state's response, regardless of the temporal setting. In looking to the past, precedents for the displacement caused by the freeway building and urban renewal programme in the 1960s can be found in the slum clearance undertaken by the railways, shipping companies, and London's Metropolitan Board of Works in the nineteenth century. Until quite recently, as then, council managers and planners have attacked the physical symptoms rather than the structural roots of poverty and poor housing conditions. Shortly it will be seen that speculation in the inner city and fringe property markets during the early 1970s in Britain, Australia and the United States involved the same sort of unregulated opportunism, misallocation, and wastage that was the hallmark of speculative building in London, and Melbourne, and Sydney in the late nineteenth century. London's housing 'crisis' in the 1880s has recurred periodically since (c.f. the Milner-Holland enquiry in the early sixties); similarly, the title of Fried's report (1972) *Housing Crisis USA* should indicate that the inability to satisfactorily house its population is not solely a British failing. And lastly, Forrest *et al.* (1979) have made it fairly plain that there is nothing especially novel or unprecedented about structurally induced inner city decline.

5

Monopoly Capitalism and the Transition to Post-Industrial Urbanization

Preview

The main task of this chapter is to outline the structural setting for the ensuing discussion of the sources of inequality and redistribution within cities (Part III). Because of the underlying bias throughout Part III towards the allocation and consumption of housing and collective services, this chapter consciously emphasizes the processes responsible for the production of urban phenomena and structures. Because recent urban development is more immediately relevant to the concerns of Part III, scant consideration will be given to the phase of capitalist formation leading up to the Great Depression in 1929, enabling due consideration to be given to the two major epochs that have characterized monopoly capitalism since 1945. For almost three decades after the last war the predominant economic trend, even though it was punctuated at time by 'hiccups', was expansionist. Thus the years between 1945 and 1975 were marked by general prosperity; steady or rising rates of profit; an improvement in the real incomes of working class households; and a significant enlargement of government programmes within advanced capitalist societies. Characteristically, the restructuring and uneven development that took place was symptomatic of reasonably healthy economies with 'growing pains'. Except for a little seasonal and structural unemployment, the labour force was fully employed in most countries; workers that lost jobs due to restructuring were generally reabsorbed in another sector or region within the economy.

Enough time has now elapsed to be sure that the economic events of the mid-1970s mark a watershed in the ascent of monopoly capitalism. The destabilization caused by the collapse of the US dollar as the international currency standard and the resetting of crude oil prices by OPEC, is apparent in the erratic behaviour of a wide range of economic indicators. These external shocks to the balance of payments of all countries were accompanied by the election in Australia (1975), Britain (1979), and the US (1981) of three governments whose conservative complexion and contractionary monetary policies deepened the recession, and added substantially to the chronically high unemployment created by the 'deindustrialization' already underway within the manufacturing sectors of the advanced capitalist economies. By 1980, therefore, it was clear to Castells and others that 'We have already entered a new stage of development of the world capitalist system which will be at least as different in comparison with the last 30 years as the post-second world war period was in respect of the pre-1929 period' (Castells, 1980: 127–8). As capital has attempted to pull out of the nose-dive of an accumulation crisis (O'Connor, 1981b), a number of tendencies linked with capital restructuring have solidified as pointers to future forms and conditions within advanced capitalist societies.

If capital is to go on being represented as the architect of spatial structures in chapter 5 then clearly it will be necessary to determine in what sense aspects of the urban transformation in Britain, the United States and Australia are expressive of the two phases of monopoly capitalism recognized above. It is possible to show, without needing to resort to a degenerate form of functionalism, that the process of capital accumulation (or capital formation), especially during the peak decades of the fifties and sixties, owed much to the proliferation of the automobile-dependent suburb and the redevelopment of undercapitalized central area space (cf. the office boom, 1968–74). The second half of the chapter is given over to examining the processes, and their impact upon urban regions, associated with the accelerating transition in monopoly capitalism from a national to a *global* division of labour/order of spatial integration. But firstly it is necessary to outline the key structural elements and tendencies of monopoly capitalism before moving on to decide how they have conditioned urban development in the postwar era.

Monopoly capitalism on the industrial downslope

'The true character of capitalism has to be rediscovered by each new generation' (Blackburn, 1972: 114). The ascendence of monopoly capitalism was probably accomplished by the late 1960s. Mandel (1975), for example, makes out a case for late capitalism on the strength of the contemporary structural characteristics displayed by the North American and West European economies. In all advanced capitalist economies the multiplicity of firms that comprised the competitive market under nineteenth-century conditions has long since been replaced by monopolistic and oligopolistic organizations that form a hydra of interlocking industrial and financial groups. The evidence for the steady extension of concentration and centralization[1] in manufacturing and finance, which culminated in the merger boom of the 1960s, is overwhelming (Scott, 1979: 48–104). By the end of the sixties, the top 100 industrial corporations in the US owned 25 per cent of all industrial corporate wealth[2] (Heilbroner, 1980: 297), while the top 100 British firms doubled their share of net manufacturing between 1949 and 1970 as a result of merger activity – up from 20 to 40 per cent (Prais, 1976). Concentration of ownership has been a long-standing feature of the Australian economy. By the early 1960s the degree of concentration in Australia was probably greater than in any other industrial country, and certainly far ahead of that in the US, Britain or even Canada (Logan *et al.*, 1981: 49). And by the mid-1970s a mere 200 of the 32,000 manufacturing firms in Australia contributed half the total value added and employment; while roughly half of mining output and one third of manufactured goods were produced by foreign-owned companies. The concentration of capital, therefore, is one of the most persistent and enduring processes within the capitalist mode of production. Indeed, the three largest corporate mergers in US history took place in 1981–82 when Du Pont acquired Conoco for $US7.8 billion, the US Steel Corporation bought out Marathon Oil for $US6.2 billion, and the Occidental Petroleum Corporation merged with the energy utility, Cities Service Co., for $US4 billion.

The passing of strategic control in industry and finance from capitalist families to corporate managers can be looked upon as another defining facet of the change-over from competitive to monopoly capitalism. As shareholding became more and more dispersed in the expanding company, the all-important strategic control gradually passed from majority ownership to minority control, then eventually to management (Scott, 1979: 37–40). In less than 30 years the proportion of Australian company shares owned by individuals has dropped from 80 per cent to about 30 per cent in 1980. This coincided with the penetration of the 'industrials and miners' between 1950–80 by the institutional investors. Crouch's (1979) investigation of the 20 most important shareholders in the top 100 Australian companies listed in 1979 revealed that between them 29 life offices, bank nominee companies, superannuation funds and trustee companies held 1,165 of the 2,000 shareholdings scrutinized. Between them these represented some 20 per cent of the market value of all listed company shares because of the enormous degree of concentration of market capitalization in the 100 largest companies (i.e., $A22.95 million of

[1] Strictly speaking, according to Marxism, the concentration of capital is measured by an increase in the average size of firms, while the centralization of firms refers to a reduction in the number of firms within any one industry or sector.

[2] Corporate concentration in the US is not matched by market concentration. In each of 213 individual product markets the top four firms only increased their market share from 41.2 per cent in 1974 to 41.9 per cent in 1966. Horizontal mergers tend to be deterred by the Sherman Anti-Trust legislation (Heilbroner, 1980: 299).

the $A24.35 million of all listed companies). Related research confirms that this level of institutional investment in Australia is similar to that of Britain (and Japan), but much higher than in the United States. Table 5.1 lists the proportions of the share capital of ten of Britain's top 50 manufacturing companies owned by funds under the control of the four major clearing banks, seven insurance companies and nine merchant banks. It reveals that a handful of finance houses, many of which are interlocked, controls between approximately 20 and 30 per cent of Britain's industrial leaders.

Table 5.1 Institutional investment in British industry, 1980–81 (percentage of share capital)

Company	Rank by market value	Clearing banks (4)	Insurance companies (7)	Merchant banks (9)	Total
Beecham	4	2.6	8.4	8.6	19.6
Racal	8	1.8	12.9	12.9	27.6
Unilever	11	1.9	9.4	6.2	17.5
Plessy	15	3.2	10.9	13.4	27.5
Thorn-EMI	16	2.9	13.3	10.7	26.9
BTR	17	3.4	7.0	14.7	25.1
Glaxo	23	2.6	9.0	12.6	24.2
Blue Circle	31	2.8	14.7	10.5	28.0
BOC	32	3.1	10.6	8.0	21.7
GKN	44	2.3	10.9	6.7	19.9

Source: Minns (1981: 2)

The establishment of the corporate colossus in economic life – the number of US industrial corporations with sales topping one billion US dollars rose from 120 in 1970 to 227 in 1976 – is only one side of the structural change that has brought monopoly capitalism to full maturity. The other is the long-run secular decline in manufacturing employment and the corresponding expansion of jobs in the services sector (table 5.2). This shift in workforce composition has its basis in technological and organizational developments directed towards increasing productivity in industry and office work, and in the widening range of government, business, professional, and personal services. Whilst it is apparent that the growth in service occupations has been in progress since the mid-nineteenth century in economies like the United States (Fuchs, 1968), a stage has been reached where it seems appropriate to speak of *The coming of post-industrial society* (Bell, 1974). For Bell a key consideration in dating the change-over to a post-industrial society was the indication, based on projections, that the non-manual, white collar component of the American workforce would exceed 50 per cent by 1980. Employment in the 'service-rendering'

Table 5.2 Changes in workforce composition: United States, United Kingdom, Australia, 1960–80 (million)

	1960	1965	1970	1975	1980
United States					
Population	180.67	194.30	205.05	215.97	227.63
Civilian employment	65.78	71.09	78.68	85.85	99.30
Manufacturing	20.39	21.11	20.75	19.46	21.94
%	31.0	29.7	26.4	22.7	22.1
Services[a]	38.23	42.99	48.08	56.05	65.46
%	58.1	60.5	61.1	65.3	66.0
Female participation rate					
% females, working age[b]	42.6	44.3	48.9	53.2	59.7
% married	30.5	34.7	40.8	44.4	50.3
United Kingdom					
Population	52.56	54.52	55.52	55.98	56.01
Civilian employment	24.26	25.33	24.38	24.65	24.37
Manufacturing	9.10	9.25	8.47	7.62	6.93
%	37.5	36.5	34.7	30.9	28.4
Services[a]	11.41	12.31	12.68	13.95	14.42
%	47.0	48.7	52.0	56.6	59.2
Female participation rate					
% females, working age[b]	48.6	51.0	52.1	55.5	57.6
% married	n.a.	n.a.	31.3	33.9	35.9
Australia					
Population	10.28	11.34	12.51	13.77	14.62
Civilian employment	n.a.	4.63	5.40	5.84	6.25
Manufacturing	n.a.	1.40	1.42	1.37	1.33[c]
%	n.a.	30.3	26.4	23.4	22.2[c]
Services[a]	n.a.	2.32	3.00	3.49	3.77[c]
%	n.a.	50.1	55.5	59.7	62.5[c]
Female participation rate					
%females, working age[b]	n.a.	40.0	46.5	50.1	52.6
% married	n.a.	27.0[c]	37.0[c]	42.4	43.7

[a] Financing, insurance, real estate, and business services; community, social and personal services; wholesale and retail trade, and restaurants and hotels; transport, storage and communications
[b] Females 15–64 years
[c] Estimates
Source: OECD (1973 and 1982)

sector now exceeds employment in the 'goods producing' sector of the economy by a factor of two or three in Britain, the United States, and Australia (table 5.2). It should be mentioned, however, that not everyone agrees with Bell's interpretation of the shifts in workforce composition. Gershuny (1978: 97), for example, estimates that about half of employment in the service sector in the UK in both 1961 and 1971 was 'goods-related'. His point is that just because automation is eliminating directly productive jobs, while more workers are engaged in supervising, controlling, transporting, research, selling, and book-keeping, one cannot assume that the importance of the industrial sector is diminishing.

In a bid to remain competitive, management in the factory and the office is continuously upgrading technology and modifying the labour process. The developments that have had the greatest influence in changing the composition of the workforce[3] in the advanced capitalist economies include: (a) the shift from direct production to non-production jobs as more and more operations are automated and blue collar workers are transferred off the assembly line to machine-tending, repair and maintenance tasks ('deskilling'); (b) the adoption of the Fordist assembly line in the consumer goods industries; (c) the application of Taylor's time and motion methods in clerical and services work; (d) the absorption of women into clerical and sales occupations; (e) the ascendence of professional and technical workers in the information services. Therefore,

Along with an impressive increase in high-level nonmanual jobs, normally assigned to males, capitalism has created a vast number of entirely new occupations in the lower nonmanual group, whose pay and working conditions are unfavourable relative to previous non-manual standards but which, being increasingly assigned to women just entering the labour force, do not lend themselves to meaningful comparisons with the past. Two income families have also mushroomed, and only careful study of the occupational patterns prevailing in such families and of the political orientation of nonmanual

---

[3] Neo-Marxists take their accounts of the division of labour much further with obviously functionalist hypotheses relating to the maintenance of *control* through the deskilling of work (Braverman, 1974) and the fragmentation or segmentation of the labour market (Boreham and Dow, 1980). In the case of the former, Braverman concluded that the deskilling of work was an inevitable tendency given the capitalist organization of the labour process. Kelly (1982) rejects the inevitability of deskilling. The economic limitations of the assembly line are obvious in the consumer goods sector – electric appliances – where extensive product differentiation and built-in-obsolescence obviates the need for long uninterrupted production runs; and in capital intensive industries like chemicals, where the switch to autonomous working groups has helped to reduce the size of the workforce.) In the case of the latter, labour market segmentation by sex, ethnicity, or race, is depicted as a variant of the 'divide-and-rule' strategy which is adopted by management in its exercise of control over labour (see the review by Blackburn and Mann, 1979: 1–34).

females can clarify the implications of these changes. (Gagliani, 1981: 281)

This has meant a change from a society at the turn of the century in which most women 'stayed at home' to one in which a majority of working-age women now work outside the home (table 5.2).

Understandably these developments entailed a gradual realignment of class and gender relationships – and sometimes the social terrain of cities – within advanced capitalist societies. Aspects of this will emerge in the treatment of postwar suburbanization; but, depending on the predilection of the theorist, social change since the 1950s has either paved the way for a kind of *embourgeoisement* of affluent elements of the working class (Zweig, 1961, 1976), or led to the *proletarianization* (Edwards *et al.*, 1975; Edwards, 1979) of all but the managers and technical experts amongst the white collar workforce (due to the routinism of office work): with the development of office machines in the 20th century 'the labour market for the two chief varieties of workers, factory and office, begins to lose some of its distinctions of social stratification, education, family and the like' (Braverman, 1974: 353). According to Touraine (1971), this leaves the dominant classes in a post-industrial society in charge of the control of information, and the dominated classes alienated rather than exploited, because they lack access to information and are unable to participate in decision-making of fundamental importance.

In what sense, then, do the postwar cities of Britain, the US and Australia bear the same marks of monopoly capitalism? After examining the prolonged phase of suburbanization, which culminated in a speculative frenzy in fringe land and central area office space (1968–74), attention will be turned to the urban and regional restructuring that followed the economic disruption of the mid-1970s.

Postwar suburbanization: 'turning cities inside out'

The neo-Marxist account of the forces behind suburban development after the Second World War stood the existing explanation of suburban growth on its head. Prior to that, studies of suburbanization exuded a bias towards the determining role of consumer preferences. Households were seeking a change in their housing situation commensurate with their improved real income and rising social aspirations, and suburban homeownership was infinitely more attractive than the deteriorating rental stock and aging municipal services available in the central cities. The suburbs offered 'a new, free-standing, well-equipped, carefully designed and attractively landscaped house, with ample yard space to play and garden. They also offered an escape from the city; a more wholesome environment, and a more neighbourly community . . . the best available financial investment' (Checkoway, 1980: 37–8). While there is no question that these sorts of considerations did motivate home seekers, it has also become clear, thanks to the radical testimony of Baran and Sweezy (1966), Checkoway (1980), Harvey (1975), O'Connor (1974), Stone (1978), and Walker (1981), that they were severely restricted in their residential investment and location decisions by a range of structural effects that left them with few real alternatives. A rather colourful image is conjured up in the aftermath of US suburbanization of the American middle class being rounded up by 'large operators and powerful economic institutions supported by federal government programmes' (Checkoway, 1980: 39) and herded off to the suburbs. The aim here is to separate out the fact from the fantasy in the radical analysis of US suburbanization and relate it, in turn, to the Australian (mostly) and British experience.

Realization crises: 'so long as it's good for business'

The credit for one of the most stimulating alternative hypotheses of postwar suburbanization belongs to two Marxist writers collaborating within the American tradition. Baran and Sweezy (1966) argued that the American economy after the war was constipated because of the inability of the domestic market to absorb the industrial surpluses which quickly built up when the mighty war machine in the US turned back to peace-time production (their realization crisis of *underconsumption*). According to them, the labour and capital absorbing activities promoted by successive governments in the 1950s and 1960s (the Marshall aid programme in Europe; the 'Cold War' rearmaments'; suburban capital formation) were designed to keep the American economy on the boil (figure 5.1). Harvey (1977) and Walker (1981) subsequently took up the 'underconsumptionist' proposition in relation to suburban development, which was only touched upon fleetingly by Baran and Sweezy (1966: 300–5), and developed it more fully. With the onset of post-industrial urbanization the American city becomes a consumption artifact, designed to stimulate consumption, as much as a workshop designed for industrial production. To facilitate mass consumption the state and specialist finance institutions engineered a massive switch of investment into the secondary circuit (Walker, 1981: 404), thereby avoiding a crisis of over-accumulation in the primary circuit *and* stimulating fresh demand for industrial goods in the housing (building materials, domestic appliances, furnishings) and transportation (cars, road building equipment) sectors.

Although this view of the state as underwriter of postwar suburbaniza-tion holds up surprisingly well under American conditions, it is not nearly so helpful in coming to terms with suburban processes in either the UK or Australia. For one thing, the US economy has been intermittently plagued

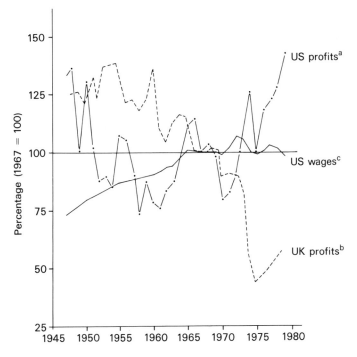

Figure 5.1 Profit rates and wages in the United Kingdom and the US, 1945–80
[a] After tax profits as a proportion of stockholders' equity for all US manufacturing corporations
[b] Real profits as a proportion of net domestic income for all UK industrial and commercial companies
[c] Average after-tax earnings of US production and non-supervisory workers employed in private industry
Source: Cowling, 1982: 153; and Marcuse, 1981: 343

by excess capacity since 1954, while the British government was not really required to support effective demand until the mid-1960s (figure 5.1) (Cowling, 1982: 172–3). As it happens, immediately after the war the problem in the US housing industry was more one of shortages than underutilized capacity (Checkoway, 1980: 30). Legislators and analysts alike saw federal subsidies to the housebuilding industry as a way of encouraging the installation of new plant and equipment and stimulating the entire economy. While the political rhetoric and enabling legislation in the 1949 and 1954 Housing Acts laid out a strategy for slum clearance and the rebuilding of inner city neighbourhoods, the federal subsidies flowed overwhelmingly into suburban housing development. In the five-year period 1950–54, when the number of low-rent public housing starts dropped back from 75,000 to 20,000 units annually, there was a steady liberalization of the funding for suburban housing. Congress raised the authorized ceiling for FHA home mortgage insurance year by year; increased the incentive for the production of three and four bedroom houses; and relaxed FHA terms on loans for single-family dwellings in suburban and outlying areas (Checkoway, 1980: 31–2). Moreover, as home ownership rates grew in the US, federal administrations came to appreciate the electoral significance of tax deductions tied to owner-occupied dwellings. This powerful orientation in the US towards home owners at the expense of tenants, new construction in the suburbs in preference to the rehabilitation or selective redevelopment of inner city housing and the largest builders in the industry, had far-reaching consequences for the metropolitan built environment.

The federal highway programme in the US was also of paramount importance to postwar suburbanization. The federal government, responding to pressures from the American Road Builders Association, the American Trucking Association, and the American Petroleum Association, diverted its entire transport budget of $US156 billion to roads between the years 1944 and 1961 (O'Connor, 1974: 105). The serious federal commitment to highways, though, dates from the 1956 Federal-Aid Highway Act, which provided 90 per cent federal support for the construction of the 65,165 km Interstate Highways and Defence System. At its peak in the 1960s, highway construction consumed well over a third of all federal grants to state and local governments; and, during the decade 1966–75, over two-thirds ($US43 billion in all) of the long-term capital authorized by Washington for urban public investment was earmarked for highway construction, financed through the Highways Trust Fund (Boast, 1980: 76). The urban expressway system constructed as part of the Interstate Highway programme acted as an umbilical cord by connecting dormitory suburbs with downtown office jobs (see Caro, 1974: 395–458). Just as importantly, the intercity expressways mandated under the 1956 Highway Act required that central city bypass routes be built into the urban highway network, especially in the congested northeastern seaboard conurbations. By the early seventies more than 80 of these circumferential *beltways* had been constructed in the outer sectors of US metropolitan areas under the interstate highway programme (Muller, 1981: 169–75). So much of the new suburban development in the form of regional shopping centres, industrial and office parks and apartment estates has gravitated to the interchanges along the beltways that they now constitute the 'main street' of American suburbia. Thus, in the US, and in Australia (where high speed road connections with the CBD went abegging), the suburban mode of existence was designed around the car, with suburban households now married to the car for life.[4]

As well as radically altering the structure of US metropolitan areas, the massive federal subsidies for highway construction were highly regressive. Firstly, as a disproportionate share of the tax revenues was siphoned off for urban freeway construction during the 1960s there was a running down of the public transit system on which poorer central city commuters relied (Leven and Abend, 1971: 36–46); and, secondly, the social costs to inner area families displaced by road building is incalculable. What is known, however, is that of the total sum invested in private urban renewal and highway construction projects causing social dislocation,[5] only $US34.8 million in relocation payments, or less than one per cent of the direct federal outlay, was allocated to the 250,000 US families displaced each year (US Department of Housing and Urban Development estimates cited in Mollenkopf, 1978: 140).

The 'underconsumptionist' account of postwar suburbanization is of dubious relevance to the British situation, where the state through its planning instrumentalities actually set out to contain the spread of Britain's cities after the war. Urban containment (Hall *et al.*, 1973), which was key element of the British Labour government's 1947 planning system, sought to protect and preserve farming land and rural areas close to cities by controlling urban sprawl. Indeed, the planning controls cut the average annual expansion of the urban land area from the 1934–39 level of 24,290 hectares to a postwar figure of 14,575 hectares. The physical containment of British cities after the war contributed to a structural distinctiveness that sets them apart from the leapfrogging subdivisions and straggling suburbs of the US and Australian metropolitan areas. Documents like Duncan Sandys' historic circular on Green Belts in 1955

---

[4] Because of the elimination of public transport alternatives, 'divorce' from the car is not an option in the outermost suburbs and exurbs of the United States and Australia. Between 1932 and 1956 General Motors (GM), often in conjunction with Standard Oil of California and Firestone Tyre, launched an investment programme enabling it to control and dismantle the 100 electric trolley and transit systems operating in 45 US cities (Snell, 1974). In 1932 a GM subsidiary, United Cities Motor Transit, was formed with the sole function of buying electric transit systems, converting them to GM buses and finally reselling them to operators who would buy only GM replacement stock. Similarly, in 1936 a GM holding company, National City Lines, was formed to destroy Pacific Electric, an electrified rail system based in Southern California, but carrying 80 million passengers in 56 US cities.

[5] In New York alone, between 1946 and 1956, 320,000 residents were evicted for 'show-piece' projects like the Lincoln Center, the United Nations complex, and the Fordham Pratt, and Long Island University campuses, and 250,000 by the arterial cross–city express-ways that penetrated Manhattan (Caro, 1974). For a particularly vivid account of the disembowelling and subsequent blighting of East Tremont – a cohesive Jewish community of 60,000 in the Bronx – by the Cross-Bronx Expressway see Caro's chapters, 'One Mile' and 'One Mile (Afterward)' (Caro, 1974: 850–94).

encouraged cities to build high and dense, since it became increasingly difficult to obtain enough building land within their own boundaries, or through overspill schemes under the 1952 Town Development Act. 'As a result, inner city housing bore a large part of the burden of urban containment' (Dunleavy, 1981: 73).

Although the material environment built by suburbanization processes in Australia during the 1950s and 1960s is much closer to the American suburban stereotype, it is difficult to reconcile these processes with the 'underconsumptionist' *raison d'être* for suburbanization. Firstly, the postwar programme of reconstruction embarked upon in the late forties by Chifley's Labor administration soon fizzled out due to the reluctance of a succession of Liberal-Country party governments to underwrite the physical, and non-productive social infrastructure needed in the developing suburbs. Secondly, there has been an historical tendency for Commonwealth and state government investment to be overconcentrated in the core area of the state capitals at the expense of the outer suburbs which were growing at such a frantic pace during the 1950s and 1960s. Perpetual backlogs in servicing including unconnected sewerage systems, overcrowded schools and hospitals, backward public transport and a 'stillborn' urban freeway system, and undeveloped parks and reserves, were symptomatic of the retardation of public investment in the postwar suburbs.[6] Not surprisingly, Szelenyi (1981a: 588) rates Australia as 'probably the most underdeveloped country in the western capitalist world in terms of collectively used non-productive urban infrastructure'.

Far more of a case can be built up around the proposition that postwar suburban development in Australia reflects a muted commitment on the part of the Commonwealth and state governments to the social reproduction of labour. For example, the South Australia government, through the auspices of the South Australian Housing Trust (SAHT), housed the families of workers employed by BHP in the steelworks and shipbuilding yards at Whyalla, by General Motors-Holden (GMH) at Elizabeth, and by Chrysler at Tonsley Park; whereas the Victorian government attracted GMH to Doveton on Melbourne's south-western fringe by agreeing to construct public housing nearby for the workforce. Otherwise, the Commonwealth progressively widened its range of subsidies and programmes to ease the accute postwar housing shortages (300,000 dwellings) and extend home ownership, which had remained at a constant level below 50 per cent throughout the interwar period in Australia (Mullins, 1981). The package of measures designed to keep new housing starts at a

---

[6] As it happens, the Australian state governments were much more diligent in meeting the requirements of Sydney and Melbourne's manufacturing sector and fostering suburban development in the 1920s. Public investment in urban infrastructure ran at four to five times prewar levels, with electrification a top priority so that exporting producers could remain competitive on the world's markets (Berry, 1982).

high level quite unconsciously biased metropolitan growth after the war in favour of suburban and fringe development (Badcock, 1982): public funds were earmarked for new construction; the housing commissions energetically promoted house sales by offering low interest, long-term loans to working class families with little prospect of obtaining mortgage finance from private lenders; preferential rates and conditions were available for war service homes; the lending policies of co-operative building societies and savings banks were liberalized, subject to the purchase of a newly constructed dwelling.

Whatever motives we might attribute to government housing policy – Kemeny's (1978a) statement, for instance, suggesting that the finance institutions engineered various self-serving policies at a time when their own housing finance instruments still lack sophistication is a little too ingenuous – there is no disputing that in Australia: public housing investment has at times served to stabilize the supply side and absorb excess capacity within the building and construction sector (Carmody *et al.*, 1979); growth in home ownership has paid off handsomely for the financial institutions; possession of domestic property does constitute a modest source of accumulation; the express commitment to home ownership as the preferred tenure has 'differentiated the whole structure of policy and the very appearance of Australian cities from those of Britain and the United States' (Mendelsohn, 1979: 262).

Mass producing the suburbs

The suburban development that took place in the United States and Australia dwarfed anything experienced in the late nineteenth century, when the commuter rail and tramways were pushing outwards, or during the 1920s, when motorized vehicles freed commuters from the restraints of fixed-track transport for the first time. Overall, housing production in the United States exceeded 15 million units in the decade 1950–59, compared with 7.4 million and 2.7 million in the two previous decades, 1940–49 and 1930–39. Between 1950 and 1955 the US population grew by 11.6 million people, and 79 per cent of the growth was in the suburbs. The total volume of new residential construction in the suburbs outstripped new housing in the central cities by a factor of three during this period (Checkoway, 1980: 25).

It is more or less self-evident that the postwar suburb is built upon the foundations of the private ownership of housing, cars, domestic appliances and furnishings. Suburban development accounted for an impressive proportion of postwar capital formation in Australia. Neutze (1977) calculates that urban development accounted for 52 per cent of the gross fixed capital formation in Australia between 1970–71 and 1973–74. The value of buildings completed within the Sydney metropolitan area during the same period was distributed as follows: City of Sydney (14.1 per cent); Inner Ring (19.2 per cent); Middle Ring (25.2 per cent); Outer Ring (41.5 per cent). Even allowing for the strikingly high level of 'privatization' in the Australian suburb (Kemeny, 1978b: 1980), public expenditure on physical and social infrastructure forms an important source of demand for capital goods. Besides, economic performance depends upon the maintenance of a high level of private consumption in those sectors centrally involved in constructing and equipping dwellings in the suburbs – building and construction, automotive, white goods. This has been achieved by skilful strategies on the part of the manufacturers of consumer durables to maximize market penetration, and by a streamlining of the mechanisms available for mobilizing investment capital in the property sector, and consumer credit in the sphere of private consumption (hire purchase, credit cards, personal loans). As Galbraith (1967) intimates with his 'fallacy of consumer sovereignty', all these strategems have been necessary for the full realization of demand. Australia trails only the US and Canada in the use of credit. A Commercial Banking Corporation survey completed in 1981 found that the average Australian household now commits 43.3 per cent of its disposable income to pay off debts (home mortgage, car repayments, hire-purchase) compared with 22.8 per cent in 1960 (*Age*, 1981: 3).

Suburban subdivision and house construction after the war were characterized, in particular, by the adoption of innovations in mass production, prefabrication and standardization, with a view not only to enlarging scale, but shortening completion times, and improving productivity within the housing industry, which has always been chronically low due to the intensity of labour employed. These developments flowed on logically from the restructuring of the house building industry. Nationally, in the United States, 'large builders' with 'annual volume greater than one million dollars, more than 100 dwellings completed, and more than 100 workers' (Checkoway, 1980: 24) increased their combined market share from five per cent of the 400,000 new housing starts in 1939, to 64 per cent of the 1.55 million starts in 1959. Specialist merchant builders like Levitt and Eichler, for example, increased their personal market shares from more than a third of all homes completed in 1950, to over three quarters by 1960 (Walker and Heiman, 1981: 70). Likewise, Australia's 'large' builders (A. V. Jennings, Hooker Corporation) accounted for 60–70 per cent of the 60,000 dwellings added to the housing stock at the periphery of metropolitan Sydney between 1971–77. In the late 1960s many of America's largest corporations made inroads into the land subdivision, housing construction, and real estate management fields by taking over established performers like Levitt and Sons (ITT). Three hundred of the top 1,000 companies penetrated the housing industry between 1960–75, no doubt in a search for product outlets, tax benefits, and long-term investment opportunities for surplus capital in a promising property market (Feagin, 1982: 53–4). Walker and Heiman (1981: 71) report that 'At the peak of corporate involvement in 1972, five of the twenty largest US corporations were building and marketing homes and another five were engaged in land development.' Likewise, Ball (1982) estimates that towards the end of the 1970s in the UK, housebuilding firms constructing over 500 dwellings on an annual basis increased their market share to one-third of the total national output. Wimpey Homes Holdings and Barrett Developments dominated the industry with 11,000 dwellings apiece (Ball, 1982: 36). The development of suburban housing estates in Australia rests on the twin pillars of land acquisition and subdivision, and the production of housing stock. The production of land and housing is financed by a range of financial institutions that grew prodigiously along with the rapid rise in home ownership after the war. The home ownership rate rose from 52.6 per cent in 1947 to nearly 70 per cent by 1961, where it has rested since. In the ten years after 1946, Australia's major trading banks almost trebled their housing advances, the building societies increased theirs five-fold, and the life offices theirs by more than seven-fold (Kemeny, 1978a: 92). But the institutions that benefited most from the issuing of mortgages for *final* consumption were the saving banks (whose investment in housing rose from $A32 million in 1945 to $A2,392 million in 1972) and the permanent building societies (with housing investment growing from $A19 million to $A1,701 million in the same 28 year period). Since then the banks and building societies have continued to extend their domination of the housing finance market, with the banks owning no less than 54.7 per cent of all newly raised mortgages in 1976, and the building societies 30.3 per cent (Kemeny, 1978a: 92).

Both the Australian finance companies, which loaned to developers on a joint-venture basis, provided bridging finance to builders, or even got caught up in the property development business themselves in the early 1970s, and the permanent building societies were instrumental in fuelling the fringe land and housing boom of 1968–74. The permanent building societies, which were required to place 70 per cent of their depositors' funds in property, expanded enormously between 1968 and 1973 with net annual receivables increasing by 452 per cent over the period (Daly, 1982b: 49). Similarly, during the property boom the real estate assets of the finance companies rose from $A684 million to $A2,689 million, representing a leap from 21 to 47 per cent of total assets (Daly, 1982a: 73). When it became apparent late in 1972 that there was enough office space under construction in Sydney and North Sydney to meet projected demand to the beginnings of the 1980s, there was a surge of untied capital into the fringe land market of Australian cities. In a 12 month period loans to developers for the acquisition and development of land rose from $A202.8 million in the third quarter of 1972 to $A515.1 million in the third quarter of 1973 (Kearny, 1975: 16). This merely continued a trend that had developed during the late 1960s. The financial links between the finance and development companies had grown so intertwined, so incestuous, that when the property market collapsed in 1974 the shock waves continued to reverbate within the Australian economy until the end of the decade. Home Units of Australia, Cambridge Credit Corp., Associated Securities Ltd, and Mainline Corporation wiped themselves out in 1974, while the First National City Bank of New York had to mount a $A150 million salvage operation on behalf of the Industrial Acceptance Corporation (Gottliebsen, 1976). Between 1975 and 1978 at least $A260 million was written off as bad debts by the major finance companies (84 per cent from the 'property' sector), while in 1979 the failure of the Finance Corporation of Australia brought down the venerable old lady of Australian banking, the Bank of Adelaide.[7]

Comparable mayhem occurred in the British property market, which built up to a peak in 1973 following the easing of credit restrictions on the trading banks by the Bank of England in 1971, and in the United States, where the banks plunged into real estate during the heady years of the late sixties. In the years, 1969–73, small investors abandoned industrial shares and turned to the banks' Real Estate Investment Trusts (REITs) as a means of maintaining the value of their savings during a period of rising inflation. The assets of the REITs grew from almost nothing to nearly $US21 billion during these years (Stone, 1978: 203). Before the demise in 1973 of one of the largest apartment and condominium developers, Kassuba, many of the trusts had achieved spectacular returns and capital gains, riding high on the building boom during the early seventies (Feagin, 1982). The point about these intemperate bursts of unregulated growth in the suburban land and housing markets of large cities is that they pressurize housing and service provision, redistribute real income (chapter 7), and create strategic problems for urban managers: 'Decisions made in haste, under pressure and with an unrealistic view of the future have set the mold for the subsequent decades of recession or slow growth' (Daly, 1982b: 44).

Seduction of the working class . . . bondage of suburban housewives . . .?

According to the radical exegesis, the spread of home ownership, and suburbanization as its material condensate, has contributed to political stability in the capitalist democracies by creating 'a large wedge of debt-encumbered home owners who are unlikely to rock the boat because they are both debt-encumbered and reasonably well-satisfied owner occupiers. Home ownership . . . as a device for achieving social stability went

---

[7] These companies had all used property valued at overinflated prices as collateral for further borrowing; and, when prices slumped they were left grossly overgeared and holding large 'banks' of undeveloped fringe land and no convertibles or cash against which they could draw to meet the escalating interest repayments (see Daly, 1982a: 78–98).

hand-in-hand in the post-war period with the drive to stimulate consumption through suburbanization' (Harvey, 1977: 125). Suburbanization, as neo-Marxists would have it (Edel, 1982; Walker, 1981), has divided and fragmented the working class organically and politically: the suburb is the touchstone of the middle class ideology and values that are gradually absorbed by working class owners of domestic property. But class allegiance amongst the manual working class in Britain, and certainly in Australia and the US where class demarcation was never as ingrained, has continued to weaken since the 1950s with the entry of married females into the labour market (table 5.2), a noticeable growth in the savings of working class households, and the extension of home ownership. This is apparent in the class ascription and voting behaviour of a sample of 8,147 Australians surveyed in the late 1970s (*Age*, December 1977). A finer breakdown of the data revealed that only 55 per cent of the lower blue collar workers (production-process workers) thought of themselves as working class, while more skilled tradesmen thought of themselves as middle class (47 per cent) than working class (41 per cent). The pattern is duplicated in Britain, where Rose (1980) has shown that the influence of social structure on voting behaviour at each general election since 1959 has almost halved in 20 years. As Rose (1980) puts it, 'The most important divisions now run within the working class. Among manual workers, home-owners and non-union members tend to be conservative, and council tenants and union members tend to remain Labour. Old clothcap and bowler hat distinctions between parties are being replaced by a multiplicity of income and life-style differences, such as housing and ownership of consumer goods.' There is no doubt that the overall improvement in living standards and educational opportunities in Britain have contributed to a weakening of the traditional power base of the British Labour Party; but, in view of the discouragement of urban containment in the 1950s and 1960s, it would be inadvisable to argue too forcibly for suburbanization as an agent in the fragmentation of the British working class. And in Australia, where the 'working class' have been decanted *en masse* to the suburbs as a result of public housing policy (Badcock, 1982), they are segregated from the middle class by the property market. This has an inhibiting effect upon the 'contamination' process; and public housing estates in the outer suburbs, though quite often socially disunited due to the high proportion of 'broken' households, remain Labor to the core.

Feminists working in urban studies take exception to the narrow class orientation of Marxist discourse – its 'gender-blind' – because they say it obscures what for them are the equally important domestic relations of production such as the sexual division of labour found in the home (see the special issues of *Signs*, **5**, 3 (1980) and the *International Journal of Urban and Regional Research*, **2**, 3 (1978) on women and the city; also Baldock and Cass (1983)). The physical form of postwar suburbs in Australia and the

United States and the abdication of their designers (all male) to the automobile has made for wholesale changes in the pattern of relations within the home. Jane Jacobs (1961) had a different focus in eulogizing the richness of social and domestic relations within Greenwich Village in the heart of Manhattan, but many of the qualities she praised are missing from the postwar suburb: the juxtaposition of housing and industry which provided opportunities for men to participate more fully in family life and share household duties; the absence of cars from local streets and close supervision that fostered streetplay; the mutual support of women and sharing in times of adversity; the pedestrian scale and local availability of goods and services; the greater degree of 'informalization' in childcare and parenting. More outspoken critics of postwar suburbanization in Australia (Allport, 1983; Harman, 1983) argue that the sexual division of space that has resulted from the decentralization of urban activities reinforces labour market segmentation because married women are locked into suburban manufacturing jobs by an insufficiency of child care and convenient public transport.

Without being overly deterministic it can be said that much of the mass-produced tract and 'battery' housing found respectively in the outer and inner ring suburbs of Australian cities is destructive of domestic relations and the life experience of many women and children, not to mention the dehumanizing effect of the postwar tower blocks built by public housing agencies: see Rainwater (1971). In the rawish fringe suburbs of Australian cities women working at home have been incarcerated on housing estates bereft of adequate medical and social services, local shopping, public transport, and child-minding facilities while the 'breadwinner' took the family car to work. A different set of problems faces women with children in the medium density, three-floor 'walk-up' home units that were built in conjunction with the redevelopment of inner suburban areas within Sydney and Melbourne during the 1960s (Cardew, 1970): groceries, washing, kids have to be lugged upstairs; play areas for children are scarce; the units, which were mass produced to a formula, are poorly sound-proofed and spartan; the rented, as distinct from the privately owned stock, houses a transient population for whom escape becomes a compulsion.

Studies that set out to explore nuances of this kind and place them in the broader context of gender relations are in their infancy. What can be said, however, is that they are being guided by an agenda that includes the domestic relations of production, the gender pattern of spatial inequality of access to urban services and resources, and the relations of urban planning to such relations and inequalities (Allport, 1983).

The suburbanization of manufacturing employment

Although the postwar city did not forfeit its prime position as the locus of production within advanced capitalist economies there was a large-scale decentralization of employment within the urban labourshed. Behind the dispersal of economic activity lies the rationalization of production and distribution, the plant shutdowns, the incorporation of new capacity and the reorganization of manpower that follows in the wake of a corporate merger. In the UK, for example, the 100 largest industrial firms increased the average number of plants within their organization from 27 to 72 between 1958 and 1972, whilst the mean number of employees per plant fell from 750 to 430 (Cowling, 1982: 76). At the heart of the postwar suburbanization of manufacturing was a partial separation of the branch plant production processes from the head office control and planning functions, and with this a splitting of the blue and white collar sectors of the corporate workforce. These organizational changes were supplemented by new forms of automated production and goods handling that rendered much former factory accommodation in the old inner manufacturing districts obsolete. So manufacturing and warehousing reassembled their operations in free-standing, single-floor premises oriented to the motorway network, container yards, and air freighting facilities (Stanback and Knight, 1976: 28–37). In the US, in particular, the completion of the suburban circumferentials within the interstate highway system and improvements in trucking greatly increased the attraction of the suburban industrial estate. Berry and Kasarda (1977: 236) estimate that the 1960–70 gain in blue collar employment for the suburbs was 29 per cent versus a nearly 13 per cent loss for the central cities, with the suburban ring outstripping the central city in white collar job gains to the tune of 67 to seven per cent. The blue collar job loss stepped up in the 1970s with the City of New York shedding over 300,000, or almost 40 per cent of its manufacturing workers between 1969–76. This same pattern is found in other highly industrialized cities like St Louis, Detroit, Cleveland and Philadelphia (Muller, 1981: 137).

This generalized picture of manufacturing decentralization in large metropolitan regions is based upon *net* changes in establishments, output or employment. Analyses that penetrate beneath this superficial impression reveal much more of the complex industrial dynamics of factory openings, closures and relocation across the whole of the metropolitan area including the central city (Christian, 1975; Lloyd and Mason, 1978; Struyk and James, 1975). For example, the net loss of 172 manufacturing plants that Bull (1978) records in a study of Clydeside, 1958–68, conceals gross changes of 711 plant deaths and 529 plant births. In addition, 607 establishments transferred their production during the ten year period to new locations within Clydeside. Excluding plant births, these adjustments represented over half (52.6 per cent) of all the plants located in Clydeside in 1958 (Bull, 1978: 94). Bull also cites unpublished evidence to show that this pattern is consistent with other UK and US cities: in Greater

Manchester, between 1966–72, 41 per cent of all the original plants had relocated or closed within the six-year period; in a two-year period, 1967–69, 11.5 per cent, 7.6 per cent and 10.2 per cent, respectively, of a total 1966 stock of 39,128 plants in the New York SMSA (Standard Metropolitan Statistical Area) relocated, closed or opened. The implication of these and other studies is that it is incorrect to view the suburbanization of manufacturing as a process simply involving plant deaths and/or intra-urban transfers from the inner city and plant births in the outer suburbs.

'Forests of glass citadels': property capital and the remodelling of the CBD, 1968–74

The momentous reshaping of the CBD core that was going on throughout the postwar period in most cities climaxed between 1968 and 1974 with an office building boom in Britain, the United States, and Australia. A forest of glass citadels sprouted up in the downtown precinct of cities of national economic importance. Millions of square metres of office space were added to the downtown areas of US cities: on average the office space of 20 central cities grew by 42.9 per cent between 1970 and 1978, with New York, Chicago, San Francisco, Philadelphia and Houston leading the way (Black, 1980a: 108–9). The total British stock of office space grew from 26 million square metres in 1967 to 32 million square metres in 1972 (Ambrose and Colenutt, 1975: 19); over one half of all the office space in Sydney's CBD was constructed in the 15 year period 1960–75. This redevelopment of the commercial core rested on the confluence of a number of developments that were not inconsistent with the maturing of monopoly capitalism. Firstly, the operational and organizational needs of the giant business and government corporations changed as they consolidated their market position and bureaucratic power in the sixties. Secondly, vital matching developments in facilitative technologies – solid state electronics, integrated circuitry, microprocessing – took place in the office-based service sector. Lastly, the property development sector came to prominence as finance (interest-bearing) capital sought out new investment opportunities for profit-taking.

The headquarters office has become the nerve centre of the industrial and financial conglomerates that formed during the 1960s. The pyramidal organization of corporate power within the US space economy comprises a set of national and regional groupings at the heart of which sit the banks (Friedland, 1980): seven of the ten most central corporations in the US national network are banks including Morgan Guaranty, Chase Manhattan, and the First National City Bank of New York; whilst the five most prominent regional groupings all had banks at their core (Scott, 1979: 88). Understandably, the corporate head office is drawn to those cities that concentrate financial intermediaries and locally owned branch plants. By the mid-1960s, 708 of the top 1,000 industrial corporations in the US had their headquarters office in 130 central cities. The national average was five per city; 31 cities had only one national headquarters office; 40 had none. In turn, the concentration of head offices has stimulated the growth of ancillary activities such as business services (accounting, legal, financial, data processing, consulting and technical advice, marketing and advertising), institutions facilitating the operation of markets (stock and futures exchanges, brokerage firms), and central and state/local government agencies.[8]

By the mid-1970s service and administrative workers alone, all of whom had to be based in offices, had grown to a third of the British, US, and Australian labour-force (table 5.2). Also, the introduction of business machines stepped up the per capita consumption of floor space in office blocks by something like three per cent a year throughout the 1960s in the UK. Demand for office space could no longer be satisfied by the existing office accommodation in the CBD, much of which dated from the inter-war years. The special-purpose, fully airconditioned, open-space, naturally lit, office with high-speed elevators was designed to cater for the varied needs of office users. Plot ratios (floor space: site area) that governed the degree to which office blocks could be stockpiled in the downtown precinct varied from 5:1 in the heart of London, to 12:1 in Sydney, and a maximum of 22.5:1 in Manhattan. This office revolution and physical restructuring of the CBD is an outward sign of the underlying transition to post-industrial appurtenances. As a consequence, Mollenkopf (1978: 121) has been prompted to aver that 'the economy of the largest central cities has shifted from a factory basis of organization to one of office-based command and control functions.'

Some of the most consequential shifts in the locus of strategic control that were part of the corporate reorganization during the 1960s took place in those sectors that now have the greatest say in the restructuring of urban space. Firstly, a relatively autonomous 'property sector' managing the development process and production of physical infrastructure, and based on specialized property development and investment groups, has emerged in the advanced capitalist economies (Ambrose and Colenutt, 1975; Boddy, 1981: 268). Prior to the 1960s there were very few large property companies and urban redevelopment proceeded on a self-financing basis

[8] With the installation of landlines and the computerized transmission of information many of these functions, which were obliged to congregate in the CBD to maximize their access to 'up-to-the-minute' sources of information, short-term finance, and users of processing services, have been able to relocate in suburban centres and office parks (Alexander, 1982; Muller, 1981: 143–58). In fact, the advantage of a central city location for many office functions has been undercut to such an extent that by 1978, 170 of *Fortune's* top 500 American corporations were based in the outer suburbs compared with 47 in 1965, 56 in 1969, and 128 in 1974 (Muller, 1981: 148).

with most firms building for their own occupation. In the mid-1960s, asset-rich industrial companies were steadily edged out of the development field by specialists in property redevelopment, who began to tap the accumulating surpluses of the finance companies that had previously restricted their lending to hire-purchase. The stock-market valuation of the British development industry soared from £103 million in 1958, £833 million in 1968, and then to £2,644 million in 1972 (Ambrose and Colenutt, 1975: 35).

Thus a separate 'fraction' of capital, property capital, was created out of a mutually profitable liaison between finance companies in the process of expanding their range of services, and the development companies engaged in land subdivision and the construction of office towers and regional shopping centres. At first the finance companies supplied short-term loans to tide the developer through the construction phase; then, as real estate shaped up as the high-flier in the investment league in the mid-1960s, the competition between the finance companies and other institutional investors intensified. By the mid-1970s the Australian finance companies held 27 per cent of their total assets in real estate and were commiting 50 per cent of their funds on current account to development purposes (Cullen and Hardaker, 1975: 38). The second source of funds that opened up for property development in the cities was controlled by the insurance companies, pension and superannuation funds, and investment trusts. Investment by the British insurance companies in 'land, property and ground rent' rose from nine to 16 per cent of total assets between 1964 and 1974; and then from four to 12 per cent in the case of the pension funds during the same decade (Boddy, 1981: 277). In Australia, between 1956 and 1975, the total property assets of the life insurance companies climbed from $A60.6 million to $A1969.2 million (Sandercock, 1978b). In the case of the seven largest insurance companies, property investment grew from 2.5 per cent of the total portfolio in 1956, to 8–12 per cent in 1965, and 20–26 per cent by 1975. Significantly, a substantial portion of the life offices' property holdings was concentrated in the CBD with the share reaching 82 per cent for the Australian Mutual Prudential, Australia's leading company. In an inventory of 585 office buildings constituting Sydney's CBD in 1973, Daly (1982a: 44) established the following distribution of ownership: UK property developers (40) and insurance companies (17); other foreign owners (26); Australian banks (46), developers (35), insurance and superannuation funds (43), and government (65); Tooths-Toohey's, a large holding company (16).

As with the speculative mania in the fringe land markets of Australian cities, Sydney's office boom, which reached its zenith in 1972–73, was driven to unrealistic heights by an overheated economy. According to Harvey (1978: 120), 'The extraordinary property boom in many advanced countries from 1969–73 . . . is a splendid example' of the diversion of investment into the built environment '. . . as a kind of last-ditch hope for finding productive uses for rapidly over-accumulating capital'. Though not incompatible with Harvey's general argument about over-accumulation, what Daly's (1982a) meticulous reconstruction of the processes that rebuilt over one-half of Sydney's CBD office space in a 12-year burst does show, is that the forces acting upon the built environment are a good deal more complicated than Harvey's superficially attractive pre-occupation with capital switching from the primary to the secondary and tertiary circuits would seem to suggest. To begin with, 'The underlying cause of interest in sites for office buildings was Sydney's rise as the financial centre in line with the structural changes taking place in the Australian economy' (Daly, 1982a: 38). Accommodation was needed for the financial intermediaries, accountants, and consultants servicing the mining industry that was expanding rapidly in the late 1960s. On the supply side, the building boom was fuelled by the surfeit of speculative capital within the Australian economy and not just a lack of interest on the part of investors in industrial stocks. The volume of interest-bearing capital in circulation between 1968 and 1974 was multiplied many times over by changes in the structure of overseas capital markets and pressures caused by domestic economic policy. Firstly, when the UK economy plateaued at the beginning of the 1970s, British institutional investors switched capital raised at 5 to 6 per cent on London's Eurodollar market to real estate in Australia, which was yielding 8.5 to 9.0 per cent in 1970–71 compared with 4.5 per cent in the overcrowded British market. British banks became major shareholders in the finance companies and provided lines of credit and stand-by facilities: in 1972, 13 of the 17 members of the London Accepting Houses Committee were shareholders in Australian finance companies (Daly, 1982a: 6). In the five years to 1971–72, $A502 million of foreign capital entered the banking, finance and property sector; whilst by 1973, five of the top nine development companies in Britain were active in the Sydney market (Daly, 1982a: 47). On the domestic scene, the inflationary pressures, which had built up under the influence of the mining boom, were aggravated when the McMahon government allowed the rate of growth in the money supply to 'blow-out' from 5 per cent per annum in 1970/71 to 14 per cent in 1972/73 (Cullen and Hardaker, 1975: 38). To make matters worse, before the federal election in 1972 there was a huge speculative inflow of between $A1.5 billion and $A2.0 billion in anticipation of a long overdue revaluation. By themselves these developments led to a 25 per cent rise in the volume of money in circulation in 1973. A critical proportion of the foreign capital found its way into the central city property market: 'The country was awash with money and with the failure of the mining boom on the stock markets property remained the one great focus of investors attention' (Daly, 1982a: 110).

Changes in banking and financing practices also contributed to the abundance of funds available for property development in the early 1970s. As the development companies lifted their profits, the bank subsidiaries (with the support of their normally conservative backers) and non-bank financiers fell over themselves to secure profit-sharing and joint-venture arrangements. With inflation mounting the finance companies were also under pressure to lift their earnings rate. Secure in the knowledge that they had respectable banking subsidiaries behind them, the property companies were enticed into operating on absurdly high gearing ratios (80 to 100 per cent) so that they could stretch the development dollar further and speed the turnaround of their borrowings (shades of Melbourne's land boom in the late 1880s).

By 1973 cracks were beginning to appear in the edifice of monopoly capitalism and an end to the world wide property boom was just over the horizon: in London investment yields had fallen to 3.5 to 4.0 per cent by June, 1973; in the first quarter of 1973 the first outflow of capital from Australia ($A62 million) was recorded for 11 years. The collapse in Australia was hastened when the Whitlam government set about tightening the money supply early in 1974 in an effort to soak up excess liquidity and curb the developers and speculators. The toll among developers and finance companies has already been mentioned; but it is also reflected in the fact that 44 per cent of the office space constructed between 1970–76 remained vacant in 1976. The worldwide property boom in the late 1960s signalled the arrival of a new order in international finance. As Daly (1982a) points out, with the property markets of major cities in the advanced capitalist economies moving together in syncromesh for the first time in the early 1970s, the countercyclical impulses may have been ironed out of the capital transfer system for good.

Cities and regions and the 'fallout' from the global integration of capital

In the mid-1970s the pressures that had been building up within the capitalist system finally erupted leaving almost all economies in varying states of disarray. In the view of one 'middle of the road' economist, Robert Heilbroner (1980), a structural crisis is underway which will inflict 'changes in seismic magnitude' upon the advanced capitalist economies. Of course the term *crisis* should be used advisedly because it does bear connotations of a terminal phase for capitalism; yet capitalism has proven remarkably durable, which is the point of much of the otherwise traumatic restructuring that was triggered by the oil price shock in the last quarter of 1973. What needs stressing most of all, as monopoly capitalism ascends for its own survival to an even higher level of concentration and centralization, is that the structural adjustments and uneven development that were part and parcel of the 'growing pains' of reasonably healthy economies during the 1950s and 1960s have been replaced by extremely rapid structural change, and involve massive economic dislocation, regional devastation and human casualties akin to that last experienced by the advanced capitalist economies during the 1929–35 Depression. The process of adjustment for capital involves a reassignment of production in key industry groups to the lowest-cost wage regions irrespective of where they are internationally, and the global integration of sourcing, sub-contracting, and capital flows.

Capital convulses: the new international economic disorder

In the last quarter of 1973 the Organization of Petroleum Exporting Countries (OPEC) quadrupled, and then tripled again in the first part of 1979, the price of crude oil. The OPEC countries stood to gain an additional $US80 billion for their oil exports in 1974–75, and a further $US120 billion following the price rise in 1979 (Harris, 1981: 32). The massive transfer of wealth that resulted from the revised oil prices ruptured the pricing structures of industrial producers and savaged the balance of payments of the non-oil developing countries. The severity of the oil price rises can be gauged from their impact upon inflation and unemployment in a core group of OECD countries (figure 5.2). But that is not to say that the oil price shock was the only factor at work; it simply laid bare and then acted upon the structural weaknesses latent in monopoly capitalism. First of all there was a general deterioration in the performance of the industrial sector in Britain and the United States in the middle of the 1960s (figure 5.1). Company profits in British industry were halved between 1965 and 1975 (Cowling, 1982), while the ratio between after tax profits and stockholders' equity in US manufacturing companies fell sharply in 1968–69, rebounded, and plummeted again following the oil stock in 1974–75.[9] Secondly, the growth of the Eurodollar market in the late 1950s added a new ingredient to the international finance system by providing a huge pool of credit available for recycling free of the inter-ference of national governments. At the same time the world debt was escalating, with the US, in particular, building up a massive deficit in order to finance the Vietnam War during the 1960s. The inflationary spiral that carried over into the 1970s and rippled outwards to destabilize many national economies was fuelled by excessive government and private

[9] Radical economists like Harris (1980; 1981) lay much of the blame for the fall in profits upon the failure of British and US industry to upgrade its productive capacity throughout the 1950s and 1960s (by 1975, when investment as a proportion of GDP in Australia, the US, and Britain hovered at 10, 15 and 18 per cent in West Germany it was 23 per cent, and in Japan, 35 per cent). Stilwell (1980: 59). The OECD secretariat, on the other hand, stresses the squeezing of profits by wages and non-wage benefits paid to employees, and the growing tax burden imposed by the welfare state.

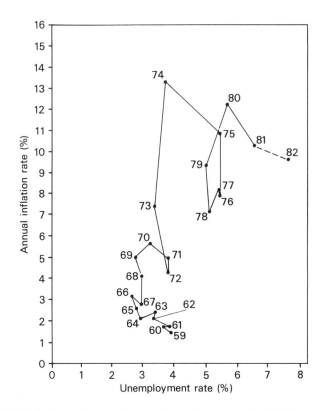

Figure 5.2 Inflation and unemployment rates in seven major OECD countries, 1959–82 (Canada, France, Germany, Italy, Japan, United Kingdom, United States)
Source: OECD, 1982: 47

borrowing. By 1980 government borrowing in the United States had risen to 20 per cent of total borrowing and consumer debt was outpacing consumer income by 50 per cent (O'Connor, 1981b).

The slump in demand for capital goods occasioned by the OPEC price reviews during the 1970s was actually matched by a rise in world industrial output with much of the planned investment coming on stream in Japan and the newly industrializing countries. In two decades the Japanese established dominance first in textiles and clothing; then in steel, ship-building, and vehicle production; and, finally, in semi-conductors, video equipment and robotics:

In the first half of 1980, motor companies in Japan produced 5.6 million vehicles, 1.4 million more than the first half year output of the hitherto largest world manufacturer of vehicles, the United States.

Japanese companies also manufactured more steel than the United States, becoming at least for a moment, the second largest steel producer in the world after Russia. . . . In the same period, Japanese shipbuilding yards took fully half the new ship orders in the world. (Harris, 1981: 30)

While the group of 23 newly industrializing countries (the frontrunners include Hong Kong, Singapore, South Korea, and Taiwan in East Asia; Mexico, Venezuela, Brazil in Latin America; Yugoslavia and India) only account for about ten per cent of world manufacturing trade, they are now mounting a serious challenge to the advanced capitalist economies in textiles, clothing, electronic components, leatherwear, and construction. The success in undercutting manufacturers in OECD countries is based upon high rates of domestic investment in growth-promoting infrastructure and new technology, and the granting of access to transnational corporations to pools of cheap non-unionized labour. Table 5.3 shows

Table 5.3 Percentage change in the national shares of total industrial output for a group of industrialized capitalist economies, 1950–73

	1950	1960	1973
United States	51.2	43.8	29.8
Great Britain	8.9	7.5	4.8
West Germany	5.8	9.1	14.1
France	4.3	4.9	7.5
Italy	2.0	2.9	3.6
Japan	n.a.	4.2	10.0
All industrialized capitalist economies	90–91[a]	89.5	88.7
Developing economies	9–10[a]	10.5[a]	11.3

[a] Estimates
Source: Compiled by Annel (1981: 65) from World Bank Statistics

that Britain is fast becoming an industrial 'spentforce', while the postwar recovery of the West German and French economies together with Japan's industrial awakening, has whittled away the United States' obvious economic superiority in the 1950s.

Capital switching: 1 The worldwide redivision of labour and 'de-industrialization'

In the 1960s, the transnational corporation with its much greater diversification and global outlook replaced the industrial conglomerate, with its inward-looking vision of the domestic market as the flagship of monopoly capital (Cohen, 1981; Crough and Wheelwright, 1982). The formation of the transnational corporation has a three-fold purpose: to control the supply of primary commodities as a counter to marketing cartels like UNCTAD; to secure and expand market positions in the face of regional tariff walls; to exploit low-wage labour regions viz. the new international division of labour (Anell, 1981). Much has been made of the new international division of labour (Fröbel *et al.*, 1980), and while it is increasing in importance as the transnational corporations break-down the production process and farm out the most labour-intensive work to low-wage regions (Lall and Streeten, 1977), another investigation by the Commission of the European Communities (1979) indicated that only about one-tenth of the foreign investment was sensitive to the low-wage inducement (this rose to one-third in the case of foreign investment in Asia). Fröbel and his co-workers (1980) list 225 firms in the West German textile and garment industry that owned foreign subsidiaries in 1974–75. An UNCTAD (1975) survey established that, between 1971 and 1974, the number of employees engaged by US, West European, and Japanese manufacturers in developing countries increased from 22,000 to 80,000. Crouch and Wheelwright (1982) estimate that by the beginning of the 1980s there were over 600 Australian-based companies operating 'off-shore' with a combined investment in excess of one billion dollars.

The establishment of new, export oriented production reflects the genuine shift that is underway from a national to a global determination of location. 'World market factories' are established in 'free production zones' – Fröbel *et al.*, (1980: 22) counted 79 operating in 25 developing countries in 1975 – that offer the transnational corporations exemption from taxes and duties, relief from rates, freedom from foreign exchange controls, preferential tariffs and financing, and leaseable floor space and infrastructure. Thus, comparative advantage now operates at the global scale for goods produced for the world market (cf. the 'world car'), bringing with it an interlacing of subcontracting and criss-crossing of capital flows between the subsidiaries of the transnationals:

> Increasingly, *trade is between corporations and not nations*, and is being conducted on the basis of the comparative advantage created and manipulated by the very corporations that reap the benefits. The flows of trade, their direction, volume and pricing, are more and more at the discretion of global corporations, which make these administrative decisions internally for the purpose of maximizing global profit, with little regard for their effects on particular countries. (Crouch and Wheelright, 1982)

Anell (1981: 83–4) presents evidence that suggests as much as 45 per cent of all world trade is now between transnational subsidiaries and that between 50 and 80 per cent of the manufactured goods exported from Asia are subcontracted.

Competition from labour-intensive goods produced in the 'newly industrializing countries' has added a new dimension to the long-term decline in manufacturing that is depicted in table 5.2. Those data show that between 1960 and 1980 the manufacturing workforce of the United States remained static at about 20 million, while employment in the UK's manufacturing sector declined by almost a quarter and Australia's by about five per cent. Many of the plant closures and much of the disinvestment that pre-figured in inner city decline on both sides of the Atlantic throughout the fifties and sixties were due mainly to structural degeneracy and technical obsolescence. A shift-share analysis of the British conurbations shows that between 1952 and 1973 the structural or 'industry effect' was dwarfed by the conurbation or 'local effect', which totalled 1.3 million jobs (Lever, 1981). What this means is that the British conurbations failed to attract their predicted share (300,000 jobs) of national employment. Probably, Cameron (1980: 63) reasons, because of a fall in the demand for urban agglomeration economies, for large labour complements, and for technical linkages. The structural influence in the 1960s, such as it was, tended to be confined to industries in mining, shipbuilding, and textiles (Townsend, 1982: 1393).

The full import of 'de-industrialization' within the advanced capitalist economies was much clearer by the second half of the 1970s; and, although all the OECD countries had suffered the ill-effects of restructuring by the mid-1980s, it was Britain, no doubt because of its antiquated industrial base, and Australia, in part because of its proximity to the Asian centre of 'new' production, that caught the full force of 'de-industrialization'. Manufacturing employment in Great Britain is estimated to have dropped by at least 1.15 million (16.2 per cent) in just two years to July, 1981. The exceptional nature of the economic downturn in Britain is reflected in the level of redundancies which climbed from levels between 150,000 and 180,000 workers in the last half of the 1970s, to 493,800 and 532,000 in 1980 and 1981 (Townsend, 1982: 1392). Employment in the nationalized UK steel industry has fallen from over 300,000 to a little more than 110,000 in the space of four years (1979–82). All told, 'de-industrialization' in Australia cost the country 237,000 jobs in manufacturing and construction between June 1974 and June 1979, representing the elimination of one job in every seven from the sector (Sheehan, 1980: 209).

Although there is little doubt that those industry groups and regions under threat from imports and international competition from Japan and the 'newly industrializing countries' have been amongst the hardest hit, it is now apparent that the 'de-industrialization' process is no longer simply confined to traditionally declining industries and regions. 'Previous differences between growing and declining industries, and hence between growing and declining regions, have narrowed considerably if not disappeared' (Keeble, 1981: 460). In the United Kingdom the worst percentage losses of employees in 1980 were recorded in categories as diverse as steel tubes (28.1 per cent); general iron and steel (26.4 per cent); cotton spinning and dobuling (19.4 per cent); dresses, lingerie, infants wear (18.8 per cent); broadcast receiving and sound reproducing equipment (17.4 per cent); and motor vehicle manufacturing (15.8 per cent) (Townsend, 1982: 1395). Moreover, the discarding of labour is beginning to take on a significance in the labour-intensive services. Notwithstanding the general expansion of services in the post-industrial economy (table 5.2), and some job-creation due to technological developments, the incentive remains for heavy users of labour in the office sector (banking, insurance, government) to replace base-grade employees with word processing equipment, computerized filing systems, and automatic bank telling services. Self-service equipment – vending machines, the 'home entertainment centre' – is also replacing workers in the realm of the personalized services – cash register operators, service station attendants (Gershuny, 1978). For these reasons it seems most unlikely that the advanced capitalist economies will see a return to full employment, even beyond the middle of 1984 when unemployment within the 24 OECD member countries is expected to peak at 35 million (OECD, 1982). Certainly, when manufacturing output eventually recovers very few of the laid-off workers will find jobs to return to, since industrialists are being forced to computerize their production lines and introduce robots[10] to match the fierce competition from Japan and the 'newly industrializing countries'. Seabrook (1982: 6) concludes that 'increasingly the essential work of production can be carried out more effectively with the decreasing participation of the British working class, whether this production is transferred to workers in other parts of the world, or whether through technological innovation.'

The urban and regional impact of 'de-industrialization' widened considerably in the early 1980s as the process made inroads in those industries that were amongst the most dynamic during the years of industrial expansion. The precariousness of single-industry cities like Newcastle, Woollongong, and Whyalla (iron-steel-coal) and Adelaide, with its restricted industrial base (vehicle assembly and components, and 'white

---

[10] At present Japan leads the world in the usage of automated robots with 67,000 systems operating in 1981, followed by West Germany with 11,500 and Switzerland with about 8,000 units. This is just the beginning, though, as the Japanese pioneers in the field are planning to triple their combined output to about 150,000–200,000 units annually during the next four to five years. Many of these robots will be purchased by manufacturers in Britain, the United States and Australia as part of a labour replacing programme.

goods') has been apparent for some time. But in the 1980s, Australian cities with a disproportionate amount of manufacturing employment were also touched by 'de-industrialization': the closure of the General Motors-Holden plant at Pagewood and British Leyland's Waterloo plant in 1979–80 together eliminated 3,000 jobs from Sydney's inner suburban labour market.

Townsend's (1982) shift-share analysis of employment change in Britain, 1980–81, also reveals that the industrial recession is 'fundamentally a national phenomena', with the worst burden of manufacturing unemployment occurring in Wales, the north west, Yorkshire and Humberside, and the West Midlands. Structural shifts of a new kind showed up with electrical and mechanical engineering replacing textiles and clothing as the most important source of redundancies after 1980. As a result, unemployment in the West Midlands could exceed any other part of Britain except Northern Ireland and Wales (Taylor, 1981). This represents an unforeseen collapse for a conurbation that was envied in the late 1960s for its 'high-employment, high-wage sub-economy, based upon vehicle building and light engineering'. Whilst in the north east, the impact of contraction in traditional industries like mining and quarrying has been accentuated because of plant closures in the new industries introduced as part of the Assisted Areas regional programme[11] in the 1960s – plastics, rubber-based production, hosiery and knitted goods, and some light manufacturing. Moreover, research indicates that about two-thirds of the closures involving more than 30 redundancies in 1979 in Tyne and Wear were instigated by parent companies divesting themselves of branch plants acquired during the merger boom of the late 1960s (Pimlott, 1981: 53).

The employment dislocation caused by the rationalization of industry on a global scale is now being displaced onto the state in the form of additional unemployment payments – £40.5m daily in mid-1982 for Britain – and job-creation programmes (table 5.4). In as much as the unemployed are spatially concentrated in cities and regions (Massey and Meagan, 1982; Stilwell, 1980: 105–26), without these 'bandaids' (and possibly in spite of them) there is a heightened threat of social breakdown at the community level (Harrison, 1983; Williams, 1982), and growing violence directed against property and privilege. The summer months of 1981 saw the outburst of rioting in predominantly black neighbourhoods in British cities with exceedingly high levels of youth unemployment (Brixton and Southall

[11] Another feature of 'de-industrialization' in the UK is the *already* high rate of closure amongst plants established in 'peripheral' regions like the north west, Scotland, and the north, and Wales. The loss of 40,000 jobs in the assisted areas of these four regions between 1977 and 1979 were due to closures and redundancies in factories established under postwar regional policies (Townsend, 1982: 1400).

158   Capital as the Architect of Spatial Structures

Table 5.4 Percentage levels of unemployment in selected countries, 1975 and 1982–83

	December 1975	October 1982	January 1983
United States	8.5	10.2	10.8
Britain	4.8	12.8	13.8
Australia	5.0	5.0	10.1
West Germany	4.9	7.2	10.2
France	n.a.	8.3	n.a.
Italy	3.5	8.6[a]	n.a.
Canada	7.1	12.6	n.a.
Japan	2.1	2.5	2.5

[a] July
Source: OECD and current periodicals

in London, and Toxteth in Liverpool). In 1982, unemployed workers invaded the Parliament Buildings in Canberra, and the Melbourne Club, while Miami, Florida, was shaken by rioting in a black neighbourhood.

Capital switching: 2 The new financial order and regional shifts in the United States

'Mankind now has a completely integrated, international financial and informational market place capable of moving money and ideas to any place on this planet in minutes' (Walter Wriston, Chairman of Citibank in Sampson, 1981: 19). This capability, which utilizes technologies in telecommunications, the satellite relay and recovery of information, and high-speed data processing, grew along with the development of the Eurodollar and petrodollar market. Capital can now be transferred instantaneously between investment centres and corporate organizations connected in the network. At the apex of the international finance system are the genuinely global cities, New York, Tokyo and London, which sit astride a second-order group of international centres of banking (Osaka, Hong Kong, Singapore, Paris, Frankfurt, Zurich and San Francisco). The emergence of these cities as top-flight investment centres is directly related to the vast increase in international business generated by the transnational corporations and client governments in the 'newly industrializing countries'. This has altered the previous pecking-order within the capitalist urban hierarchy as cities that acquired their economic stature when production had a national orientation are overtaken (Cohen, 1981).

Sydney moved ahead of Melbourne in the late 1960s as the chief conduit through which foreign investment entered Australia (Rich, 1982: 100–4; Taylor and Thrift, 1981). In the United States, New York has outstripped all the other regional centres in the sphere of international business services, whilst San Francisco has developed along with the growth of Pacific trade. Banks in New York and San Francisco have 54 and 18 per cent of foreign bank deposits in the US, compared to 31 and 13 per cent of total US bank deposits (Cohen, 1981). The foreign assets of the West Coast banks grew from $US7 billion to $US32 billion between 1969 and 1974 (Cohen, 1977: 221). And in the United Kingdom, the City of London, with its reservoir of trust and expertise in banking, was invigorated by the growth of the Eurodollar and petrodollar markets:

> By 1979 the City of London employed 500,000 people and was earning almost £3 billion in invisible exports from insurance, banking, commodity trading and shipping; a performance contrasting starkly with the wretched conditions of the British economy in general. In a sense the City of London has been operating above and outside the British economy, and its links are with the exchanges and markets of the other world financial centres. Eighty per cent of the Euro-currency business conducted in London is through foreign banks. . . . (Daly, 1982a: 5)

The big money movers in all these centres are the international banks, the life offices combined with the superannuation and pension funds, and the financial directorates of the industrial corporations which place idle money on the 'spot-money' market, or switch it continually between currencies.

The global integration of the international banking system and sovereign states was cemented in the mid-1970s with the recycling of the huge Arabian oil surpluses which were deposited with reputable banks of New York, London and Zurich. In 1976 a Senate Foreign Relations Committee enquiry established that the six largest US banks held OPEC funds totalling $US11.3 billion, with $US3.2 billion shared amongst the next 15 (Sampson, 1981). Uncharacteristically, because borrowing by the banks' traditional clients (industrial corporations, utilities, urban municipalities) was checked by high interest rates in the mid-1970s, over 60 per cent of the petrodollar pool was loaned to the governments of several 'newly industrializing countries' that had large development programmes underway and were confronted with balance of payments difficulties when oil prices jumped. Between 1970 and 1975, 95 per cent of the growth in earnings of five of the top banks was due to their increase in international earnings (Cohen, 1981: 299). Or looked at another way, by 1977 over $US45 billion had been siphoned from the domestic economy, representing loans to the developing countries by commercial banks in the US.[12]

It is this sort of detail that lends bite to Boast's (1980: 73) general observation that the American capital market for urban and regional development 'is embedded in nationally and internationally integrated economies'. And since the commercial capital market supplies approximately 90 per cent of externally funded urban capital, cities must compete against each other for funds: 'Those that create conditions conducive to private economic prosperity can compete successfully on the market, while those that have declining local economies are less able to attract market investment funds' (Boast, 1980: 73). Structural shifts and a growing regional imbalance within the US economy are making the competition between cities for new private investment increasingly uneven. The regional discrepancy that is causing most concern is between the old manufacturing belt with its 'rustbowl' cities like Cleveland, Detroit, Toledo, Akron, Newark, Youngstown, and Buffalo, and the Southern and Pacific Coast states. While it would be wrong to assume that a direct exchange has occurred, it is not entirely coincidental that between 1965 and 1975 the north-east and north central regions lost 3.9 million inhabitants due to inter-regional migration while the south and west regions together gained 3.9 million immigrants (the south 2.5 million, the west coast 1.4 million persons) (Lowry, 1980: 174). And although Black (1980a) can demonstrate that on some indicators the economic performance of particular north-eastern cities places them above the national average, Garn and Ledebur (1980: 212) confirm that four-fifths of the 50 most distressed large cities in the US are situated in the north central and north-east regions (the 'Frostbelt'). The most convincing demonstration that the regional contrast between the Frostbelt's large manufacturing cities and the emergent 'Sunbelt' cities is widening is supplied by table 5.5. In the half decade, 1970–75, when national manufacturing employment fell precipitously in absolute terms, only the southern and western regions recorded growth – and a modicum at that. There are two components to the manufacturing growth in the Sunbelt: firstly, the constituent states

[12] Altogether the developing countries (excluding OPEC) owed commercial banks $US75 billion in 1977. By 1982 the world's banking system was deeply enmeshed in the deficit financing process, and the leading central banks had a full scale debt crisis on their hands. In the last quarter of 1982 they had little choice but to reschedule the foreign debt of Poland ($US25 billion), Mexico ($US78 billion), and Brazil ($US89 billion), in order to prevent a default that would have brought the international monetary system tumbling down. Argentina, Chile, Venezuela, Turkey, South Korea, Belgium and Canada all have similar problems. Thus the global integration of capitalism is all but complete. Apart from the penetration of the communist block by transnational corporations, the COMECON owes $US75 billion to western bankers: 80 per cent of Poland's export income is now tied up in servicing foreign debts; the equivalent ratios for Hungary and East Germany are 60 per cent and 40 per cent.

Table 5.5 Regional shares of the change in US manufacturing employment, 1960–75

Region	Absolute change (thousands)			Percentage share of national change		
	1960/65	*1965/70*	*1970/75*	*1960/65*	*1965/70*	*1970/75*
North-east	−110.1	264.9	−936.2	−15.2	12.0	−63.9
North central	189.7	624.5	−579.8	26.2	28.2	−39.5
South	520.6	951.5	23.9	72.0	43.0	1.6
West	122.7	372.5	25.1	17.0	16.8	1.7
US total[a]	722.9	2213.4	−1467.0	100.0	100.0	100.0

[a] Excludes Hawaii and Alaska
Source: Compiled by Rostow (1977: 93), from US Department of Labor, Employment and Earnings Statistics

have attracted a significant share of the newly established low-wage industries as well as inducing many to shift from the heavily unionized and high-wage north-eastern cities; secondly, the Sunbelt has snared corporations in the fast growing sectors like scientific instruments, electronics, biotechnics, aerospace, petrochemicals and agribusiness (beef, poultry, processed fruit and vegetables).

Much of the capital investment necessary for this growth originated in the north-eastern states where it was also needed. For instance, Cohen (1977: 221) contends that so much of the industry in the Sunbelt cities was financed and is still controlled from the north-east that they are entitled to 'dependent nation' status. He found that 42 per cent of the largest corporations in Texas used 'out-of-state' bankers based mainly in New York, Chicago and California. Similarly, a disproportionate share of the superannuation funds collected from union members in the north-eastern states is being placed by the portfolio managers in the Sunbelt cities. In effect their savings are helping to underwrite the disinvestment in north-eastern industries and cities that will lead to a further round of job losses and accentuated urban fiscal stress.[13]

Government policies have also acted to stimulate and reinforce these divergent regional tendencies in the USA. The Sunbelt states have prospered from all phases of federal enterprise during the last two decades, partly by playing off the Democratic and Republican administrations who both needed the southern constituency to govern. Having secured the 'lion's share' of federally funded R & D, aerospace and defence installations (75 per cent of all US Government R & D is based in Texas, Florida and California; 70 per cent of aerospace production is located between Houston and Florida), the southern and Pacific states now monopolize the

[13] There is an obvious parallel in Australia where the portfolio managers of the life offices are bypassing the labour-intensive industries that employ their policy-holders to place funds in resource and property development in Western Australia and Queensland.

recurrent grants, contracts, and salaries in R & D and defence on a per capita basis (Vaughan, 1980: 358). For example, 44 and 50 per cent of all the defence and R & D contracts let by the Federal government are won by corporations producing in the 15 southernmost states. On the other hand, current cutbacks in Federal, state and local funding are aggravating the run-down of urban infrastructure in the north-east at the same time as municipal bond issues are being undermined by a series of other Federal measures (All Savers Certificates, Individual Retirement Accounts, accelerated depreciation and 'safe harbour' leasing laws). Federal, state, and local spending on infrastructure dived by about 25 per cent from $US32 billion in 1972 to $US23 billion in 1981 (*Newsweek*, 1982: 33). Physical infrastructure in New York City has deteriorated to such an extent that the repair bill to put right the inoperable bridges, roads, water and sewer lines could exceed $US40 billion (Lewis, 1982). On top of this, 'the write-offs permitted for new investment in plant under the Reagan administration are expected to increase by $9.7 billion in 1982, $18.3 billion in 1983, and $30 billion in 1984' (Marcuse, 1981: 339). The illogicality of a strategy that calls for tax cuts and subsidies to resuscitate the private sector at the same time as it runs down the physical infrastructure upon which business depends has not escaped some observers (*Newsweek*, 1982: 29); not to mention the destructive effect of accelerated depreciation upon manufacturing employment in the north central and north-east states. According to a highway industry group, The Road Information Program, the aggregate cost to the private sector in lost revenue from inadequately maintained roads and bridges is $US30 billion annually.

Capital switching: 3 Reinvestment in inner area housing space

The restructuring of capital brought about by a recession does not force all investors into economic retreat; nor does it lead to disinvestment in all urban localities. At the same time as the suburban dream was disintegrating for many families in Australia and the United States, other newly formed households were alerted by the energy crisis to the possible dangers of being stranded on the outskirts of overextended metropolitan regions. Just as new investment continues at respectable levels throughout the American Sunbelt and in the resource-rich Australian states, certain inner area neighbourhoods in the early 1980s still attract the private reinvestment that has come to be identified with 'gentrification'.

'Gentrification' is the term that is applied to the re-colonization of inner area neighbourhoods and the restoration of their mainly Georgian and Victorian dwellings by youngish, middle class households. Adult members of the household are likely to work in a central city office and perform one of the 'white collar' functions associated with tertiary sector activity, i.e. administrative, managerial, professional, clerical, or business and community services (Mullins, 1982; Laska and Spain, 1980). Known alternatively as 'revitalization' in the US, the phenomenon began in the 1960s with the restoration of Victorian row houses around Capitol Hill in Washington DC and in Boston's South End; and with the conversion of lofts in the vicinity of New York's Greenwich Village, which has always been an artists' colony. Patchy private-market renovation has since been reported in most US cities: two Urban Land Institute surveys conducted in 88 central cities with more than 150,000 residents reveal that the proportion of cities with some gentrification rose from 65 to 86 per cent between 1975 and 1979 (Black, 1980b). With the exception of pockets of inner Boston, Atlanta, Washington DC and San Francisco, neighbourhood rejuvenation is still something of a novelty in most US central cities.

Extensive tracts of Georgian and Victorian housing stock have also been restored in London (and subsequently in regional cities), especially in boroughs like Camden, Islington and Kensington, which are close to the old upper class bastions in the West End (Williams, 1976). This is shown by an increase between 1971 and 1977 in the proportions of professional and managerial workers residing in the boroughs: up from 18 to 24 per cent, from 9 to 12 per cent, and from 23 to 30 per cent for Camden, Islington and Kensington respectively (reported in Roof, **4**, 2, 1979: 41). Much of this reinvestment in dilapidated rental accommodation was stimulated by government grants for housing improvement under the Housing Acts 1969–74 (Balchin, 1979; Bassett and Short, 1978; Hamnett, 1973). Taken overall, the improvement of inner area housing in British and US cities has been highly localized and runs counter to the predominant trend which is overwhelmingly one of disinvestment. In North America, inner city decline has culminated in abandoned housing (Leven *et al.*, 1976; Stegman, 1972), whereas in Britain sustained housing shortages have forestalled the abandonment of housing that signifies the completion of the cycle of neighbourhood decline. By way of contrast, comprehensive reinvestment in inner land and structures is now the norm in the Australian capital cities and it seems highly probable that the momentum of the spontaneous gentrification that began in the late 1960s will be sustained into the 1980s by the *expectation* of rising fuel prices (King, 1980) and state government encouragement.[14]

[14] The current emphasis in Australian metropolitan planning policy, which nicely reflects the austerity of the times, is upon 'urban consolidation'. The commitment to urban consolidation has come with the realization that: (a) because of falling occupancy ratios, there is now underutilized infrastructure and service capacity in inner zone suburbs; (b) there will be a greater need for smaller dwellings (flats, units, duplexes, town houses, apartments) as the population ages; (c) compact cities are more fuel efficient; (d) there is now such intense pressure on the inner city housing stock that a majority of Australia's urban poor face the prospect of becoming stranded in the outermost suburbs unless a sufficient stock of low-rent public and private dwellings is constructed in the inner zone (Archer, 1980; Bunker and Orchard, 1982; Reid, 1981).

Because the gentrification process is not yet fully understood, a theoretical presentation would be premature (though see Smith, 1982). However, several promising leads are being explored empirically, all of which presuppose a significant redirection of housing finance from the outer suburban to the inner city sub-markets. It is in this sense that capital switching and uneven spatial development is currently taking place within the capitalist city. Investigations have shown that it is not so much second-time home buyers transferring their equity from a peripheral to an inner city neighbourhood that is responsible for revitalization, but the housing investment undertaken by households *electing* to remain in the inner city when switching from renting to ownership. An *Annual housing survey* conducted by the US Bureau of Census in 1976 indicates that 70 per cent of households who purchased homes within the same central city were relocating nearby, with only 18 per cent of central-city buyers moving back from the suburbs (reported in James, 1980: 148). Similarly, on the basis of their work in London, Hamnett and Williams refute the hypothesis that most gentrifiers are households moving back into the city: 'They have not been forced by distance and fuel costs to seek inner-city location, although they may have been aware of the implications of suburban residence' (Hamnett and Williams, 1980: 482). And whilst it has been argued elsewhere that the 'deterrent' effects of a fringe location are magnified by the topology of Australian cities (Badcock and Urlich-Cloher, 1981), some provisional calculations from an analysis of some 7,800 property transactions over a decade for the inner suburbs of Adelaide, suggest that no more than 16 per cent of house purchases were made by buyers living in outer suburbs.

The extensive gentrification reported within Australian cities (Badcock and Urlich-Cloher, 1981; Kendig, 1979; Logan, 1982; Maher, 1979; Mullins, 1982) has a lot to do with the distinctive initial conditions found in the inner area zone. Here prospective home buyers found: housing in much better conditions and less crowded than in the old British or US industrial cities, with arrears of maintenance but, nonetheless, suitable for rehabilitation; an absence of the disincentives commonly encountered in the racially troubled and often inhospitable inner areas of US cities; and not the same obligation to directly subsidize services for the welfare-dependent poor, as is the case in many inner city municipalities in the United States. By the mid-1970s the range of positive externalities associated with reinvestment in the inner zone neighbourhoods of Australian cities was such that they had become highly attractive as a general location, irrespective of residential quality within the immediate neighbourhood. Community services and social infrastructure have been upgraded and expanded; suburban shopping streets redeveloped; the arts, entertainment and leisure pursuits assiduously promoted (Mullins, 1982); and local government penetrated by articulate and highly motivated community activists (Logan, 1982; Sandercock, 1978a).

It has to be said that these are amongst the more transparent supply-side effects in which the opportunities for accumulation by 'fractions' of commercial and domestic property go largely unnoticed. From the late 1960s onwards, the lending institutions allocated proportionately more of their mortgage finance to 'established' dwellings as confidence in the inner city housing market gradually picked up. Then, in both the United States and Australia towards the end of the 1970s, the rise in the production costs of suburban sites and new housing shifted price relativities in favour of the *undercapitalized* remnant housing stock built in near-city localities at about the turn of the century (James, 1980: 146–8; Badcock and Urlich-Cloher, 1981: 53–4). In the years before 'professional' traders and investors entered the inner city housing market, 'trend-setters' could obtain low to moderately priced dwellings with arrears of maintenance. But once bank finance for housing in older areas was more freely available in Australia, and investors had come to appreciate the opportunity for capital gains, house prices and turnover rates soared in the renovation and redevelopment submarkets.

It is no accident that the most feverish activity in the inner city housing market coincided with the general surge of speculative capital into real estate at the beginning of the 1970s. 'Bona fide' renovator-occupiers were joined by professional traders, and the shrewd operators who adopted a consistent investment strategy irrespective of whether it was London (Counter Information Services, 1973a: 40–4), Washington DC (James, 1980: 138), Melbourne (Centre for Urban Research and Action, 1977), or Adelaide (Badcock and Urlich-Cloher, 1981). The Centre for Urban Research and Action's (1977) investigation of the residential property market in inner Melbourne between 1970 and 1975 established that, while 60 per cent of the 'professional' investors recorded gross capital gains in excess of $A1,000 per month, only eight per cent of the owner-occupiers exceeded this figure (Centre for Urban Research and Action, 1977: 29; 42). While these pressures were relatively short-lived, middle class demand for inner area housing stood up well right to the end of the 1970s in Australian cities, largely because of doubts about the long-term outlook for fuel costs (King, 1980). In Sydney the hyperactivity that characterized all land and housing markets in the early 1970s returned again in 1978–81. The revival of Sydney's property market, which was fuelled by an extraordinary inflow of foreign investment capital (see Daly, 1982a: 31–2), placed much greater strain than ever before on the poorest sections of the innermost housing stock. With much of Sydney's inner housing in the hands of the middle classes, investors turned to the least likely suburbs: the number of sales in South Sydney, Leichhardt and Marrickville – all industrial and warehousing areas – increased from 719 in the June quarter of 1978 to 1,177 in the June quarter of 1979 (Daly, 1982a: 31–2). Local government areas that have traditionally concentrated Sydney's low-rent boarding and lodging accommodation, including Waverley, South Sydney, Sydney City, and Leichhardt, all registered house price increases above 20 per cent during the financial year 1978–79.

What this is leading up to, of course, is an assessment of the impact of gentrification upon the working class communities that have traditionally occupied the neighbourhoods that are in the process of being reclaimed and colonized by the young, mainly professional elements of the middle class. Because it is so difficult, if not impossible, to estimate accurately the numbers of households forcibly displaced by gentrification, the overall significance of displacement in the housing mobility of poor families is a source of dispute (see the debate between Sumka (1979) and Hartman (1979)). Sumka (1979: 484) cites estimates drawn from the *Annual housing survey* which suggest that over 500,000 US households (or two million persons) are displaced each year; or not more than four per cent of all movers, whichever figure is more palatable. Plainly, the level of displacement will depend upon the tightness of the housing market which varies from city to city; nonetheless, in those cities where gentrification has gained a foothold there is an unavoidable depletion of the long-term supply of low-cost accommodation as dwellings are transferred from the rental to the owner-occupancy sector. The problem is especially acute in Australian cities (Centre for Urban Research and Action, 1977), where commercial and institutional reinvestment has probably produced as much displacement as gentrification (Badcock and Urlich-Cloher, 1980; Kendig, 1979). In relation to gentrification, 20 per cent of all the rented units sold between 1970 and 1979 in inner Adelaide were lost to the rental submarket. Of the 2,370 rental units sold by landlords during the decade, 38.6 per cent were transferred to owner-occupiers (unpublished survey data). There is no question that within large Australian cities the traditional rights of access to inner area housing that the working class enjoyed because it was the remnant stock are endangered. Private *and* public reinvestment[15] is occurring on such a scale within the inner zone of Australian cities that a reshuffling of class shares of space is a foregone conclusion.

What is needed in view of this is a careful analysis in class terms of who are likely to be the 'winners' and 'losers' from the vigorous competition for inner city housing space. It will not be enough to produce a prognosis that simply pits blanket categories of 'working' class against 'middle' or 'upper' class. To do so is to ride roughshod over important within-class differences with respect to property and access to the means of collective consumption. The growing middle class presence and the upward revaluation of inner city residential property – three times the consumer price index (CPI) in inner Sydney since 1967 – has treated property

---

[15] Kendig (1979: 82) puts the non-residential building investment in inner Sydney between 1969 and 1975 at $A991.2 million, or 40.6 per cent of the metropolitan total.

'fractions' differently. Amongst the working class, many long-time Australian-born, as well as more recently arrived migrant home owners, welcomed the opportunity to realize the capital gains, and move to much newer housing in the suburbs. Likewise, during the 1960s many working class tenants were rehoused to their satisfaction by the housing commissions in the middle suburbs, or even purchased their own dwellings under rental-purchase programmes operated by the public housing agencies. It is the 'residual' working class renting privately within the inner city, many of whom can be considered to form an underclass of 'non-working poor' that are most vulnerable to gentrification and commercial reinvestment. In particular, the loss of boarding and lodging accommodation has drastically reduced the supply of cheap, short-term housing that is most suited to the needs of 'skid-rowers', transients, migratory workers, homeless youths, the marginally handicapped, and families in need of emergency shelter (Badcock and Urlich-Cloher, 1979; Centre for Urban Research and Action, 1979). Nonetheless, even amongst the 'non-working poor' significant variations in the degree of access to centralized housing can be found, owing to the belated efforts of state and local governments to build up the public stock of inner city rental accommodation (see Badcock, 1982; and Milligan and McAllister, 1982). For instance, the admittedly few pensioners and lone-parent families enjoying security of tenure, subsidized rentals, and well-placed housing in Australia's inner suburbs obviously have greater disposable income and a higher level of amenity than those households still on the housing commission waiting lists or renting privately.

For their part, middle class home buyers have done very nicely out of the rejuvenation of the housing market within the inner suburbs of Australian cities. They have seen the value of their assets appreciate rapidly through the capitalization into property prices of positive externalities, as well as their own 'sweat equity'. Since 1967 the average value of a 'standard' dwelling within six km of Sydney's CBD has risen by 665 per cent, compared with the CPI which gained 228 per cent. Between 1976 and 1981, when the CPI rose by 60 per cent, an average inner area dwelling in Sydney increased its value by 162 per cent (Hickie, 1983: 21). And in metropolitan Adelaide, between 1979 and 1982, the price increases recorded for average dwellings in the inner, middle and outer zones were 31.6, 35.0 and 10.1 per cent respectively (unpublished data, South Australian Valuer-General's Department, 1983). Lastly, it goes without saying that 'fractions' of property capital, including investors in the rental sub-market, the 'town-house' developers, the professional traders, and home restoration specialists, are among the prime beneficiaries from inner city revitalization. Those investors astute enough to read and 'play' the market profit handsomely: with the appearance of some restoration and evidence of neighbourhood rejuvenation, investor-renovators enter the home improvement submarket, while developers demolish nearby dwellings of little architectural merit to make way for town houses and flats.

Recapitulation

This chapter has examined postwar urban development under conditions of monopoly capitalism. In particular it has focused upon the branches of capital responsible for the transformation of three key segments of advanced capitalist cities: the producers of and institutional investors in land and housing in the outer suburbs; the role of corporate finance in unison with the property development sector in reshaping the office core of globally integrated cities; the multiplex investment directed at selected residential areas within the inner city. Part of the brief was also to show that similar capitalist institutions and mechanisms do not always make for common urban outcomes (low income housing on the outskirts of Australian cities); that government policy (urban containment in Britain) may give rise to indigenous expressions of essentially the same process (suburbanization); that different local conditions commend alternative patterns of investment (the rise of Sunbelt in the United States; new life for old suburbs in Australian cities). It is to be hoped that this treatment of city forming processes has adequately prepared ground for the next stage of the analysis, in which the distributional consequences of urban phenomena are considered at closer range.

Part III

Sources of Inequality and Redistribution Within Cities

Part III endeavours to determine in what sense and to what degree the use of urban space and social provision within cities are subsidiary sources of inequality and redistribution. If the way cities are structured affects a redistribution of income, then the susceptibility of individuals and households to these transfers is governed chiefly by where they reside; and, for most people, the money wage is the real arbiter of what amounts of space they will consume and which particular neighbourhoods they will live in. It is argued in chapter 6 that, notwithstanding its varied derivation, inequality has its basis in the structure of the labour market and the institutions that perpetuate such an arrangement within advanced capitalist societies. This is the crucial framework of relations that sets the level of dependency of households upon the state, dictates how they will fare in the finance and property markets, and predisposes their assignment to various sectors of the urban and housing markets. Whether or not the provision of housing is appropriate to the needs of all households depends on the efficacy of the supply side, in broad terms: fiscal policy, the production of land for housing, availability of housing finance, and the selection and allocation procedures of private and public sector institutions.

It is from this perspective that chapter 7 sets out to examine the ways in which the urban land and housing markets operate to redistribute real income, and how the housing assignment process has an important bearing on the household's more general command over resources in the urban environment. One of the aims is to show how land and housing markets reproduce and compound the primary inequalities originating in the labour market. The land/housing market differentiates, and at worst segregates, households with respect to the acquisition of wealth and property rights, and determines where the household will be located with respect to an extensive range of community resources that are supportive of a genuinely fulfilling way of life. Income is also transferred within cities when changes to the pattern of access costs and externalities materialize as capital gains (or losses) to domestic property. Chapter 8 describes the process whereby governments have gradually assumed responsibility for the provision of essentially non-productive urban infrastructure required by capitalist societies. In the chapter attention is drawn specifically to the unevenness of state provision by sectors and locations and the inequities that flow from it. Inequitable provision between and across cities has its basis in the differing approaches of governments to welfare functions, public finance, and the delivery of social services. It is particularly through its housing programme that the state sets the pattern of access for the most dependent households to these unevenly distributed opportunities and resources.

The point of chapter 9 is to show that residents are not necessarily the passive recipients of collectively provided services or the investment decisions of private capital, and that they can and do intervene in the shaping of the urban environment. It deliberately sets out to counter the nihilism that attends some analyses of urban change; for example, the view that if a struggle succeeds against the interests of capital it is only because it has unwittingly aided the accumulation process. Moreover, depending upon their power, the actions of coalitions of residents can and do affect the access and opportunities, and redistribute the real income of other households in urban society. Groups with a vested interest in the property market organize (sometimes along class lines, sometimes not) either to attract or to oppose private and public investment within their locality.

6

Structural Underpinnings of the Residential Assignment Process

This chapter serves a dual purpose: its chief assignment is to show how the distribution of income and wealth between classes and households, allied with entry to and position in the labour market, governs household revenue; for this is the principal determinant of housing demand. It affects the wage earner's ability to provide housing for the household, and has a major bearing on the placement of the household within the various sectors of the city's land and housing markets. This is matched on the housing supply-side by a multiplicity of institutions which perform equivalent structural functions. Some of these are directly concerned with the formulation and implementation of aspects of state housing policy – central government departments of housing, council housing agencies, building societies, and the house building industry – while others are indirectly responsible for shifts in economic or political circumstances that inevitably affect the state of the housing market, and may even undermine carefully devised housing reform. The fine-tuning of the economy undertaken by the Exchequer or Treasury seldom, if ever, takes account of national housing goals. Hence, an important part of understanding the 'residential assignment process' involves some knowledge of the institutional framework behind housing provision, and the political and economic forces which so often enmesh it.

In the process of describing the structural underpinnings of the residential assignment process some conclusions can also be drawn about the relative contribution of spatially linked sources of inequality to material inequality as a whole. Donnison (1976) lists five sources of inequality, only two of which are spatial in kind: the life-time cycle of earned income; the stratification process in capitalistic societies; urban-rural and inter-regional disparities; the uneven distribution of resources within cities; and discrimination. The reader may recall that chapter 2 concluded that the most damaging and persistent inequalities are structural and that space functions, at best, compound these structurally produced inequalities. In order to lend perspective to the arguments developed in chapters 7–9 some overview is needed of the full range of distributional mechanisms that prescribe the living standards of groups in society (table 6.1).

Economic resources of the household

The plan in this section is to elaborate upon the main sources of household income and wealth (table 6.1) as a precursor to the discussion of how they in turn govern access to housing (i.e., 'ability to pay'). Firstly, there is a short account of those social institutions and conventions that sustain the system for dispersing income and wealth in capitalist societies; some general observations are then made about the resulting distributions of income and wealth; and, finally the planned redistribution of the income earned in the labour market is examined.

Educational success, occupational destination, and remuneration

The structural linkages that operate *at the level of aggregates* within advanced capitalist societies are well rehearsed (Connell *et al.*, 1982;

Table 6.1 The composition of household resources: a ranking of the principal sources of original and redistributed income (i.e. inequality)

First-order sources

Pre-tax earnings in the form of fees, wages and salaries, investment income and inherited wealth.

Second-order sources

Capital gains from domestic property, especially in times of inflation.

Third-order sources

Incidence of tax, tax relief, cash transfers by government. Social security payments to elderly and invalidity pensioners; unemployed, sickness, and supporting mothers benefits. Family allowances, child endowment etc. Income support supplements and social wages paid to workers assigned to job creation and retraining programmes.

Fourth-order sources

There are two main kinds. Benefits-in-kind, including government services and area funding (the income-effect of public housing, state education or medical treatment varies according to need and social access). Fringe benefits and perquisites in the workplace such as superannuation, supplementary endowments, a company car, subsidised housing, workers compensation etc.

Fifth-order sources

Indirect redistribution produced by imperfect capital, housing and urban land markets. Externality, or 'spill-over', effects which may be positive or negative are capitalized into the value of domestic property. Variations in the price and physical accessibility of resources.

Halsey *et al.*, 1980; Illich, 1976; Stewart *et al.*, 1980; Wedderburn, 1974). Material differences in living standards in capitalist societies seem most directly to reflect the hierarchical ranking of roles in the employment system and the exclusion of certain sections of the population from that system.[1] Entry to, and the position that one eventually occupies in the workforce, invariably provides a commentary on a person's educational record.[2] Mincer (1974: 66) has shown how the annual earnings of white non-farm males in the United States vary quite consistently with the number of years of completed schooling. This comes about partly because the family, via its ascriptive and socialization functions, provides a springboard to the education system with its differential access to achievement and certification (Faia, 1981). The educational systems of capitalist societies have evolved to ensure that in the long-run, at least, as many graduates as possible can be absorbed wherever the greatest needs exist in the labour market. Hence, by the time they graduate, high school students have been prepared either for admission to a tertiary institution or left to find their level in the labour market. Of course substantial social mobility has occurred during the last half-century in capitalist societies, notwithstanding the handicap of class background. What has remained largely unaltered in Britain though, when compared with Australia and the US, is the relative chance of those born into different social classes reaching the top (Halsey *et al.*, 1980). The significance of occupational inheritance within the family is that 'occupation' is really the fulcrum used to lever economic resources from the labour market.

Sectoral and regional rigidities in the labour market

The labour markets of capitalist economies are riddled with institutionalized rigidities such as wage controls and wage bargaining, cartels, trade union requirements, and regulations relating to recruitment and training practices. Thereby, wage inequalities are often frozen into place between workers with similar levels of skill and performing identical tasks (as between male and female employees). Historically, powerful unions in strategic industries have succeeded in extracting more favourable wages and conditions from employers (at the expense of unorganized guest workers, females, and blacks. See Harrington, 1962.) Dockers, refinery maintenance workers, coalminers, and airline pilots are amongst the pace-setters in Australia and the United Kingdom.

Because the housing market tends to concentrate unemployment, place of residence can also be a hinderance to obtaining work (the 'housing

---

[1] Of course the resilience of inherited wealth serves to shelter the members of some families from the vagaries of the earning system.
[2] Education, it must be said, is not the sole determinant of advancement. Career development and promotion in employment says as much about success in an occupational role.

trap'). The poverty of unemployed workers may be sufficient to im-
mobilize them geographically, confining them to a local labour market
plagued by a mismatch of skills on the demand and supply sides, and
where job opportunities may be in decline (Bramley, 1979; McGregor,
1979).[3] Plainly the vitality of the regional economy determines whether or
not a redundant worker can re-enter the labour market without migrating
(Donnison with Soto, 1980: 45–6).

In short, this is the web of dependencies that goes far to determine not
only a worker's level of earnings, but also his/her access to a range of
opportunities, including housing, within an urban society. Not un-
exceptionally, occupational status is placed at the nexus of this web of
dependencies: the wide variability in 'access to opportunities' that actually
flows from position in the UK labour market is illustrated in a table
originally constructed by Berthoud in 1976 (table 6.2). The table also
summarizes the correspondence that has already been revealed between

Table 6.2 Occupational destinations, opportunities, and living standards (UK, early
1970s, percentage)

	Managerial and professional	Other non-manual	Skilled manual	Semi-skilled	Unskilled
Male unemployment rates, 1971	2	3	4	5	12
Earning less than £45 per week, 1974	7	25	13	27	45
Middle-aged men with limiting long-standing illness, 1973	11	19	20	24	33
Poor reading ability at age 11, Inner London, 1971	7	15	22	31	38
In housing without exclusive use of bath or shower and WC, 1973	5	12	12	18	21
Households without a car, 1972	15	48	45	69	82

Source: Berthoud (1976)

[3] While this cannot be seriously disputed for free standing labour markets, like regions
within a spatial economy, there is certainly less agreement about whether the localization
of unemployment within cities is due to spatial constraints. Cheshire (1981) prefers to
believe that because of social segregation the incidence of unemployment varies between
different areas within the city.

educational background, employment status, occupation and earnings, and variations in housing conditions and physical mobility. The characteristic features and sources of inequality have now to be thrown into relief: the approach will be to examine some of the data that describe the pre-tax distributions of income and wealth, followed by a review of the planned redistribution, obtained under capitalist market conditions.

Original income and wealth under capitalist market conditions

Some of Peter Townsend's calculations (table 6.3), based on his massive study of poverty in the United Kingdom towards the end of the 1960s, provide a useful first approximation of the origins and breakdown of household resources. They are drawn from an elaborate sample survey of 3,260 households and 10,048 individuals in 1967–68 (Townsend, 1979). Firstly, table 6.3 shows that net earnings from employment and self-employment make up almost half of the household's total resources. Secondly, it shows that, 'The income equivalent of assets held, including the value of owner-occupied housing less any capital repayments outstanding, was more than a fifth of the total, making a substantial contribution to living standards' (Townsend, 1979: 225). Thirdly, it reveals that employer welfare benefits in kind form about 5 per cent of the total, or 11 per cent of net earnings from employment. Fourthly, social transfers in the

Table 6.3 Estimated breakdown of resources accumulated by UK households over a twelve month period, 1968–69

Type of resource	Gross disposable resources (%)
Net disposable cash income (less property income)	
Net earnings from employment	44.5
Self-employment income	4.2
Employers pension	1.8
Social security cash benefits	7.3
Miscellaneous payments	0.3
Sub-total	58.1
Imputed income	
From assets (annuity value)	22.8
From employer welfare benefits in kind	5.0
Value of social services in kind	11.6
Value of private income in kind	2.5
Sub-total	41.9
Total	100.0

The value of annuities is based on the imputed capital value of owner-occupied housing rather than the rental value.
Source: Townsend (1979: 226, table 5.27)

form of social services in kind, and cash benefits, account for 11½ per cent and seven per cent of total resources respectively.

These aggregates for Britain's statistically 'representative' household provide an underlying justification for the ranking given to the main sources of inequality in table 6.1. Moreover, though cash earnings assume their rightful position as the cardinal source of household resources, Townsend's analysis emphasizes that the others should not be overlooked; notably, the value of domestic property and social transfers.

It has been established that a regular and adequate income is of paramount importance for full and effective participation in society. This is amplified in figure 6.1, which displays the shares of total *pre-tax* (original) income going to five equal-sized groups of 'tax-units'[4] in the United Kingdom in 1978/79. There is a telling relationship between the proportion of a tax-unit's pre-tax income that is gained from working, and its share of total taxable income: the top quartile, which accounted for half of the total income in 1978/79, derived 90 per cent of it as recompense for working; whereas, the poorest 25 per cent, in receipt of only 8.1 per cent of total pre-tax earnings were nearly as dependent on state pensions and non-taxable benefits (representing 66 per cent of their income before tax). Figure 6.1 is expressive of the damaging social cleavage, which is common to Britain, the United States, and Australia, between those workers that enjoy job security, good levels of pay, and sometimes substantial fringe benefits,[5] and the labour market's cast-offs who periodically fall victim to public expenditure priorities (Stretton, 1979; Townsend, 1980). The exclusion of around one in every ten workers from paid employment, falling participation rates among the elderly and disabled, and employment difficulties among single parents are responsible for the maintenance of an underclass comprising married females and their children, and young unskilled manual workers (Showler and Sinfield, 1980; Windshuttle, 1979). Although some of the ageing may join them because of a lack of work it is mainly the inadequacy of their pension entitlements that consign them to the ranks of the poor. According to evidence presented to the 1977

---

[4] A 'tax-unit' is defined by the Central Statistical Office (1981a: 86) as a married couple or a single person over school-leaving age and not at school.

[5] To earnings must be added the industrial fringe benefits, or 'perks', tied to a specific job. Representing income inkind, fringe benefits tend to flow to workers roughly in proportion to the status of the occupation. Superannuation contributions by an employer, sick pay entitlements, a company car, housing and educational subsidies, and travelling expenses are typical examples. In an era of high marginal tax rates these sources of 'undisclosed' income serve to widen the differentials, or inequalities, already existing in the levels of earnings. Following a nine month study of occupations and industries with the highest and lowest fringe benefits, Jamrozik and Leeds (1981) established that such benefits in Australia can be worth between 10 and 20 per cent of the average worker's total income, and in the case of executives, can reach 30 per cent. They calculated that a worker on an income of $A300 a week or more receives four times the value of the benefits available to the worker on a weekly income of $A180.

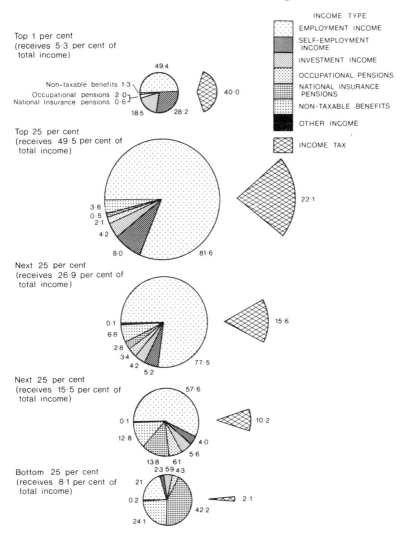

Figure 6.1 Income by source and tax paid as a percentage of the pre-tax income of
quartile groups, UK taxpayers, 1978–79
Source: Central Statistical Office, 1981a: 83

Royal Commission on the Distribution of Income and Wealth (the
Diamond Commission), 60 per cent of Britain's poorest families were
those without any earners.

In turning to the *distribution of wealth* in the three countries of interest
(table 6.4) the degree of inequality is even more pronounced than was the
case with the distribution of original income (figure 6.1). While there is no
doubting that the spread of home ownership has reduced the complete

Table 6.4 Distribution of wealth in Australia, USA and the UK (percentage shares)

	Australia		USA	UK	
	1915	*1967*	*1964*	*1951–56*	*1975*
Top quintile	89.72	53.51	76.64	89	81.8
Top 10%	n.a.	36.63	62.79	79	62.4
Top 5%	66.22	24.57	51.63	67.5	46.5
Top 1%	34.46	9.26	31.44	42.0	23.2
Concentration ratio[a]	n.a.	0.52	0.76	0.87	n.a.

[a] The concentration ratio is a single measure of inequality ranging from 0–1. Developed by Gini, it is the ratio of the area between the Lorenz curve and the 'egalitarian line' (where each family receives the same income), to the area of the triangle below that line.
Sources: Meacher (1980); Podder (1978: table 4.19)

monopolization of wealth by a handful of families, and that some sort of shakedown has occurred in the top 20 per cent of the asset-rich (compare Australia in 1915 and 1967, and the UK in 1951–56 and 1975), the fact remains that in spite of a general improvement in living standards, not much of society's wealth has percolated down to the lowest quintile in any of the three countries under consideration. Consider the position in the United Kingdom in 1975, for instance, with four-fifths of the population holding only 18 per cent of the total personal wealth (Meacher, 1980: 122).

Except to the privileged minority that still owns and controls a disproportionate share of total personal wealth, the domestic property market represents one of the principal means of accumulating wealth. Although the increase in home-ownership should not be overlooked, property incomes in the UK since the mid-1950s have increased disproportionately to earned incomes, with housing growing from 20 per cent of gross personal wealth in 1960 to 41 per cent in 1976 (Webster, 1980: 249). During the decade 1955–65, the contribution of property incomes to total household incomes in the UK rose from 10.6 to 13.2 per cent (Townsend, 1979: 121). Capital gains in the domestic property market (imputed income) are channelled to owners on a sliding scale: the larger the asset, the higher the absolute yield. The increments to capital held as housing accrue as a rule from: enforced savings, future buyers; investors, large and small, altering the capital stock of cities; preferential taxation provisions for home buyers; grant-aided home improvements undertaken by the owner (see chapter 7).

*Planned distribution: incidence of income tax, cash payments
to beneficiaries and benefits in-kind*

All capitalist societies have a welfare system designed by the state to redistribute income (cash and in-kind). As table 6.1 suggests, redistribution of income is affected by the whole fiscal system; that is to say, by all taxes, direct or indirect, collected by central/federal, state and local government, and all types of governmental expenditures. The redistributive impact of most of these fiscal measures is intentional and usually traceable; however, other transfers may be unforeseen and quite difficult, if not impossible, to trace. Income tax is the largest single source of government revenue in Britain, the US and Australia, so it offers considerable scope for redistribution. Broadly speaking there are two main ways of redistributing national income: through the incidence of income tax, tax relief and cash payments to beneficiaries; and as benefits in-kind (table 6.1).

There is mounting evidence of a significant leakage of potential government revenue that otherwise could be committed to public programmes. The range of concessional deductions allowed under the taxation schedules in Britain, the United States and Australia represent one of these leaks. Tax evasion represents the other leakage: corporations, professionals, consultants, small businessmen and operators in the private sector are presented with more opportunities for understating their taxable income than wage and salary earners. The evidence charting the growth of tax avoidance in Australia during the 1970s is unequivocal (figure 6.2). The director of the Centre for Research on Federal Financial Relations at the Australian National University and chairman of the Commonwealth's Committee of Inquiry into Inflation and Taxation, states that he has '. . . estimated conservatively that something like 20 per cent of personal income tax nominally payable is being lost to revenue through avoidance and evasion, usually by high-income taxpayers other than wage and salary earners' (Mathews, 1982: 13). He adds that it is not an exaggeration to say that nearly all the major social and economic problems which currently beset Australia, including the lack of distributional equity arising from the failure of the taxation and social welfare system to operate as intended, have their origin in this loss of revenue control.

The most systematic, though by no means flawless, estimate of the effect of taxes and benefits in-kind on household income is provided by the British Central Statistical Office (1981b). The CSO argues that, 'when the benefits of public spending which these taxes finance are taken into account the net effect of government activity is generally equalizing – resources are distributed from working households with relatively high incomes to low income families mainly dependent on state transfers' (Sandford, 1980: 14). A number of welfare economists including Le Grand

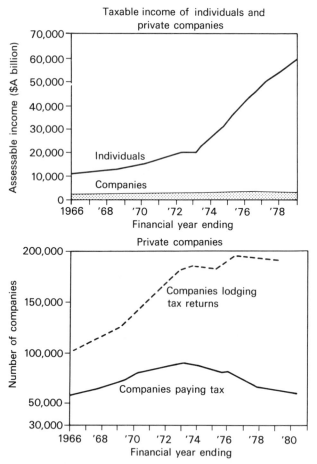

Figure 6.2 The growth of tax avoidance in Australia, 1966–81
Source: based on data compiled by the Costigan Enquiry into Tax Avoidance, 1982

(1982), O'Higgins (1980) and Pond (1980b) have voiced their scepticism. They claim that the CSO analysis, parts of which are summarized below, is incomplete because it omits 'tax expenditures' (allowances, tax relief and subsidies)[6] from the accounts. Whilst more generally, Field *et al.* (1977) and Le Grand (1982) have attempted to demonstrate, without complete success, that the middle classes do better out of the health and educational services than the working classes.

---

[6] Tax allowances are of greatest real benefit to the prosperous who pay high marginal rates of taxation. According to the House of Commons Public Expenditure Committee, the aggregate worth of the different tax allowances that could be calculated amounted to £26 billion for 1978–79, compared with Britain's total public expenditure of £65 billion (Townsend, 1980: 15).

The CSO analysis of the Family Expenditure Survey for 1979 concluded that the share of total income going to the bottom 20 per cent of households improved from 0.5 per cent (pathetic?) to 7 per cent (paltry?) following redistribution (Central Statistical Office, 1981b: 104).

Benefits in-kind normally take the form of social, health, housing and educational services delivered by the state. As suggested above, the income effect of government provision may be pro-rich, with higher than average income households obtaining greater benefits, on balance, than households with low income (table 6.5). A major factor in this is the greater consumption of education by the highest three quintile groups in table 6.5 (an average of £430 compared with £185 for the lowest two quintiles). There is only part consolation in the fact that these benefits in-kind represent the highest proportions of final income for households with the lowest incomes, and tend to be reasonably sensitive to those households with particular needs. Likewise, the largest average benefit from the council housing subsidy in Britain went to the single retired adults, one parent families, and large families dependent upon public housing assistance. These household types made up 43, 54, and 44 per cent of local authority tenants respectively in the 1979 Family Expenditure Survey.

The ladder of redistributive effects has been descended (table 6.1) to the point where those that are readily identifiable as spatial in-kind are reached. Although they have been assigned a low ranking within the idealized scheme, some of the effects can at times loom much larger than they ordinarily would in the set of deprivations visited upon poor households. Because the incidence of these income transfers (unlike the majority of those above) varies according to where the householder resides, the residential assignment process is now proximal to the discussion.

Table 6.5 Average amounts received as benefits in kind by UK households, 1979

£ per household	Selected quintiles, households by original income			Average for all households
	Bottom fifth	Middle fifth	Top fifth	
Education	110	400	440	330
Welfare foods	20	30	30	20
Health	460	390	370	390
Council housing 'subsidy'	150	110	80	110
Other	0	30	80	40
Total	730	970	990	890

Source: Central Statistical Office (1981b: table E, 106)

Housing needs and economic circumstances

More space than is customary in urban texts has been devoted to looking at what households earn in capitalist societies because this is indispensable to a thorough understanding of how they will fare in the urban land and housing markets. Leaving aside, for the moment, the structural inflexions that separate one housing system from another under capitalism, there is often an uncanny correspondence between the position occupied by workers in the labour market and their spatial destination in the housing market. It is visible in a myriad factorial ecologies left to us: even a healthy respect for the ecological fallacy (Janson, 1969: 316–21) cannot detract from the consistently high correlations obtained between measures of workforce participation, occupational status and income, and area of residence.

There is an essential reality that is hard to gloss over and that is, it does not seem to matter how the provision of housing is approached in capitalist economies, the housing market is stratified mainly according to the lines laid down in the labour market. True, some households register a measurable improvement in their housing situation and financial standing once they have qualified for state housing assistance,[7] but for those others denied this access the housing market acts to heap additional disadvantage upon the inequality embedded in the earnings system. Although many of the 'non-working poor' are relegated, as if by default, to their housing, it is important perhaps to stress that not all housing consumers are totally beholden to housing institutions in this way. There has been a rather tedious debate about how much choice and discretion households actually exercise in consuming housing. Naturally American and Australian researchers active in the sixties were impressed by the range of housing opportunities that the majority of home seekers seemed to be presented with (Johnston, 1971; Timms, 1971). Alternatively, British workers were obliged to come to terms with much larger public and private rental sectors, and a home purchase sector monopolized by a single institution, the building society. Somewhat facetiously, Niner and Watson (1979: 335) liken the household in many of these studies to a 'mere pawn', at the mercy of the urban managers, who control access to housing, and are themselves subject to government supervision and capitalist fiat. Karn (1979: 172) feels that: 'To polarize the argument in this way is in itself a distortion. People are neither totally free to choose to rent or buy, nor are they totally prevented from exercising any choice, especially if they are willing to

[7] The effect of council housing provision in some parts of British cities has been to reduce the correlation in the bottom half of the income distribution between income deprivation and housing deprivation (Evans, 1980: 194). This follows large scale clearance of the worst slums and the rehousing of the poorest families in council housing, which at least conforms to current standards and includes all basic amenities.

accept relatively poor housing and/or to set aside very large proportions of their income for buying.' Murie's suggestion that 'the total decision space of individual households is *reduced* prior to the exercise of choice or preference by eligibility factors, job factors, shortages and previous housing experience' (Murie, 1974: 121) gets much closer to the truth.

Housing as an opportunity set

The matter of access is approached provocatively and represents the housing market as a set of opportunities from which households make selections, *if they have the wherewithal*. The insistence on the priority of institutional constraints has had the effect of shifting attention away from the decisive limitation on access to housing which is found in the system of earnings. The prior view overlooks the positive inducement given by the state to home owners, consistent with its drive to extend property ownership in Britain, Australia and the United States. It focuses upon the institutional constraints acting upon the poor; while agreeing that housing systems must ultimately be judged by how they house the poor, there is a danger that housing provision is neglected as a whole. 'Thus in matters of *housing* the primary inequality concerns the income level which conditions access to the type of housing market,' to which Castells (1978: 21) adds, 'but it does not stop there'. And nor shall we: almost all the households that miss out on decent housing in our societies do not receive a sufficient income. It follows that because of their economic circumstances many households exercise no real choice in respect of housing sector (public/ private) and tenure (ownership/rental), though they may have some say about the type, quality and location of the council dwelling they occupy:

> Recent research has suggested that perceptions of the estate are of more salience than type of dwelling but, other things being equal, houses are likely to be more popular than flats, central than peripheral areas, modern than old-fashioned dwellings and 'respectable' than 'rough' neighbourhoods. Two factors which are of relatively little significance in the public sector are price and size of dwelling: rent structures are usually relatively flat with only modest variations according to quality while housing departments are generally only willing to allocate accommodation of the 'correct' size (English, 1979: 116).

Even though the last part of chapter 6 shows how access can be restricted by government policy and housing managers, the fact should not be ignored that to other home-owning households – now a majority in all three countries of interest – these institutional mechanisms actually represent an enabling framework, or an *escalator* to a significant means of accumulation.

Housing costs

The form of accommodation appropriate to a household's needs will usually take account of both the number of, and relations between members of the household, the stage of the family's development and the life style preferences of its members. If society takes the view that a 'need' is a socially accepted aspiration, then it follows that 'the faster that one is met the faster do new aspirations arise' (Cullingworth, 1979: 31).[8] It is these needs, *adjusted for price and ability to pay*, that set the level of housing costs for the household and are converted into aggregate demand.

Figure 6.3 segments the housing market into the main sectors: outright owner, home buyer, and public and private tenants. Although the outlay on housing rises with income in the case of both buyers and private renters, it represents a reducing proportion to higher income families. It also appears that while higher income households have better housing they do not pay much more for it, partly because they enter the sector earlier in their housing careers (Neutze, 1981: 113). Figure 6.3 contains two other significant pieces of information: firstly, the weekly housing costs of private tenants exceed those of home owners for all except the lowest income level; and, secondly, public tenants have much lower housing costs than private tenants. The influence of tenure on housing costs is also transmitted through the age of the household head; since older heads are more likely to have paid off or substantially lowered their mortgage payments, which in the event reflect historic costs.

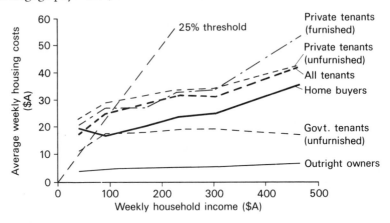

Figure 6.3 Average weekly housing costs of Australian households classified by tenure, 1975–76
Source: Australian Bureau of Statistics, 1978: Table 4.4

[8] Steadily rising aspirations have long run implications for housing provision, because this means that there will always inevitably be a portion of the housing stock in need of improvement in order to keep up with revised aspirations and housing standards.

Ability to pay and access

Housing studies generally report an almost universal preference for owning rather than renting and for detached dwellings as opposed to other
types (Stretton, 1974). Having said that one does not have to be particularly astute to appreciate that 'To state that "most people want to own
their own home" begs the important question of on what terms and at
what cost' (Murie, 1974). It is ability to pay that is crucial in the household's entry to home ownership. Britain's Family Expenditure Survey
demonstrates quite conclusively that access to various sectors of the
housing market is based upon what people can afford to pay. For example,
35 per cent of households living in privately rented accommodation in
1978 were getting less than £2,100 compared with 28 per cent in council
homes and flats, 27 per cent of outright owners, and 2 per cent of families
still paying off a mortgage (Hillman, 1980: 17).

And yet some households will go to extraordinary lengths to own their
own home, as the owner–occupancy rates for different national groups in
Australia indicate (table 6.6). It is interesting that these rates are achieved in
spite of below average earnings (table 6.6), and more restricted access to
formal sources of housing finance. Similarly, Asians in British cities also
make an inordinate sacrifice to achieve owner occupier status even though

Table 6.6 Home ownership[a] and wage levels in Australia by birthplace

City	Non-English background[b]	Australia	UK/Ireland	Italy (percentages)	Greece	Yugoslavia
			Country of birth of household head			
Sydney	20.7	71.8	68.3	85.9	78.9	81.0
Melbourne	26.3	72.1	71.8	92.2	85.9	80.5
Brisbane	9.7	76.0	74.6	96.4	–	–
Adelaide	16.8	70.9	70.1	94.7	98.0	84.8
Perth	16.2	72.7	72.3	90.3	–	80.9
Hobart	8.2	70.2	80.7	–	–	–
AUSTRALIA		71.6	69.6	90.0	83.8	79.6
Weekly earnings[c]				*Dollars*		
Male:						
median		225	246	205	203	220
mean		249	269	218	220	246
Female:						
median		184	195	158	155	164
mean		194	204	166	158	174

[a] Outright owners and buyers
[b] Percentage of total households with heads born in non-English speaking countries
[c] Full-time employees in all jobs
Source: Australian Bureau of Statistics (1981a)

they generally have great difficulty in attracting mortgages from conventional lenders and thus face excessively high interest charges (Karn, 1979). This intense desire to be a home owner, which is characteristic of many immigrant households, probably owes as much initially to an urge for residential security and stability as it does to an awareness of the possibilities for accumulation.

However, it is as a means of accumulation that home ownership separates itself from other forms of tenure. Moreover, much of the inequity arising from the imperfections in the housing market involves the transfer of income from all other tenures to owner occupancy (see chapter 7). For these reasons, the cost of access to owner occupation represents the most decisive consideration for aspiring home owners. Kendig (1981: 20) has prepared a table of access costs which is based on a survey of 700 moving households in Adelaide (table 6.7). Plainly the 20 per cent deposit typically required for a home loan, plus the transaction costs, represents a formidable financial hurdle to households with below average incomes. These households are concentrated in the private rental sector: in the case of the 198 private tenants interviewed for Kendig's survey, 'only 16 per cent had sufficient assets and income to buy a modest house on usual terms from a bank or building society' (Kendig, 1981: 48).[9]

Lastly, one section of Kendig's work makes crystal-clear how the economic circumstances of a household dictate access to a particular tenure. It (Kendig, 1981: 135–9) is based on a modified analysis of

Table 6.7 Median housing cost by tenure ($A)

| | | Weekly housing outlays | |
Tenure	Access costs[a]	Recent movers	All occupants[b]
Owner-occupied	8,090	67.9	17.9
Publicly rented	20	19.0	15.0
Privately rented	120	36.5	33.1

[a] Figures for recent movers only. For owners, 20 per cent of the average house price for the deposit plus 4 per cent of sale price for transactions costs; for public tenants, actual bond paid; for private tenants, actual bond plus one months rent
[b] For owners, mortgage repayments of $7.1 and rates and maintenance and repairs; for public tenants, actual rent; for private tenants, actual rent $23.4 plus maintenance and repairs
Source: Kendig (1981: 20, table 2.2 based on 1977 Survey of Movers)

[9] Yet half the renters had enough income to meet loan repayments on bank terms and almost had enough for repayments on loans; the point being that 'unless households on low incomes have access to heavily subsidized finance, the financial barriers to home ownership are prohibitive and many are forced to rent permanently' (Kendig, 1981: 72).

variance[10] which enables the user to discriminate amongst a number of predictor variables, in order of importance of the statistical contribution that they make to an explanation of tenure selection. 'Wealth', or size of the assets held by the household, turns out to be by far the most important discriminant of tenure choice (figure 6.4): only five per cent of those with less than \$A1,500 worth of assets could afford to buy, as opposed to 68 per cent of those with assets over the amount. Households simply cannot purchase without the deposit. The other constraint that operates is total household income, rather than the head of household's income, since the lump sum necessary to pay a deposit and transaction costs must be accompanied by a flow of income sufficient to meet mortgage repayments. This reflects a significant shift in the policy of lending institutions in Australia because, in the past, they have been reluctant to take a wife's earnings into account. Thus the home ownership rate is noticeably higher amongst the 'asset-rich' households with higher incomes (73 per cent against 45 per cent). Note that it is only at this subsequent stage that life cycle plays any part in tenure selection (figure 6.4), leaving a group of households preferring to rent because it enabled them to travel, save for a better home, or plan for marriage.

Financial standing and place of residence

Housing costs are neither uniformly distributed in space nor maintain

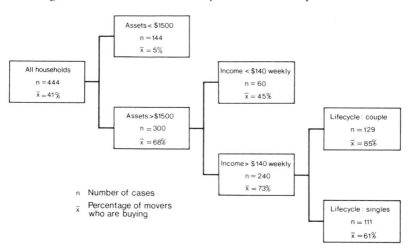

Figure 6.4 Discriminants of tenure choice amongst Adelaide home buyers
Source: Kendig, 1981: 136

[10] Called AID (Automatic Interaction Detector), the method was developed by Sonquist and Morgan (1970). The first split in figure 6.4 shows which variable is the most important determinant of tenure and which cut-off value for the variable best separates renters and buyers.

constant proportions through time: table 6.8, for example, suggests that even when regional disparities in wage rates are taken into account, local economic conditions and housing markets produce differences that can be of real consequence to intending home buyers. In the early 1970s house price inflation peaked in the London and Sydney regions, whereas the most recent acceleration of housing prices in Australia has been confined to Sydney (table 6.8). As to be expected the impact of these differing pressures on the local housing market also shows up in each of the other submarkets: for example, in 1975–6 the rents fixed by housing commissions in Australia ranged from a low of $A13.55 in Adelaide, to a high of $A19.28 in Melbourne. Likewise, the average yearly rentals fixed by rent officers in England in 1978 registered the following differences: around £310–15 for Yorkshire, Greater Manchester and Lancashire; £458 in Devon and Cornwall; £499 in Surrey and Sussex; and £594 in Greater London (Hillman, 1980: 17).

Spatial variations in the structure of housing prices *within* cities generally reflect both the replacement cost of the building and the value of the site. The value of the site combines estimates of its physical endowment, together with the level of amenity found within the surrounding environment, with an evaluation of relative accessibility to jobs and services of all kinds. Because households have to pay a premium for the convenience of centrality – it may take the form of high density living – income acts as a locational liberator. Even the most casual observer will have established that in the long-run competitive land and housing markets deliver the best locations and environments to the wealthy. In David Harvey's (1973: 171) memorable phrase, 'The rich can command space whereas the poor are trapped in it.'

Take the way first-time home buyers with modest savings and incomes have commonly been assigned to a fringe location within Australian

Table 6.8 The cost of home ownership in British and Australian cities, 1971–80

| | \multicolumn{5}{c}{House price/earnings ratio} | | | | |
	UK	Greater London	Sydney	Melbourne	Adelaide
1971	3.20	3.67	n.a.	n.a.	3.37
1972	3.72	5.05	n.a.	n.a.	3.27
1973	4.51	5.94	n.a.	n.a.	3.74
1974	4.43	5.20	4.6	4.2	3.82
1975	3.73	4.12	4.1	3.6	3.68
1976	3.40	3.64	3.8	4.0	3.66
1977	3.34	3.60	3.7	3.5	3.58
1978	3.37	3.65	3.6	3.3	3.36
1979	3.67	4.14	3.8	3.0	3.25
1980	n.a.	n.a.	4.9	2.9	3.10

Sources: Greater London Council 1980: 32, table 3.2; Australian Bureau of Statistics (1981b); Real Estate Institute of Australia

capital cities. They were enticed there solely by the availability of cheap housing, slipping down the land price curve until they found their level in the market. Whilst this represented the best way of minimizing their costs of entry (fixed), it earned with it a continuing impost in the form of higher movement costs (variable). It is interesting that many hopeful home buyers in the London region have been similarly constrained to make the same 'choice': 'one way in which potential borrower's overcome deficiency of current income which unacceptably restricts their borrowing, is to substitute higher travel costs for loan repayment charges to find cheaper properties in more distant locations' (Pennance and Gray, 1968: 58).

Harvey has likened the residential assignment process to a space packing problem: if the unoccupied housing stock (vacancies and newly constructed dwellings) represents the geographical disposition of housing opportunities within the city (n), then the most desirable dwellings and sites are going to be taken by the wealthiest class of households (1). The amounts they offer for the highest quality housing set the level of prices within the market. It follows that once the most desirable housing has been removed from the market the next income class (2) will have to make their selections from a housing stock reduced by $n-1$ dwellings. With the second income class clearing the market the vacant stock will shrink even further to $(n-1) + (n-1-2)$ dwellings and so on. . . . Harvey's idealization of the residential assignment process bears a resemblance to the 'Tiebout hypothesis' (Tiebout, 1956) which relates social segregation in the US metropolis to unequal public provision at the local government level. The assumption is that, given the patchiness of public provision on an area-by-area basis within American cities, homogeneous groupings of public goods within local jurisdictions will attract households that are stratified by income class. Indeed, there are now a number of studies that link residential choice and the stratification of households with variations in the taxes levied and services provided at a local level (Eberts and Gronberg, 1981; Reschovsky, 1979). Thus the housing and residential opportunities presented to the lowest income classes by this 'free' market form of allocation must always be the residue: that is, the least desirable stock in the most marginal locations. How these households that are relegated by the earnings system to the bottom of the housing market actually fare, in practice, relies mainly upon the efficacy of state housing provision in capitalist societies. As a general rule, the meaner the economic circumstances of the household, the greater its reliance upon the public housing sector. It is in this context that locational considerations tend to become an afterthought. So before broaching the subject of inequity in urban land and housing markets, I will show how the housing opportunities of the poorest households in the community can be severely circumscribed by state housing policy and the enabling institutions on the supply-side.

The institutional and policy framework

The field of housing studies has expanded 'exponentially' during the last decade or so. There is no pretence that this literature can be comprehensively reviewed here; in the event, it would amount to a duplication of the heart of that fine text on *Housing and residential structure* by Bassett and Short (1980: 55–154). I propose to distill the essence of 'housing access' from a selection of these materials, expressly with an eye to the locational repercussions of institutional arrangements and policy measures. This is an area which is complicated by the broader issues of autonomy in relation to housing management, shifting attitudes to public expenditure, and the capriciousness of capital markets. The housing sector cannot be isolated from the economy as a whole. Nor is housing policy immune from the lateral impacts of policy drawn up in other government departments, which frequently means that housing managers are frustrated in the pursuit of objectives by process beyond their control. The fact is that housing often becomes the battlefield for intersector scurmishes within the capitalist economy to the lasting detriment of families in need of housing assistance.

The organization of housing

Housing is not really a single market but a number of submarkets that are highly interdependent. These submarkets are partitioned by tenure and sector, namely private owner; private rental; public rental; public purchase. While the ratios between these submarkets are liable to fluctuate with changes in economic conditions and government policy, the long-term trend in Australia, the US and the UK has been marked by a gradual extension of home ownership within the private sector. For example, between 1960 and 1973 dwellings in owner-occupation rose from 42 to 52 per cent of the total stock in the UK, whilst dwellings rented in the public sector rose from 26 to 31 per cent, and privately rented dwellings declined from 32 to 17 per cent (Niner and Watson, 1979: 341). The most recent breakdown available to the author (table 6.9) says as much about the commitment to home ownership of successive governments in each of the countries under consideration as it does about the ability of families to pay for it. Although home ownership rates in Britain still lag behind the equivalent Australian and US rates a considerable shift in housing priorities has occurred since a bi-partisan position was adopted on owner-occupation in the mid-1960s (Community Development Project, 1976). Nonetheless, housing provision in the UK remains much more collectivistic than in Australia, or the United States, where the public housing sector can only be described as stillborn (table 6.9).

Table 6.9 Organization of the housing market in the UK, Australia and United
States (percentages)

	Owner occupation			Rental		
	Outright owner	Mortgagor	Total	Government	Private	Total
UK 1978[b]	23	30	53	34	13	47
Australia 1980[c]	38.3	33.6	71.9	4.8	20.2	25[a]
United States 1976[d]	27.1	37.6	64.7	1.6	33.7	35.3
United States 1979[e]	–	–	66	–	–	34

[a] 3.1 per cent of private households occupy accommodation rent-free, or on some other basis
Sources: [b] Tenure of households, General Household Survey, 1978 (Central Statistical Office, 1980: 197)
[c] Survey of Housing Occupancy and Costs, 1980 (Australian Bureau of Statistics, 1981b: 4)
[d] Annual Housing Survey (Bureau of the Census, 1978)
[e] Sternlieb and Hughes (1980: 13); estimates

It is not too much of an exaggeration to describe the assortment of
institutions that have evolved to provide housing as a labyrinth. While the
responsibility for the framing of national housing policy normally rests
with central government, the execution is largely a matter for the States in
Australia and the US, and municipal councils in the United Kingdom.
Cullingworth (1979: 1) estimates that in the UK, for example, there are:
460 local government bodies; developmental agencies like the new town
corporations, the Scottish Special Housing Association and some 2,000
housing associations; financial institutions such as the Public Works Loans
Board, the Housing Corporation and 380 building societies, as well as the
joint stock banks and the insurance companies. These are joined in the
private sector by real estate agencies; countless landlords, ranging from
sizeable companies to individuals owning a few houses or sub-letting part
of their own dwelling; and some 88,000 building and construction firms.
Because this distribution of organizational power is so complex housing
opportunities vary greatly, 'not only according to the distribution of
income, but also according to the constraints which differing geographical
locations place upon organizations and people, and according to the
varying ideologies of the agencies on which the government's policies
depend for their implementation' (Harloe *et al.*, 1974: 169). I will look
briefly in turn at the public sector institutions followed by those operating
in the private sector.

Public sector institutions and access

Most of the important studies of access to public housing have emanated
from the United Kingdom (English, 1979; Gray, 1976, 1979; Lambert *et
al.*, 1978; Murie *et al.*, 1976) which is not especially surprising given the
amount of council housing in the UK. These studies have helped to
document the tremendous range of accommodation and environments
that constitute council housing. Even though council housing tenants are

drawn largely from the working class, the scale of the programme has contributed to a perceptible overlapping of income and class between tenures (Holmans, 1978). In 1971, 81 per cent of council households were headed by manual workers (against 58 per cent for all tenures); likewise, by 1976 the sector contained 43 per cent of all the households in England and Wales in the bottom quarter of the income distribution (Gray, 1979: 200–1). All the same, the entrance rules have tended to favour large families and elderly people and this has up until now worked against large numbers of single, working and childless couples becoming local authority tenants.[11] It seems that now demand for council housing has eased somewhat, 'determining which applicants shall have particular houses' has taken over from 'who shall become council tenants' as the chief concern of housing allocation in many local authority areas of Britain (English, 1979: 117):

> Housing departments usually attempt to meet individual needs and desires in terms of nearness to employment or relatives, for example, but this does little to counteract general preferences. A few areas have draconian policies of severely restricting choice by automatically offering the first suitable vacancy (from an official point of view) to the applicant at the top of the waiting list with substantial penalties for refusal. This procedure would not generally be regarded as good housing management practice and it does not appear to be widespread. In the past desert, through the process of grading, very often determined who should be allocated the best housing; but this practice seems to be diminishing in importance.[12]

The assignment of public housing tenants to a particular part of the city is an inseparable aspect of the decision, 'Who shall have which house?', while the postwar insistence on containing the outward growth of British cities (Hall *et al.*, 1973) meant that much of the housing lost through clearance was replaced *in situ* at higher densities, some of the council 'overspill' was constructed at the edge of the built-up area. Here, if they were unfortunate, the new arrivals could face a battery of problems that

[11] Some of the sternest critics now claim – unfairly perhaps – that the council sector in Britain has become a welfare net for those unwilling or unable to provide themselves with adequate private sector housing: 'from creditable and idealistic origins it has descended to a miserly output of often poorly designed and constructed homes for "underprivileged" groups (Community Development Project, 1976: 28).

[12] This post-dates the period of comprehensive clearance and renewal (1954–73) when 1.5 million dwellings were demolished or closed in Great Britain (Cullingworth 1979: 81–6). Naturally the obligation to rehouse displaced residents led to some invidious practices such as 'grading' (Lambert *et al.*, 1978: 50–5), 'queue-jumping' (Gray, 1976: 39), and the 'dumping' of problem tenants in other sub-standard housing awaiting demolition or on unpopular estates (Gray, 1979: 225).

arguably find their most exquisite expression on the housing commission estates ringing Australia's largest cities. High land prices, an insistence on assembling parcels of land large enough to return scale economies in estate development, and a fixation on the part of Australian governments with home ownership have 'resulted in the creation of foresaken suburban wastelands on the far periphery of metropolitan settlement' (Mendelsohn, 1979; 273).

The siting of public housing in the United States is a reversal of the locational principle that has been so assiduously pursued until recently by the housing commissions in Australia: if public tenants in Australia are urban outcasts, in the US they have been interned in austere high-rise blocks on small downtown sites. These massive housing complexes are commonly bereft of support services while management, for too long, did little to encourage a sense of permanency or community. Because such a high proportion of public housing tenants are nonwhite in the US, to many critics urban renewal and the associated rehousing programmes have smacked of a cordon sanitaire:

> The U.S. Commission on Civil Rights found (in 1967) that of the quarter of a million low-rent housing units that have been built by city public housing authorities in the nation's 24 largest metropolitan areas, in only one – Cincinnati – has the city housing authority been permitted to build outside the central city. There, the authority has provided low rent units in a Negro enclave in the suburbs. (Sloane, 1968)

Housing allocation procedures are such that applicants with the least acute needs tend to obtain acceptable housing in the more convenient locations, while destitute households have to accept housing on the estates with high turnover and vacancy rates (that is, those that concentrate households with multiple deprivations and attract undue stigmatization). The most notorious examples of these 'hard-to-let' council housing estates in the UK, which were constructed in the 1960s to Parker-Morris standards, include the massive Hulme Estate in inner Manchester, the 'Piggeries' in the Everton district of Liverpool, and Killingworth which is located on the edge of Newcastle upon Tyne (Taylor, 1979). Anyone seeking American parallels are directed to Lee Rainwater's (1973) devastating sociological portrait of Pruitt-Igoe, a high-rise public housing tract in St Louis that was finally dynamited less than two decades after its construction in 1954. Although there is nothing to compare with this experience in Australia, some of the earliest high-rise estates constructed in Melbourne's inner suburbs have vacancy rates exceeding 15 per cent, whilst a number of the outlying housing commission suburbs have an overrepresentation of deprived households.

In the sphere of housing management both Gray (1979: 204–9) and Cullingworth (1979: 8–14) appear to be in general agreement that local authorities in Britain cannot be accurately described as agents of central government:

> Perhaps of all the aspects of state housing, it is management which, in an immediate sense, allows local authorities the greatest degree of discretion and autonomy from external forces, and in particular central government. In this field local authorities operate with a minimum of legal control, the legislative framework being phrased in such a way as to allow considerable freedom in deciding who should be housed, when and where. (Gray, 1979: 205)

Beyond this, at any one time a good proportion of the state and local governments are going to be of a different political complexion to the central administration.[13] That this political difference between two levels of government can have an affect upon access to public housing is dramatically illustrated in the case of policy relating to the sale of council housing. In March 1979, the Environment Secretary in the British Labour government, Peter Shore, announced drastic curbs on the sale of council houses which had risen to 27,000 in 1978.[14] Labour housing policy in Britain was then overturned in the 1980 Housing Act by the incoming Conservative government.

Although the Tories are philosophically committed to a reduction in the level of direct public intervention, Murie (1982) is emphatic that the series of measures undertaken in 1979–81 does involve direct intervention. The 1980 Housing Act introduced a new subsidy system under which the Secretary of State can determine the increase in local contribution (rent and rates) to be assumed in calculating the housing subsidy for local authori-

[13] Wilcox (with Richards, 1977: 27) shows that in the case of the London region, Labour and Conservative controlled all levels of central government, the GLC, and the London Boroughs Association in only six of the years between 1965 and 1976.

[14] Although Cullingworth (1979: 107) points to 'changing attitudes', the objections to the sale of public housing stock are manifold: (a) if houses are sold at a discount the original public investment cannot be recouped, which leaves an economically emaciated tenant population to carry the debt burden; (b) it reduces the scope for cross-subsidization between the poorest and better-off council tenants; (c) sales to low-income tenants on 100 per cent mortgages, subsidized interest, long-term loans and the like are financed at the expense, perhaps, of rent rebates; (d) to segregate the most deprived households in a single identifiable sector of the housing system is socially divisive; and, (e) not only does it deplete the number of vacant dwellings for letting to the needy, but local authorities are left with the stock that will not sell because it is unattractive or in the wrong location. It can be said in relation to the last point that by 1977, Australian public housing had sold about 34 per cent of total completions from 1945, with sales often as high as 80 per cent on the NSWHC and VHC estates enjoying prime locations (Jones, 1980: 184). This alienation of inner area stock has contributed to the spatial bias in public housing within Australian cities (Badcock, 1982).

ties. (The effect of this in 1981–82 was to increase council rents throughout England by about £2.95 per week per dwelling.) Also, the first Chapter of the 1980 Housing Act included a Right to Buy clause impelling councils to sell their housing stock in all localities: 'In anticipation of some opposition from local authorities, the right to buy provisions were backed by powers for the Secretary of State to intervene, carry out and charge for the implementation of council house sales in any local authority in certain circumstances' (Murie, 1982: 160). Most importantly, the Conservatives wielded the Housing Strategy and Investment Programme (HIP) 'weapon' much more ruthlessly than their Labour predecessors, who introduced it in 1977 in order to control the level of capital expenditure in housing. As a result of the Exchequer's tighter control over all housing capital expenditure, local authority dwelling completions in England, for example, fell from 105,164 in 1976 to 67,138 in 1980. Thus, in 1980, for the first time, Britain's council housing sector actually declined (by 8,000 dwellings). According to Murie (1982: 157), the period 1979–81 'marks an important watershed in the development of the British housing market'. The Conservative's policy of 'privatization', which envisages a residual role for council housing, promises in the long run substantially to affect the nature of the housing service and patterns of inequality in housing (Murie, 1982: 170).

The power of central government to stymie housing programmes at the state and local levels has become more and more apparent in recent years as the shadow caste by the public expenditure crisis in the capitalist economies has lengthened. The quite massive programmes of public rental construction that had been sustained through the fifties and sixties in Britain and Australia began to falter in the early 1970s.[15] In the period 1968–73, the production of council housing was halved in the UK. This coincided with the diversion of investment and labour into home improvement; an involuntary cutting back of council housing targets as cost yardsticks (an adherence to which Exchequer grants had been made conditional in 1968), and costs moved further part; and a steady rise in the cost of borrowing capital funds (Mellor, 1977: 112–14). This general picture was duplicated in Australia in 1973–74, with two added complications: a housing boom was slowing the rate at which the state housing authorities could let tenders; and 'uncontrollable' land prices were limiting access to home ownership, thereby placing more pressure on the waiting list for public housing. The *coup de grâce* for state and local government housing programmes came with vigorous Treasury and Exchequer cutbacks. This has made the task of servicing the debts incurred on capital development increasingly difficult, if not impossible in the face of rising interest rates, and in the UK over 70 per cent of local authority housing

[15] About 3.7 million dwellings were constructed by the local authorities between 1956 and 1973 in the UK (to partially replace the 1.4 million demolished in slum clearance schemes).

revenue is absorbed by debt charges, and only 30 per cent of that redeems the capital with the balance consisting of interest repayments (Lambert *et al.*, 1978: 151). At the very time when most public housing authorities in Britain and Australia have unprecedented permanent debts the central governments are shifting fiscal responsibility from their treasuries to the local state (under the Housing Finance Act, 1972, and the Commonwealth States Housing Agreement 1978–81, respectively). The effect is to transfer to public tenants a large part of the cost of building programmes that was previously considered a central government responsibility. The White paper (HMSO, 1980) on *The Government's Expenditure Plans 1980–81 to 1983–84* reveals just how far the British Government intends to go in winding back expenditure on public housing: the intention is that housing expenditure as a proportion of total government expenditure should fall from a level of 10.0 per cent in 1974–75, to 3.91 per cent in 1983–84. This represents a decline from £7,154 million to £2,790 million in 1979 prices, or a reduction of 61 per cent. Likewise, the Commonwealth outlay to the Australian states for public housing expenditures has fallen from a peak of $A652.2 million in 1974–75 to $A231.2 million in 1979–80. The Victorian Housing Commission's predicament as a result of central government stringency is fairly typical: during the financial year, 1981–82, it received $58.4 million under the Commonwealth States Housing Agreement, and yet had to meet interest and redemption payments of more than $61 million.

Private sector institutions and access

On the whole, the private housing sector in countries like Britain, USA and Australia is dominated by an enabling framework set up and regulated by the state to facilitate home ownership. It matters, therefore, that housing provision in the main private sector submarkets – owner occupancy and renting – can be disrupted: in the case of new housing by blockages in the production pipeline; capriciously, as a result of imbalances and bottlenecks within each of the submarkets; and, more generally, by a scarcity of capital for producers and credit for consumers. This ties output and turnover in the private housing sector to the state of the capital market, especially the institutions that lend housing finance.[16] Access to private housing, therefore, is largely determined at two levels. It reflects the general availability of housing finance, of which interest rates are the best barometer. Because of the considerable scope for manipulating the money supply and pursuing other public expenditure objectives the

---

[16] Financial intermediaries include building societies, insurance companies and investment trusts which, together with landlords, enable the producers of housing to recover their investment and households to consume the housing while they are paying it off; that is, they purchase a flow of housing services as well as property rights.

state must accept a measure of the responsibility for a scarcity of housing funds (Townsend, 1980). The banking system and financial intermediaries operate within the parameters set by Treasury. The interest rate is the mechanism which, completely dispassionately, determines the distribution of housing finance amongst competing income groups; that is, while each rise in the mortgage rate makes access to home ownership more difficult for *all* households, it eliminates those would-be home buyers with the lowest incomes from the market altogether. Selectivity also operates at another level in the private housing sector. If, as happens in Australia, government regulation holds mortgage rates below the general rates for borrowing then the lending institutions must resort to a method of non-price rationing for allocating home loans. There is ample evidence to show that in fixing rules to minimize what they perceive as lending risk, many of the lower income groups are excluded from home ownership (Carter, 1978: 55). In addition to this, there is also an undeniable restriction of access that can be traced to the discriminatory practices of real estate agents and landlords.

Broad structural differences exist in the home mortgage markets of the UK, Australia and the United States. The United Kingdom has a three-tiered system. The building societies, which have a commanding position in the market (table 6.10), usually charge a single cartelized mortgage rate to all borrowers that meet their eligibility criteria. By borrowing short and lending long they offend a cardinal principle of sound finance. The banks and insurance companies, on the other hand, shorten the repayment period and charge higher mortgage rates. In Karn's (1976: 18–24) opinion: 'One only slightly overstates the position in saying that governments and non-profit bodies (including the building societies) cater for the . . . average situation, the easy case. It is the private market which mops up the exception, the abnormal, the difficult.' Karn's reference to government involvement in mortgage lending is to the local authorities, which constitute the third tier of housing finance in Britain. Despite her implied criticism, local authority lending has at times been especially important for aspiring buyers with low and uncertain incomes or those who want to buy

Table 6.10 Mortgages granted for owner-occupation, England and Wales, 1972–75

	1972		1973		1974		1975	
	000s	%	*000s*	%	*000s*	%	*000s*	%
Building societies	617.8	79.7	494.5	76.7	390.7	77.0	597.4	80.9
Local authorities	45.2	5.8	59.4	9.2	14.9	14.9	102.0	13.8
Banks	89.0	11.5	64.1	9.9	3.4	3.4	17.7	2.4
Insurance	23.3	3.0	27.0	4.2	4.7	4.7	21.5	2.9
Total	775.3	100.0	645.0	100.0	507.6	100.0	738.6	100.0

Source: Greater London Council (1980: 33, table 3.4)

old properties.[17] However, this source of home finance has almost dried up since the peak in 1975 when over 100,000 mortgages were advanced by local authorities (table 6.10).

Compared to Britain the financial market for home purchase in the United States is 'a Gordian knot composed of a multiplicity of institutions with many threads of federal and state legislation' (Bassett and Short, 1980: 92). Savings and loans associations (S&Ls), which follow the commercial banks and life insurance companies as the third largest financial institutions in the US, are the biggest source of mortgages with 56.9 per cent of housing loans nationally in 1978. Next come the commercial banks (17.4 per cent), mortgage companies (15.6 per cent), and life insurance companies (1.5 per cent) which generally seek out the higher yielding investments. In an effort to improve the access of households with moderate incomes the federal government underwrites the subsidized loans made by the non-profit S&Ls (through the Federal Home Loan Mortgage Corporation), and provides support to the commercial banks and insurance industry (through the Federal National Mortgage Association). Chastened by the reaction to their public housing programme (Anderson, 1967; Wilson, 1967) Federal Housing Administrations in the US turned increasingly to the subsidization of private lending as a way of improving the access of low- and moderate-income households to housing finance. About 70–80,000 loans granted to low- and moderate-income households by the Farmer's Home Administration were underwritten annually by the Federal Government through the 1970s (table 6.11). Before the FHA scheme, mortgage loans covered as little as one half to two thirds of the purchase price which meant that families commonly had to take out second, if not third, mortgages to make the settlement. With FHA insurance available against mortgage defaulting the lending institutions offered more favourable terms. Apart from the insuring of private mortgages, from time to time specially tailored programmes were also devised like the Section 221 (d) 3, which funded a below market-interest-rate (BMIR), and Section 235 subsidies (see Bourne, 1981: 196–97).

The structure of the house finance market is different again in Australia with the savings (41 per cent) and trading (16 per cent) banks, and building societies (30 per cent) dominating overall, despite variations from state to state (Australian Bureau of Statistics, 1981c). Perhaps the most important change in the structure of Australian housing finance has been the launching of savings bank subsidiaries by the major trading banks, and their remarkable growth since the mid-1950s along with the expansion of home ownership (Kemeny, 1981).

---

[17] In 1978, for example, 85 and 93 per cent of local authority loans in England and the Greater London Council area were for pre-1919 dwellings compared with 23 per cent from building societies throughout the country (Greater London Council, 1980: 30).

Table 6.11 Federally subsidized housing production in the US, 1969–77 (new construction starts and rehabilitated units)

Housing production/programmes	Fiscal year								
	1969	1970	1971	1972	1973	1974	1975	1976	1977
Total subsidized production	202,700	328,010	482,970	429,790	331,830	171,660	128,840	137,840	217,440
HUD[a]	166,950	276,970	397,400	338,190	234,170	90,520	46,540	51,130	130,030
FmHA[b]	35,750	51,220	85,570	91,600	97,660	81,140	82,300	86,110	87,410
1–4 Family, total	48,120	128,280	233,110	211,990	154,110	86,480	70,110	82,020	74,740
HUD[a]	15,050	80,320	150,180	124,940	65,920	15,110	5,080	7,960	4,610
Sec. 235	7,980	70,180	137,590	113,300	57,640	8,420	1,800	3,200	3,080
Sec. 115/312	5,760	8,760	12,250	11,600	8,260	6,680	3,200	4,740	1,630
Sec. 221(h)	1,320	1,470	340	40	20	10	80	20	–
FmHA[b]	33,070	47,960	83,930	87,050	88,190	71,370	65,030	74,060	70,180
Low income	n.a.	n.a.	n.a.	61,730	56,680	38,070	46,400	49,680	46,120
Moderate income	n.a.	n.a.	n.a.	25,310	31,520	33,300	18,630	24,380	24,010
Multifamily, total	154,580	199,730	249,860	217,800	177,720	85,180	58,730	55,220	142,700
HUD[a]	151,900	196,470	247,220	213,250	168,250	75,410	41,480	43,170	125,420
Public housing	80,290	87,880	99,700	53,930	36,700	26,150	17,100	11,110	12,020
Sec. 8	–	–	–	–	–	–	–	11,750	106,310
Sec. 236	1,000	91,390	106,980	113,060	95,070	37,090	17,240	16,570	6,640
Rent supplement	16,640	22,530	16,800	12,480	11,740	4,520	2,510	1,380	390
State asst. projects	3,410	1,800	9,860	28,690	23,530	7,360	4,410	2,360	n.a.
Sec. 221 (d) (3) BMIR	43,590	26,870	11,640	3,880	520	120	–	–	–
FmHA[b]									
Without Sec. 8 asst.	2,680	3,260	2,640	4,550	9,470	9,770	17,270	12,050	17,280

[a] Department of Housing and Urban Development
[b] Farmer's Home Administration
Source: Compiled by D. Liskotin for Sternlieb and Hughes (1980: 22, exhibit 9)

The investment strategies of all housing finance institutions are notoriously conservative, motivated as they are by risk aversion. Consequently, the selection criteria utilized by the lending institutions give preferential treatment to households with the greatest savings and favour specified types of housing and areas of the city over others. These include unnecessarily large deposit requirements, ceilings on the loan-to-valuation ratio and the proportion of income to be committed to repayments, and conservative valuations of properties (Carter, 1978: 55). The discriminatory effect of these considerations can be seen in some statistics supplied by the State Savings Bank of Victoria (Garlick, 1978): in 1976–77 only 33 per cent of SSBV loans were granted to applicants with income equivalent to average weekly earnings or less; conversely, 67 per cent of SSBV loans are granted to a group representative of only 33 per cent of wage and salary earners. A 1980 survey of 5,862 applications for housing finance conducted in Victoria (Institute of Applied Economic and Social Research, 1981) indicates that 54.2 per cent of the unsuccessful applications involved failure to meet eligibility requirements. Reasons for the rejection of applicants included: 'poor security offered' (188); 'savings disqualification' (170); 'insufficient equity' (68); and, 'inability to meet repayments' (63). In only seven per cent of cases was the rejection attributed solely to a lack of sufficient funds on the part of the *lender*. While in the UK:

> potential borrowers likely to be penalized by building society rules are those who can only afford, or only wish to buy, old (pre-1919) property, especially if this requires improvement or repair or is in an area with doubtful future; those who cannot provide a 10 or 15 per cent deposit; those whose incomes are low relative to the amount they need to borrow; and manual workers lacking skill who are thought to be particularly vulnerable to redundancy or loss of overtime and who lack assured incremental salary scales. The chances of all 'marginal' cases are worse when funds are scarce and 'safe' lending opportunities exceed the potential supply. (Niner and Watson, 1979: 333)

This has gone hand-in-hand with 'redlining', or the black-listing of selected parts of British cities, which effectively debars prospective property holders in these areas from qualifying for building society loans (Boddy, 1976; Williams, 1978). This deliberate disinvestment on the part of lending institutions is thought to be a much underrated factor in the deterioration of many inner city neighbourhoods on both sides of the Atlantic. In the USA it has prompted the passing of legislation by Congress – the Home Mortgage Disclosure Act of 1975 – that now requires all depository institutions to disclose the number and value of all mortgage loans in each SMSA. Analyses based on this evidence for a number of American cities make it clear that the mortgage lending activity that does not attract FHA insurance 'is very low in the older, low- and moderate-income, minority, and racially changing urban areas' (Tomer, 1980: 501). However, the federally assisted mortgage lending, under the 235 programme introduced in 1968,[18] appears to be higher in census tracts undergoing racial transition (leaving it open to interpretation as a catalyst to neighbourhood decline).

One of the major problems facing all potential borrowers of housing finance is that the home mortgage market is inherently unstable because the volume of lending largely depends upon the success of the intermediaries in attracting depositors' funds. In 1973–74 when the minimum bank lending rate in the UK climbed to 13 per cent, it was accompanied by a home mortgage drought. This pattern was repeated in Australia during the first part of the 1980s. The rising mortgage rates in Australia were due to a tightening of the money supply coupled with the state governments' promotion of resource development. In their bid to attract development capital for the 1980s the state government utilities and semi-government authorities offered higher interest rates than the savings banks or building societies. As a result of these pressures on mortgage interest rates: only about half of Australia's households were able to afford to buy a home at the time – down from about 80 per cent towards the end of the 1960s (CSIRO, 1981); the number of home loans fell; mortgage defaulting increased alarmingly; and, the lower income households and young home buyers were allocated a declining share of housing funds.

Most of these households 'mark time' in the *private rental sector* – some continue to live with parents – thereby putting additional pressure on a declining form of tenure. This withering of the private rental sector began at the turn of century and is characteristic of the housing systems of all three countries under consideration. In the UK, between 1951–77 alone, the number of dwellings rented from private owners fell from 6.3 million to 2.2 million. Because of its age[19] and poor condition much of the private

[18] Under the 235 programme the FHA was provided with a 'special risk insurance fund' and authorized to issue insurance to low- and moderate-income families whose irregular income or credit histories prevented them from meeting normal FHA credit standards and to insure mortgages in older, declining urban areas (Fried, 1972: 70). Prior to 1968, when the conditions for FHA backed mortgages were relaxed, the 40 per cent of the population whose housing needs were greatest received only 11 per cent of FHA insured loans. The programme, however, is not without its problems. Thousands of Section 235 houses in unsafe and poorly serviced neighbourhoods have been abandoned by families who found that they could not afford to renovate them or meet the repayments. Moreover, Aaron (1972: 140) contends that some of the assistance has gone to middle-income families eligible for ordinary federal subsidies or mortgage insurance. For these reasons, in 1973 the Nixon administration shifted the emphasis from supply (or construction) subsidies like Section 235 grants to cash assistance (or demand subsidies) for eligible households (table 6.11).

[19] In 1971, in the UK, at least 68 per cent of households renting 'unfurnished' and 51 per cent renting 'furnished' lived in dwellings built before 1919 (Murie *et al.*, 1976: 189).

rental stock in British and US cities has suffered the depredations of comprehensive clearance programmes, abandonment, and conversion. Likewise, state intervention at the local and national level has been directed at the private landlord partly because much of the unfit housing was concentrated in the sector, and partly because of the patent need for tenant protection.[20] The typical response of landlords to rent controls, debilitating property taxes, and falling profitability,[21] whether in Britain (Murie *et al.*, 1976: 179–89) the US (Stegman, 1972: 9–42), or Australia (Kendig, 1979), has been undermaintenance of their properties thereby hastening the deterioration of the private rental stock and aggravating housing stress. Elsewhere close to the centre of cities like London, Washington DC and San Francisco, Sydney and Melbourne, private rental housing in a retrievable condition has been improved and converted for owner occupation ('gentrification'), or transferred to public ownership ('municipalization'). Cullingworth (1979: 98) reports that a total of 3.7 million rented dwellings in England and Wales were sold to owneroccupiers between 1914 and 1975.

This contraction of the private rental sector is perturbing because of the role that it has traditionally performed in the housing system. Private tenancies have provided a basic form of shelter for the highly mobile single people and childless couples, for immigrants, the elderly, itinerants and visitors, and others who do not want, or are not admitted to others sectors (Berry, 1977). Notwithstanding the level of homelessness or housing stress detected by the Milner Holland committee in a tight private rental market like London, few other sectors offer the same ease of access:

> The one advantage of the private landlord is that he does not expect home hunters to have spent five years living in London, and perhaps two years in the borough, before putting them on a waiting list. His main test is how much the customer will pay. This is, of course, little consolation to a family with two children competing against four secretaries for a flat with a rent of £40 a week. (Wilcox with Richards, 1977: 94)

While private rental accommodation represents the easiest point of access to the housing system, to the destitute family bond money and rent in advance, or a landlord's objection to children, may become an insuperable barrier to entry. Further, because accommodation at the bottom of the

---

[20] Many of the worst excesses of harassment and eviction which culminated with the Rachman scandal in 1963 came to an end in the UK with the promulgation of a series of Rent Acts (Banting, 1979: 14–65).

[21] In periods when housing values are rising rapidly, the yield from the capital appreciation of property increases in significance, relative to rental income, as an item in the landlord's return. This can more than compensate for low or controlled rents.

housing ladder tends to be so basic, on top of economic hardship families have to cope with the added indignity of seedy, run-down surroundings, over-crowding, multiple-occupancy, and the sharing of domestic facilities. The most acute conditions are generally found in furnished lettings scattered through the nineteenth-century housing stock of London's inner boroughs (Adams, 1973; Greater London Council, 1981), and in Australia, in the boarding and lodging sector (Badcock and Urlich-Cloher, 1980; Centre for Urban Research and Action, 1979).

Because of the feebleness of the federal government's public housing programme in the US (table 6.11) most of the urban poor are renters occupying nonsubsidized units in the private housing market. The comparatively few households that do qualify for rent supplements under the Housing and Community Development Acts (1974, 1977) must rent an apartment in a building in which the landlord has agreed to participate in the Section 8 housing assistance programme. A Section 8 rent supplement is paid directly to the landlord on behalf of a low-income tenant, who would otherwise have a 'fair market rent' in excess of 25 per cent of total household income. Inevitably this ties the rent supplement to the 'hard-to-let' multi-family housing in the poorest neighbourhoods of US cities.

Estate agents bring buyers and sellers together, value property, arrange mortgages for buyers, and manage rental property. Their actions constitute yet another occasion in the round of positive reinforcement that buttresses existing socio-economic patterns: 'Where households *can* live is primarily determined by their income and credit rating, but estate agents play the subsidiary role of directing household's attention towards areas commensurate with their means, and discouraging them from higher- and lower-income areas' (Bassett and Short, 1980: 86). By and large the process of segmenting the housing market territorially and by price range is both an intuitive and subtle one. However, market situations do arise where estate agents adopt an active 'gatekeeping' role. Williams (1976) has placed on record the very energetic involvement of estate agents in the rejuvenation of housing in the West End boroughs of London. They were often the prime movers in the property improvement process, capitalizing on centrally funded improvement grants and persuading building societies to reinvest in 'promising' neighbourhoods. Even more extreme forms of market 'subversion' have been commonplace in the United States. There has been extensive documentation of discriminatory practices in the ethnic submarkets of American cities where 'block-busting' is a typical example of a ploy devised to hasten the exodus of whites and the deflation of property values. Once estate agents have white families on the run they 'score' from higher turnover rates and inflated markups on the properties sold to incoming blacks. In 1969, according to Davis and Donaldson (1975: 145), twelve real estate firms and salesmen were indicted for block-busting in the Brooklyn and Queens section of New York City.

That completes an admittedly selective compilation of the sorts of institutional and policy effects that prescribe the degrees of access enjoyed by households in the housing market. To recapitulate, the aim has been to show how the inequality arising from position in the labour market is reinforced by the institutional arrangements for the provision of housing in capitalist societies. Because the susceptibility of households to a range of subsidiary sources of inequality – centering on property ownership and collective provision within cities – is determined by the nature of housing occupied and where it is located, it has been necessary to expose the structural dependency of the residential assignment process.

Household destinations and the geography of social class

Up until now the residential structure of capitalist cities described in chapter 5 has tended to be taken for granted; but the household's locational decision, even when it is arbitrary, represents a response to the existing class geography of the city. The structural forces outlined above normally predispose households to social niches commensurate with their class background. Because new housing is mostly built for a single social class, it 'follows that the newer the houses, the more likely is the area to be homogeneous in social class' (Young and Willmott, 1975: 193). Apart from that it helps to remember that the ageing of the housing stock and a relatively high rate of population turnover are necessary, though not always sufficient, conditions for a dilution of social homogeneity.

Residential location has the greatest implications for social inequality in cities when the redistributive impact of imperfect land and housing markets, and the costs and benefits arising from resource provision have a distinct class, and therefore locational bias. The processes that are generative of class geographies of the city were identified in chapters 4 and 5. The most revolutionary and far-reaching development, city-wise, came with the lifting of the technological embargo on intra-urban movement in the mid-nineteenth century (Fales and Moses, 1972). This liberated manufacturing firms and the propertied classes and they ventured outwards in opposite directions, leaving the poor behind until the introduction of working mens' fares towards the end of the century. Physical distance could now be used to remove any lingering doubts about the social distance between classes by stamping social distinctions indelibly into the fabric of the city. This was the embryonic process that now, in its full maturation, is responsible for social polarization and the broad social gradients that transect capitalist cities. Because there are extensive tracts within any city either bereft of, or with run-down physical and social infrastructure, social segregation prevents poorer households from even getting close to the better quality public goods.

However the social geography of cities in capitalist societies does take *different* forms depending upon how these processes are refracted by local conditions and circumstances. In chapter 5 it was observed that for ageing industrial cities on both sides of the Atlantic the predominant class pattern is bowl-shaped: intergenerational mobility and rising aspirations have incited progressive numbers of households to leave behind the cramped, run-down factory barracks and tenement housing and move with jobs to the suburbs. This irresistible trend in the American city, where race also intercedes, has produced perhaps the most polarized, divisive, and inequitable form of socio-spatial patterning. With black suburbanization so halting and patchy due to the opposition of all-white suburbs the image of a doughnut remains valid. Australian cities, as has been seen, are fashioned differently with the lower income households tending to be pushed to the outer suburbs. Yet they remain palpably bipartite in their arrangement: primary social gradients trending northeast – southwest, east-west, and southeast-northwest can be discerned in figure 6.5 for Sydney, Melbourne, and Adelaide, respectively. While it is to be expected that the continuity of the regional social gradients should be broken by physical features and objects in the built environment, when all these irregularities are smoothed out of the social topography of cities, the core areas of the highest and lowest social classes display the greatest spatial separation.

There are no signs of this social segregation abating on a regional scale. The steady clarification of the richest and poorest suburbs alluded to by Stretton in *Ideas for Australian Cities* (1970) has since been measured by Stilwell and Hardwick (1973). Although residential upgrading near the heart of Australian cities currently leaves a temporary illusion of social heterogeneity, the long-term prospect for a genuine sharing of the inner area housing space is bleak without large-scale intervention by the housing commissions. What is less clear at present is how the dual income household phenomenon will blur the occupational status, as distinct from economic class, composition of urban sub-areas. A working wife not only enables blue collar families to purchase housing, but more of it, in a wider range of suburbs.

It is now relevant to move to a consideration of the two main circumstances whereby households with unequal earnings and assets, or perhaps even those with the same wage levels, are subjected to additional injustices as a broad consequence of where they live. This happens because in large cities the land and housing markets have a capacity to redistribute further the earnings and wealth of households (chapter 7), as does the provision of social and physical infrastructure by governments (chapter 8).

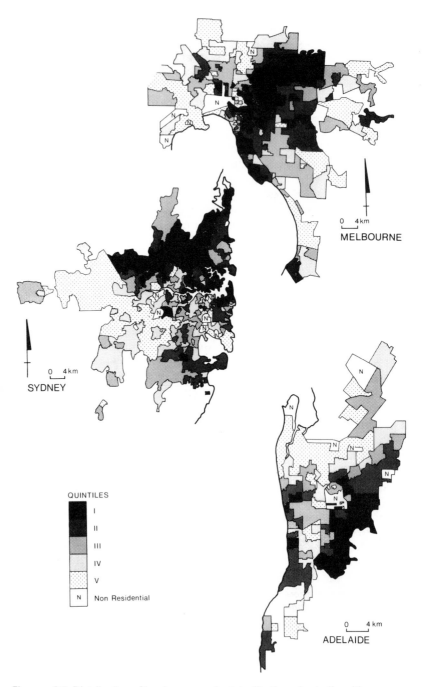

Figure 6.5 Distribution of 'socio-economic status' in three Australian cities
Source: redrawn from Logan et al., 1975: 77–79, 81–83

7

Inequality in Urban Land and Housing Markets

Introduction

Although it has been argued so far that the fountainhead of inequality in capitalist societies is found in the labour market, that by no means exhausts the fund of inequality. As the effect of institutional constraints on housing access was explored, an awareness should have been emerging that housing finance and ownership mechanisms also provide a means by which: 'banks, building societies, insurance companies, government agencies and other institutions distribute and redistribute among the citizens up to a third of affluent nations capital and up to a quarter of many people's spendable income' (Stretton, 1978b: 81). Much of the mobilization of this redistributed income and wealth takes place within the land and housing markets of cities through the institution of property. It is the redistributive function performed by property that constitutes the central preoccupation of this chapter. Australian urbanists have been made particularly aware of the considerable potential of the urban land and housing markets as mechanisms for redistribution, arguably because the effects have been exaggerated under Australian conditions. This chapter, therefore, draws heavily upon Australian materials.

Stretton (1976: 222) has been perhaps the most unequivocal: 'the structure of cities distribute costs and benefits as drastically as the structure of income does.' While it should be clear from table 6.1 that we cannot entirely agree with Stretton, nor should these effects be written off as some discussants choose to do. The redistribution of household income, even after taxation and benefits in-kind have been allocated, has its origins in the imperfections that afflict land and housing markets as well as in the complicated locational interdependencies that are found in large cities. Land, housing and capital markets are highly interactive by nature (Daly, 1982b). Indeed, much of the redistribution that is traceable to imperfections in the urban land and housing markets follows upon government intervention that has failed to understand these interdependencies and therefore to foresee the redistributive consequences of policy:

It is the irrational nature of the public finance policy of land use and development which is at the heart of our housing problems. We attempt to tax according to capacity to pay, spend this money on public services and then devise a housing policy which enables higher income groups to receive a disproportionate share of housing-related services and to pay lower and sometimes negative real prices for them. (Pat Apps quote in Dickinson, 1981: 18)

For convenience of exposition this chapter is divided into four parts; but because the mechanisms dealt with are so interdependent it goes without saying that there is considerable overlap between each of them. The first, which deals with land, will show how urban development processes may lead to transfer payments from public to private beneficiaries, while those centering on the production of land can contribute to a redistribution between housing submarkets by feeding into the new home-owners' costs of establishment. The second part will extend the consideration of housing inequity as between owners and tenants. Thirdly, there is a need to comprehend the transfer of wealth that follows when certain areas and housing submarkets outperform others to the income advantage of their participants. This reflects the import of externality effects which are capitalized into property values. The fourth topic concerns the more general structural adjustment and ensuing redistribution that accompanies changes in the price of accessibility within cities. Some of the more recent evidence will be reviewed indicating that the threat of escalating fuel prices is modifying the structure of the residential property market in Australian cities.

Production of land for housing and redistribution

Although in the course of examining the impact of externality effects on property values it should become clearer that the interaction of any segments of the land[1] and housing markets can generate transfers of real income, this section will reveal how the land conversion process can be redistributive. The production of land for urban purposes, and especially land for housing, is quite a complicated process involving the subdivision of rural holdings at the periphery of cities and the servicing of individual building allotments. That this process is redistributive owes a lot to the peculiar nature of land as a commodity and to the imperfections that seem to bedevil the land development system in the cities of market economies.

---

[1] Visualize the urban land market as a composite of three distinct but interrelated submarkets: (a) the 'fringe' land market in which rural uses are converted to urban uses; (b) the market in the established stock of land and dwellings; and, (c) the redevelopment submarket which may involve a change of use.

Redistribution is most severe at times when market pressures drive land prices ahead of gains in average income and other factor prices. These conditions, which prevailed in Britain, the United States, and Australia during the early 1970s, can give rise to the following forms of redistribution:

1 since shares of land in general are unequal, with peripheral land concentrated in the hands of a minority, a disproportionate rise in land values implies a redistribution of aggregate wealth towards the owners of land;
2 speculation, representing the most regressive and least defensible form of redistribution (investors, who generally undertake little or no improvement to their property holdings, reap windfall gains from soaring land prices and by withholding land from the market aggrevate the shortages and fuel the upward spiral);
3 'involuntary' transfers from those government departments that make extensive use of land – housing, education, hospitals, parks and recreation – to private investors;
4 in turn 'sitting' owners, developers, and speculators all stand to receive the 'unearned increment' that results from the provision of government services and community development;
5 as a part of the land-house package, inflated land prices contribute to a redistribution from new to established home owners.

A proper insight into the mechanisms responsible for these transfers has to be based upon an appreciation firstly of the distinctiveness of land as a commodity, as well as some background knowledge of the interventions that convulsed the property market in Britain and Australia in the early 1970s.

The value of land

Land is a peculiar commodity in that: it cannot be done without as all activity must occupy a space; it is fixed geographically, and unlike other capital goods cannot be moved around; although any site attributes or improvements can be modified, the land itself, in being consumed, has a definite permanency and indestructibility; ordinarily it changes hands relatively infrequently. It is because of these properties that land has such appeal as a form of accumulation. Not only does it provide the opportunity to store and accumulate wealth but 'absolute location confers monopoly privileges upon the person who has the rights to determine use at the location' (Harvey, 1973: 158–60). The determination of 'permitted use' or a plot-size ratio by a planning authority, or the outcome of 'negotiated rezoning', significantly alters the value of a site at the stroke of a pen.

Unlike most other commodities, therefore, the value of urban land is determined more by its scarcity and capacity for intensive use – or yield – than by its cost of production. In a growing urban economy producers can adjust to the demand for additional land in either of two ways – by using land more intensively or, as technological improvements permit, by expanding the urban area. The expansion that takes place on the periphery of cities pushes up the value of previously developed land closer to the centre. Hence, inner city dwellers pay a premium for accessibility and convenience. As a rule, the larger the urban area, the greater the differential between the value of undeveloped and developed land at the edge of the city. It is in this situation, as was the case in Australia throughout the 1960s and 1970s, that lower income earners seeking the cheapest building blocks for housing collide with investors bent on capturing the unearned increment or the development value of the land.[2] There is no doubt that investment in land on the fringe earmarked for urban development can be highly lucrative, even if supply and demand are in reasonable balance. Mellor (1977: 57), for example, estimates that the cost differential between rural land (with planning approval for conversion) and urban land in the UK is in excess of 1:10.

Land price inflation

The ill effect of land price inflation was most noticeable during the property booms that peaked in Britain and Australia between 1972–74. The reaction of both governments to the recession which bottomed in 1970–71 was to expand the money supply. In the case of Britain much of the additional money, which was pumped into the economy to stimulate industrial output, found its way into land and property (Massey and Catalano, 1978: 164). Apart from that, in the UK the money in circulation was swollen by US investment in the Eurodollar, whilst in Australia the collapse of mining stocks and shares in 1972 left 'idle' money searching for safer investments. The excess liquidity in both economies was soaked up by the land and housing markets. In Australia, finance companies, which had previously invested in the production side of land and housing development, lifted their lending for the purchase of housing and building blocks by 100 and 200 per cent in the 12 months between mid-1973 and mid-1974 (Cullen and Hardaker, 1975: 40). In both Australia and UK the demand for building sites was relayed through the used housing market. But because of the massive increase in market activity there was no way the supply of either raw land or serviced sites could keep pace with demand. Inevitably the rises in the price of residential land in Britain

---

[2] Until such time as public services like access roads, water, sewer and electricity mains, and schools are supplied to subdivisions the expectation of capital gains remains unmet (this is sometimes referred to as the 'hope' value).

(figure 7.1) and Australia (table 7.1) surged ahead of earnings and other costs.

Imperfections in the production of housing land

The responsibility for rises in land prices relative to other costs does not lie solely with government monetary policy. Neutze (1972) has constructed a series of indices for housing and land prices in Australia over the period of 1948–49 to 1969–70 and his measure of the site component of the land-house package rises by 274 per cent between 1952–53 and 1966–67, easily outstripping any other indicator. The available evidence (table 7.2) would seem to indicate that in Australia, followed by Britain, the cost of land

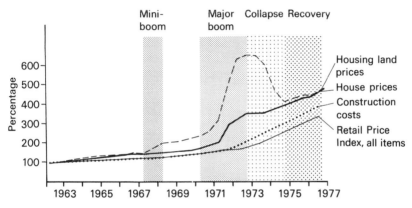

Figure 7.1 Trends in the component parts of housing costs, UK, 1963–77
Source: Hyman and Markowski, 1980: 1122

Table 7.1 Land prices, building costs, wages and consumer prices in Australia, 1970–80

	Land prices			Building costs	Average weekly earnings	Consumer price index
	Sydney	Melbourne	Adelaide			
1970–71[a]	100	100	100	100	100	100
1971–72	121	103	110	104	110	107
1972–73	172	138	136	111	120	113
1973–74	212	217	185	129	140	128
1974–75	213	242	219	157	175	149
1975–76	261	281	245	183	200	169
1976–77	264	339	286	205	225	192
1977–78	288	n.a.	257	220	251	210
1978–79	359	n.a	236	225	271	228
1979–80	493	n.a	246	233	298	251

[a] Index: 1970–71 = 100
Sources: Land prices, based on vacant lot prices: Valuation Departments; building costs, average six state capitals (per square metre): Australian Board of Statistics (ABS); average weekly earnings: ABS; consumer price index, weighted average six state capitals: ABS

has risen out of all proportion as a percentage of the total house price (Drewett, 1973b: 214). By the mid-1970s in Sydney the price of a home site accounted for almost half of the cost of an average dwelling.

Imperfections and failures in the fringe land market also lie behind the comparative escalation of prices for building allotments. With regards to British experience, Drewett (1973b: 219) puts the main reasons for the distortions down to speculation, legislation and taxation; whereas in Australia, higher standards of residential subdivision, inefficiencies in conversion and servicing, and excessive speculation all contributed to the hyperinflation in fringe land. The most immediate reason for land price inflation in Australian cities in the early 1970s was the decline in the production of allotments. This occurred to a marked degree in Adelaide in 1969–70 and 1970–71, in Perth in 1971–72, in Sydney in 1970–71, and in Melbourne from 1970 to 1972.

Building allotments in Australia also became costlier throughout the 1950s and 1960s as the standards of subdivision and servicing were raised, and with the transfer of the major responsibility for residential subdivision from the local council to private developers. These increasing developer requirements – the provision of access roads, storm water and sewerage within new subdivisions – greatly increased the initial (front end) cost of land development. During the last 15 years the land and services component of the housing package has increased from less than a quarter to about a third (Paterson, 1974: 30). According to Neutze (1978b: 73), making the developer mainly responsible for the provision of urban infrastructure has fuelled land-price inflation in three ways. Firstly, there is the direct effect with the passing on of the additional costs of development. The first of the two indirect effects was to substantially increase the holding charges on

Table 7.2 Variations in the ratio of land to total house price: Australia and the UK during the 1960s (%)

United Kingdom	1960	1965	1970
NW England	4–10	10–14	20–26
W Midlands	8–10	11–13	18–24
Outer London (W)	10–12	16–21	25–38
S Hampshire	8–12	13–14	21–25

Australia	1968	1971	1973
Adelaide	25	27	29
Brisbane	21	23	31
Hobart	27	21	26
Melbourne	29	31	32
Perth	34	38	33
Sydney	34	41	47

Sources: for UK: Developer Survey reported in Drewett (1973a: 216, table 7.2); for Australia: Housing Industry Association, 1973

unsold allotments. A South Australian report on the stabilization of land prices (Bentick, 1973) calculated that holding charges (at 10 per cent per annum) added 8.9 per cent and 14.9 per cent to the price of a site in Adelaide and Sydney respectively. The other indirect effect results from the greater involvement of local, metropolitan and state authorities in approving development applications. Although this has been necessary to eliminate a range of other inefficiencies in the production of fringe land, the added complexities and time taken to consider an application have increased the costs of development (figure 7.2). An apparent reluctance at the level of the local planning authority to designate sufficient land for residential development also led to acute shortages in Britain throughout the sixties. To make matters worse, in 1967 the Labour government set up a land commission to stabilize land prices and the release of land. Its levy division was empowered to charge a betterment levy (at 40 per cent) on all transactions resulting in a realization of development value. Perversely, between 1967 and 1970, when the land commission was dissolved by the incoming Conservative government, land prices doubled. Drewett (1973b: 223) estimates that by 1970, and discounting for inflation and devaluation, the combined effect of local and national legislation added £1,000 to the cost of each dwelling purchased in the south east (Outer Metropolitan Area) of England.

The fringe land market attracts the sort of speculative activity that can trigger off a land boom (Clawson, 1962; Harvey and Clark, 1965; Hyman and Markowski, 1980; Schmid, 1968). The speculative purchase and holding of land out of the market is guided by the speculator's and landholder's expectations of land price rises relative to holding costs, which in turn reflect the market rate of interest and the rates and tax charges payable on the land less any income which it yields (Archer, 1974: 209). What sets speculators apart from other land owners is that they acquire land primarily for resale and normally have no intention of improving it, or little interest in it as users. The really huge gains come from a change in zoning or the granting of planning permission to commence the development of a site, especially where it acquires a mono-poly value as is the case with a regional shopping centre. For instance, the speculative value of 'white' land in Britain (not designated for any use and not Green Belt) varies between one-fifth and one-tenth of the market value for land with planning permission. Drewett (1973b: 221) sets the apprecia-tion of land values above farm values at between 200 and 400 per cent. The effect of the Sydney Outline Plan, which was designed to rationalize urban development in metropolitan Sydney, was to telegraph the progressive release of land. Because it removed so much of the risk inherent in property speculation it served the purpose of a punter's 'form guide'. Besides, the speculator in broadfields knows that when serviced lots are in short supply he/she can expect the value of broadacres to rise up to three to

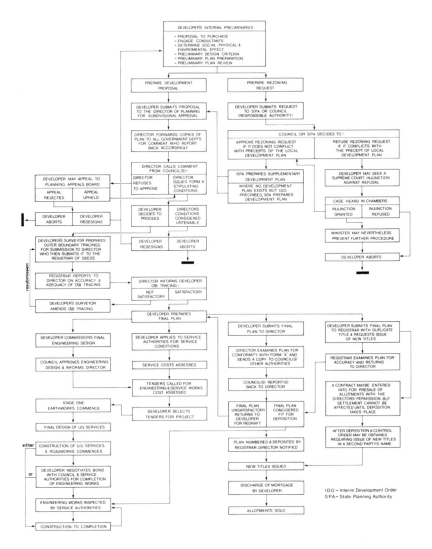

Figure 7.2 Institutional monitoring of the urban land development process in South Australia

Source: adapted from a chart compiled by Jennings Industries, Australia P/L

four times as fast as the price of allotments, just so long as servicing costs are relatively stable (Bentick, 1973). Not surprisingly the average prices of land released on the outskirts of Sydney trebled between 1969–71 (Sydney Morning Herald, 1972: 4).

Apart from directly fuelling land price inflation,[3] speculation distorts the fringe land market by holding raw land and serviced sites off the market. This eventually leads to 'leap frogging', or a proliferation of scattered subdivisions beyond the areas where land is being held off the market. As well as generating unnecessary costs by way of increased development, operating and travel costs, 'leap-frog' subdivision is one of the main causes of the sprawl around North American cities. In an interesting exercise Archer (1973) calculates that five land-owners, who held 216 hectares out of the fringe land market of Lexington, Kentucky, and received about $US317 per hectare a year for their efforts between 1956 and 1963, generated additional social costs which they did not have to pay of about $US3,345 per hectare annually on a 81 hectare leap-frog subdivision. These costs had to be born by the residents of the detached subdivision.

Because the public sector is such a large user of land in cities – possibly upwards of 40 per cent in the US and Australia (Neutze, 1977) – excessively high land prices can have a deleterious effect upon the provision of government services. With speculation rampant, public authorities seeking large sites have to operate in a market which fosters profiteering, and compete for those same sites with developers that can pass their costs on to homeseekers.[4] This situation forces massive transfer payments that the community can ill-afford from the public purse to private opportunists. In effect a housing commission, education department or hospital's board can pay grossly inflated prices and be accused of squandering taxpayers' money; or it can refuse to pay the price asked and leave new suburbs unprovided for; or it can locate the facility on less accessible, lower cost land. When the Victorian Housing Commission (VHC) shifted its emphasis in 1973 from higher density redevelopment in Melbourne's inner suburbs to lower density housing estates, it entered the fringe land market at the worst possible time. In 1973–74, the VHC paid $A20.63

---

[3] Resale rates ranging from 45 per cent in Adelaide (Wastell, 1980: 27) and 50 per cent in Wollongong (Cardew, 1977: 86), to 75 per cent in Melbourne (Paterson, 1974: 24) were reported at the height of the land boom in the early seventies in Australia. A doubling and trebling of prices between sale by a developer to the first (speculatively intentioned) owner, and the ultimate home builder was commonplace in Melbourne between 1971–74 (Paterson, 1974: 30).

[4] The NSW Housing Commission went for 18 months without acquiring a single block of land in the Sydney area in 1971–72 (Sydney Morning Herald, 1972). As an illustration, over half a 106 hectare block earmarked by the Sutherland Shire Council for low-cost public housing had been collared by speculators by the time the allocation was made for its purchase by the NSWHC in 1972.

million for 1,338 hectares which had changed hands the previous year for $A5.93 million. As a consequence of the VHC's land acquisition (and incompetence) scarce resources were wasted and fewer families housed:

> the waste of public money is . . . not limited to the purchase price but is compounded by holding charges which have added at least another $5 million and by the fact that much of the Pakenham land, for which the VHC paid $2.5 million, is subject to flooding and two-thirds of that land has since been rezoned for farming use only. To these figures need to be added the money lost by the VHC's failure to charge rent or agistment fees for the lands held, the waste of time and skill of public servants of various departments and statutory boards who have attempted in the intervening years to bring the land into productive use, and the enormous sums required to redirect headworks and services to make some of this land acceptable for residential purposes. (Sandercock, 1979: 41–2)

And now, with homebuyers showing much less interest in fringe development as fuel prices escalate, the VHC is having to market new home sites on the Goonawarra estate at Sunbury at up to $A4,800 below their cost of production (Wilson, 1981: 5).

The redistributive function of housing

The mixture of unstable land prices and interest rates that dominated the 1970s has highlighted the exceedingly regressive nature of the bipartisan policy of encouragement to home ownership in Britain, Australia and the United States. Even though horizontal redistribution does occur within each tenure division the economic significance of access to home ownership, and hence the all-important distinction between owner-occupiers and renters,[5] overshadows all other redistributive mechanisms within the housing system. When the capital appreciation of domestic property outpaces other revenue bearing investments, 'A family may gain more from the housing market in a few years than would be possible in savings from a lifetime of earnings' (Pahl, 1975: 291). Once again much of the redistributive potency of home ownership seems to flow haphazardly and inadvertently from government measures:

> These policies were intended to make owner-occupancy *possible* for most people, but they have had the effect of making anything except owner-occupancy disastrous for the people concerned. Almost anyone who opts, by choice or necessity, for not being an owner-

[5] The division in the UK opposes owner-occupiers/public tenants against private tenants.

occupier, is almost invariably acting in a way which is demonstrably irrational in terms of his own long term scope for maximizing real wealth and income. These effects arise primarily from imperfections in the financial intermediaries sector, together with special treatment of owner-occupiers by the income tax system. The arrangements which a household makes to provide itself with shelter commits the household to taking a ticket in an income redistribution lottery which may prove to be hugely to its advantage or hugely to its detriment (Paterson, 1975a: 28)

Tenure divisions and redistribution: owning versus renting

The wealth creating capacity of domestic property (over and above the intergenerational transmission of wealth) is at its greatest when property values race ahead of general price levels (Saunders, 1978: 243–5). It is sometimes argued that unlike a mortgagee, for whom loan repayments represent obligatory savings, the tenant can invest the amount surplus to his/her housing costs. This assumes, of course, that for the same weekly household income the interest repayments on a housing loan exceed outgoings on rent. But this is not the case (figure 6.3); therefore, the typical tenant does not have income, net of rent, to invest in wealth creating ventures. And that is why entry to owner-occupation is so prized in the 'property owning democracies'.

When land and house prices rise faster than returns on any of the competing forms of investment it is impossible for non-owners to match the returns accruing to owners of domestic property. One estimate reported in Webster (1980: 249) indicates that over the short period 1964–70 in the UK, the average owner would have been at least £1,200 (1979 prices) better off than the average tenant. Following on from that, partly to catch up with the exceptional rise in earnings in 1970, house prices rose by 21 per cent in 1971, and by a further 18 per cent during the first six months of 1972. So in the UK, between 1960 and 1976, housing's share of gross personal wealth rose from 20 to 41 per cent (Webster, 1980: 249).[6]

Taxation benefits of home ownership

Taxation policy as it affects housing is arguably the most potent redistributive device of all. First, neither the capital gain nor the imputed income from owner-occupied housing is taxed in Australia, Britain, or the United States. Thus the definition of income for the assessment of income tax includes the total income of renters as well as the rental income of landlords, but not the income in-kind of homebuyers (i.e. the flow of housing services connected with the use of a dwelling). This produces

---

[6] While part of the change is due to the swelling of owner-occupation the redistribution that also occurs within the propertied classes must not be overlooked.

inequity between home-owners and renters in the proportion of their real incomes taken by tax. Reece (1975: 219) has estimated that personal income tax in Australia would be about 15 per cent higher if imputed income from home ownership was taxed. He observes that the value of this tax foregone ($A1,500 million in 1977–78) outstrips the value of the Commonwealth housing 'subsidy' to householders in the public sector (i.e. $A390 million advanced in loans to the States in 1977–78 under the Commonwealth States Housing Agreement). This is an exemplary case of hidden, undeclared transfers exceeding in importance the targeted transfers in-kind of the welfare state. In Britain the Meade (1978) enquiry put the revenue lost through the non-taxation of imputed income at £1,500 million in 1976. Both Robinson (1980) and Hughes (1979) have attempted to gauge the distributive effect caused by the failure to tax the imputed income and capital gains flowing to owner-occupiers. Not unexpectedly the subsidy favours the wealthy households, which was worth £191 to households with an annual income of £6,240 or more in 1977 (Robinson, 1980: tables 2–4). By contrast, poor owner-occupiers with annual incomes below £2,080 only received an estimated £28 on average.

Further economic discrimination between owner-occupiers and renters is contained in the British and American taxation systems where the interest on mortgage repayments on the family home are treated as a tax deductible item. These mortgage interest relief schemes are quite regressive since the higher the household income and the greater the initial outlay on the housing the higher the tax concession.[7] In the US, for example, of a total estimated housing subsidy of $US20.56 billion in 1972, nearly two-thirds represented tax relief of various kinds (Bourne, 1981: 210). Most of this subsidy went to households with above average incomes: even after the direct subsidy to public housing (and presumably poorer households) is taken into account, the average subsidy ($341) to households with incomes above the median exceeds the subsidy ($275) to households with below median income levels. More of the distributional impact of housing-related tax provisions in the United States is uncovered in a background paper prepared by the Congressional Budget Office (1978). In the graph prepared by the Congressional Budget Office (figure 7.3):

> Most such benefits tend to fall to the middle-income home owner, except for the accelerated depreciation allowance for owners of rental housing which increases with income. The least regressive of the tax-related provisions appears to be the deferral of capital gains on house sales while the most inequitable is the tax deductability of local property taxes for home owners. (Bourne, 1981: 210–11)

[7] Except for a minor means-tested scheme which operated between 1972–78, Australian governments have resisted interest deductability as a method of providing tax relief.

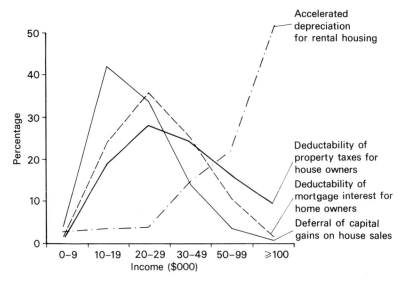

Figure 7.3 The distribution of benefits from housing-related tax provisions by income group in the US, 1977
Source: Bourne, 1981: 211

Whereas in the UK, the estimated value of mortgage interest relief allowed to owner-occupiers has grown from £235 million in 1969/70 to £1,450 million in 1979/80 (Whitehead, 1980: 91). Further, mortgage interest relief is distributed such that wealthier owner-occupiers with household-heads earning £6,000 or more in 1974–75 received over six times as much on average per household as those earning £1,000 or less (Department of the Environment, 1977: 214, table IV.37). Townsend (1973: 37) also provides an illustration of the possible combined value of tax relief to British home owners: late in 1971 a government spokesman estimated that tax relief for a standard rate income tax payer on a 20 year mortgage at 8 per cent interest would amount, altogether, to £2,009 on a £5,000 mortgage, £4,109 on a £10,000 mortgage, and £8,038 on a £20,000 mortgage.

Transfers from depositors to borrowers

A third mechanism for redistribution that profits owner-occupation can be found in the financial measures that cushion mortgages against the full impact of inflation upon housing interest rates. The direct controls imposed by governments in the UK and Australia on the nominal rate of interest for housing loans has meant that the real charge to the borrower has often been zero or even negative at a time when property values have been rapidly appreciating. It is the depositor with the lending institutions that bears the cost of interest subsidies to the homebuyer:

Under inflation, the lenders are the main losers, so that the smart money is not in housing. Private housing is currently subsidized by unsophisticated lenders and by the public sector and *prima facie* this leads to overconsumption. Any value which people place on the use of private space is certainly built into the value of the housing stock. (Paterson, 1975a: 29)

Transfers from new to established home-buyers

With the cases considered so far it is fair to say that there is a predominance of vertical redistribution; that is, the income or wealth advantage accrues to the households with more resources at the expense of those with fewer. Situations will now be considered where the redistributive effect is at least as much horizontal as vertical, which means that households in *otherwise equal* circumstances are treated differently purely on the basis of their position in the housing market.

In periods of inflation impressive capital gains are made by the established and previous owners 'trading-up' at the expense of new buyers who have to pay current prices for housing. Well established home buyers are likely to have lower loan repayments since these are fixed in money terms from the date of purchase, and comprise mainly interest in the early years leaving the reduction of the principal for later on. Because loan repayments increase at less than the rate of inflation while at the same time incomes are rising along with increase in the cost of living, established home owners reap bonuses in the form of reduced real housing expenditures and increased savings (Kendig, 1981: 93). This real discrepancy in the housing expenditures associated with duration of ownership is apparent in table 7.3. Contrast the average weekly mortgage repayments of Australian households that purchased housing before 1960 ($11.77) with those that purchased in 1980 ($68.46).

Table 7.3 Average weekly mortgage repayments ($) of home buyers according to date of purchase: Australian state capitals

Separate house purchase commenced	Capital city						
	Sydney	Melbourne	Brisbane	Adelaide	Perth	Hobart	Total
Before 1960	12.82	11.73	11.24	8.58	11.76	14.35	11.77
1960–64	21.87	20.62	15.28	16.56	14.58	13.34	18.86
1965–69	29.33	22.66	19.68	21.02	23.49	21.15	24.29
1970–74	44.62	35.59	30.78	30.18	32.21	26.37	36.77
1975–79	63.68	63.70	50.62	50.50	54.50	45.68	59.04
1980	81.29	61.47	60.50	58.07	69.64	52.43	68.46
Average	49.35	45.09	38.62	36.36	40.90	32.89	43.86

Source: Australian Bureau of Statistics (1981b: 9, table 6)

Concessional interest rates and eligibility

Those people, including politicians, who argue that the economies of Britain, the US and Australia in their present depressed state can no longer afford to subsidize public tenants at the same levels as in the past conveniently overlook the subsidies that flow to eligible (deserving?) home buyers.[8] Almost 40 per cent of first-time buyers in Australia received some kind of government subsidized first mortgage. The most heavily subsidized loans are channelled through the Home Builders' Account (HBA) and the Defence Services Homes Scheme (see Mendelsohn, 1979: 274–5). Although most of the HBA loans are reserved for households that could not otherwise afford to buy their own home, in the case of war service homes, because assistance is not tied to social need, the subsidized funds flow to a much broader cross-section of income groups. The value of these concessional interest rates, which can range from 3 to 5 per cent below bank and building society rates, is not to be taken lightly when it is realized that prevailing interest rates (12.5 to 15 per cent) double the original price of a dwelling.

One of the conditions for the approval of a subsidized loan until recently has been that it goes towards the purchase of a newly constructed dwelling, the aim being to help overcome the postwar housing shortage and stabilize the building industry in Australia. The proportion of the subsidized loans tied to new housing varied from about 60 per cent in Victoria to 90 per cent in South Australia. In terms of equity the effect cut two ways: while it represented a form of positive discrimination to buyers of new rather than existing housing, with the expansion of Australian cities it simultaneously imposed a permanent levy on those same households in the form of extra travel costs. The tying of subsidized finance to new housing was gradually relaxed during the 1970s so that now the loans approved for existing dwellings outnumber those for new dwellings by 2:1 in Victoria (Garlick, 1978: 155–7).

Horizontal inequity in the rental submarkets

The Commission of Inquiry into Poverty (1975) unearthed evidence of the particularly uneven treatment received by households *forced* to rent accommodation in the private as opposed to the public rental sector. Table 7.4, which is adapted from the Commission's Report (1975: 164, table 10.5) sets out the proportions of rent paying households with

[8] The irrefutability of this assertion was demonstrated in March, 1982 when, with an election campaign underway in the state of Victoria, the federal government announced a package of measures – a tapering tax rebate, improvements to the Home Savings Grant scheme, and a new 'low-start' mortgage plan – which was designed to provide relief to recent home buyers suffering from record interest rates. No assistance whatsoever was extended to welfare housing.

Table 7.4 Adult income units by type of rental accommodation in Australia: numbers below 120 per cent of poverty line before and after housing costs

		Annual income			
		Before housing		After housing	
Rental group	Adult income units (thousands)	Total poor (beneath 120% of poverty line) (thousands)	(%)	Total poor (beneath 120% of poverty line) (thousands)	(%)
Housing Commission	183	51	26	29	17
On HC waiting list	71	20	10	21	12
Not on HC waiting list	768	126	64	123	71
Total	1022	197	100	173	100

Source: Commission of Inquiry into Poverty (1975: 164)

incomes below 120 per cent of the poverty line before and after their rents are taken into account. It shows that after housing costs 71 per cent of Australia's 'poor' tenants in 1972–73 were housed by the private rental sector. This reflects, firstly, the fact that private rentals are determined by the current value of property whereas in public renting, until 1978, rents reflected the total mortgage debt of the housing authority,[9] and, secondly, it is indicative of the moderating effect in the longer term of subsidized rentals upon poorer households. So long as public rentals were so advantageous there was little incentive for housing commission tenants to vacate their dwellings following an improvement in their financial position and make way for the new needy. This situation, which in effect locks the neediest households out of the public housing sector and deprives them of the benefits of rental rebates and the like, is grossly inequitable. To make matters worse, it has been exacerbated by the sales programmes and locational principles pursued by the public housing bodies in Australia since the mid-1950s.

The policy of selling public housing to 'sitting' tenants to increase ownership rates has the effect not only of reducing the absolute quantities of rental stock available but also of depleting tenancies in the most accessible urban locations. Jones (1980: 184) estimates that over a third of all the housing constructed by the states since 1945 has been sold. This alienation of public housing resources has been most pronounced in Sydney and Melbourne, with the greatest proportion of sales occurring on the better

[9] Public tenants benefit from historic costs once a housing authority operating over several decades has assembled a stock of houses on which the public debt is comparatively low. In the private sector, however, the difference between the current worth and the original cost of a dwelling accrues to the landlord.

positioned cottage estates in the middle suburbs. Of the 47,251 dwellings built by the NSWHC in Sydney, 24,480, or 52 per cent, had been sold by mid-1973; however, the respective proportions typically reach 92, 83 and 65 per cent in suburbs like Maroubra, Ryde and Manly-Warringah (*Sydney Morning Herald*, 1972: 8). On the other hand, the Victorian Housing Commission had sold 72 per cent of its metropolitan flats by 1977. The Victorian sales programme continued right up until the end of 1980, a year in which all 800 dwellings completed by the VHC were sold. As a result of this extensive 'asset stripping' the VHC forfeited the opportunity to create more than 70,000 low rent vacancies in inner Melbourne on an annual basis during the 1980s (Jones, 1980: 184).

The shortsighted sales programmes contributed to an over-concentration of rental accommodation on the fringe housing estates which, for their part, were due to a determination to house as many applicants as possible rather than from a genuine concern for social needs. Even in the case of the SAHT, which never embarked on wholesale 'asset stripping', public tenants on average (15.1 km) reside twice as far from the centre of Adelaide as private tenants (7.2 km) (Kendig, 1981: 19). There-fore, it is fair to claim that in this respect the public housing bodies defaulted on their tenants by passing on to them the costs of access to jobs and services. Public housing estates that have been alluded to in these terms include: Green Valley, Mt Druitt and Campbelltown in Sydney; Broadmeadows, Sunshine and Waverley in Melbourne; and Elizabeth and Christies Beach in Adelaide.

The real cost to public tenants of 'fringe' housing

To those households in dire need of public housing assistance the strategies adopted by the housing authorities represent, locationally-speaking, a foreclosure of choice. Increasingly the fringe housing commission estates are concentrating more and more of the single parent households and the 'non-working poor'. A recent estimate for Mt Druitt, a NSWHC estate on the outskirts of Sydney, revealed that about half of the 90,000 residents comprises single parent families and that they constitute up to 60 per cent of all the new settlers (Rowley, 1981: 21). The costs attached to living on these housing estates include: poorly scheduled and co-ordinated trans-port services; the physical isolation of mothers and children in one-car families; a shortage of local employment for both male and female work-ers; a paucity of community resources (Bryson and Thompson, 1972; Brennan, 1973). To be more specific, in Sydney in 1971 under 15 per cent of the residents of Green Valley and Mt Druitt worked locally (Manning, 1978: 69). Four out of five of the remaining workers are forced by a combination of dispersed blue-collar employment and inadequate inter-suburban bus services to purchase vehicles on credit that they can ill afford. The alternative for the households that cannot meet the interest repayments on a vehicle is a backward transport system beset by a range of debilities: 'As a result work travel is a doubly severe burden in the typical low income outer suburb' (Manning, 1978: 170).

There is general agreement (Windshuttle, 1979; Stilwell, 1980; Vipond, 1980) that the very high rates of unemployment amongst the youth that have grown up on these outermost public housing estates are due not only to the mismatch of skills and jobs within the labour markets of the western suburbs, but also the costs and frustrations associated with competing for jobs elsewhere in Sydney and Melbourne. In 1978, for every vacant position there were 41 and 58 unemployed persons registered with the Liverpool and Mt Druitt offices of the Commonwealth Employment Service. The equivalent ratio for the Sydney region, which includes Newcastle and Woolongong, was 16:1 (Stilwell, 1980: 119–121). Therefore, teenagers unable to find local employment and without private vehicles often have 'to battle with the unreliability of public transport' (Vipond, 1980: 340) if jobs in accessible areas are accepted.

Capitalization of externalities into property values

One result of the high degree of interdependency found between activities and locations within the city is that the investment and disinvestment decisions of the owners of land and property in the vicinity have the power to alter significantly the value of third party property. This is known as an externality or 'spill-over' effect. Classically it refers to costs generated in the course of production that are avoided by the producer because they can be externalized. Motorists, for example, are not required to meet the full costs of the air pollution or traffic congestion that they help to create in cities. Because of the juxtaposition of activities within cities there is immense scope for both positive and negative externality effects. Scott is so convinced of the salience of negative externalities to the functioning of cities that for him they constitute the crux of the urban question, as suggested by the title of his book *The urban land nexus and the state* (Scott, 1980). One suspects that this has almost become an article of faith for Scott, not the least because it is so difficult to isolate and measure the magnitude of externality effects; in the event, Scott 'can offer little evidence of massive negative externality' (Ball, 1981b: 1454). The approach here will be to proceed from a few general illustrations that hopefully will reveal something of the unpredictable nature of 'urban externalities', to the attempts made mainly by urban economists to measure the capitalization of externality effects into property values. This should at least leave us with an interim assessment of the redistributive capacity of externalities in an urban setting.

'Urban externalities'

Externality effects range from the sublime to the ridiculous. For example, the local real estate agent anticipated that when a modest Cotswold cottage just 200 metres from Prince Charles's Gloucestershire home was placed on the market in March, 1982, that its position would add at least £10,500 to its nominal value of £21,000. And who would have guessed that the growth of Australia's live-sheep export trade to the Middle East would have such an adverse effect on the amenity value of North Haven, a relatively new housing development on the Le Fevre Peninsula in Adelaide? North Haven just happens to be downwind from the holding pens and loading facilities at Port Adelaide that are being built to facilitate the transhipment of over a million head of sheep yearly.[10] Positive externalities have the opposite effect on property values: it has already been noted that speculators and developers set out to capture the 'unearned increment' produced by public investment on adjacent or nearby sites, or by the general development of the locality. Similarly, Young and Willmott point to the very personalized benefit that accrues to the occupants of properties that fringe the private squares or great commons like Regent's Park, Green Park, Hyde Park and Kensington Gardens in the West End of London: 'Almost every one of the Great Common lands of London . . . was public for walking on within the prescribed hours but private all the year around and all the clock round for the views over it. Public property gave a spatial bonus from the community to those who already had private privilege' (Young and Willmott, 1975: 45). Likewise, the alienation of large stretches of the foreshore of Sydney Harbour has secured for the lucky few an even more exclusive dominion over a public resource.

The thing that sets urban externalities apart from externality effects in general is that they assume the form of spatial fields. It is the characterizing properties, then, of intensity, extent, and rate of distance-decay (Papageorgiou, 1978) that actually determine how an externality field will affect surrounding activities and property owners. This is sometimes called the 'neighbourhood effect'. Not unnaturally, the more a community feels it has to lose from disruption and threatened property values, the more intense and uncompromising its reaction will be. Thus, it is typical for well endowed and residentially stable neighbourhoods to defend themselves more vociferously from encroachment than transient, resource deficient areas (Dear *et al.*, 1980).

Measurement of externality effects

The measurement of externality effects represent a considerable technical challenge: it is one thing to elicit and scale the reactions of local residents to

[10] How's that for 'unearned *ex*crement'?

the addition or closure of a public facility in their neighbourhood (Dear *et al.*, 1977); it is another to quantify the effects of a gradual process of neighbourhood improvement or deterioration upon property values, or separate out the independent effect of several overlapping externality fields. Urban economists and geographers are now using regression analysis to estimate the equivalent of these values, which are known as the hedonic, or implicit, housing/property prices. The underlying assumption is that the actual expenditure on each individual property contains a buyer's evaluation of the structural characteristics of the building and lot, as well as the public goods and environmental amenities associated with it. Hence, by regressing these different effects against the prices paid for housing it is possible to derive an estimate of how much, on average, each one contributes to the capital value of properties in differing spatial markets. The field dealing expressly with externality effects has been dominated by Americans to date (see Ball, 1973, for a related investigation into the determinants of house prices). The value of their findings lies not so much in what they tell about the generality of cases, as in pointing to the relative orders of magnitude that one might attach to urban external effects.

Environmental amenities and disamenities

Starting with the simple case of a 'view', Gillard (1981) analysed 392 houses sold in Los Angeles in 1970 and found that a view added $3,887 to the price of a residential property, or a little more than the presence of a fireplace and somewhat less than a swimming pool. He remarks, 'Given the fact that the mean selling price of the housing units in the sample was $US42,128, the view-lot premium was not trivial' (Gillard, 1981: 219). Anderson and Crocker (1971) along with Ridker and Henning (1967) in studies restricted to air pollution, and Diamond (1980b), Li and Brown (1980), and Mark (1980) in more general studies that included measures of air pollution, have all examined the negative effect of particulate pollution on property values. It is interesting to compare the results from three of the studies which were undertaken for St Louis. Ridker and Henning (1967), using measures of the sulphation levels applying to census tracts in 1960, obtained estimates ranging from $966 to $1,800 for each milligram of SO_3 per 100 square centimetres per day. Anderson and Crocker (1971) compared the effects of air pollution on property values in three cities: Washington DC, Kansas City and St Louis. They costed the negative effect of sulphur dioxide pollution, also for 1960 property prices, at between $300 and $700. Lastly, Mark (1980: 114) calculated for a sample of 6,553 sales of single-family homes in 1969–70, that a reduction in the air pollution level of a neighbourhood by one ton per square mile per month of settled particulates was worth between $28 and $35.

The St Louis (Mark, 1980) and Boston (Li and Brown, 1980) studies also provide estimates of the impact of noise levels around their airports on property values. Mark (1980: 113) found that a typical St Louis household was willing to pay a premium of between $1,517 and $1,610 to avoid living with a NEF 35 noise exposure contour, and $2,093 and $2,459 to avoid living in an NEF 45 contour. This represents a discount of 8.5 and 14.0 per cent respectively. In the Boston study (Li and Brown, 1980: 135) a doubling of perceived loudness – an increase of 10dbA corresponds to a doubling – produced a drop of $460 in the value of a dwelling (in 1971 prices).

Quality of local schools

There is also a related group of studies that has registered a price effect of local public schools within certain parts of US cities (see Jud and Watts, 1981). Grether and Mieszkowski (1974: 141) report a highly significant relationship between a measure of reading skills and house prices. From a regression model for 830 New Haven house transactions between 1962–69 they predicted that if the standard house were to be moved from a school district which ranked in the fiftieth percentile on a regulatory reading test to one in the nintieth percentile its value would increase by approximately $3,000 in mid-1970 prices. Likewise, Jud and Watts (1981: 462–3) established that school quality, measured by third grade reading level, exerts a strong statistically significant influence on house levels in Charlotte, North Carolina: the coefficients on reading scores indicate that an increase in performance of one grade level would raise housing values 5.2 per cent over the full sample and 6.2 per cent in the non-ghetto sample of single-family residences. The implication of this is that an increase of one-half grade level in student achievement levels in the public school system would be worth $675 (1977 values) to the average home-owner in Charlotte, or $48 million across the city as a whole.

Zoning policy and the effect of non-residential land uses upon house values

The evidence from studies of the effect of non-residential land uses on the prices of adjacent housing is less straightforward. The expectation is that incompatible and deleterious activities depress the value of residential property and therefore should be segregated; after all, that is what the system of land use regulation and controls is all about (Babcock, 1966). In their work on Boston, Li and Brown (1980) get much closer conceptually and numerically than earlier attempts (Crecine *et al.*, 1973; Grether and Mieszkowski, 1980; Reuter, 1973) to the probable effect that non-residential activity has upon housing values. They recognize that in practice the surrounding land value surface will incorporate not only the external costs (negative effects) but also the benefits (positive effects) of accessibility to commercial centres, various mixes of industry, and major highways. In a set of diagrams, reproduced below (figure 7.4a–c) and based on their regression coefficients, Li and Brown are able to demonstrate that the net effect of proximity to commercial establishments, industry and major highways is not a simple, monotonic function of distance. Proximity to industry, for example, incurs 'mixed blessings'. The coefficient for the logarithmic distance from industry shows that sales prices decline by $1,366 for each doubling of distance (curve B in figure 7.4a), whereas the negative externality effect dissipates very quickly (curve A). On balance, a house located about 550 metres from industry commands the highest premium in the Boston sample. As figure 7.4b illustrates, the negative effect of commerce upon nearby housing values is offset somewhat, especially in the immediate vicinity of a shopping centre, by the positive effect of accessibility. Lastly, the effect of being close to a major highway produces a complete reversal of the pattern obtained for industry (figure 7.4c). Curve C in the diagram shows that so far as the capitalization of the effects into property values is concerned, the least profitable location for housing is about 300 metres from major highways (i.e. thruways in the Boston study).[11] These diagrams nicely convey the redistributive cross-currents that remain largely as unpriced externality effects until such time as property changes hands.[12]

Lastly, both Peterson (1974) and Stull (1975) report significant price effects that derive from local government attitudes to community growth (chapter 9). In their study of 50 municipalities in the San Francisco Bay Area, Wolch and Gabriel (1981: 1260) estimate that a pro-growth stance on the part of a suburban council depresses 1976 house values by about $US4,200 (this approximates eight per cent of the average house value in the sample). As well as this, about $3,000 is added to the mean value of home prices as the proportion of land subject to a minimum size-size clause increases from nine to ten per cent of a municipality's developable land (this is the exclusionary zoning effect). They conclude that 'After controlling for traditional determinants of house prices, land use controls implemented by the local state together may account for approximately 14% of the price of a typical Bay Area home' (Wolch and Gabriel, 1981: 1261).

[11] Li and Brown (1980: 137–9) suggest that even though noise levels will be higher within this corridor, the higher net value near major thruways reflects the potential for eventual conversion to a more intensive and productive use.
[12] It is not until externality effects are translated into exchange values that householders can really be sure what price they have had to pay for the new airport, the freeway at the bottom of the garden, or the nuclear power station in their area; or what the recently completed school, swimming pool, or streetscaping has added to the value of their properties.

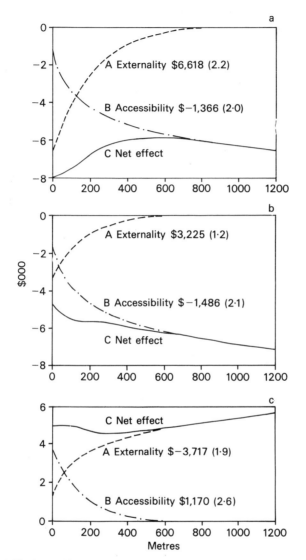

Figure 7.4 The joint effect of externalities and accessibility on property values near (a) industry, (b) regional shopping centres, and (c) a major thruway in the south-eastern sector of the Boston metropolitan area
Source: Li and Brown, 1980: 136–8

Although much more work remains to be done, from the evidence reviewed it is difficult to sustain a case for 'massive externalities' – negative or positive. Nonetheless, externalities are built into all property values to a greater or lesser degree. The ones that really claim attention definitely have the capacity to significantly depress property values in 'high risk' districts or to fortuitously boost the yields to corporate investors in urban real estate. However, as Edel and Sclar (1975: 384) point out in their study of trends in Boston's property market, urban externalities capitalized into house values do not compare very favourably with the stock market as a means of wealth accumulation. Hence, it seems highly improbable that externality effects within cities are responsible for massive transfers of real income or wealth within capitalist societies.

Redistribution, accessibility and the changing cost advantage of relative location

The remaining source of redistribution which requires attention is the purest of the 'spatial' effects yet identified. No one takes issue with the notion that the real income of the household varies according to locational accessibility and proximity; nor is there any question that real income is redistributed between residents living in different parts of the city as comparative advantage, in terms of movement costs, shifts from one location to another through time.

Physical accessibility (access to . . .)

The main interest at this point is with the costs – monetary, time and discomfort – and barriers associated with overcoming distance within cities. But the inequalities that spring from the unequal costs of moving about the city can be partly traced back to discrepancies in the level of access to private vehicles. Schaeffer and Sclar (1975) argue that America's metropolitan regions have become so geared structurally to universal automobile ownership that those people without cars suffer a chronic disadvantage. Multiple ownership within many households disguises the fact that over a fifth (22 per cent) of all families living in metropolitan areas own no car, and in the central cities nearly a third (32 per cent) of the households are carless. Although based on the 1971 US Census, Schaeffer and Sclar (1975: 105) do not envisage a marked improvement in these proportions. Unremarkably, the lack of ownership is greatest among the poor and aged. Nationally, over half (56 per cent) of those with incomes below $3,000 in 1971 were carless, and nearly half (45 per cent) of the households with heads 65 years of age and older own no car. Hillman and his co-workers (1973: 53–6) have uncovered further evidence of the very wide range in levels of access to cars in a survey of six communities selected from different orders of the UK urban system. In defining levels of access, possession of a driver's licence and household car ownership were taken into account. The figures of direct relevance are presented in table 7.5. They confirm the low levels of access enjoyed (endured?) by housewives and pensioners to what is usually the most convenient and comfortable mode of transportation.

Table 7.5 Levels of access to cars in three UK urban communities (percentages)

Household	A New Town ward (13,200)[a]			An outer suburb, city of 0.3 m (21,000)[a]			An inner London borough (14,000)[a]		
	1[b]	2[c]	3[d]	1	2	3	1	2	3
1 + car	64	–	–	46	–	–	43	–	–
Car owning household									
licence-holder	37	8	18	31	5	3	26	14	4
non licence-holder	25	44	6	15	24	3	16	26	4
Non car-owning household									
licence-holder	7	3	6	6	2	3	5	n.a.	n.a.
non licence-holder	31	45	71	48	68	91	53	60	91

[a] population
[b] %adult population
[c] %housewives
[d] % pensioners
Source: Recompilation of Hillman *et al*. (1973: tables 3.2–4)

In order to underline the importance of access to a private vehicle I will briefly record the findings from a section of Young and Willmott's work on families in metropolitan London. They determined with the aid of a regression model that after taking account of age – rather youthfulness – car ownership made the greatest difference to an index of the total leisure activities engaged in by the male head of household during the previous year. To their surprise 'car ownership added most, more so than our other big three, class, income and education' (Young and Willmott, 1975: 223–6). Although they are only dealing with the range of activities which the car can multiply just by adding to a person's geographical reach, it raises the spectre of a doubly severe deprivation for those who are both poor and carless. As well as living in the least congenial districts they are handicapped in their opportunity to get away from them; whereas households who enjoy almost unrestricted mobility have the most pleasant environs. One perceptive advertisement on Australian television promotes its product as an 'escape machine'.

Price of accessibility and movement costs

Movement costs are an unavoidable part of the household budget: transport expenditures averaged 19.51 per cent per household in the Household Expenditure Survey, 1975–76 (Australian Bureau of Statistics, 1978). Although there is a tendency for transport expenditure to be moderately income elastic the greatest variation in movement costs is due to where the household lives in the city, and where its members have to move to on a daily basis in earning their living. This is the major non-discretionary element in household travel costs. It is in the context of the journey-to-work in Australian urban regions that the redistributive relevance of land costs, public housing policy, and the bias of financial institutions to new housing becomes apparent.

Because Australian cities are so dispersed and their urban transport systems so comparatively backward the residents in the outer areas are frequently obliged to pay an unduly large premium for poor accessibility. Black (1977) has compared the locational inconvenience with respect to journey-to-work travel in 1971 of seven Sydney suburbs: Marrickville, an inner area 6 km from the CBD; Hurstville and Sans Souci, two middle distance suburbs (16 and 18 km south-east of the CBD); and four outer area suburbs – St Ives and Pennant Hills, high status North Shore suburbs 20 and 22 km from the CBD, are compared with the two low status suburbs, West Parafield and Blacktown, which are 28 and 35 km from downtown Sydney. Crude differences in employment accessibility are indicated by the median travel times for each suburb. They range from a minimum of 3.4 km for Marrickville residents to a maximum of 16 km for St Ives residents. Between these extremes were the following median travel distances: 6.6 km (Fairfield); 7.5 km (Sans Souci); 9.8 km (Pennant Hills); 10.8 km (Hurstville); and 12.5 km (Blacktown).[13]

Quite clearly the impost of extra travel costs falls unevenly upon workers living in the outer suburbs: firstly, it is more likely that those choosing to live there of their own volition will normally have the incomes that allow them to be largely indifferent to the added travel costs;[14] while, amongst those households relegated by a public housing assignment or coaxed there by cheaper land costs, only those with jobs nearby escape the

---

[13] More is actually learnt of the concentration of inconvenient worktrips by focusing on the proportion of workers who travel more than 16 km to work: 0 per cent (Marrickville); 5 per cent (Sans Souci); 6 per cent (Hurstville); 15 per cent (Fairfield); 26 per cent (Pennant Hills); 42 per cent (Blacktown); and, 50 per cent (St Ives) (Black, 1977: 48).

[14] Even in Adelaide where the problem is less acute, the annual commuting costs for two representative outer suburbs (Flagstaff Hill and Christies Beach) were calculated at $A1,175 and $A1,000 per person compared with $A440 for the inner area suburb of Hackney (Australian Institute of Urban Studies, 1973: 71).

imposition of poor access to work.[15] Consequently, households in Sydney's western suburbs are required to spend twice the proportion of their income and time on commuting to work as the metropolitan average (table 7.6). As a proportion of income, the fixed costs of car ownership in these households can be up to one third higher than the Sydney average, even though the car ownership rate is much lower. In a very real sense, residential location can involve a transfer of income in aggregate terms from those households living in the least convenient parts of a city to those that are fortunate enough to command the prime locations. In this respect, at least, low income households in the outer reaches of Australia's farthest-flung suburbs are worse off than their counterparts in either North America or the United Kingdom.

Table 7.6 Transport costs and ownership levels in Sydney's western region, 1971

Suburb	Percentage of household income		Motor vehicles per 100 persons
	Work trip costs[a]	Vehicle expenses	
Green Valley	9.0	11	23
Mt Druitt	11.4	12	23
Penrith	10.1	11	25
Lalor Park	10.0	9	20
Metropolitan Sydney	5.6	9	37

[a] Sum of costs plus value of travel time incurred
Source: Commonwealth Bureau of Roads (1975: 107, table 7.7)

Changing relative accessibility within cities

Point-to-point accessibility within cities is constantly changing: new routes are constructed, or services augmented to improve the accessibility of outlying areas and join previously unconnected parts of the urban network; metropolitan growth poles generate new traffic and reorientate the direction of traffic flows; developments in transport technology and fluctuations in the relative cost of getting around in cities have stretched and squeezed space through time (Schaeffer and Sclar, 1975). The net effect of all these developments is to quietly redistribute real income according to where households live and work within the urban system.

[15] Such households are under no illusion about the hidden cost of poor access. Kendig (1981: 116–18) records that the one-way worktrip times of new homebuyers in Adelaide rose from 17 to 25 minutes after moving, compared with a median time trip of 14 minutes for buyers of established dwellings. When asked to state the biggest disadvantage of the 'new' place of residence, 60 and 55 per cent respectively of the buyers of new 'private' and housing trust homes nominated accessibility. 'The most frequently mentioned disadvantages were lack of access to public transport (19 per cent), long journey-to-work (15 per cent), poor access to shops (8 per cent) and poor access to the city centre (7 per cent). (Kendig, 1981: 117).

This is affected in two ways: through adjustments in the form of changing fares and fuel prices to the daily commuting costs of households; and, indirectly, through the responsiveness of the property market to shifts in the relative accessibility of each location within the city. Evidence that this has gone on in conjunction with improvements in urban transportation for over a century or more is provided in two longitudinal studies of residential land values in Chicago (Mills, 1969) and Boston (Edel and Sclar, 1975). With respect to the Boston area, for example, the higher rate of value increases occurring at greater distances from central Boston in the recent decades (table 7.7) implies a regressive distribution of capital gains between home–owners:

Table 7.7 Estimated changes in house values by distance from central Boston (percentages)

	Centre	3 miles	6 miles	9 miles	12 miles
North-south gradient					
1930–40	−57	−45	−38	−34	−34
1940–50	+172	+172	+116	+126	+169
1950–60	+12	+47	+58	+50	+16
1960–70	+50	+31	+34	+54	+115
1930–70	+97	+126	+184	+244	+343
Western gradient					
1930–40	−36	−32	−27	−27	−34
1940–50	+131	+121	+125	+146	+200
1950–60	+26	+47	+50	+33	−8
1960–70	+96	+90	+100	+130	+117
1930–70	+265	+324	+392	+445	+978

Source: Edel and Sclar (1975: table VI)

If the very center of the metropolitan area (only partially characterized by owner occupied housing) is excluded, then the areas with higher income residents (the suburban fringes) have shown the highest rates of increase in house values in most decades. There is evidence too, from the house value regressions, for slightly faster appreciation in farther western suburbs than in farther northern or southern suburbs. Thus even among suburbs, the more affluent appear to benefit the most. (Edel and Sclar, 1975: 380–1)

The escalation of fuel costs that followed the OPEC priceshock in 1974 has been an important catalyst to a renewed shift in the pricing of urban accessibility. The momentum of postwar suburbanization has been sustained by the dispersion of car ownership amongst all but the lowest income groups, the availability of abundant cheap motoring fuel, and a massive investment in urban roads. Over two decades, between 1955 and 1973, the cost of petrol in the US continued to decline in real terms and consume less of household income (Bruce-briggs, 1974). Similarly, during a time (1960–75) when public transport fares rose by 50 per cent relative to the Consumer Price Index, private motoring costs fell by 25 per cent in Australia (Lane, 1977: table IV). Although this price shift freed urban firms and households from the locational constraints imposed by a radial transport system, at the same time it left the outermost residents of Australia's sprawling cities almost entirely dependent upon the automobile. Simultaneously, the running down of investment in public transport that has accompanied falling patronage, together with the dispersal of residences, employment and other activities, has guaranteed dependence on the private car in the outer areas of Australian cities.

The real rise in liquid fuel prices posted in the late 1970s (Ogden 1980) removed one of the main sources of encouragement to urban dispersal in Australia. What is more, the expectation of an uncertain future in relation to motoring fuel threatens to redistribute real income to a degree never envisaged when the car dependent outer suburbs were developed. A real rise in motoring costs erodes the income of outer area households relative to inner area households. Bannister and Ogborn (1978) have explored the impact of rising fuel prices on the rent surfaces associated with housing and employment in a selection of industry groups in metropolitan Adelaide. Their predictive model is able to forecast the changes in travel costs, residential rents, and employment rents, assuming an increase of one cent/km and consumption at the rate of 10 km per litre (this corresponds to a rise of 50 per cent over the 1978 price). The general effect is to make central land more valuable and to accentuate the peaking of rents around the main centres of employment. The authors (Bannister and Ogborn, 1978) worked out that the average change in total travel cost incurred by residents approximated $A1,000 in 1978 prices. The average incidence for the metropolitan area as a whole breaks down into: travel costs (50 per cent), residential rents (44 per cent), and employment rents (6 per cent). But the constituent proportions can vary from an 80 to 20 per cent split between residential rents and travel costs for inner area residents to a 20 to 80 per cent split between employment rents and travel costs in the outer suburbs – it is assumed that the increment to residential rents will be zero at the edge of the city (figure 7.5). They also estimate that in the case of the inner city residents this would produce a transfer payment of about $80 yearly from tenants to landlords (as higher rents) whilst the capital benefit would only accrue to a home owner when the property was sold. Figure 7.5 affirms that outer area residents bear the full amount of increased travel costs and that there are no capital gains to be realized by home-owners.

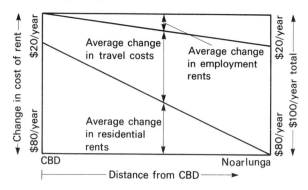

Figure　7.5　The mix of travel-related changes in motoring costs incurred by residents living at various points removed from the centre of Adelaide
Source: Bannister and Ogborn, 1978: 8

Shifts in price relativities as a function of accessibility

So far as Australian urban households are concerned these changes are not merely impending, they have already been registered in the property markets of the main centres:

> Households' *expectations* of increasing private motoring costs, and their fears of disruption to private vehicle use, are leading to higher relative valuations of convenient residential locations, and shifts in the physical distribution of the population, so that lower income households may increasingly find themselves in the less convenient locations in the city. (King, 1980: 1)[16]

This raises doubts about the prospects for a continuation of the capital gains recorded in the outer suburban property markets of Australian cities between 1972 and 1977. During this period the value of housing beyond 12 km of central Adelaide, for example, appreciated by an annual average of 33.02 per cent. King's analysis of Melbourne's property market also confirms that during these years 'the greatest escalations in average house prices tended to occur in those urban fringe LGAs (local government areas) where there was substantial new development' (King, 1980: 26). He records annual rates of price inflation between 1972 and 1977 from 35.8 to

[16] The results of two recent housing surveys in Melbourne (Melbourne Metropolitan Board of Works, 1981) and Sydney (Maddocks, 1978) also support this impression. There appears to be a swing underway reversing the tendency throughout the 1960s and 1970s to downgrade accessibility factors in considering housing preferences (Bryson and Thompson, 1972; Daly, 1968; Gibbings, 1973; Highway Research Board, 1969): 'People *are* preoccupied with accessibility issues; about that the results leave no doubt. They are also voting with their feet for better accessibility, as the market clearly reveals' (Melbourne Metropolitan Board of Works, 1981: 34).

39.1 per cent for eight of the 12 LGAs that form the outer cordon of metropolitan Melbourne.

Since 1978 the regional pattern of house price appreciation in Australian cities has begun to respond to the shift in the cost advantage of different locations brought about by the rise in private transport costs. In Adelaide, where, like Melbourne and unlike Sydney, property values as a whole did not keep pace with inflation between 1977 and 1981, relative price movements in the inner areas were nevertheless almost double those achieved in outer areas. House values in some outlying LGAs have remained stagnant or even fallen in absolute terms between 1977–81 (the annual average increases for Elizabeth, Salisbury, and Noarlunga were 0.08, 2.3 and 1.3 per cent respectively). This situation is broadly comparable to that reported in both Melbourne and Sydney (*National Times*, 1980), except that in Sydney inner area property values have soared above that city's median house price. It should not be necessary to dwell upon the redistributive implications of these developments: if the trend to higher private transport costs is irrevocable, and it appears to be in the long run, there will be a leakage of real wealth from those home-owners in the comparatively inaccessible outer areas to the suburbs with the best provision of public transport and other services.

As a postscript it might be said that one cannot help being struck by the singularity of the Australian urban experience: the conditions that have given rise to the inequities and redistributive effects that we have devoted so much attention to in the last part of this chapter are not duplicated elsewhere. Firstly, a majority of the poor in the US and Britain enjoy a spatial bonus, if nothing else, by living near the heart of their cities. Secondly, although the outer suburbs of US cities are arguably more car dependent, and almost as dispersed, they are much more affluent than their Australian counterparts on the whole and therefore better equipped to cope with rising fuel costs. Lastly, because Australian cities have been developed at such low densities, 'fringe dwellers' are not as well served – nor are they likely to be – by convenient public transport alternatives as is the British commuter from the suburbs.

Resumé

A lot of ground has been covered in the last two chapters. It might help to tie together and crystallize the arguments that have been developed with a final illustration of the full import of the 'residential assignment process' in capitalist cities. In an interrogation of the distributional effects of variable ingredients upon access to housing, King (1980) shows just how restricted locational choice has become in a large city like Melbourne. It is also a compelling demonstration of how the housing market segregates house-

Table 7.8 Impact of fluctuations in household income, interest rates and property values on locational choice in Melbourne, 1967–77

	Gross family weekly income[a] (relative to average male unit in Victoria) ($)	Maximum weekly repayments (family income/4) ($)	Maximum savings bank interest[b] (%)	Maximum available loan (25 years, quarterly rests) ($)	Maximum affordable property value (assuming 80% ratio loan) ($)	LGAs in which average property value obtainable		LGAs in which median property value attainable	
						Houses	Flats	Houses	Flats
1967	32.90[c]	8.23	5.75	5650	7070	0/53	0/18		
	49.35[d]	12.34	5.75	8480	10600	19/53	5/18		
	65.80[e]	16.45	5.75	11310	14130	44/53	10/18		
	98.70[f]	24.70	5.75	16960	21200	53/53	18/18		
	131.66[g]	32.90	5.75	22610	28270	53/53	18/18		
1972	48.85[c]	12.21	7.00	7470	9340	0/55	0/38		
	73.30[d]	18.30	7.00	11210	14010	20/55	16/38		
	97.70[e]	24.43	7.00	14950	18690	44/55	31/38		
	146.55[f]	36.64	7.00	22410	28020	55/55	38/38		
	195.40[g]	48.85	7.00	29890	37360	55/55	38/38		
1977	99.80[c]	24.95	10.50	11430	14290	0/55	0/45	0/57	0/48
	149.70[d]	37.43	10.50	17150	21430	0/55	1/45	0/57	1/48
	199.60[e]	49.90	10.50	22860	28580	1/55	5/45	3/57	12/48
	299.40[f]	74.85	10.50	34290	42860	38/55	38/45	47/57	45/58
	399.20[g]	99.80	10.50	45720	57150	50/55	45/45	56/57	48/48

a for calendar year
b at June of year
c ½ average
d ¾ average
e average
f 1½ average
g 2 average
Source: King (1980: 50, table 4.4)

holds spatially. The calculations set out in table 7.8 establish in which Melbourne suburbs 'representative' households, under 'standard' lending conditions, could afford to buy housing in each of the years 1967, 1972 and 1977. The households are 'representative' in that household income is related to male average weekly earnings in 1967, 1972 and 1977. Lending conditions are 'standard' to the extent that: the housing loan is available at the prevailing savings bank interest rate; repayments must not exceed 25 per cent of household income; the household must have a 20 per cent deposit, together with the transaction costs. These are conditions most relevant to lower income households, single income families, and first-time home buyers.

Table 7.8 reveals that in 1967 the household on average male earnings could afford the average priced house in all but nine of Melbourne's 53 LGAs (the flat market was more restricted with access possible to only eight of the 18 LGAs). There was a steady attrition of the locational choice of home buyers in Melbourne so that by 1977 the household on average male earnings could afford to purchase a house/flat in only one/five of Melbourne's LGAs.[17].

The significance of this sort of locational preclusion by the housing market lies in the way it also restricts the physical access of already resource-poor households to the public and private goods and services which are unevenly distributed within cities. In advancing to a consideration of how government provision effects the distribution of 'urban' resources we are consciously building upon a foundation that recognizes that some households in our largest cities have to bear the *cumulative* brunt of: a widening income gap; unequal access to housing finance; growing differentials in land and housing prices; and, a deterioration of big city living and movement costs.

[17] There are, as King points out, a number of options which may help marginally to improve this otherwise dismal locational choice. A household can boost its gross income with a second job and/or wage earner, though these options involve some disruption of family life, perhaps the postponement of children, or reliance on supplementary child care. Secondly, a household can settle for poorer housing conditions such as a flat or a smaller block of land. Thirdly, it may apply for subsidized finance or enter higher-risk loan arrangements like vendor terms financing.

8

State Augmentation and Collectively Provided Services

Introduction

The provision and location of urban resources was implicated in the previous chapter about spatial externalities and the income effects associated with access to jobs and services. This chapter will deal exclusively with those urban resources that take the form of goods and services provided by the state. Chapter 3 showed how the state in capitalist economies has come to intervene, whatever the reason, in the spheres of production, consumption, and social control; hence it is apt to talk in terms of an augmentative role for the state. Let there be no mistake: a sufficiency of good quality *social* consumption goods and services within easy reach of the urban household can make an immense difference to its members. Indeed, households with limited personal resources (i.e. access to private consumption goods and services) and mobility may well measure their quality of life in terms of the quality of the public goods and services available locally. Peter Townsend (1979: 36) paints a picture of fatherless families with identically low cash incomes in Britain, but with noticeably differing access to other resources. There are those who live in the slum areas of cities in very bad, overcrowded housing and are served by local schools, hospitals, public baths, and libraries built to nineteenth-century standards. Conversely, there are those who live on new council housing estates on the fringe of cities or in new towns, in good housing with their spacious and well equipped schools and hospitals, with comprehensive community services and ample open space. Clearly the standards of living of these sets of families are not all equivalent.

By venturing to the East Side of Manhattan with Charles Reich one can begin to grasp something of the contradiction in Galbraith's aphorism, 'public squalor amidst private opulence':

> In New York City, on Sixty-seventh Street, east of Second Avenue, there is a public library that serves the neighbourhood. It is small, seedy, inadequate; the books are greasy, the chairs, lighting and tables

are poor, the whole building has an air of shabby neglect. When seen recently, it was obvious that nothing had been done to it in the twenty-five years since it was seen previously, and probably for much longer. Yet in these same twenty-five years, towering apartment houses have been built in the neighbourhood, involving expenditures of many millions of dollars, and chic shops, restaurants and theatres have appeared. Twenty-five years have brought an explosion in publishing, in knowledge, in education, in the need for adult education. They have brought new culture and arts. And so, the wretched library which has stayed the same for twenty-five years (except for the inevitable deterioration of age) has actually fallen behind. It is much less valuable to the neighbourhood now than it was then, and even then it was pitifully inadequate. (Reich, 1972: 146)

Alternatively, those readers who grew up in an Australian suburb during the sixties may find it easier to relate to Mathews's depiction of the postwar backlog in local government services (and of those that qualify, still more will need to switch the gender of Mathews' suburban dweller):

a typical suburban dweller in one of our cities may be seen each morning walking or driving down his expensive concrete drive, past carefully manicured lawns and shrubs to his front gate. There, in a strong metamorphosis, he will step or drive into a mud puddle or, in the dry season, a dust hole . . . He will then take his place in an uncomfortable and overcrowded bus or train, or if he is driving his own car he will force his way into congested traffic lanes. Only when he reaches his destination – say a commercial office building – will he exchange the discomfort of the public domain for the standards of comfort he expects in his own home or place of work. (Mathews, 1967: 256–7)

Although these conditions will have changed for the majority of suburbanites by the 1980s, they are still real enough for households living in the outermost suburbs of Australian cities.

The main objective of this chapter is to try and establish how gross imbalances like these arise; and, more generally, how the mismatching of resources and needs in cities comes about. Connected with this is the ongoing interest in redistribution; but the equity issues of public finance are bypassed here to ponder the redistributive implications of variations in local government charges (fiscal incidence), relative to capacity to pay (fiscal capability), and spatially destined government expenditures. These expenditures have a multiplicative effect on the quantity and quality of public goods and services, irrespective of whether they are funded by the private capital market or by central, state, or local governments. To begin with we will focus on the individuation of public provision within cities that stems from systemic differences in the forms of government in Britain, the US and Australia and their methods of funding urban resources. This leads on logically to a discussion of some of the rather more specialized distributional effects like metropolitan fragmentation, the fiscal imbalance between the central city and suburbs, and locationally discriminatory public provision. Of necessity, this is a fairly technical discussion in which we set out to discover just how much urban inequities owe to governmental relations, institutions and mechanisms.

Public (or 'collectively provided') goods and services

Those urban resources provided by governments are called public (or social) goods to distinguish them from the goods and services supplied by private producers. Education, transport services and electricity supply, for example, are really 'private goods' that have been endowed with public interest. Because the private sector tends to undersupply goods with 'public' characteristics, they now have a legitimate status as 'merit' goods implying more consumption – of low-cost housing, schooling, or hospitalization – than the consumer could otherwise afford (Margolis, 1968: 597). On the other hand, these services also guarantee that society is safely reproduced in its own image.

Bennett (1980: 28–31) recognises three main spatial traits that can affect access to public goods and services: tapering, jurisdictional partitioning; spillover. Tapering is the distance decay effect in another guise. Quite simply, because travel cost and inconvenience increases with distance from the point of supply, provision to households on the spot cannot be equated with supply to all who wish to have access. Even though a uniform charge is fixed for all users within a catchment they do not enjoy the same level of access to fire, police and ambulance services which are supplied from static points on a transport grid. The effect of the territorial compartmentation of public goods and services within cities, that is jurisdictional partitioning, is to limit general access to them. Alternatively, when the benefits bestowed by a particular good or service are available to people living outside the government area, a spillover is said to occur. These effects represent the spatial ingredients that fortify the area and class-biases already present in the allocation of public goods and services.

Organizational forms of government and the machinery of urban public provision

The message here is that *who* gets *what* public goods and services in capitalist cities rests just as much with governmental structures and policies – the *how* of resource allocation – as with *where* households reside in the city. In so far as the flow of resources to the local level is concerned, the allocational outcome is mediated by systemic differences in the government and administration of the public economies of countries like Britain, the US and Australia. The intention is to show what a difference considerations like the structure of public finance and the nature of intergovernmental relations can make to the allocation of resources among and within levels of government, but especially at the lowest level of urban government where it matters most to households.

This may seem reasonably obvious except that one of the more persuasive theories of the state (see chapter 3) does not accord any particular importance to institutionally defined questions such as the relationship between the central and local levels of government, the composition of public expenditure, or the mechanics of allocation. A reading of Marxist structuralists in the Althusserian mould – Poulantzas and Castells – gives such a strong impression of economic determinancy that the state's political institutions are left with very little latitude in the area of economic management and resource allocation. They insist on a homogenized vision of the state which reduces the functions of government to the reproduction of the capitalist relations of production. This disembodiment of the state carries with it the risk that all government agencies will be assimilated without differentiation, 'into an apparently monolithic "state apparatus" in which the central–local distinction often disappears and local government is treated simplistically as the "local state", a kind of microcosmic example of Marxist analyses' general theory of the state' (Dunleavy, 1980b: 127). Indeed, this is the fate of local government in Cynthia Cockburn's (1977) study of Lambeth, a south London borough: she maintains that as a miniaturized version of the central state, the primary function of local institutions (in Britain, at any rate) is to reproduce labour power.

Throughout this chapter it will be seen that governments discharge comparable tasks somewhat differently depending both upon how they are historically constituted and the types of machinery they inherit; and that these systemic differences can materially affect living conditions from suburb to suburb within cities. In the realm of revenue-sharing alone 'there is a great variance among the ways that national governments go about controlling and influencing how cities obtain a share of the national pie' (Ashford, 1980: 6):

> In absolute terms, the magnitude of dependence varies from the high of Britain and France, which provides respectively about 45 and 40 per cent of local revenues from national taxes, to the lows of Germany and the United States, which provide roughly a fourth of local (urban) revenues.[1] No sooner does one embark on the systemic

---

[1] Amongst the advanced capitalist economies Sweden, with two-thirds of local expenditure coming from the centre, indulges in the biggest exercise in resource switching.

comparison than do the intrasystemic differences begin to loom in importance . . . No two countries, for example, could have more different territorial divisions than Britain, now with about 450 local governments, and France, with over 360,000. Similarly, a simple time series shows that Germany has managed to keep the transfer to low levels fairly constant for the past thirty years, while in the United States the national government was providing only about 10 per cent of local and state revenues in 1950.

Significant differences are also encountered in the functions performed by local government. Education, housing and police protection, which take up more than half the use of funds in the United Kingdom and close to one-half in the United States, are not included amongst the tasks of Australian local government.

One way of deciding how resource allocation within the public economy of urban areas is arrived at in Britain, the United States and Australia is by viewing it through the multiple lenses of (a) the constitutional framework of government; (b) intergovernmental financial relations; (c) fiscal policy toward urban capital formation. The essential elements of the discussion are summarized in table 8.1 which, at best, can only be representational.

The constitutional framework of government

The UK has a unitary system of government in which 'local and regional authorities possess devolved rather than federal powers' (Bennett, 1980: 349). Following the reorganization of local government between 1965 and 1974 the number of local authorities was reduced by two-thirds from about 1,500 (table 8.1). If the Greater London Council is left to one side,[2] then the English and Welsh urban areas, for example, are divided into 36 metropolitan districts with fiscal responsibilities for education, personal social services, housing, refuse collection and environment, followed by six metropolitan counties (with additional functions such as transport, fire and police, and consumer protection). Thus the government of urban areas in Britain is primarily discharged by second level institutions in a unitary state.

Although the US and Australia both have federal systems of government they exhibit differences in relation to the division of powers as they affect the governing of cities. 'In legal terms, the American municipalities have the same subordinate status to the States as their Australian counterparts. In practice, however, they enjoy a great degree of autonomy' (Parkin, 1983), and generally overshadow the states functionally in

---

[2] The Greater London Council incorporates 33 boroughs including the City of London.

Table 8.1 The political framework within which urban resource allocation takes place in the UK, US and Australia

State	System of government	Tiers	Locus of power	Number of government jurisdictions	Average size of LGA	Financial relations	Composition of local government revenue
United Kingdom	Unitary	Central County District	Local government formally subordinate to central government	36 Metropolitan districts 6 Metropolitan counties 47 Counties 333 Districts GLC (33 metropolitan boroughs)	122,000 persons	Direct central expenditure, general grants (Rate Support Grant)	Grant aid 45% User charges 30% Rate income 25%
United States	Federal	Federal State Local	'Co-ordinate and independent within spheres' (Wheare, 1973)	(within US SMSAs, 1972) 444 Counties 3,462 Townships 5,467 Municipalities 4,758 School districts 8,054 Special districts (US Bureau of the Census, 1975)	2,668 persons (Jones, 1981)	Federal expenditures, revenue-sharing tax credits, superannuation, Community Development Block Grant Program	Grant aid 30–35% Property & sales taxes 30–35% Utility and user charges 30–35%
Australia	Federal	Commonwealth State Local	Powersharing with a Commonwealth monopoly of the public fisc and the states dominating law-making	937 LGAs municipalities, shires (Jones, 1981)	16,400 persons (Jones, 1981)	Income tax sharing, matching and Section 96 grants	Rates 50–60% Grant aid 12–15% Miscellaneous charges 25–35%

the sphere of urban resource allocation. Thus, local governments are the primary organs of US urban government. This lowest tier of US government shows the materialization of some of the most cherished American values – the worship of self-determination and local autonomy, the ethos of privatization, and the principle that the user should pay. While incorporation procedures vary markedly from state to state in the US – some states have so-called anti-incorporation laws which give a municipality the power to annex adjoining unincorporated areas – residents in many states retain the right by law to form a breakaway municipality or service area by petitioning for incorporation, so long as they obtain the majority approval of at least 25 per cent of the affected ratepayers. Hence government in the United States is a pastiche of 50 States; the District of Columbia; some 450 county, 3,500 township, 5,500 municipality, and 4,800 school as well as 8,000 other special purpose districts (e.g. water/sewerage reticulation). It really is a hotchpotch of myriad overlapping jurisdictions in which the underlying purpose seems to be to restrict delivery solely to a group of ratepayers handpicked by the housing market, and thereby avoid the issues and costs of redistribution. Taken to the limit this approach to resource allocation becomes unashamedly self-serving.

Australia's brand of federalism can best be looked upon as a mutation. Mathews (1980: 197) goes so far as to call Australian federalism with its 'unitary and highly centralized fiscal system, and an aggressively federal and political administrative system', a 'federal paradox'. Section 51 of the Australian constitution invests fund-raising powers in the Commonwealth, leaving the states with formidable policymaking responsibilities in the area of programme implementation and administration. Few of the Commonwealth's powers are constitutionally 'exclusive', and Commonwealth financial dominance has been evolutionary rather than a necessary consequence of the wording of the document (personal communication, A. Parkin). For example, the Commonwealth tightened its grip on revenue-raising when the state governments relinquished their income and excise taxing powers to the Australian government as a 'temporary' wartime expediency and failed to regain them after the Second World War.

Where does local government fit into this framework? They are statutory creatures of the states, constituted by Acts of State Parliament, and therefore legally subservient to them. 'State governments continue to limit municipal autonomy through various review, guideline, auditing, planning and appeal procedures, and local governments often act effectively as enforcers of State-mandated standards in such areas as health and sanitation' (Parkin, 1983). With about 930 local government bodies at present, the structure of local government broadly reflects the English pattern prior to 1974. As the duty-roster of Australian government gradually took shape local government ended up with the 'leftovers'; that is, the mundane services like the provision of local streets and drainage, rubbish collection, park maintenance and the issuing of library books. Gradually in the 1960s and 1970s these activities have been expanded in a modest way to include social welfare services such as the appointment of health officers and social workers by some councils. The limited liability of local government in Australian public affairs is born out in the following data which were compiled by Parkin (1983): as of 1978–79 – the latest year for which even crudely comparable data were available – Australian municipalities accounted for only about 7 per cent of total public sector spending. In the USA the comparable estimate was about 26 per cent, while in the UK, with only two tiers of government, the corresponding figure was about 30 per cent.

Hence the business of urban government in Australia is dominated by the states. In contrast with the British and US situations, the states in Australia run the public education, health and transport systems. State authorities build and manage highways and housing and provide those universally local services in America, fire and police protection. Moreover, a number of *ad hoc* state bodies also supply the water, sewerage and electricity services within the cities. Significantly, the very services that American scholars take for granted will be provided at the local level, where they are supposed to display the greatest sensitivity to community aspirations, needs, and ability to pay, 'are those most strongly entrenched as State level responsibilities' in Australia (Parkin, 1982: 136) – schools, public housing, law enforcement, urban development, public health and welfare.

Intergovernmental financial relations

Both the means available to and the success of local governments in raising or attracting revenue are obvious keys to the adequacy of public provision at the 'grassroots'. Local authorities can tap three main sources of revenue – the taxes they levy, charges made for goods and services they provide, and grants from central or state governments (Hepworth, 1978). Their expenditure must be financed out of this revenue or else made up by borrowing on the private capital market. The actual proportions obtaining amongst the various sources of local government revenue say quite a lot about underlying political ideologies as well as indicating where the locus of power lies in the government superstructure.

The vast assortment of general and special local authorities to be found in America's metropolitan regions, coupled with an array of federal and state aid programmes, demands an exceedingly cautious approach to generalization about intergovernmental fiscal relations in the United States. For example, in Hawaii 80 per cent of the cost of delivering services is borne by the state government; whereas, only about 25 per cent of New

York City's revenue came from the State of New York during the first half of the 1970s. By the late 1970s there were over 400 individual legislative authorizations providing federal funds to local governments, of which 70 bypassed the states completely (Bacharach *et al.*, 1980: 46). They included funds allocated under the State and Local Fiscal Assistance Act of 1972 (with two-thirds going to local government); the Community Development Block Grant Program (1974), which fed aid directly to distressed urban neighbourhoods; urban development action grants; and assistance aimed at stimulating lagging local economies through capital works expenditure and allocations under Titles II and VI of the Comprehensive Employment and Training Act, 1976–77. All this is supplemented by state assistance to local authorities, mainly in the form of categorical grants, plus the direct state spending on education, public welfare, law enforcement, and health services which does not show up as intergovernmental transfers. Despite this growth in federal and state aid to urban governments, table 8.2 shows that local municipalities in the US are still heavily

Table 8.2 Sources of city government revenue, US, 1960–75[a]

	1960	1965	1970	1975
Federal grants	3.0	3.9	5.3	11.1
State grants	12.5	13.5	18.9	21.8
Property taxes	34.8	32.2	27.9	21.8
Sales and gross receipts	8.2	8.8	7.4	7.6
Licences	4.7	4.7	6.4	5.9
Charges and miscellaneous	14.9	15.1	15.5	15.2
Utility revenues	19.2	19.0	15.8	13.6
Insurance trust revenue	2.7	2.8	2.8	3.0
Total revenue ($ million)	14,915	20,318	32,704	59,744

[a] All urban municipalities and their dependent agencies except other local governments overlying city areas
Source: US Bureau of Census (1978: 310)

reliant on property taxes for their revenue. Largely because of this feature of local government revenue in the United States, councils are preoccupied with attracting private investment to fortify the local tax base and increase revenues (or, conversely, with halting private disinvestment which depletes per capita revenues).

With structural decline and disinvestment depleting the tax base of the nineteenth century manufacturing cities in the north and north-east, many central city governments are now confronted with a widening gap between the growth in public expenditure and their taxable capacity.[3] Urban fiscal

[3] Up until the late 1960s it was generally true that despite the outmigration of healthy households and firms the taxable capacity of the central cities exceeded that of the suburbs that enveloped them (Kirwan, 1980a: 26–7).

stress grew increasingly acute during the 1970s as the central cities' social welfare bills soared with mounting structural unemployment; whilst municipal labour costs and service charges on local government debts were hit by inflationary pressures. Boast (1980: 82–3) estimates that the ability of the 55 largest US cities to internally finance their own current operations steadily fell away from a level of 87 per cent in 1955, to 84 per cent in 1962, 79 per cent in 1967, and 75 per cent in 1972. Table 8.3 confirms that there is a link between the condition of the urban public economy and the reliance of metropolitan governments in the US upon direct federal aid. Indeed the 1978 estimates for direct federal aid, and the per capita value of that aid, highlights the severity of the urban fiscal 'crisis' for particular cities in the US. Yet, in spite of the contrasting levels of federal assistance received by these sample 'declining', 'stagnant' and 'growing' cities, it appears that the federal government still does not return revenue to taxpayers in proportions that match their income tax

Table 8.3 Direct federal aid as percentage of total revenue for selected cities, 1957–78

	1957	1967	1976	1978 (estimated)	Per capita federal aid	
					1976 ($)	1978 ($)
'Declining' cities						
St Louis	0.6	1.0	23.6	56.1	86	228
Newark	0.2	1.7	11.4	64.2	47	291
Buffalo	1.3	2.1	55.6	75.9	163	239
Cleveland	2.0	8.3	22.8	60.3	65	190
Boston	negl.	10.0	31.5	30.2	204	219
Unweighted mean	0.8	4.6	29.0	57.3	113	233
'Stagnant' cities						
Baltimore	1.7	3.8	38.9	46.4	167	225
Philadelphia	0.4	8.8	37.7	53.8	129	204
Detroit	1.3	13.1	50.2	76.8	161	274
Chicago	1.4	10.9	19.2	42.1	47	117
Atlanta	4.3	2.0	15.1	40.0	52	167
Unweighted mean	1.8	7.7	32.2	51.8	111	197
'Growing' cities						
Denver	0.6	1.2	21.2	25.9	90	150
Los Angeles	0.7	0.7	19.3	39.8	54	134
Dallas	0.0	negl.	20.0	17.8	51	54
Houston	0.2	3.1	19.4	23.8	44	71
Phoenix	1.1	10.6	35.0	58.7	57	117
Unweighted mean	0.5	3.1	23.0	33.2	61	105

Source: US Advisory Commission on Intergovernmental Relations (1978: table 1)

contributions. Further calculations by Boast (1980: 84), indicating the 'over-taxing' or 'underrewarding' of northern cities in relation to western cities, are consistent with a 'progressive federal income tax structure and federal spending patterns tilted towards the South and West.' In 1969, according to Boast, federal personal income tax payments represented only 45 and 52 per cent of federal outlays received by Pacific and south-western cities, compared with ratios of 63, 67 and 73 per cent for north-eastern, south-eastern and north central cities respectively. Clearly the declining older industrial cities of the north and east are disadvantaged by the present federal revenue-sharing arrangements. And in the chilly climate of Reagan's homespun monetarism, there is little point in the distressed cities holding out in the hope of receiving federal assistance at the same levels that applied during the 1970s. From a peak in 1978, federal grants-in-aid have fallen as a percentage of all government outlays from 17.3 in 1978 to 15.8 in 1980 (US Office of Management and Budget, 1980).[4] To place the full implications of these cut-backs in context, some of the most distressed US cities drew three-quarters of their general revenue from the US Treasury in the late 1970s (table 8.3).

Significantly, although British inner cities have also been beset by the same problems of structural decline and suburbanization they have not been crippled fiscally, as have many of their US counterparts. Kirwan (1980a; 1980b) and Bennett (1982a; 1982b) suggest three main reasons for this. Firstly, the level of metropolitan fragmentation is much less in Britain than in the USA (table 8.1). As a result of the reorganization of local government in the mid-1970s, the suburbs and centres of most British cities are now contained within the same administrative jurisdiction which facilitates equalization at the level of the metropolitan district or county. Secondly, metropolitan government gives British local authorities plagued by centralized urban stress access to large and increasing tax bases; allows rate poundages to be fixed at levels similar to other local authorities; and service expenditures to be maintained at high levels (Bennett, 1982a). Thirdly, the level of central government involvement in local finance is very high. Since 1975/76, central government transfers to local authorities have never dropped below 50 per cent of total local current account expenditure.

The main form of rate supplementation in the UK is the Rate Support Grant (RSG), which accounted for about 85 per cent of total Exchequer assistance to local authorities in 1979/80 (Smith, 1981: 254). Because the Rate Support Grant, in taking variable local resources and needs into account, has been relatively successful in equalizing local financial

---

[4] Reischauer (1981: 33–36) explains that discretionary spending on targeted community aid is much more vulnerable to fiscal paring than 'mandatory entitlement' programmes like social security and defence (the electoral impact is also less likely to be so wide-reaching).

burdens,[5] the fiscal strain of inner city decline in Britain has been shifted, in part, to the national tax base (Bennett, 1982b: 1303). In 1981/82 the RSG, which formerly comprised three separate elements – needs (60 per cent), resources (30 per cent), domestic (10 per cent), was collapsed into a domestic rate relief grant and the *block* grant. The domestic rate relief is hypothecated, meaning that local authorities are obliged to use it specifically to reduce the rate poundage on domestic property (where rates are judged burdensome). The *block* grant now seeks to simultaneously equalize local authority differences in the tax base, or fiscal capacity, and expenditure on 'needs'. The calculation of the level of the needs element (see Hepworth, 1978: appendix II) makes use of weighted indicators that are sensitive to annual adjustments in local authority housing, dependency ratios, student numbers etc. Naturally changes to the formulae, such as those which favoured the Labour-dominated inner city councils in the 1978/79–79/80 allocations, are challenged by local authorities facing cutbacks in their needs grant. Predictably, shortly afterwards the new Conservative government reviewed the RSG in order to limit need payments to local authorities considered well-enough endowed to fund more of their own spending: namely, the London councils and the metropolitan districts (Bennett, 1982b: 1290).

Intergovernmental relations in Australia are characterized by an unusually high degree of fiscal centralism. Although most of the major prerogatives for public expenditure in the cities lie with the states, the Commonwealth is the only level of government empowered to tax personal and corporate income, excise and sales. In 1978–79 the Commonwealth share of total taxation amounted to 79.9 per cent, which compared with 15.8 and 4.3 per cent for state and local government respectively (Jones, 1981: 48). Thus, in a very real sense, federal government in Australia controls the public sector 'purse strings'. Obviously this forces local government to be much more self-sufficient in expenditure matters than their UK counterparts; but then they have less extensive duties. With the gradual improvement in the intergovernment transfers to the lowest level of government during the last decade, the combined Commonwealth and state contribution to local council revenue in Australia rose from 18.2 per cent in 1969–70 to 25.8 per cent in 1978–79 (Jones, 1981: 177). Despite the Whitlam government's commitment to a strengthening of the third tier of government between 1972 and 1975, local authorities have remained firmly under the tutelage of the states.

This overshadowing of local government by the states has left an

---

[5] The effectiveness of the resources element of the RSG as an instrument of equalization can be judged from data presented by Foster *et al.* (1980: 189): after introduction in 1948 the coefficient of variation of rate poundage of county boroughs fell from a pre-war average of 25, to 12 per cent after the war.

indelible imprint on Australian cities. Urban investment undertaken by the states has always favoured the core of the metropolitan primates at the expense of the proliferating suburbs. The overcentralization of expenditure is visible in the concentration of each state's public services in the CBD, as well as their hospitals (Lawrence, 1972) and welfare administration (Mendelsohn, 1979: 37), and in the neglect of the outer suburbs by the statutory authorities responsible for sewerage, public transport and road construction (Perlgut, 1982). The states' departments and statutory authorities in general have proven either very slow, incapable or unwilling to budget for the capital expenditure requirements of councils in rapid growth urban regions like the western suburbs of both Melbourne and Sydney, and Adelaide's northern and southern suburbs. In a region like western Sydney, which has had to absorb 750,000 people between 1947 and 1980 (or three Canberras), the present backlog of capital works in residential areas released prior to 1978 is in the order of $A20 million. Additionally, Payne (1981: 8) has calculated that the 28,600 lots released for housing in western Sydney since 1978 carry frontend costs of $75 million. As shown in the next section a programme of urban fixed investment of this magnitude imposes an immense capital burden upon outer area councils.

It was expressly for this sort of reason that the Whitlam government revamped the Australian Grants Commission in 1973. A total of $A56 million in specifically targeted grants was allocated in the first year of operation (1974–75), with the objective of equalizing council revenue and fiscal 'needs'. With the accession to power of the Liberal government in 1976 there was another shift in intergovernmental financial relations towards general revenue sharing arrangements and away from specific purpose grants. Untied funds rose as a proportion of Federal-local transfers from one-third of the total grant in 1975–76 to over one half in 1979 (Jones, 1981: 191). Notably the Fraser government's 'new federalism' entailed tax sharing under the Commonwealth-Local Government (Personal Income Tax Sharing) Act, 1976, which now delivers two per cent of personal income tax to local bodies. But even though the money comes from Canberra, the transfer mechanism has restored to the states much of their previous ascendancy in urban public expenditures. There is obviously an extremely heavy rural bias in the Grants Commission formulae applied at the state level that exaggerates the importance of road expenditures and low population densities. As a result, while the NSW-wide average for LGAs in 1981–82 was $24.88 per capita, inner city councils like Sydney and South Sydney, with high infrastructure costs due to redevelopment only received $23.63 and $22.26 per capita. Similarly, the Western Sydney Regional Organization of Councils, with its massive capital works programme and pressing social needs, only received a combined per capita grant of $18.92. Perlgut (1982) concludes that with glaring disparities like these some parts of Australian cities are not receiving their fair share of Commonwealth revenue sharing funds.

The unequal burden of urban capital formation

The extent to which urban governments are required to borrow on the private capital market in order to finance housing stock, infrastructure, utilities and the like, can have a lasting impact on the quality of life within their jurisdictions. Borrowings for capital expenditure, as distinct from expenditure on current account, are conventionally deployed to offset short-term or seasonal fluctuations in revenue, or to finance fixed investment in urban infrastucture and stock. A third reason for borrowing, which is frowned upon because of the risks involved, is to meet public expenditure on current account items. It is this dubious, even desperate practice, adopted increasingly by US city treasuries in the seventies, that was most immediately responsible for the 'urban fiscal crisis'. In simple terms, this approach to 'deficit financing' involves the salvaging of current account deficits by borrowing and issuing new debt in order to pay off old debt (Shefter, 1980: 198–203). In the case of New York City (NYC) things came to a head when the 11 NYC clearinghouse banks jointly refused to bid for NYC securities following the default of the New York State Urban Development Corporation in the spring of 1975 (Boast, 1980: 79).

In the US, during the period 1966–75, the private capital market supplied $193 billion of the $257 billion in long-term capital to the cities while the federal government supplied $64 billion as 'additions to state and local assets' (Boast, 1980: 76). Significantly, 77 per cent of all the capital borrowed from the federal government was used for financing economic infrastructure – while over 90 per cent of the funds for social infrastructure and subsidy purposes came from private market lenders. It can be argued, therefore, that instead of using direct loans to create redressive resource flows, the federal government abdicated to the market the responsibility for the financing of educational and health services. Furthermore, the private market can put a stop very quickly to any city's efforts to redistribute resources from the haves to the havenots by refusing to purchase its bonds and securities. This has been the fate of the declining industrial cities with the highest level of welfare dependency in the north-east and north central regions of the US: 'cities that pay for expanded public services with a declining tax base are penalized with higher market costs and less access' to the all-important urban capital market (Boast, 1980: 80). The vulnerability of sick central cities to fiscal strangulation only fully dawned upon their administrators when the capitalist economies were convulsed in 1974 by the unfamiliar combination of hyperinflation and recession.

Local authorities in Britain must obtain central government approval to borrow finance for capital expenditure programmes in 'key sectors', including housing, education, major roads, police and social services. The capital, which is borrowed for fixed investment and to refinance existing debts, accounts for about a quarter of the total local authority expenditure on an annual basis (Kennett, 1980: 65). Local authority capital expenditure in 1974–75, for example, was divided between housing (62 per cent), transportation (14 per cent), and education, libraries, science and arts (12 per cent) (Hepworth, 1978: 45). Approximately half of the longer term borrowing emanates from the Public Works Loan Board (PWLB), a statutory body that allocates funds voted by Parliament. Otherwise councils may float loans on the domestic capital markets or borrow foreign currency subject to Treasury approval. Like urban public corporations in the United States, British municipalities have not been able to emerge unscathed from the ravages of stagflation. Their outstanding loan debt escalated during the 1970s so that repayments on borrowings now account for over a fifth of total local authority revenue expenditure (Kennett, 1980: 66). The hardest pressed cities tend to be those squeezed financially by a combination of falling revenue from rates and rising demands for services from the poor and elderly who are not amongst the migrants – Liverpool, Leeds, Birmingham, Manchester and Sheffield (see Rose and Page, 1982).

Notwithstanding Kirwan's (1980b: 94) verdict that 'local fiscal crisis in Britain has been avoided at the cost of national fiscal stress', the future does not bode well for the ratepayers of councils that have to service escalating debt charges from static incomes (Eversley, 1972). Kennett (1980) believes that Kirwan's assessment may be too sanguine, especially now with central government cuts in public expenditure threatening to transfer more of the financial strain to the public economies of British cities. It can no longer be expected that the Rate Support Grant will insulate urban councils from periodic shocks delivered by rapid inflation and volatile interest rates.

Quite different factors lie behind the financial straits in which some Australian urban authorities find themselves. Apart from a handful of older inner area municipalities faced with the task of renewing worn-out infrastructure and keeping up with demands for improved social services, the capital burden imposed on local government can be traced directly to the complications of *rapid* growth. Local councils in the fastest growing outer suburbs, which also happen to be amongst the poorest, have had to live with the problems of funding the crippling frontend costs of suburban development for at least the past 25 years. Because rate revenue is unavoidably low in the early stages of development this produces cashflow problems and heightens the reliance on capital loans. To make matters worse, since the mid-1970s outer area councils have fallen victim to Commonwealth penny-pinching, limitations on their borrowing power, as well as a number of inflationary effects.

Firstly, despite the Fraser government's expansion of revenue-sharing, the value in real terms of Commonwealth assistance to local government in 1980–81 was 15 per cent below its 1975–76 level. Secondly, local authorities seeking Loan Council approval for 'normal' borrowings are facing mounting competition for borrowing rights from semi-government bodies constructing the roads, rail, electricity generation and transmission equipment for resource-based development in Australia. Hence, in 1981–82 councils in the western Sydney region received only 70.3 per cent of the $48.7 million requested even though 'in virtually all cases the councils have been able to line up the lenders for the full amount of the money they wish to borrow' (Perlgut, 1982: 3). Finally, hyper-inflation has affected the operations of urban local governments with heavy capital expenditure in the following ways: (1) new plant and equipment is more expensive to purchase than acquisitions made before inflation; (b) in the case of the Western Suburbs Regional Organization of Councils (WSROC) it has doubled the interest repayments for servicing loans; (c) it has increased the WSROC contributions to NSW statutory authorities to the point where, for some member councils, they approach the combined receipts from the Local Government Assistance Fund and Commonwealth taxsharing. Councils are levied to meet the cost of services delivered to their areas. In NSW this may include: contributions to the Board of Fire Commissioners and the Bush Fire Fighting Fund for fire protection; the Department of Environment and Planning for open space and parks purchased on their behalf; street lighting costs; and upkeep of roads maintained by the Department of Main Roads. Perlgut (1982: 30) calculates that 45 per cent of the combined government grant to WSROC councils in 1981–82 was returned to the State of New South Wales in contributions to statutory authorities.

Resource allocation in politically divided cities: the incidence of costs and benefits

Some of the individuality in governmental structures and fiscal relations that we have described combines with spatial effects within the urban setting to exacerbate existing disparities in wealth and service levels. The plan in this last section of chapter 8 is to point out some of the distributional consequences that flow from political fragmentation and the compartmentation of fiscal capacity. Of special interest are the spillover effects that contribute to the fiscal exploitation of the central city by the suburbs in the United States, and the equitableness of public provision at the community level. This involves measuring the incidence of costs and benefits associated with both the raising of revenue and the provision of services against accepted norms for 'equalization', or put another way 'territorial justice'. Bleddyn Davies (1968: 16) suggests that the criterion for 'territorial justice' should be 'to each area according to the needs of the population of that area'.[6]

Political fragmentation of metropolitan space: a means for manipulating who gets what public goods and services

Is metropolitan government organized in a way that facilitates the pursuit of redistributive policies? Or has an organizational form been created that *ipso facto* inhibits redistribution and buttresses the tendencies to localism, insularity and the concentration of income and wealth that are inherent in the housing and land markets of capitalist cities? Undoubtedly a centralized form of government is better suited to the prosecution of redistributive objectives *if that is what society wants* (i.e. in itself it does not guarantee that redistribution will occur). Conversely, redistribution is hardest to achieve, while at the same time the most conspicuous differences in the provision of and access to government services within cities are found, under conditions of exaggerated political subdivision. These conditions, which generally provide a very effective deterrent against redistribution, are met most often in the United States. There a process of 'balkanization' has left metropolitan regions with a patchwork quilt of compartmentalized governments and overlapping service areas of all kinds (table 8.1). Because the American system of localized urban government probably comes closest to 'localism' in practice it is worth taking time to consider the implications for the redistribution of real income in cities (see also Cox, 1973). Unlike the Australian arrangement, which is fairly highly centralized by international standards, and urban government in the UK, which occupies a position midway between 'centralization' and 'localization', there are no well-developed compensatory mechanisms built into the structure of government such as Britain's Rate Support Grant, or the centrally supervised public provision that obtains at the state level in Australian cities (see Parkin, 1982: 79–81).

In a paper aimed at bringing the relationship between jurisdictional fragmentation and inequality into sharper focus Hill (1974) tested several pertinent hypotheses for 127 'eligible' municipalities in US metropolitan areas.[7] To start with, his summary statistics confirm that the distribution

[6] Bennett (1980: 93–5) demonstrates that while this may be sufficient for private needs, or the personal services that Davies deals with, it falls down as a principle for assigning public goods.

[7] The US Bureau of Census only releases income data for municipalities with populations in excess of 2,500 persons. Hill (1974: 1563) estimates that on these grounds alone, one half of all the municipalities within American SMSAs were precluded from the study. This introduces unfortunate distortion with the distributional significance of these 'undersized' municipalities dwarfing their numerical contribution to total metropolitan population (three per cent in 1960): they include a disproportionate number of the very wealth and/or very poor residents of US metropolitan areas.

of median family income can be highly variable from municipality to municipality within any metropolitan area. In 1960, the standard deviation in municipal income averaged $920 across Hill's 127 SMSAs. At best, the SMSA with the least inter-governmental inequality had a standard deviation in municipal family income of $14, while in the worst SMSA a standard deviation of $3,128 was recorded. Hill postulates that a number of underlying structural conditions give rise to these observed variations in municipal income inequality. With the aid of multiple regression analysis he (Hill, 1974: 1567) determines that the most important contributors to governmental inequality within US metropolitan areas ($R^2 = 0.58$) are as follows (standardized regression coefficients in parentheses): the relative size of the nonwhite population (0.601); the proportion of families with annual incomes over $10,000 (0.455); the degree of municipal fragmentation (0.342); the extent of family income inequality (0.289). On the strength of his analysis Hill concludes that 'Family income inequality is translated through the dual mechanisms of residential segregation and political incorporation into inequality in the distribution of wealth, and therefore, the capacity to produce public goods and services among governments in the metropolis' Hill, 1974: 1565).

Urban education in the United States: 'What you pay for, is what you get'

The principles of localism and citizen involvement in the management of local affairs find their clearest expression in the American school district. There is the expected variation from state to state in the degree of administrative and fiscal autonomy vested in the elected school boards. Johnston (1979: 33) reports that in 23 states school districts are entirely independent, in 16 they are semi-dependent, and in 7 they are partially independent which leaves only five with a centralized education system. On top of this are parallel variations in the level of state aid flowing to school districts (Kirst, 1982). States like California, in response to court orders to 'level up' per pupil spending ratios across the state, increased the level of state aid from 32 to 65 per cent of the combined state/local expenditure between 1970 and 1979. However, in states like Michigan and Florida the allocation of state aid to school districts remained at a constant level throughout the 1970s (45 and 55 per cent respectively). This means that there is no guarantee that school districts will be compensated for the striking variations in locally derived taxes for education that are a natural corollary of the income segregation of urban communities. For example, when averaged across 49 states the mean assessed value per pupil in the richest school district exceeds that of the poorest district by a factor of 17.3 (Johnston, 1979: 38). Some of the interdistrict disparities in fiscal capacity have come to light as a result of litigation testing the Fourteenth Amendment of the US Constitution which prohibits discrimination; or if more liberally construed, unequal treatment.[8] For example, in arguing that educational expenditures based on property values was unconstitutional, the 1971 *Serrano* suit contrasted the fiscal position of two Los Angeles school districts (Kirst, 1982). The assessed property value per pupil, the tax rate levied, and the educational expenditure per pupil varied as follows for Beverley Hills and Baldwin City respectively: $550,885 and $3,707; $2.38 and $5.48; $1.232 and $577. A similar picture emerged in the case of Rodriguez vs San Antonio Independent School District (table 8.4).

Table 8.4 Fiscal differentials between Texan school districts

Market value of taxable property per pupil in district	Tax rate per $100 ($)	Tax yield per pupil ($)	Number of districts
>$100,000	0.31	585	10
$100,000–50,000	0.38	262	26
$50,000–30,000	0.55	213	30
$30,000–10,000	0.72	162	40
<$10,000	0.70	60	4

Source: Lineberry and Sharkansky (1974: 223)

The whole issue of funding education by means of a property tax is given an extra twist when student needs in unevenly endowed districts are set against fiscal capacity. In a study of school districts in New York State, Akin and Auten (1976) illustrate that the outcome across an urban region can be unmercifully regressive: those municipalities (like old central cities and poorer suburbs) with a limited fiscal capacity and/or above average student needs may well incur proportionally higher tax rates and yet still not match the educational standards extant in well-off school districts.

Central city-suburban disparities: the inverse relationship between fiscal capacity and community needs

In one of a series of studies which have the evaluation of central city fiscal distress as their major objective (Bahl, 1978; Oakland, 1979; Peterson, 1976; Teitelbaum, 1982), Nathan and Adams (1976) also construct an index designed to disclose the intra-metropolitan disparity between con-

---

[8] While these law suits were unable to produce a redistribution of property wealth from high spending to low spending areas (thereby respecting the 'tax revolt' movement of the mid-seventies) they did require many states to supplement expenditure on education in deprived school districts. In addition, in some states property tax relief has been targeted at school districts with high fiscal effort but below average per student expenditures; but, in this situation, property owners win at the expense of school children (Kirst, 1982). Other decisions (*Seattle* vs *Washington*; *Levittown* vs *Nyquist*) have acknowledged the special needs of disadvantaged and handicapped pupils residing within hard-pressed cities.

ditions in the central city and suburban areas of US urban regions. The index is a ratio between the composite scores obtained by the central city and suburbs on six measures of socio-economic conditions; namely, unemployment levels, proportion of dependents educational attainment (population under 18 and over 65 years), average income, incidence of family poverty and overcrowded housing. An index of central city hardship relative to the balance of the SMSA was calculated for 55 of the nations 66 largest metropolitan areas at the 1970 Census. A value of 100 in table 8.5 would signify identical socio-economic conditions for both the central city and suburbs of an SMSA. Table 8.5 reveals that more than a quarter of America's most populous SMSAs have indices of 200 or more, 'denoting especially marked city-suburban divergencies' (Nathan and Adams, 1976: 50). By the same token it is a fact that some suburbs are not much better off than their parent city, whilst the contrasts between some suburbs can be just as noteworthy as between central city and suburb.

From table 8.5 it is also clear that a good proportion of those SMSAs with the greatest central city-suburban disparities are those with central city boundaries dating from the nineteenth century and now encasing poverty-impacted cores. The separation of central cities from the metropolitan tax base by ossified political boundaries is arguably the root cause (Oakland, 1979: 328) of the phenomenon measured by Nathan and Adams.

> . . . it remains an inescapable fact of federalism that if localities try to redistribute income to a much greater extent than the other localities, or if they run abnormally large deficits and incur subsequent high interest and debt retirement costs, there is a good risk that the tax-paying population will simply pick up stakes and leave the locality in a fiscal situation that is much more precarious. (Gramlich, 1976: 417–18)

Because the housing market in the US concentrates the welfare-dependent poor in the central city, and City Hall cannot tap the taxable wealth of the suburbs, it is not uncommon to find a 70 per cent differential in the tax rate struck by the central cities compared with suburban municipalities (Oakland, 1979: 328). This gives rise to the situation in New York City, which has over 70 per cent of the state's welfare recipients, where City ratepayers must shoulder a disproportionate share of public assistance and medicaid. In 1975, their per capita contribution was $199 compared to only $28 in the rest of the state. While the City of New York had to pay for 75 per cent of the statewide local share of public assistance and medicaid, other localities, with 58 per cent of the state's population and 30 per cent of all welfare recipients, only had to meet 25 per cent of all local costs (reported in Gifford, 1978: 580–81).

Table 8.5 Indices of central city hardship relative to rest of SMSA, selected US metropolitan areas

Primary central city of SMSA	Central city hardship index	County areas in SMSA	Total SMSA population 1970 (thousands)	Central city (%)
Newark	422	3	1,857	20.6
Cleveland	331	4	2,064	36.4
Hartford	317	1	664	23.8
Baltimore	256	6	2,071	43.7
Chicago	245	6	6,975	48.2
St Louis	231	7	2,363	26.3
Atlanta	226	5	1,390	35.8
Gary	213	2	633	27.7
New York	211	5	11,572	68.2
Detroit	210	3	4,200	36.0
Philadelphia	205	8	4,818	40.4
Boston	198	1	2,754	23.3
Milwaukee	195	4	1,404	51.1
San Jose	181	1	1,065	41.9
Columbus, Ohio	173	3	916	58.9
New Orleans	168	4	1,046	56.7
Akron	152	2	679	40.5
Ft Worth	149	2	762	51.6
Cincinnati	148	7	1,385	32.7
Pittsburgh	146	4	2,401	21.7
Denver	143	5	1,228	41.9
Jersey City	129	1	609	42.8
Oklahoma City	128	3	641	57.2
Indianapolis	124	8	1,110	67.1
Toledo	116	3	693	55.4
Los Angeles	105	1	7,036	40.0
San Francisco	105	5	3,110	23.0
Syracuse	103	3	637	31.0
Allentown	100	3	544	20.1
Portland, Oregon	100	4	1,009	37.8
Dallas	97	6	1,556	54.3
Houston	93	5	1,985	62.1
Phoenix	85	1	968	60.0
Salt Lake City	80	2	558	31.5
San Diego	77	1	1,358	51.3
Seattle	67	2	1,422	37.3

Source: Calculated by Nathan and Adams (1976: 51–2) from 1972 US Census data

A further explanation known as the central city 'exploitation hypothesis' has been proffered to account for the disproportionately high taxes paid by central city ratepayers. It is attributed to Hawley (1951) who recognized that there is a beneficial spillover of central city expenditures to suburban residents who commute into the city for employment, shopping and entertainment as well as availing themselves of the public goods and services funded by central city taxpayers. However, these benefit spill-overs must be discounted by the gains to the central city in enhanced property values, retail sales, and other expenditures by non-residents. Although there have been various tests of the 'exploitation hypothesis' it remains unproven: 'Relatively few studies, for example those of Neenan (1970) and of Greene *et al.*, (1974), have concluded that suburbs do indeed make a net gain at the expense of the central cities; and each of these studies requires the weighting of a particular welfare basis to be accepted in adducing the magnitude of benefits' (Bennett, 1980: 423).

Comparable, though not crippling, central city-suburban disparities also characterize many of Britain's nineteenth-century industrial cities. Prior to the 1974 local government reform, Greater Manchester's central city and industrial suburbs possessed industrial and commercial property from which to subsidize their less productive domestic property (table 8.6). This helped to keep the rate bills for householders lower on average than elsewhere in the conurbation, despite the fact that the central city had the highest rate poundage (£1.02 for every £1 of assessed value) due to the

Table 8.6 Fiscal capacity and effort in Greater Manchester, 1973–74

District	Value of property per ratepayer (£)		Rate poundage	Average rate bill (£)
	Domestic	Non-domestic		
Manchester	59.65	107.22	1.020	60.84
Stockport	61.79	57.68	0.855	52.83
Stretford	63.41	135.20	0.895	56.75
Urmiston	74.97	132.23	0.798	59.83
Sale	81.72	30.50	0.900	73.54
Altrincham	74.02	62.14	0.950	60.24
Hale	115.37	23.37	0.995	114.79
Wilmslow	96.49	48.47	0.905	87.32
Alderley Edge	109.33	36.50	0.960	104.96
Cheadle and Gatley	96.22	36.90	0.875	84.19
Hazel Grove	110.23	44.60	0.870	95.90
Marple	81.59	22.03	0.895	73.02
Bowdon	118.79	28.24	0.925	109.88

Source: Johnston (1979: 40). Based on Department of Environment data on rates and rateable values

relative concentration of needs. The more serious disparity arises, however, when domestic rates are adjusted for taxable capacity: 'In no suburban area is the rate bill twice that of Manchester, and so, assuming that average incomes in the suburbs are at least twice those of the central city, suburban fiscal effort is relatively low' (Johnston, 1979: 41).

Although disparities in relation to the incidence of local government costs (rates), benefits (services), and fiscal effort, have been reported for Australian cities (Groenewegen, 1976; Law, 1975; Manning, 1973) they are somewhat different in nature to the central city-suburbs pattern that predominates in the United States and Britain. Most importantly, the labour-intensive social services used by the central cities' service-dependent poor are provided by the state and Commonwealth governments in Australia. Even though the central city councils forego considerable rate income on property owned by the federal and state governments,[9] and notwithstanding 'freeloading' commuters from the suburbs,[10] the non-domestic downtown tax base is prosperous enough to support most public expenditure requirements.

Both Groenewegen (1976: 122–5) and Manning (1973: 20–74) concur about the uneven incidence of fiscal (rate) effort across the metropolitan area of Sydney. Groenewegen's calculations place LGAs with the highest and lowest aggregate property values at the opposite ends of his tax effort index: the following poor LGAs accompanied by their rank, were at the top – Botany (2), Campbelltown (3), Auburn, (4) Penrith (5), Leichhardt (6), and Liverpool (7), while the bottom ranks were filled by Sydney's richest LGAs – Hunters Hill (39), Kuringai (37), Mosman, (33), Woollahra (31). Manning (1973) arrives at the same general conclusion about the distribution of fiscal effort within Sydney: 'Despite all the rhetoric about the benefit principle[11] the costs of local services are regressively distributed, so that municipal operations almost certainly take more than proportionately from the poor and give more than proportionately to the rich' (Manning, 1973: 70). Therefore, as a general rule, the lower the aggregate prosperity of Sydney ratepayers, the higher the rate levied and the lower the fiscal yield per capita. Related studies by Law (1975) and Perlgut (1982) have confirmed that ratepayers find local government taxes

[9] By 1977 only 22.4 per cent of the land area of the City of Sydney was rateable. Leaving aside roads and parks, about 36 per cent of the City area was exempted from rates because it was owned by government users, education and health institutions, churches and charities. Estimates suggest that in 1980 these exemptions represented about $18.3 million in revenue foregone.

[10] The spillover problem is probably most accute for the City of Sydney where 15,000 ratepayers have to provide facilities to support a daily influx of 180,000 office workers and 50,000 students, and the roads to move 500,000 vehicles into and through the city core (City of Sydney, 1980).

[11] i.e. the beneficiary should pay for the benefit received.

especially burdensome where there is a conjunction of low local prosperity and rapid growth, and councils that set a very high rate to achieve per capita yields well above those in older suburbs exhibiting comparable levels of prosperity.

Locationally discriminatory public provision

Underlying any evaluation of 'territorial justice' is the distinction between equal distribution, which gives everyone the same level of services, and an equitable distribution. An equitable arrangement is one that leaves households in life circumstances more nearly equal than before the service was provided. This places the criterion of equity in service distribution much closer to a genuinely egalitarian 'standard of "equal results" ' (Rich, 1979: 152). Pinch (1979) echoes this need to measure 'outcomes' (defined as 'the effects of services upon individuals and community'), since the provision of services is not entirely congruent with inter-authority patterns of expenditure. For various reasons expenditures are not foolproof indicators of the extent of services: administrative overheads and costs of delivery vary between areas; councils do not operate with equal effectiveness and efficiency, and they hold differing opinions about standards of provision.

When it comes to the distribution of public services every community can no doubt provide examples of preferential treatment, misplaced priorities in allocation, and deliberate withholding or neglect. Caro (1974: 318, 509) provides two flagrant examples of locationally discriminatory provision. The bridges built across Long Island's parkways in the 1930s were just low enough to prevent buses from carrying blacks from Manhattan's tenements to Long Island beaches. Although 255 playgrounds were created in NYC in the 1930s, only one was provided in Stuyvesant, one in Harlem, and none in South Jamaica (three neighbourhoods which housed the City's 200,000 black children). Jackman (1979) has shown that London receives a proportionately generous 'clawback' through the needs element entitlement of the Rate Support Grant. London's share of the needs grant total rose from 16.5 per cent in 1974–75 to 21.6 per cent in 1978–79. Over the same period, the metropolitan districts' share increased from 25.3 per cent to 26.5 per cent while the shire counties' share fell from 58.2 per cent to 51.9 per cent (Foster *et al.*, 1980: 257). As this is difficult to justify on a 'needs' basis, one can only conclude that the grant system had been politically manipulated to benefit the London electorates (Kennett, 1980: 50–5).

But leaving aside these all too familiar cases where service provision mirrors electoral fortunes, and even assuming the most disinterested allocations, 'it is rarely, if ever, possible to provide public services on a uniform or ubiquitous basis' (Bennett, 1980: 28). For one thing, practicalities force public authorities to trade off the pressure to centralize resources on economic grounds (efficiency and scale) against the need to disperse resources uniformly (equitably) so that users are not disqualified purely on the grounds of access.[12] For another, because most of the social infrastructure built into the fabric of cities is long-lasting, households occupying the older parts of those cities have to live with those standards of provision for several generations. Then there is the related problem that arises when private capital formation (suburban housing) outpaces public investment in social infrastructure. Whilst the profit motive ensures that retailers and shopping centres are quick to carve up newly created trade areas in the suburbs,[13] there is no such inducement to the suppliers of public goods and services. This suggests that much of the patterned imbalance in the distribution of public services can be linked to structural effects rather than to any systematic victimization or neglect of working class suburbs by government bureaucracies.

The past decade has furnished enough material (notably Black, 1977; Davies, 1968; Levy *et al.*, 1974; Lineberry, 1977; Smith, 1977; Troy, 1981) to round out this chapter with a few succinct observations about the justice of public provision within cities. In this it helps to recognize that public services tend to divide into those that are ubiquitous and normally supplied at uniform standards of provision and those where much greater variation in public largesse is condoned by local government. The former generally includes all the usual public utilities (urban transit, telecommunications, electricity, water supply and sewerage), and may extend to police and fire protection. Although one is instinctively suspicious of 'samples of one', this difference between water, sewerage, and fire protection, and libraries and parks, shows up in the recorded values for the coefficient of variation in table 8.7. Although common law precepts in the United States, for example, require 'equal and adequate' service provision however one might define that (Lineberry, 1977: 43–5), it is more likely that the statutes setting minimum standards in relation to water and sewerage reticulation 'originally arose from the need to protect public health and hygiene standards and had little to do with equity *per se*' (Rees, 1981: 102). In the event, while 99 per cent of all dwellings in England and Wales now receive piped public water supplies and nearly 95 per cent are

---

[12] While the ability to reach facilities is clearly a necessary condition for usage, it does not in itself ensure utilization. Apart from the fact that many government services now attract a nominal fee-for-service, young mothers, for example, with adequate access to transport may nevertheless be home-bound by restricted access to child-minding facilities.

[13] We should note that this does not hold for all private services: where primary health care is provided on a competitive basis – as in Australia and the US – general practitioners are less responsive to local effective demand, especially in the poorer suburbs. In Australia this behaviour produces a maldistribution, with GPs per capita declining with distance from the city centre (Cleland *et al.*, 1977; Donald, 1981; Freestone, 1974; Lawrence, 1972; Morris, 1978).

Table 8.7 Measures of service distribution, San Antonio, 1972

Service measure	Mean	Standard deviation	Coefficient of variability	Ranges Maximum	Minimum
Fire					
Fire distance	1.04	0.52	0.50	2.75	0.25
Libraries					
Library distance	1.73	0.96	0.55	4.25	0.25
Library volumes per capita	1.09	2.06	1.88	9.03	0.34
Library personnel per 1,000 population	0.72	1.32	1.83	5.84	0.17
New books per 1,000 population	0.45	1.04	2.32	4.33	−0.08
Library expenditures per capita	1.85	4.09	2.21	17.66	0.48
Parks					
Park distance	0.99	0.64	0.66	3.40	0.15
Park development	4.51	5.43	1.21	19.62	0.10
General evaluation	5.68	1.93	0.34	8.00	1.00
Pool distance	4.57	3.13	0.68	9.00	1.00
Pool quality	7.50	0.64	0.09	9.00	6.00
Playground quality	4.85	2.90	0.54	8.00	1.00
Sportsfield quality	4.97	2.86	0.58	9.00	1.00
General evaluation	5.68	1.93	0.33	9.00	1.00
Water					
Housing units with public water (%)	99.18	1.73	0.02	100.00	89.90
Sewers					
Housing units with public sewers (%)	95.82	7.57	0.08	100.00	52.90

Source: Lineberry (1977: 107)

connected to the sewerage system, parts of the outer suburbs of Perth, Sydney and Melbourne still remain unsewered, and in Adelaide lack filtered water (see Rees, 1981: 88–91).

Public services like hospital care, schooling, libraries and parks are much more liable to display marked differences in quality from suburb to suburb (table 8.7). However, very little evidence has been tendered to support the dual proposition that service disparities are necessarily cumulative or that there is a consistent relationship between standards of public provision and socio-economic status. Here are a few 'representative' findings extracted from a selection of studies of service distribution within cities. An investigation of libraries, schools and street maintenance

in Oakland, San Francisco (Levy *et al*., 1974) 'found a pattern of distribution that favoured both extremes'; that is, while some mechanisms were
biased towards the rich and/or poor, none favoured the middle
(Wildavsky, 1979: 383). The conclusion that Lineberry, (1977: 184–7)
draws from 14 American studies, including his own, is that '*pockets* of
discrimination can be found, but probably not *patterns* of discrimination'.
While he adds that the evidence is most ambivalent for libraries, it is also
worth noting that these studies omit facilities like hospitals, public swimming pools and community centres which are less ubiquitous in their
distribution. Pinch is somewhat surprised by the results of his investigation of the provision of residential accommodation, domiciliary care, and
the 'meals-on-wheels' service in Greater London boroughs: 'In light on
the initial speculations, perhaps the most remarkable features of the results
presented above is the relatively high degree of association between needs
and resources' (Pinch, 1979: 218). And while Black does identify some
important sources of educational inequality, which will be commented
upon directly,

> The general conclusion is that the provision of government schools in
> different parts of Sydney, measured in terms of their location and
> quality attributes, is, on *average*, a fair one between areas. However,
> there is as much variation in standards between individual schools but
> this is disguised when average values for study areas are calculated. ∙ . . .
> Accepting that inequalities do exist, there is no evidence that the State
> Education Department has allocated resources in such a way as to
> discriminate against residents of lower socioeconomic status areas.
> (Black, 1977: 139)

This result for Sydney is not too inconsistent with what one would expect
from a reasonably centralized system of public servicing.
  However, a verdict of 'no consistent class bias' should not obscure the
persistence of chronic service deficiencies in selected areas; nor the need for
a probing of administrative ineptitude. Whilst inner Sydney's schools
have deteriorated structurally, are located on cramped sites surrounded by
deleterious activities, and are inappropriate to changes in teaching practices
(Badcock, 1977; Walker, 1979), it is the outer region that exhibits the
greatest deprivation of educational resources. Even when one makes a
generous allowance for the pressures created by a rapid expansion of the
school population within a region like Sydney's western suburbs, the 'class
size' (staff/student ratios) data reported by the author (Badcock, 1977: 330)
were unacceptably high in the mid-1970s. Public sector tardiness in servicing Sydney's western suburbs has already been raised in another context;
but this same criticism can also be levelled at the NSW Department of
Education and the NSW Hospitals Commission. A new report on the state

of community services in western Sydney (Long, 1982: 6), contends that 4,300 additional pre-school places would have to be created immediately, at an estimated cost of $35 million, just to restore access to child care in the western suburbs to the same level as that enjoyed in the rest of Sydney ('Yet there is currently no capital funding available from the NSW Government for new child care projects in the region' Long, 1982: 9). This parlous state of affairs is matched in the health sector. Although the need for a decentralization of hospital beds in metropolitan Sydney was recognized as far back as 1912, the NSW Hospitals Commission has, by its own admission, continued to channel hospital funds into central expansion (Donald, 1981: 77). The current per capita subsidy to each of the metropolitan sub-regions stood as follows in 1981–82: inner ($347); northern ($129); southern ($144); and, western ($67). The NSW average stood at $141. While these differentials are partly justifiable in terms of the concentration of 'super speciality units' in the heart of Sydney, they also relate to the gross maldistribution of hospital beds in the metropolitan area.[14] While the state average is 6.1 public and private beds per 1,000 persons, the equivalent proportions for the inner and western sub-regions are 24 and 3.8 beds per 1,000 persons. Accordingly, early in 1982 the NSW Government announced that it planned to close 678 hospital beds in the inner city area in order to fund the provision of 670 beds in the western sub-region over the next three years. It goes without saying that the reaction of the sectional interests most affected by the proposal was highly emotional, not least amongst the Macquarie Street specialists that practice 'within a stone's throw' of Crown Street Hospital (one of those threatened).

In a similar vein, it is when the location of major installations like airports, stadia and hospitals, and the routing of public transit corridors, bridges, and highways is at issue that Castells's 'means of collective consumption' really takes on added distributional meaning. It is not surprising, therefore, given the importance of these government expenditures to the quality of our daily lives that they should engender such intense lobbying and competition, and even hostility, between rival groups of residents. The politicization of resource provision within cities forms the centrepiece of the next chapter.

---

[14] As Donald (1981: 81) states 'Perhaps the most ludicrous aspects of Sydney's maldistribution of hospital facilities is the centralization of paediatric and obstetric accommodation', when the greatest demand is on the urban fringe and not in the aging inner suburbs.

9

Urban Conflict and the Property Market of Capitalist Cities

The outcome of the conflict that periodically breaks out between the different 'fractions' of property competing in the urban land and housing markets vitally affects the access and opportunities, and redistributes the real income and wealth of other property and non-property 'fractions' in the city. It goes without saying that power, resources and skills – the potential to effectively promote economic interests and realize objectives – are not evenly spread between contending property 'fractions' (see Simmie and Hale, 1978). In endeavouring to explain, if not predict, who wins and who loses in these urban struggles, social theorists have rather indiscriminantly drafted into service contemporary Marxist ideas about the relationship between capital and the state (see chapter 3). Much of this work is quite tendentious so in this chapter a few key ideas will be taken and evaluated empirically. The evaluation will be built up around two case studies: the first shows how coalitions of domestic property owners have foiled attempts to 'open up the suburbs' and in the process have succeeded in denying access to unwanted households; in the second, it will be shown how the 'green bans' movement centred in New South Wales enforced the abandonment and/or revision of several state government projects and much corporate urban redevelopment that would have drastically restructured the property market and impaired the quality of life in the inner city and suburbs of Sydney. But firstly it is necessary to decide what is meant by *urban* conflict or struggle.

Towards a definition of urban struggle

Chapter 3 outlined the Marxist thesis that urban restructuring is a crucial element in creating the conditions for capital accumulation because it helps to speed up the circulation of capital (Lamarche, 1976; Lojkine, 1976). Private and social investment in cities creates new, and alters existing exchange and use values. For this reason 'capitalist investment has to negotiate a knife-edge path between preserving the exchange value of past capital investments in the built environment and destroying the values of those investments in order to open up fresh room for accumulation' (Harvey, 1978: 123–4). Because the 'stakes' (opportunities for accumulation) in the urban development process can be so immense, market investment decisions tend to generate a distinctive form of political action: development rights are hotly contested by property developers and their financial backers; industrial capital despoiling or polluting can come into conflict with property capital; local promoters of growth and domestic property owners frequently feud; different property 'fractions' are spasmodically drawn together and mobilize politically to achieve limited ends in relation to domestic property. The term urban struggle is reserved for these forms of political action and conflict in order to separate them from the more common forms of political struggle that are mostly devoid of urban content. Firstly, there is genuine class struggle, such as that arising out of state intervention in the wage labour-capital relation – struggles over prices and incomes legislation, the regulation of trade unions, subsidies to ailing industries, etc. Then, secondly, there is the political mobilization which is prompted by state action taken in relation to social provision – struggles over cuts in social services, the management of council housing, provision of day care facilities, levels of health care and so on. . . . Because these forms of political struggle are acted out in the urban arena they have been mistakenly represented as *urban* politics/ struggles. In the first case by French structuralists like Castells and Olives; in the second case by Saunders and Dunleavy who are both British political scientists. This came about because for a time in the 1960s and 1970s community mobilization and resident action arguably overshadowed work-based union action as the most outstanding form of social conflict in the advanced capitalist economies. Social conflict within an urban setting ranged through the kaleidoscope from the full-scale mobilization of Parisian workers and students in 1968 and the devastating riots in America's black ghettoes in the latter part of the 1960s to the occupation of building sites, rent strikes and squatting campaigns in London, and the formation of resident associations and their integration into local politics.

'Urban social movements' as a transposition of the class struggle?

The rioting in Paris in 1968 left such a strong impression on French Marxists, like Castells and Olives, that they proposed that this form of political statement was 'no more and no less than the working out of the historic class struggle within the urban context' (Kilmartin and Thorns, 1978: 130). Indeed, they went so far as to forecast that mounting state intervention in the spheres of production and consumption might link workers and residents in local struggles, and that these would assume the status of class struggles of major importance. The concept 'urban social movement' is reserved, therefore, for urban action that is capable of producing 'structural transformation of the urban system', or 'a substantial change in the balance of forces in the class struggle that is to say, in the power of the State' (Castells, 1977a: 263). But several urban sociologists have complained that this is a very restricted, and indeed a reductionist, view of the class struggle and social change. Firstly, the consumption process (the struggle revolving around the means of collective consumption and the reproduction of labour) is always subsumed by the more general production process in Marxist analysis and does not warrant a place at the heart of the class struggle (Mingione, 1981: 66–7). The second point is that, while most 'urban' action is too ephemeral to meet Castells' specifications for a fully-fledged 'social movement', resisting urban redevelopment and the contest for public goods and services have nevertheless brought together malcontents who, in class terms, are 'unlikely bedfellows'. A third difficulty with Castells' stress on social movements as the major agent of urban change is that it denies the contribution of government institutions: 'it is urban social movements and not planning institutions which are the true sources of change and innovation in the city' (Castells in Pickvance, 1976: 203). Pickvance (1976: 203–7), who rejects this one-sided interpretation of urban effects, cites British and French evidence that attests to the importance of pressure from other than resident action groups. Similarly, he reprimands Olives who dismisses the 'urban effect' (namely adequate housing) that followed successful petitioning by an immigrant welfare association on behalf of evicted immigrants in the 'Cité d'Aliarte' (Paris) (Olives, 1976). Lastly, because resource 'targeting' and investment patterns are forever shifting within the city one would expect the momentum of 'urban' action to be relatively short-lived from locality to locality. The class solidarity implicit in Castells' 'urban social movement' is unlikely to reach maturation so long as urban-based political action is sporadic and individuated.

Consumption cleavages and urban content

Although Saunders (1979) presents a Weberian analysis of 'urban politics' and Dunleavy (1980a) girds his 'urban politics' with a neo-Marxist corset, their frameworks have a lot in common. They both subscribe to the view that political conflict arising out of consumption issues can produce antagonisms within a class with supposedly common economic interests, and may even serve to fracture the class structure (Harloe, 1981a: 11). What draws individuals and groups together in their bid to procure collectively provided services at the expense of others, is a 'sectoral' interest. As a consequence, in Britain according to Dunleavy (1980a), the traditional class-based political cleavages are in the process of being rearranged around items of collective consumption like housing, transport and education.[1] Saunders (1981a: 274) concludes that, 'Analytically, there is a 'necessary non-correspondence' between class struggles and sectoral struggles, although empirically the two may overlap'.

While not disputing that 'collective consumption processes can constitute an independent basis for the development of social cleavages' (Dunleavy, 1980a: 45–50), strictly speaking they have no 'urban' content unless their effects are transmitted to the urban property market and capitalized into exchange values (see chapter 7).

Property relations as a source of urban conflict

Urban conflict arises out of the everpresent challenge to the existing order of property relations that accompanies spatial restructuring within cities. By conferring analytical priority on real property as a means of accumulation, in preference to production relations or consumption categories, it is possible to formalize capitalist property relations in the following way:

1 State corporations and instrumentalities
   (a) government administrations in receipt of revenue from property taxes, commercial and domestic rates, etc;
   (b) statutory authorities, like highway departments, hospital and education boards, engaged in property acquisition and development;
   (c) housing authorities/commissions in receipt of rental income.

2 Commercial property 'fractions'
   (a) property development sector (including financial backers). Profits accrue in the production, construction, and marketing phases;
   (b) property holding companies that own, lease and manage (including real estate firms). Profits accrue as rental income and service charges for managing/selling property; also, returns to capital include appreciation of land and improvements;
   (c) leasees of commercial property providing the *operational* base for their enterprise.

3 Domestic property 'fractions'
   (a) landlords earning rental income from multiple ownership and deriving capital gains;

---

[1] While he admits that they are 'not strictly concerned with consumption but with regulation or management of the urban system', Dunleavy (1980a: 53) includes land use regulation and urban planning because of the way they can affect social provision and collective consumption.

(b) owner–occupiers/mortgagees who not only extract use value from an appreciating asset, but may also be eligible for a range of valuable tax concessions;

(c) non–owning tenants. Forego capital gains from property; nevertheless, tenants that derive a high use value from rental accommodation may feel extremely possessive towards it.

Urban political struggle, therefore, brings into confrontation – either individually or in alliance – property 'fractions' possessing differing degrees of power in the property market. It involves a *collective* response, with strategically limited objectives, to locality-specific issues and 'is more often defensive than aggressive' (Saunders, 1979: 127).

Some readers will have noticed that urban planning agencies are missing from the list of state bureaucracies active in the urban property market. This is because the real initiative for strategically significant urban investment lies, for the most part, with the corporate sector, governmental and private. Rather than directing market forces, the urban planning process tends to be reactive and negative; 'It can exclude uses considered undesirable but cannot ensure that desirable uses are developed. Responsibility for that decision rests with the private sector' (Logan and Ogilvy, 1981: 180).[2] The same general point applies to the administration of development controls. 'By and large a planning authority can only react to applications submitted using development control as a defensive weapon' (Kirk, 1980: 45). Hence, the statutory planning framework (Logan, 1981: 8–9) and zoning (Parkin, 1982: 37) are to no avail unless investors come forward with proposals that meet with the state's prescription for urban development. Urban planners, then, do not have an eminent domain in the sphere of resource allocation within cities (Broadbent, 1977; Kirk, 1980; Mellor, 1977: 149–66; Ravetz, 1980: 68–81). The position of the state, through its planning machinery, is more that of a 'joint-venturer': it prescribes the rules of the game, but it is for the property development sector to decide whether it will enter on those terms, or try to procure more favourable conditions for its participation.[3]

---

[2] The authors illustrate the point by relating how developers in Melbourne circumvented the 1954 Melbourne Planning Scheme with the concurrence of the Metropolitan Board of Works, on five different occasions. Instead of using the locations designated for 'district shopping', the developers established 'free-standing' regional shopping centres away from public transport routes and upon cheaper land.

[3] This frequently happens when 'planning bargaining' or 'negotiated planning' becomes an accepted practice (see Kirk, 1980: 48–51; Logan and Ogilvy, 1981: 190–2). Elkin (1974: 53–73), for example, details the 'horse-trading' that was part and parcel of the redevelopment of Centre Point and St Giles Circus in the City of Westminister, London. By giving up some of the land on the St Giles Circus intersection so that the London County Council could improve traffic circulation, Hyams, the developer, was able to lever a 'plot' ratio of 10:1 out of the LCC, twice that laid down as the 'permitted maximum' by the London Development Plan.

State intervention and property-based urban conflict

As the breakdown of property 'fractions' stands at present there is no way of foretelling under what circumstances, or on whose behalf the state might be expected to intervene. Despite the attention paid to the role of the state (see chapter 3), social theorists have yet to develop convincing accounts of state intervention. For example, the instrumentalist claim that capital is all but unstoppable in urban development is firmly rejected by Aungles and Szelenyi, (1979: 35): 'The hegemony of capital above the state apparatuses is not absolute and unconditional and, if the political pre-conditions are given, it can be challenged'. Lojkine (1977) is taken to task by Harloe (1981b: 180–3) for his highly selective use of evidence in relation to resident action. On the four occasions when Lojkine does admit material that implies 'concessions' to dominated groups, 'In each of these cases he demonstrates that the "concessions" were not what they seemed and that, in reality, they were motivated by, and in the interests of capital, conferring little or no advantage on the dominated groups' (Harloe, 1981b: 181–2).

It is also dawning on those social theorists seduced by Poulantzas's (1976b) revised version of state intervention that the concept of 'relative autonomy' fails to specify under what circumstances the state will intervene on behalf of dominant economic interests and when it will yield to popular demands (Saunders, 1981b: 32). According to Saunders, the apparent 'relative autonomy' of the state may be due to two discrete processes which need to be theorized differently:

> the reason why the state appears to act in the long-term interests of capital while also responding to the political demands of other classes is that social investment policies are developed in close consultation with capitalist interests within corporate state agencies, while social consumption policies are relatively responsive to popular pressures within representative state agencies. The interests of capital prevail in the long run because social investment takes priority over social consumption, because of the dependency of the state on future capital accumulation, and this is reflected in the subordination of local to central government. (Saunders, 1981b: 46)

Therefore, if Saunders' 'dual-state' model is valid, in the case studies that follow we can expect to find national and regional policy consistently reflecting the dependence of governments (at that particular level) on the private sector, with greater responsiveness to popular pressure evident at the local level. This means keeping a watchful eye throughout on the 'power-play' taking place between the various 'fractions' of property and the divisions of government (central, regional, local) responsible for urban planning, social investment, and social consumption, all of which have their locus in the urban property market.

Exclusionary zoning, restrictive practices and the defence of property

'Fiscal zoning' and restrictive building codes

Exclusionary zoning represents the institutionalizing of territorial inequity at its best (Babcock, 1980). In the United States, as perhaps the best known among a set of restrictive practices, it has been refined to the point where it is utilized by local government (responding to pressures from domestic property owners) to deny access to unwanted activities or households, most notably those that are low income and/or black. Yet, as Perin (1977: 3) observes, while race permeates the whole issue of restrictive zoning in the US, it would not have been adopted by so many suburban municipalities where blacks pose no real threat if there was not something in it for owners of domestic property. In the US, exclusionary policies also help to underpin municipal strategies of fiscal prudence (Bennett, 1980: 242–4). With so much of the onus falling on urban governments and their taxpayers to pay their own way in the US, suburban councils have developed 'fiscal zoning' measures, 'whereby local planning authorities seek to 'zone in' either ratepayers with high incomes or land uses which create high rate revenues, and to 'zone out' residents or uses which will contribute little to municipal coffers' (Paterson, 1975b: 390). Thus a study conducted in 11 New Jersey suburbs, which set out to gauge the reactions of 106 local government administrators (or 'community gatekeepers') to multi-family housing, found that almost three-quarters (73.5 per cent) felt low- and moderate-income housing would be unacceptable in their community (reported in Perin, 1977: 39).

The measures devised by suburban councils in the United States to prevent tax-draining activities and households from settling in their areas include large-lot zoning, the exclusion of multi-family dwellings, specification of minimum house size, the exclusion of mobile homes, and an insistence on excessive subdivision requirements. The most effective of these restrictive measures is undoubtedly the prohibition of multiple-unit dwellings (apartments or flats). Exclusionary zoning is particularly well entrenched in the New York metropolitan area, where over 99 per cent of all undeveloped land zoned for residential uses is restricted to single-family housing (Danielson, 1976: 53). In suburban Bergen County, which abuts the metropolis, only 53 hectares of developable land was zoned for apartments in 1970, compared with more than 10,976 hectares for single-family homes. In 1976–78 Burchell and Listokin (1981) analysed two sets of 40 municipalities each, randomly sampled from the largest SMSAs in the north-east, the north central, the south and the west. Their results (table 9.1) established that 62.5 per cent of the so-called 'developed' municipalities permitted the subdivision of lots under 0.1 of a hectare compared with only 39 per cent of 'developing' municipalities. Similarly,

Table 9.1 Zoning design standards set by sampled US municipalities, 1976

	41 'Developed'[a] municipalities (%)	42 'Developing'[a] municipalities (%)
Minimum lot size Land available and permitting minimum lot size:		
< 0.1 hectare	62.5	29.0
> 0.4 hectare	7.5	25.6
Minimum lot width Land available and permitting minimum lot width:		
< 21.3 metres	51.2	23.7
> 45.7 metres	9.8	26.4
Minimum floor area Specifying floor area:		
< 92.8 square metres	90.0	33.3
> 130 square metres	5.0	36.7
Permissible housing types in residential zones Other than single-family detached dwellings permitted as of right	14.6	5.1
Allowable with exemption as a permitted use:		
Explicit multi-family development	7.2	2.6
PUD[c] or cluster development	36.6	33.3
Mobile homes	10.0	30.0

[a] 'Developed' municipalities are defined as central cities/older suburbs wherein no more than ten per cent of the land remains to be developed
[b] 'Developing' municipalities are outer suburbs with over 35 per cent of their total area still available for development
[c] Planned Unit Development
Source: Burchell and Listokin (1981: 364)

the 'developing' municipalities enforce much more stringent requirements relating to the minimum permissible lot width and size of building (table 9.1). For these reasons, many suburban communities remain impervious to low- and moderate-income housing despite the enactment of 'progressive' legislation like Massachusetts' 'Anti-snob Zoning' law

(Krefetz, 1979),[4] and the 'stream-lining' of the urban development process with innovations like the Planned Unit Development (PUD).[5]

In Australia restrictive practices have a similar effect upon the location of low- and moderate-income housing, but because they do not carry the same racial overtones the use of residential and land subdivision standards as techniques of exclusion have not attracted much attention. Paterson's (1975b) assessment is based on a detailed examination of residential and subdivision standards in Melbourne which was commissioned by the Priorities Review Staff within the Prime Minister's Office. Techniques of exclusion include: building controls on flat development; the setting of minimum standards for dwelling size, boundary set-backs and external walls; excessive provision for car parking and open space; and, the over-design of the street and service systems in new suburbs. In respect of flats, for example, Paterson (1975b: 392) found that nearly half of Melbourne's municipalities restrict flat construction to specified areas. The effect of this is to exclude flat dwellers from over 50 per cent of the area of 11 munici-palities and from over 90 per cent of the area of five others (and these tend to be the areas with the better schools, parks, shopping and other amenities).

The exchange value of domestic property has also been kept intact by the 'downzoning' of substantial tracts of Adelaide's inner suburbs in response to collective agitation by middle-class homeowners (Young, 1981). The process of 'downzoning' amends the zoning of an area so as to *reduce* the permissible intensity of development; that is, from industrial/commercial to residential, or by prescribing lower density in place of medium density housing. The campaign for 'downzoning' in Adelaide's established inner suburbs (figure 9.1) was primarily directed at medium density flat development which was permitted under the Metropolitan Planning Regulations gazetted in 1971. Since these were the suburbs undergoing gentrification from the late 1960s onwards (Badcock and Urlich-Cloher, 1981), young professional newcomers formed Adelaide's first resident's associations and were instrumental in nourishing and spreading the movement to prevent any further intrusion of flat develop-ment. Hence the movement for 'downzoning' was essentially conserva-tive and motivated by self-interest.

---

[4] Even though provision was made for the construction of 14,639 low- and moderate-income housing units under the Massachusetts 'Anti-snob Zoning' Law of 1969, 10 years later only 3,000 units had been built (Krefetz, 1979: 291–2).

[5] 'PUDs typically exceed 406 hectares and have a population large enough to support a high school and shopping center (around 10,000). The PUD is both floating in location and discretionary in approval on a one-time basis. It waives restrictions on lot-size, housing type, density, and mixing of residential and nonresidential uses. The developer is subject only to an overall density limit and approval of a general plan submitted to local authori-ties' (Walker and Heiman, 1981: 68).

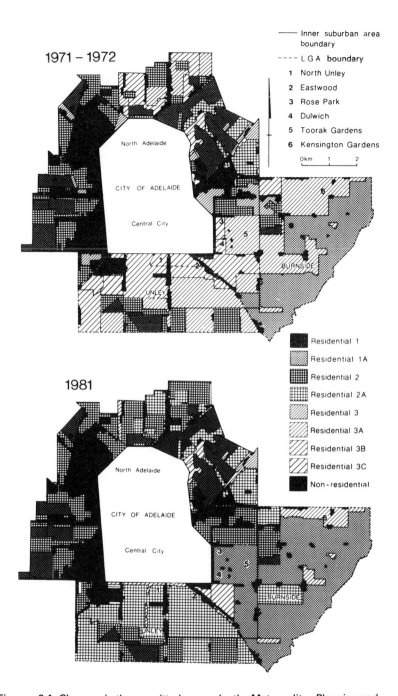

Figure 9.1 Changes in the permitted use under the Metropolitan Planning and Development Act, 1966–81, inner Adelaide
Source: Young, 1981: 19, 49

The reaction to the residents' demands for the 'downzoning' of their neighbourhoods came chiefly from these quarters: firstly, from the property development interests which stood to gain from the provision for higher residential densities in sought-after areas close to the city centre; secondly, from the councils involved; and, thirdly, from the State Planning Authority, which was perturbed about the diseconomies of urban sprawl. Burnside Council was not prepared to accede to the residents' demands without a fight because the 1971 regulations had taken over six years to formulate and a backdown was contrary to the pro-growth ethic that prevailed at the time (Young, 1981). However, as the magnitude of the groundswell of support for 'downzoning' became apparent the councillors representing the affected wards found it politically expedient to side with their constituencies against the pro-growth elements on council. The first amendments to Burnside's zoning map were gazetted in December 1973, and were followed by further amendments to 'down-zone' in 1974 and 1975 (figure 9.1). The Unley Resident's Society, on the other hand, had to wait until it finally gained control of the Unley Council in 1976 before it could push through the 'downzoning' amendments it was seeking.

'Locking-out' the corporate property developers

In the US, the power 'bloc' which was trying to break the zoning blockage thrown up around American suburbs represented formidable opposition on paper. The specialist home building firms were backed in the late 1960s by some of the USA's largest industrial corporations who saw the opportunity to boost productivity, increase market penetration, and enhance sales through involvement in 'new community' projects and PUDs. According to Walker and Heiman (1981: 73), these property development interests then joined forces with private civic groups such as the Regional Plan Association of New York, the Bay Area Council in San Francisco, the Metropolitan Fund Inc., in Detroit, and the (national) Committee for Economic Development, to campaign for the consolidation of metropolitan government and the abolition of land use, no-growth and environmental controls. A number of liberal planning lawyers committed to land use reform – Richard Babcock, Fred Bosselman, David Callies, and William Reilly – were also retained by the urban development corporations in their running battle with suburban municipalities. Even though there is no shortage of cases to suggest that commercial property interests manage to infringe, even subvert, local planning and zoning regulations (see Danielson, 1976: 36–7), one is drawn to the conclusion that the big guns of the property development corporations in the US were silenced, for a time, by the property 'fractions' defending local amenity and housing investments. It is also noteworthy that the confrontation between large developers and suburban homeowners normally draws in different tiers of government, but not on the same side: 'With increasing frequency, local environmental, labour and business interests are joining forces to challenge national and multi-national economic concerns that are relying upon the states and the federal government to overcome local opposition to their projects' (Walker and Heiman, 1981: 82, footnote 106). Superficially, this division of allegiance accords with Saunders' dualistic perspective; however, the decisions and issues relate to neither social investment nor consumption policies.

Resisting metropolitan housing strategy

A case study of exclusionary tactics drawn from London reveals that an alignment of suburban councils and domestic property owners is often sufficient to stall metropolitan housing strategy (Young and Kramer, 1978). Outer suburban boroughs like Bromley, Kingston and Sutton have been tenacious in protecting amenity, preserving social distance, and defending property values and rates. Their protagonist is the Greater London Council (before 1965 the London County Council) which, from its formation, set about attempting to acquire suburban land for public housing in order to 'export' households from overcrowded and decaying inner area neighbourhoods. The fight to exclude unwanted families from Bromley was conducted on two fronts (Young and Kramer, 1978): externally, through a network of intergovernmental relations set up to deflect the overtures of the GLC; internally, through the development of housing strategies within the policy nexus of suburban conservatism. Three times in 10 years the threat of large-scale public housing in London's outer suburbs was countered: 'Neither Labour nor Conservative administrations at County Hall succeeded in their sporadic attempts at a strategy of opening up the suburbs.' Even the Conservative housing ministers at Westminster, who were more interventionist in outlook than most, were beaten back when they went to the aid of the Conservative regime at County Hall in the early 1970s: in a series of stormy meetings at Conservative Central Office the suburban party machine 'totally repudiated the policies of their national and GLC colleagues' (Young, 1980: 242). With the suburban land acquisition programme thwarted, the GLC moved to negotiate access to the outer boroughs' own housing stock;[6] whereupon, Bromley began shifting the emphasis of its housing policy away from dependency-creating forms of tenure with a series of novel measures designed to expand private sector housing (these included 'sponsored

---

[6] The number of households rehoused by outer suburban boroughs between April 1966 and April 1969 under the 'nominations' scheme (2,548) reflects their reluctance to open up the suburbs (Young and Kramer, 1978: appendix III).

development' and the sale of council housing to sitting tenants). Thus there are two levels of the state completely divided in purpose, but with the expected roles reversed if Saunders (1981a: 269–71) is followed. It is regional government, the GLC, that is found promoting social consumption policies and mediating on behalf of powerless non-owners. On the other hand, apart from championing the interests of domestic property-owners against the GLC housing programme, the Conservative boroughs on the outskirts of London appear favourably disposed towards private housing contractors, including several national leaders (see Ball, 1982: 32).

By way of summary it should be reported that the most obvious losers (by default) from this uncompromising defence of property by the sub-urban middle class are those households obliged to live at uncomfortably high densities in US or British cities, or edged to the outskirts of Australian cities (where, in both situations, they have to suffer the meanest levels of social provision found in cities). It is not without significance, for example, that over 60 per cent of the 23,924 applicants seeking public housing assistance from the South Australian Housing Trust in mid-1982 stated a preference for accommodation in the central sector of metro-politan Adelaide.

Inner city redevelopment and the potency of urban struggle

The most dramatic forms of urban-based popular mobilization to emerge in the 1960s and 1970s were largely provoked by state programmes designed to revive ailing central city economies and improve the operational efficiency of the urban system (Mollenkopf, 1978). This reshaping of the physical and social environment at the heart of major western cities came about as a result of: (a) construction projects and the development of infrastructure undertaken by government; (b) private investment in property redevelopment that usually bore the imprimatur of the state; (c) pressures on local government (especially in the US and Australia) actively to promote the more intensive use of property so as to boost rate revenue. The impact of comprehensive urban renewal, often in conjunction with public housing projects, is recalled in numerous studies. Fincher (1981) and Mollenkopf (1981) have scrutinized the impact of the Boston Redevelopment Authority in Boston's South End. The commercial redevelopment of parts of London are described in detail by Ambrose and Colenutt (1975), Barras (1979), and Elkin (1974); while Castells (1978) and Daly (1982a) have done the same for central Paris and Sydney respectively. The other development that promised to transform not only the inner city but the whole metropolitan environment during the 1960s was the proposal to introduce urban freeway or motorway systems into the existing fabric of cities (see chapter 5). The urban transportation solutions prepared for Australian cities, for example, bore the trademark, 'Made in USA'. The cure for Melbourne involved a total expenditure of $A2,616 million: 67.7 per cent for 495 km of metropolitan freeways; a further 22 per cent for other highways, leaving only 10.3 per cent for public transport (Sandercock, 1975: 156). The lynchpin for the freeway systems designed to serve Sydney, Melbourne and Adelaide was undoubtedly the hoop of inner city connectors, which were to be built at the expense of thousands of solid homes and hectares of precious parkland.

'Green bans' in Australia – an indigenous expression of urban struggle

A diagnosis of the 'green bans' movement that took shape in Australian cities in the first half of the 1970s can help to illuminate aspects of property-based social relations, the social base of urban politics, the distribution of power (or powerlessness), and the role of the state in urban change. In both NSW and Victoria, where conservative governments had built up powerful bureaucracies and seemed especially receptive to the private redevelopment of the old city core, an unlikely coalition of interests was thrown together to prevent the unacceptable destruction of the existing social and physical fabric. While conflict over property rights lay at the heart of urban struggle in Australia, not all of the 'fractions' had a vested interest in property. The nucleus of the resident action groups ranged against the state and private developers comprised middle and working class owners and tenants who were not about to relinquish their property rights without a bitter struggle. In addition, even though local government in Australia has traditionally been the preserve of businessmen, real estate agents and small-time developers, because they were seldom, if ever, consulted by the state governments about the rebuilding of the inner city, councils like Fitzroy and Collingswood in Melbourne, and Leichhardt in Sydney, were prepared to join forces with the resident associations through the 1970s to oppose the State 'bulldozer' (Centre for Urban Research and Action, 1977: 44–64).

The bargaining position of the residential associations in Australian cities was greatly strengthened by the Builders Labourers Federation (BLF) 'green bans.'[7] In effect, by recruiting the BLF to their cause the

[7] The 'green ban' saw the adaptation of a well-known industrial tactic in the building and construction industry – if a log of claims or grievances cannot be resolved a job is declared 'black' until a settlement is reached (Hardman and Manning, 1974: 58–64). The BLF, led by a unionist who passionately believed in environmental conservation in the broadest sense (see Mundey, 1981), agreed to withhold their labour from any project that was thought to be detrimental to the environmental or historic character of an area, or likely to destroy the social cohesion of a neighbourhood. Without their labour, buildings could not be demolished and the developer could not prepare a site for development. A 'green ban' was not applied indiscriminately. The BLF intervened at the request of a neighbourhood organization, and only after a properly convened public meeting of all the affected residents had been held (Mundey, 1981: 83).

resident associations introduced the classic confrontation between wage labour (builders' labourers) and capital into urban politics (*à la* Castells). Indeed, by August 1973, so much building construction had been halted in Sydney that the Master Builders' Association attempted to have the BLF de-registered in accordance with Section 33 of the Industrial Arbitration Act. Between 1971 and 1975, the builders' labourers were instrumental in halting approximately $A3.3 billion in building construction for inner Sydney alone. While whole neighbourhoods in inner Sydney – the Rocks, Wooloomooloo, Waterloo, North Newtown, Glebe – were protected by 'green bans' for a time, in Melbourne the bans were directed more at private developers than at the Victorian government and therefore tended to be site-specific (table 9.2). Other Australian cities also had their 'green bans', but not on a scale anything like that witnessed in Sydney and Melbourne (Roddewig, 1978: 34).

Table 9.2 Pretexts for green bans in Sydney and Melbourne, 1971–75

	Sydney	Melbourne
Preservation of urban heritage	10	5
Downtown redevelopment	7	4
Retention of parks, open space	5	9
Proposed housing below acceptable standard	6	1
Anti-expressway, car parks etc.	8	1
Redevelopment incompatible with existing housing	0	3
Compensation for compulsory purchase inadequate	3	0
Source of air/water pollutants	0	2
Total	39	25

Source: for Sydney, Carmina (1975, 233); for Melbourne, Roddewig (1978, 33)

As table 9.2 shows, the pretexts for the BLF interdictions were many and varied. Projects that were conceived and financed by government departments included: highrise flats for Waterloo (NSWHC); the Eastern and Northwestern Expressways (NSW Department of Main Roads); a campus for a college of advanced education in the heart of residential Newtown (NSW Department of Education); the commercial redevelopment of the Rocks (Sydney Cove Redevelopment Authority); the resumption of Moore and Centennial Parks for a sporting complex (Sydney City Council); and, two hectares of office blocks on Navy land in Woolloomooloo (Commonwealth Department of the Interior). Alternatively, many of the 'green bans' were directed at the projects launched by private developers, who not only received the endorsement of the Askin government but also police protection for their investments when the going got rough. The 'over-building' of the Eastlakes housing estate by

Parkes Development, the planned apartments for Kelly's Bush, demolition of vernacular terrace housing along the length of the Victoria Street ridge in Kings Cross, and the proposed obliteration of historic Woolloomooloo by a $400 million scheme for highrise offices represent some of the better known cases (Figure 9.2).

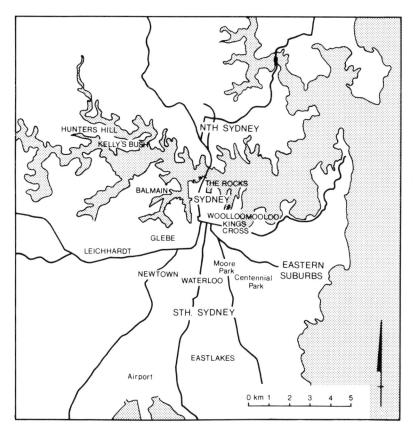

Figure 9.2 Localities within inner Sydney subject to 'green bans' during the 1970s

By the late 1970s the 'green bans' movement had petered out. This was partly due to the fact that union infighting and disagreement about environmentally inclined industrial action intensified as building activity slowed and the spectre of long-term unemployment loomed in Australia. By this time, there had been a softening of the confrontationist posture adopted by the government bureaucracies. Much was being made –

ostensibly at least – of 'citizen participation' and consultation with the aggrieved parties[8] (Parkin, 1982: 90; Sandercock, 1979).

Australian urban action: preparing a 'balance sheet'

So far as state intervention in Australian urban development during the 1970s is concerned, no clear-cut pattern emerges whereby central or regional government managed to impose its will upon subordinate sections of the capitalist economy. Likewise, plenty of instances can be cited where the 'urban outcomes' were clearly dysfunctional to commercial property capital. For example, although local government politics, especially in the old working class strongholds like Richmond, Carlton, Fitzroy, Collingswood (in Melbourne), South Sydney, and Leichhardt (in Sydney), were disturbed by policy disputes between the amenity-conscious middle class and local industrialists and businessmen during the 1970s, this did not prevent these factions from uniting to keep public housing and freeways out of their suburbs.[9] Despite the massive government contracts that would have gone to the highway and housing industries, social investment proposed by the states for the construction of urban freeways and system-built public housing did not assume priority over popular preferences in the sphere of social consumption (basically because these programmes were magnified into election issues). Significantly, the Liberal premier of Victoria gave an assurance just two months before the state elections in 1973 that the freeways would not be built in inner areas where their construction would involve substantial loss of established housing and disruption of existing communities: 'This victory for grass-roots political action suggests that for reasons of survival and self-preservation both capitalism and bureaucracy, in certain circumstances, are flexible' (Sandercock, 1975: 159).

Clearly, in this case, the implementation of the states' social investment policies did depend upon popular endorsement (but not at the lowest or most representative level of government). Equally as critical, from the states' viewpoint, was the federal Labor government's open hostility to inner city freeways. Not only was the Commonwealth able to virtually suspend all the contentious freeway routes by withholding federal grants

---

[8] Not to mention the fact that resident action has come a long way since the prototypal Carlton Association was formed in the late 1960s in Melbourne: the pool of expertise, resources, and sense of solidarity grew impressively following the formation of city-wide movements like the Coalition of Resident Action Groups which had 17 affiliates in Sydney (Nittim, 1980); the Committee for Urban Action, an amalgamation of 14 inner suburban associations in Melbourne; and the Federation of the Adelaide Metropolitan Residents' Associations.

[9] Since 1973 in the US, as a result of community action 22 metropolitan areas have cancelled 305 km of interstate highways under the Surface Transportation Assistance Act which allows the funds to be diverted to other transport programmes (Peters, 1981: 13).

for roadworks (Nittim, 1980: 245), but other weapons were available for preventing the state projects from going ahead. When the Labor government purchased the Glebe Estate – 19 hectares supporting 700 dwellings – in inner Sydney (July, 1974), the Minister of Urban and Regional Development, Tom Uren, 'found to his intense pleasure that he could frustrate the freeway builders by refusing to sell the Glebe properties. The state ministers and the Department of Main Roads had refused to accept the general arguments made by the commonwealth against the inner-city freeways but the states could not compulsorily acquire land owned by the commonwealth' (Lloyd and Troy, 1981: 187).

Even more difficult to reconcile with the especially functionalist accounts of state intervention is the Commonwealth's intervention on behalf of the working class residents of Woolloomooloo, when it acted to stop the commercial redevelopment of the area and put an end to the duplicity of the NSW government and the City of Sydney (Lloyd and Troy, 1981: 188). Because the residential population had been in decline since the 1930s and only 17.4 of the 36.5 hectares remained in private ownership, the NSW government, through its State Planning Authority, saw the opportunity to undertake comprehensive redevelopment. Generous plot ratios were set as incentives to private developers to acquire titles and consolidate sites. In 1971 a consortium of developers submitted a redevelopment proposal to the Sydney City Council that included 1.63 million square meters of office and retail space to accommodate 21,710 workers – creating, in effect, a twin CBD on Sydney Cove (see figure 9.2). A BLF 'green ban' was imposed in March, 1973; and when the Commonwealth intervened in June 1975, insisting that the locality should be reserved predominantly for residential purposes, there was a massive 'write-down' of the value of properties in Woolloomooloo. Actions taken by the consortium against the NSW government and the Sydney Council in 1982 suggests that corporate investors suffered losses[10] in excess of $A50 million as a result of the concessions made to local residents (Wilson, 1982: 1).

In each of these encounters with corporate developers the resident coalitions achieved their objectives only after the action had been broadened sufficiently to either enlist another level of government on their side, or unsettle the state governments politically. When, in the face of government obstinacy, this was not the case, the resident action movement felt its powerlessness keenly; that is, unless the BLF came to its aid

[10] The list of financial casualties included Regional Landholdings, which had been backed to the tune of $A20 million by the Moscow Narodny Bank! In this bizarre piece of international finance it is alleged that it was Sir Robert Askin, Premier of NSW at the time, who put Regional Landholdings in touch with the Singapore office of the Moscow Narodny Bank (Wilson, 1982: 1).

with the declaration of 'green bans'.[11] There were numerous episodes in Sydney during the 1970s where the NSW government would have ignored the protests of residents but for the 'green bans' – Kelly's Bush, Eastlakes, Centennial-Moore Park, the Rocks (to name a few). The campaign to save the Rocks, which is the cradle of urban Australia, represents perhaps the most impressive populist effort to curb an implacably unresponsive state government. In order to make the most of Sydney's downtown property boom in the early 1970s, the Sydney Cove Redevelopment Authority planned to displace over 100 of its longstanding tenants and develop 465,000 square metres of net usable office and retail space, three new hotels, and apartment housing to boost the residential population to 1,200 (Roddewig, 1978: 20). The campaign to save the Rocks came to a head during a fortnight in October, 1973, when: thousands of demonstrators marched through downtown Sydney to state government offices; hundreds of police were bused in to prevent the BLF and resident activists from occupying housing earmarked for demolition; the BLF stopped all work on every construction site in the Sydney metropolitan area for the duration; key unions, including the FEDFA (bulldozer operators) and the AMWU, Australia's largest, threw their weight behind the challenge to the Askin government (see Hardman and Manning, 1974; Roddewig, 1978: 34). While not prepared to admit openly that the confrontation and the 'green ban' coalition arrayed against it had caused it to modify its plans, the Redevelopment Authority progressively scaled down the scheme between 1973 and 1975.

Deciding who wins and who loses

There can be no question that as a result of federal intervention on the side of property 'underdogs' in 1974–75, both the Glebe Estate and Woolloomooloo have been preserved as areas of low income housing (see chapter 10). And as a result of the BLF's 'green bans', the Sydney Cove Redevelopment Authority has not yet displaced long standing tenants from the Rocks (though the market may in due course).[12] The only compromise was to allow the NSW Housing Commission to undertake

---

[11] The builders' labourers did not let class affinity prejudice their bans. Apart from all the support that was given to the predominantly middle class resident action in Sydney (Nittim, 1980) and their demonstration of solidarity with the working class residents of Waterloo, Eastlakes, and the Rocks, the BLF also went to the aid of residents in the very exclusive suburbs of Hunters Hill and Centennial Park (figure 9.2).

[12] The outlook for the original residents of the Rocks is bittersweet. Although residents have not been displaced by a forest of offices, two tourist hotels have been built, and those that remain have to put up with the nuisance to their daily lives as the historic area adapts to the demands of tourism. The number of visitors to the Rocks rose from 30,000 in 1970 to an estimated 1.25 million in 1976 (Roddewig, 1978: 27).

the construction of 70 flats 'for Rocks residents in the Rocks area with resident consultation and approval' (Nittim, 1980: 238).

However, these reversals for sectors of capital and government run against the pattern of urban outcomes in Australia's inner city property markets (see chapter 5). The effect of much urban action is to preserve intact the residential quality and amenity of previously working class neighbourhoods for present and future generations of middle class home-buyers. 'In Islington, for example, the Barnsbury Association, formed by middle class owner-occupiers, proved very successful in sponsoring a policy of gradual gentrification which led to the displacement of working class tenants' (Saunders, 1979: 272). And in US cities like Boston and San Francisco, slum clearance and renewal has gradually been replaced with a series of 'softer' programmes that, nonetheless, enhance the way the market works and benefit middle class houseseekers: 'Such appealing programmes as low interest rehabilitation loans, obligating savings institutions to invest in formerly redlined areas, historic preservation, brick sidewalks built by neighbourhood public works allocations, and neighbourhood down-zoning simply continue a renewal displacement process by more politically and economically effective means' (Mollenkopf, 1981: 17).

Final reflections

It is essential to be clear about 'urban outcomes'. Case studies of exclusionary practices and resistance to the redevelopment of the inner city were presented as sounding-boards for Peter Saunders' 'dual-state' hypothesis. At least two divergencies have surfaced: firstly, a model of central-local relations based on a unitary system of government is not all that relevant to federal systems such as the US and Australia; secondly, urban outcomes are encountered that are not always consistent with the hypothesized reactions of different tiers of government to the needs of capital on the one hand, and popular pressures on the other (Saunders, 1981b). Despite the synonymous interests of central government and the private sector in the performance of capital, in certain circumstances, which are often difficult to predict, dominant property fractions can suffer costly reversals.

Maybe the pursuit of a theoretical framework of sufficient malleability to accommodate these departures is futile: '. . . specific outcomes are not logically deduceable from the existence of the capitalist mode of production or from the tendency to accumulation' (Edel, 1981: 19–44).

Significantly, the strongest assertion of the central state over a section of capital forcibly reshaping the Australian urban environment coincided with the peaking of a long period of post-war prosperity. With business confidence running high there was less pressure on the various sectors of capital to act in a concerted fashion; besides, in singling out the property development industry there was no question of taking on the class interests of capital as a whole. Nor should the fact be overlooked that the incoming Labor government, which interrupted cosy relations between capital and the state spanning two decades, was committed as a reformist party to active intervention, and largely eschewed close ties with the business community.[13] It was not until the 'crisis' in 1974 that the Labor government, for its own good, had to be more attentive to the falling rate of profit in industry (witness the 25 per cent across-the-board tariff cut in July 1973). Hence, the nuances added by political and ideological differences between governing parties must find a place in any reckoning with the way capital was treated by the federal Labor government between 1972 and 1975.

On a more general note it has to be admitted that state structures and political organizations have undergone their own form of conditioning under capitalism and, therefore, should not be expected to react unilaterally to urban conflict: 'capitalism in general has no politics, only (extremely flexible) outer limits for the kinds of supports for property ownership and controls of the labourforce that it can tolerate' (Skocpol, 1980: 200).

One might surmise that the interference of the federal Labor government into the states' management of the cities in the early 1970s was not in itself perceived as a serious challenge to the prevailing order of class/property relations in Australia. And because the resident coalitions that took action to protect their neighbourhoods against private and state-sponsored redevelopment projects did not transgress those 'hidden parameters of power' (Kirk, 1980: 171), they were permitted to have a say in the shaping of the urban habitat and indirectly, in the redistribution of real urban income. But for resident intervention, supported by the 'green bans' movement, the social character and shape of the built environment would be noticeably different in many parts of the Australian city.

[13] Note, though, that these forms of intervention do not appear to have much to do with overcoming economic contradictions, arresting a decline in the rate of profit, or reintegrating the working class into the CMP as postulated by Block (1977: 6–8).

Part IV
The Rise and Fall of 'Urban' Policy

Part IV takes the process of state intervention well beyond the routine provision of non-productive urban infrastructure considered in chapter 8. Attention will shift from an assessment of the area-based initiatives in positive discrimination that dominated urban aid programmes on both sides of the Atlantic in the sixties and seventies to public intervention in the fringe land market of Australian cities under the Whitlam government, 1972–75.

The concluding section will report the demise of 'spatial' policy, not necessarily as a casualty of the state's disengagement from urban programmes, and canvas a range of alternative approaches to redistribution (including the Socialist vision as it is taking shape in Communist cities and versions of the social democratic model e.g., selected aspects of the Dutch, Scandinavian, and West German welfare systems). All this assumes that the technological change prompted by industrial restructuring, together with the dismantling of state welfare programmes in Australia, Britain and the United States, carries with it the social costs of an uneconomically deprived and alienated underclass. While it can be recognized, along with the Marxists, that such developments are intrinsic to the nature of capitalism, the prescription is different. Where property rights and individual ownership are woven into the very fabric of society, the advocacy of forfeiture is not going to win popular support. Consequently, radical change of the kind envisaged by many Marxists is tantamount in our societies to a 'cop-out' since it cannot deliver what it promises, and in the meantime does nothing to alleviate material hardship. I want to impress upon people that there are feasible alternatives to the callous monetarist doctrine that is currently in the ascendency in the UK, the United States and Australia. There is little place for *reactive* states under prevailing conditions of capitalism: what is needed is a less doctrinaire, and a more creative political response to capital. Likewise, the welfare systems of several social democratic societies offer the hope of an altogether higher sense of collective morality than that which currently prevails in Australia, Britain and the United States. That is not to infer that the organizational principles of social democratic systems are inviolate, or that they can escape unscathed from the periodic restructuring of capital; but rather, that central planning ensures a degree of resilience that is missing from economies guided predominantly by the market (US, Australia), spreads the social and economic costs of dislocation more evenly, and provides income maintenance programmes that allow people to live with dignity, even if austerely.

10

Urban Policy, Programmes and Palliatives

Urban policy is an umbrella term that tends to subsume the planning and resource allocation that is undertaken within a number of sectors of the economy including transportation, housing, construction and industrial development. In this chapter, however, the treatment of urban policy is confined to a comparatively narrow purview; namely, the area-based initiatives that were part of the broader campaign of positive discrimination in the sixties and seventies, and the measures taken by Labour governments in Britain and Australia to offset market failures and minimize the redistributive capabilities of the fringe land market within cities. Ultimately, the impact of urban policy and targeted allocation upon cities and their inhabitants must be measured alongside that of 'implicit' or 'undisclosed' public expenditure. Though not consciously conceived of as urban aid programmes, the main categories of social welfare flowing to pensioners, the unemployed, or dependent families inevitably have substantial flow-on effects since a high proportion of welfare recipients are localized within cities. For example, the percentage of the 'statutory poor' in central city areas in the US grew from 30 per cent in 1964 to 36 per cent in 1974 as a result of immigration (Kirwan, 1980a: 49). In 1975, federal assistance to the elderly and disabled totalled $US85.2 billion and $US25 billion to the poor. As a result, transfer payments comprized over 10 per cent of personal income in central cities in 1974, compared with 7.7 per cent in 1969 (Vaughan, 1980: 364). In one of the few studies of its kind, Schaffer (1973), has produced a community income statement for two neighbourhoods in NYC, Bedford-Stuyvesant, a poverty-stricken black neighbourhood with 219,000 residents, and Borough Park, a middle-income Jewish community of 186,000 residents. What is especially interesting (Schaffer, 1973: 14–5) is that while the adjusted gross income from wages, earnings and profits in the two communities was $US282.9 million and $US615.4 million respectively, the figures for government transfers (social security, public assistance, unemployment and workers compensation) were comparable ($US121.7 million versus

$US108.2 million). Throughout this chapter, keep in mind that programmes administered by a department like Health, Education and Welfare (HEW) in the United States dwarf the specific urban programmes controlled by the Department of Housing and Urban Development (HUD). Glickman (1981: 507) reports that in the 1980 financial year about $6–8 billion was spent on targeted economic development programmes, about $19 billion on area-based programmes in general, and a global sum of $336 billion on government transfers to welfare recipients.

Urban deprivation, area-based initiatives and the inner cities

Explicit recognition of 'urban problems' by the state, and the possibilities and limitations of ameliorative policy is comparatively recent in origin in most advanced capitalist societies. The 1960s and 1970s saw the formation of government departments with prime responsibility for the framing of urban policy and co-ordinating the policies of other departments that might also affect cities:[1] HUD in the United States (1965); the Department of the Environment in Britain (1970) and the Department of Urban and Regional Development (DURD) in Australia (1972). But even then, having set up the machinery, urban programmes could quickly be relegated to the status of 'left-overs' on a government's agenda. Programmes and urban policy units were likely to be opposed on ideological grounds with a change of government, or even draw fire from within the party that established them (e.g. Britain's Community Development Project). The explicit spatial destination of targeted transfers always renders them liable to charges of 'pump-priming' (*Newsweek*, 1982); and even when priorities have been finally agreed, underfunding and a lack of continuity in funding can compromise urban objectives. Fainstein and Fainstein (1979: 135) calculate that the federal government's budgetary outlays administered by HUD varied by as much as 0.10 to 0.50 per cent of the GNP between 1966 and 1976. A much greater threat to hardpressed cities and the urban poor, however, has emerged in the eighties with the effective disengagement of central government in Britain, the US and Australia from urban and regional development. The diminished status accorded urban policy and the running down of urban and housing

---

[1] In practice this could not be taken for granted. In Australia, the Treasury bitterly resented the upstart DURD, which quickly, amassed impressive powers in the sphere of resource allocation. In fact, 'The creation of DURD disturbed the cosy arrangement whereby the trinity (Public Service Board, Treasury, Prime Minister's Department), virtually determined not only the bureaucratic structure but the priorities of government' (Lloyd and Troy, 1981: 260).

programmes have been consistent, though in another sense contradictory, features of the conservative strategy for recreating conditions conducive to a new round of private investment.

The forerunners of the federal programmes that were developed to channel aid to distressed areas within US cities can be found in the experimental community action programmes set up by the Ford Foundation during the 1950s. The Ford Foundation funded a number of demonstration schemes in the 'grey' areas of cities like Oakland, New Haven, Boston, Philadelphia and Washington to try and improve the career prospects, awareness of civil rights, and self-respect of young blacks and Puerto Ricans. The encouragement of self-help and the effective participation of local groups were uppermost amongst the concerns of the project administrators. Two of the main programmes in Johnston's War on Poverty in the 1960s were modelled on these early experiments in community action. Under the Economic Opportunity Act (1964), an Office of Economic Opportunity was established to provide manpower development and training, public employment and community development programmes for minority groups and the urban poor. By the late 1960s over 1,000 projects were operating in the major US cities. Although the other demonstration programme (Model Cities) was supposed to suggest ways of ameliorating social and educational disadvantage, and unemployment rates in the ghettoes, much more effort went into renewing blighted neighbourhoods. By the end of the 1960s the Model Cities programme had been judged a failure because the available resources ($US900 million), which had to be shared amongst 150 cities, were spread too thinly and the programme of social redistribution was subverted by the welfare and planning bureaucracies based in City Hall (Eyles, 1979: 228). More than anything else, the Model Cities programme demonstrated the importance of 'linking public expenditure on physical renewal and environmental rehabilitation to the provision of social services and a guaranteed supply of housing, earmarked for low- and moderate-income households' (Kirwan, 1980a: 51).

Urban Aid in the United Kingdom

Although British social planners learned from the American experimentation with anti-poverty programmes, and in the process developed the machinery that allowed for a more concerted approach to deprivation and housing stress by central government, in the final analysis the implementation of these policies for the inner cities fell far short of the politicians' promises and ignored the structural bases of poverty. As with Johnson's War on Poverty, the anti-poverty programmes in Britain – there were ten or more area-based initiatives – grew with the awareness that the rising tide of prosperity had passed by some minority groups within the population (Berthoud *et al.*, 1981). Foremost amongst these was the Urban Aid programme which directed supplementary funds to deprived communities (Lawless, 1979). However, although the terms of the Urban Aid programme were broad enough to embrace projects as diverse as day nurseries, language classes for immigrants, holiday pay schemes, housing and neighbourhood advice centres, and women's shelters, funding was parsimonious, with applications exceeding grants by a ratio of 5:1. In the nine years to 1977 projects winning approval for Urban Aid had received a total of only £43.5 million; or in the financial year, 1972–73, no more than the equivalent of 0.1 per cent of expenditure on social services (Lawless, 1979: 31).

Both the Urban Aid and the Educational Priority Area (EPA) action-research projects, which were also set up in 1968 by the Department of Education and Science on the recommendation of the Plowden Report on Children and their Primary Schools (HMSO, 1967), were based implicitly on a pathogenic conception of poverty. This meant that in framing policy public servants assumed that poverty was basically self-inflicted; that is, that the concentration of deprivation within the least desirable parts of the inner city was the product of individual and collective disabilities borne by local residents. This same social pathology conception of deprivation informed the establishment of the Community Development Project (CDP), which was a neighbourhood-based experiment set up by Callaghan within the Home Office in 1969 to find new ways of meeting the needs of people living in areas of high social deprivation. Twelve neighbourhoods were selected for CDPs including the better known ones of Canning Town in east London, Southwark in south-east London, Saltley in Birmingham, Paisley in Glasgow, and Batley in West Yorkshire. The assumption was that at the end of five years the CDP would be able substantially to correct many of the local problems through 'better field co-ordination of the personal social services, combined with the mobilization of self-help and mutual aid in the community' (Edwards and Batley, 1978: 227). But:

> A few months' field-work in areas suffering long-term economic decline and high unemployment was enough to provoke the first teams of CDP workers to question the Home Office's original assumptions. There might certainly be in these areas a higher proportion of the sick and the elderly for whom a better co-ordination of services would undoubtedly be helpful, but the vast majority were ordinary working-class men and women who, through forces outside their control, happened to be living in areas where bad housing conditions, redundancies, lay-offs, and low wages were commonplace. (Community Development Project, 1977: 4)

Not unexpectedly, though embarrassingly for their political patrons, at the end of the five year project in 1974 the Inter-Project report firmly rejected a social pathological approach to deprivation.

By the time the CDP Inter-Project report was released in 1974 the Department of the Environment had begun another round of area-based initiatives, with the added drawcard of a 'total' approach to the urban problem. A comprehensive approach to the problems of inner city areas was felt necessary to avoid the defects present in the Urban Aid and CDP programmes. Known as the Urban Guideline studies, three of the six urban 'guinea-pigs' were the inner area neighbourhoods of Small Heath, Birmingham; Stockwell in south London; and Liverpool 8 (Toxteth). The Inner Cities programme that stemmed from this action-research in 1978 singled out three main contributors to inner city deprivation: economic decline producing higher rates of unemployment and a mismatch between the skills of the resident workforce and the kinds of jobs available; the physical decay of the area; and the preponderance of social disadvantage in the population. In launching the revamped Policy for the Inner Cities (HMSO, 1977) against a backdrop of rising unemployment, the Labour government stated that 'the time has now come to give the inner areas an explicit priority in social and economic policy'. The appropriation which stood at about $30 million under the old Urban Aid programme was raised to £125 million per year. The new Urban Programme established a three-tier hierarchy of urban areas and districts for funding. Seven special Partnership Areas, in which local governments were required to collaborate with Whitehall, received £75 million of the annual appropriation. The sub-regions chosen as Partnership Areas included the Docklands, Hackney, and Islington in Inner London, Liverpool, Birmingham, Manchester/ Salford, and Newcastle-Gateshead in the north-east. Next in line were 15 Inner Area programme authority districts, followed by another 18 districts in England and Wales (Department of the Environment, 1978a: Annex 2).

In 1980 the Conservative government in Britain sought to strengthen the initiatives to stimulate industrial reinvestment in declining urban localities (see Nabarro, 1980) by redefining the 'inner city problem'. According to the Tory party theorists, at the bottom of the malaise lay a myriad of planning controls and government regulations that were strangling private enterprise and discouraging new investment (Bow Group, 1978). Naturally, a solution required the lifting of planning controls and a moratorium on government intervention within the area of economic and physical decline. By March 1980, the 'enterprise zone' was the new panacea, with 12 such zones designated in the heart of London, Liverpool, Manchester, Clydeside, Belfast, etc. Peter Hall (Australian Urban Studies, 1982: 10), who now pleads that the 'enterprise zones' established by Geoffrey Howe, Chancellor of the Exchequer in the

Thatcher government, are a pale likeness of his original proposal for *freeports*[2] in fairly derelict areas in the inner city, has compared them instead with 'a not-very-new-version of the traditional British regional policies beginning with the UK Distribution of Industries Act 1945'. He adds that in the judgement of some planners in Britain 'it is the non-centre-piece of a non-policy'. On the other hand, the London Enterprise Zone has been described by the chairman of the development corporation as 'the most benevolent planning and taxation regulations ever dreamed of' (Cross, 1982: 711):

> Companies that move into the area will not have to pay local auth-ority rates until May 1992 (central government, through the LDDC,[3] supplies the money). Any capital invested in the area qualifies for a full tax allowance, and all projects starting within 10 years of the launch of the enterprise zone will be exempt from development land tax (normally 60 per cent of the increase in the land's value from development). The corporation offers less tangible benefits in the shape of simple planning controls.

Even though it smacks of 'clutching at straws', another group of enterprise zones were to be created in the early part of 1983. Hall (Australian Urban Studies, 1981: 11) predicts that, at best, 'they would have only a marginal effect on the fortunes of the worst UK inner city areas'.[4] In the view of CDP, the Urban Programme is one of the 'starkest contradictions of the State's position' (Community Development Project, 1977: 53). The accusation is that at the same time as it was turning a blind eye to the running down of the traditional manufacturing industries, positive discrimination was presenting an illusion of a genuine political

---

[2] The idea behind the *freeport* was to introduce into the heart of a few ailing British cities the kind of economic regime that has worked so successfully for Singapore and Hong Kong.

[3] London Docklands Development Corporation.

[4] The experience of Toxteth, or Liverpool 8, would seem to bear this out. During the course of the period, 1968–76, Liverpool 8 has been an EPA (1969), a CDP (1970), a Neighbour-hood Scheme (1971), the subject of an Inner Area study (1973), an Area Management experiment, and in receipt of £1.7 million for 146 different Urban Aid projects. In 1980 an Urban Development Corporation was set up in Merseyside as a sop to local unemploy-ment which had risen from 25,000 to 85,000 in complete indifference to a decade's worth of area-based positive discrimination. The response to the rioting that tore Toxteth apart in 1981 included: the refurbishing of council housing and industrial estates; the establishment of workshops in disused premises; the development of the site around the City's Anglican cathedral; the expansion of inner Liverpool's sports facilities for local youth. While employing local craftsmen and apprentices in the short-term, none of these initiatives are capable of creating lasting jobs. Indeed, when Heseltine, the Environment Secretary, went up to Liverpool to take charge of the rebuilding of Liverpool 8 it was suggested that 'he learned nothing that was not already known and will propose nothing that has not already been tried and failed' (*Observer*, 1981: 7).

response. In a word or two, the Urban Programme was tantamount to 'gilding the ghetto'.

Housing stress and 'targeting': more misses than hits

In the latter half of the 1960s, rehabilitation replaced the comprehensive redevelopment of inner area neighbourhoods as the preferred housing strategy of central government in Britain. The disillusionment with comprehensive redevelopment came about for a number of reasons. Firstly, it had certainly proven insensitive to the existing social fabric of many of the working–class communities that were displaced by clearance. Secondly, there was a nagging feeling that just as much unfit housing remained in the UK despite the clearance drive. Indeed, the National Housing Condition Survey, which reported in 1967, put the uninhabitable housing stock at 860,000 dwellings. But because many of the poorest dwellings remaining were widely scattered outside designated clearance areas, the 'blitzkreig' approach of block clearance was less and less appropriate. Thirdly, the cost of producing a dwelling unit on a high-rise housing estate exceeded the alternative which was to combine low-rise 'infill' flats with rehabilitated housing stock (Dunleavy, 1981). Consequently, with the Treasury facing a large trade imbalance, a deficit in the capital account and a 'run' on the pound in the late 1960s, the axe fell on the mass housing programme and a large number of housing projects were deferred (Short, 1982: 45). The number of public housing starts in Britain fell from a peak level of 191,985 dwellings in 1967 to 131,506 in 1976.

The alternative policy was promulgated in the 1969 Housing Act which prescribed a constant level of spending in the public housing sector and announced a swing in emphasis to housing improvement. Whilst provision existed in the 1964 Housing Act for housing improvement within an area framework it was not really taken up, either by the private sector or the local authorities which were distracted by the redevelopment of clearance areas. This was 'put right' by the Conservatives in the 1969 Housing Act by raising the value of the grant from £400 to £1,000, and by removing the obligation to repay the grant if an improved dwelling was sold (Cullingworth, 1979: 80–1). At the same time the 1969 Act empowered local authorities to declare GIAs (General Improvement Areas) with the aim of assisting owners to preserve the condition of their housing up to a minimum standard. A nominal sum of £50 per dwelling within the declared GIA was also made available to local authorities with which to undertake environmental 'repairs' (traffic management, tree planting, provision of play spaces, improvement of pedestrian safety).

As might be expected, the four years following the proclamation of the 1969 Housing Act saw a significant upsurge in improvement activity (up from 124,000 grants in 1969 to 454,000 in 1973). Between 1969 and 1973 a total of 1.3 million improvement grants were issued and 911 GIAs were declared, whilst the subsidies for home improvement rose from £87.7 million in 1969–70 to £568.7 million in 1973–74 (Cullingworth, 1979: 80–1). This grant-aided improvement did contribute to an overall improvement in the quality of housing in England and Wales between 1967 and 1976: however, much of the improvement occurred outside the designated GIAs, with landlords using the grants to improve property and either sell or relet at a higher rental (Balchin, 1979). By contrast, the rate of improvement within the GIAs was distinctly unimpressive. In a survey of 75 GIAs Roberts (1976) found that only 41 per cent of council housing and 18 per cent of private housing in need of improvement had been treated. To summarize, only 75,000 of the 1.65 million home improvement grants went to dwellings within GIAs between 1969–74, many of which were interwar local authority housing estates (Cullingworth, 1979: 80–1).

The 1974 Housing Act sought to strengthen the backbone of GIA policy (i.e. area treatment) which had proved to be the least successful aspect of the housing improvement programme, and at the same time prevent opportunists from profiting from the public subsidy. As well as clarifying the role of the GIA, the 1974 Housing Act provided for the designation of Housing Action Areas (HAAs). The Act required the local authorities or the nonprofit voluntary housing associations to take charge directly of housing improvement within the HAAs. In order to qualify for the more generous grants (normally 75 per cent of improvement costs, or in cases of financial hardship 90 per cent), the housing within an HAA had to be in a bad physical state and the resident population had to exhibit symptoms of extreme social deprivation. By mid-1977 only 219 HAAs containing 70,798 dwellings had been declared, such that only 10.14 per cent of the estimated 700,000 dwellings in areas suitable for inclusion in the HAA programme were under consideration for improvement (Short and Bassett, 1978: 154). Most of these were concentrated in only a few cities – London, Liverpool, Birmingham, Manchester, and Newcastle (Department of the Environment, 1976: 10–11). Otherwise, the HAA programme was hamstrung almost from the start by a shortage of local authority resources for housing and the restrictions placed on Housing Corporation spending (the source of public funds for the housing associations).

The impact of economic stagnation upon central government allocations from 1974 onwards in Britain is reflected in the respective cutbacks for 'local authority acquisition and improvement' and 'improvement grants' between 1974–75 and 1978–79: from £871 million to £480 million and from £214 million to £134 million. By the mid-1970s questions were being raised in the UK about the effectiveness of area-based programmes. A detailed analysis of the 1971 Census (Holtermann, 1975) confirmed what people like Donnison (1974) had suspected for some time – an area framework for positive discrimination in social policy runs the risk of missing out more of the poor and deprived than it includes. For example, if one takes the five per cent of Enumeration Districts with the highest concentration of pensioner households in the UK, they only contain nine per cent of all the pensioner households in the country (Evans, 1980: 195). Holtermann (1975: 39) found 'the degree of spatial concentration of individual aspects of deprivation [to be] really quite low'. There were EDs in the worst 15 per cent on three indicators (male unemployment, overcrowding, and lack of all basic amenities), but they only accounted for one-fifth of the 15 per cent of deprived persons. More general criticism has been levelled at area-based action masquerading as a total programme (Deakin, 1977). But this should not be allowed to overshadow recognition of the usefulness of relatively inexpensive demonstrations of the feasibility of community action; nor should it obscure the appropriateness of the locality as a basis of reform, especially if that means the provision of much needed facilities in poorer environments (Berthoud *et al.*, 1981: 274).

Area improvement and the preservation of working class communities in Australian cities

Because of their more specific and modest objectives, the area-based programmes of positive discrimination developed by the federal Labor government in Australia during its mid-seventies term of office could be said in general terms to have achieved what they set out to do. Firstly, an Area Improvement Programme (AIP) was established within the Department of Urban and Regional Development with the express purpose of directing federal aid to locational 'trouble-spots' within Australian metropolitan areas. By the early 1970s the mushrooming electorates in the outer suburbs had become exasperated by backlogs in basic services like sewerage, and the poverty of resource provision in the sphere of local and state responsibility. The AIP was to be the prime mover in urban and regional development (Lloyd and Troy, 1981: 180–2). The types of projects receiving assistance under the AIP included: three community television centres for the western suburbs of Sydney; a scheme to employ migrant extension officers in Sunshine, a VHC estate in outer Melbourne; beach development in Altona, Melbourne; road reconstruction in Blacktown, outer Sydney. Funding for the AIP rose from $A7.4 million in 1973–74, to $A14.9 million in 1975–76, and then plummeted to $A0.6 million in 1976–77 with the disbanding of the programme by the Fraser government.

The switch by the Liberal-Country Party coalition in 1976 to block grants within a revenue-sharing framework ('new federalism' *à la* Nixon) was consistent with its philosophical objection to centralism and positive discrimination (Carrick, 1978). However, in mitigation it must also be said that Labor Party policy-makers are no longer quite as sanguine as they were between 1972 and 1975 about funding on a needs basis. In his review of the Whitlam years, Wilenski (1980: 43) questions whether the programmes, *as constituted*, could ever 'have effectively and permanently altered the status quo in favour of lower income groups and why many of the benefits intended for that group flowed towards middle income earners.' In the primary health care sector, for example, Wilenski contends that because the state Liberal governments – especially NSW – bowed to pressure from the medical profession only 48 community health centres had been established by June 1975. Likewise, although the massive increase in Commonwealth spending in education (up from $A492 million in 1972–73 to $A2,626 million in 1974–75) 'did make schools in poorer areas more pleasant places in which to be incarcerated in the childhood years' (Wilenski, 1980: 44), it could not really alter educational opportunities without restructuring the entire education system that streams students into state schools, Catholic schools, and fee-paying private schools.

Another group of area-based initiatives arose from the Whitlam government's concern for the pressures created in the inner city housing market during the 1970s by gentrification and commercial and industrial intrusion. In 1973–74, three established residential areas of considerable historical significance, which at the time were under threat of commercial redevelopment, were acquired by the Australian government to serve as demonstration projects in community preservation. Each of the neighbourhoods housed a combination of ageing pensioners and deprived working class families, many of whom had resided in the area for several generations. Thus the disposal of the properties by the major landlords – the Anglican church in the case of the Glebe; a charity, the Family Care Organization, in the case of Emerald Hill; and the federal Department of the Interior in the case of Woolloomooloo – placed historically significant townscape at risk and jeopardized the access of low-income tenants to inner city housing and community services.

In May 1974, $A3.5 million was advanced by the Commonwealth to the Victorian government for the purchase of the 2.1 hectare Emerald Hill estate in South Melbourne. Renewal and rehabilitation was carried out by the Victorian Urban Renewal Authority using funds made available under the Commonwealth-States Housing Agreement (Lloyd and Troy, 1981: 188). The second project involved the purchase, in August 1974, of a 19 hectare church estate in the inner Sydney suburb of Glebe (figure 9.2). Acquisition of the site cost $A17.5 million and it was estimated that a further $A8.5 million would be required to rehabilitate 723 houses and 27 commercial premises and construct a further 250 infill cottages (Wagner, 1977). The estate, which was developed between 1840 and 1870, comprises mostly terrace housing for artisans with the occasional merchant's villa occupying the higher ground.

The third large scale area-treatment project took place in Woolloomooloo,

another working class suburb of inner Sydney (figure 9.2). Federal intervention in June 1975 pre-empted plans to transform Woolloomooloo into
a prestige office, commercial and apartment 'County centre' in accordance
with a redevelopment scheme prepared by the NSW State Planning
Authority in 1969. In June 1975, following interminable negotiations, the
Commonwealth concluded a tripartite agreement with the NSW government and the Sydney City Council. The Commonwealth agree to pool its
land and to provide another $A14 million to buy back property from
private developers and $A3 million for detailed planning, site develop-
ment and landscaping, while the City Council agreed to carry out detailed
planning and implementation, with management by the Housing Commission of NSW (Lloyd and Troy, 1981: 188). It can be said that the two
housing estates which are now managed by the NSW Housing Commission have secured a modicum of low-cost rental accommodation near the
centre of Sydney in perpetuity for about 12,500 residents, as well as
contributing to the preservation of vernacular nineteenth-century
housing. Before the change of central government in 1975 DURD had
also begun feasibility studies for the redevelopment of large housing
estates in Waterloo, Randwick and Marrickville in Sydney, and
Richmond in Melbourne; though not without some misgivings due to the
enormously high costs of assembling inner city properties.

Urban land policy and land reform in the 1970s

The chaotic state of urban property markets in Britain and Australia
during the 'land and property boom', 1968–74, led to renewed demands
for the government regulation of land development, if not the nationalization of land awaiting subdivision (Counter Information Services, 1973b;
Department of the Environment, 1974; Massey *et al.*, 1973). What is so
unacceptable about a property market that is out of control is that it takes
on the redistributive mode of a lottery by rewarding a few at the expense
of many. It also presents opportunities for perfidy that racketeers cannot
resist as the Royal Commission into Melbourne's land scandals has since
disclosed. In 1973, for example, on the advice of its land purchasing
officer, the Victorian Housing Commission paid $A10.63 million for a
1,334 hectare block of land on Melbourne's outskirts which twelve
middlemen had assembled the previous year for $A5.9 million
(Sandercock, 1979: 41). In effect this constitutes a transfer payment of
$A4.7 million at the taxpayer's expense. As well as the undesirable dis-
tributional effects of profiteering in land, in Britain it was widely held that
'private ownership, and more specifically its financial form, was damaging the national economy' (Massey and Catalano, 1978: 170). Indeed, their
monograph on landownership in Britain contains estimates that put the

increase in the value of land between 1972 and 1974 at the equivalent of the entire gross domestic product – £50,000 million (Massey and Catalano, 1978: 1). Not only was the diversion of investment capital into speculative property unproductive and wasteful at a time when British industry was being starved of capital, but the flow-on effect of high land prices retarded the growth of the private housing market (Counter Information Services, 1973b). Thus, the urban land policy that arose out of the various government enquiries into the operation of the 'fringe' land market (Commission of Inquiry into Land Tenures, 1976; Department of the Environment, 1975) was designed to neutralize the regressive capabilities of a capitalist land market left to its own devices.

The British Labour government's proposals for community control of land development (Department of the Environment, 1974), though highly controversial (see Massey and Catalano, 1978: 172–4), were finally enacted in 1975–76. The Community Land Act (1975) dealt with the arrangements for taking development land into public ownership. It empowered local authorities to acquire all land – with provision for exemptions – needed for 'relevant development' for the next ten years. The Development Land Tax, which became law in 1976, set up a mechanism for returning some of the capital gain resulting from public investment to the community. Land owners would be taxed on profits from increases in the value of land due to a development or change in existing use. (As might be expected, neither of these land reforms outlived the Thatcher government.)

For its part, the Australian Labor government set up a land commission programme which was modelled partly on Canberra's leasehold system and partly on the British experiment bearing the same name (in its short existence – five years or so – the UK Land Commission acquired and assembled very little land). Land commissions were to be state agencies, with financial assistance and management guidance coming from the Commonwealth. It was envisaged that each land commission would compete with, rather than completely replacing, private land developers in the production of building lots in the major growth centres and corridors (Johnstone, 1976: 17–19). It was also intended that eventually the land commissions would become self-financing, with revenue from the sale of land being used to purchase further land ahead of needs. Lastly, functions like the subdivision and physical servicing of land would be contracted out to private developers, and most of the housing on commission lots would be erected by private home builders. Hence, the only private sector operations that could possibly have grounds for feeling threatened by the land commissions were speculators and/or specialist land vendors.

Despite the best efforts of federal officers to convince the states of the advantages of a land commission, all excepting the South Australian Labor government were reluctant to participate in the programme. Because the proposed intervention in the land market had such wide popular support amongst prospective home buyers, four other states eventually agreed to participate, though on terms more to their own liking (Troy, 1978: 88–134). Rather than the independent statutory body intended by the Commonwealth they set up land councils that were responsible to a state government minister. The amounts and value of developable land acquired by the land commissions between 1973 and 1976 are set out in table 10.1. The land commission programme loans were to be repaid over a thirty-year period, with a ten-year deferral of initial payments. Provisional policies took shape as the programme got underway: the land commissions endeavoured to obtain a minor market share, around 20–25 per cent, in each sector of the outer zone of a metropolitan area and thereby lever down the lot prices of rival private developers (Murphy, 1976: 53); commission prices were based on production costs and generally were $A1,000–1,500 lower than comparable priced blocks on nearby subdivisions; all lots were made available on a restricted freehold basis forbidding the transfer of vacant land and requiring construction within two years of purchase; the land commissioner supplied developed sites to private individuals, licensed home builders, and the housing commissions.

Following the toppling of the federal Labor government in 1975 the land commissions/councils faced an uncertain future. The incoming conservative government drastically reduced the appropriation in the 1976–77 year down to $A15.1 million from $A54.4 million and $A53.6 million in 1974–75 and 1975–76 respectively. However, in NSW a new Labor government quickly acted to fill the void by passing the Land Commission Act (1976) and lending $A10 million to its new authority so that it could commence operations. Since then the Land Commission of

Table 10.1 Urban land acquired by land commission/councils in Australia, 1973/74–1975/76

State	1973/74		1974/75		1975/76		Total	
	Area (ha)	Cost ($m)	Area (ha)	Cost ($m)	Area (ha)	Cost ($m)	Area (ha)	Cost ($m)
New South Wales	0	0	65	0.82	651	8.40	716	9.22
South Australia	1,299	8.50	1,920	16.68	1,036	7.42	4,255	32.60
Victoria	0	0	354	7.98	315	4.49	669	12.47
Western Australia	0	0	4,998	9.80	52	0.46	5,050	10.26
Total	1,299	8.50	7,337	35.28	2,054	20.77	10,690	64.55

Source: Troy (1978: 140)

NSW has increased its share of lots produced in the Sydney metropolitan area from 5.2 per cent (1976–77) to 28.1 per cent (1980–81) (unpublished Land Market Indicators Report, Land Commission of NSW, 1982). By 1976–77 the South Australian Land Commission (SALC), which was producing about 40 per cent of Adelaide's house sites, had reduced its dependence on external funding. The breakdown of revenue ($A19.7 million) in 1976–77 was as follows: 31 per cent land sales; 29 per cent Commonwealth government; 21 per cent semi-government loans; 12 per cent South Australian government; 7 per cent investments and leasing. By 1979 the SALC held 5,002 hectares of raw land for future needs and was in a position to deliver long-term benefits to home buyers (a steady supply, stable property prices). But the SALC was scuttled at the beginning of the 1980s by the political economy, thereby providing mute testimony to Leonie Sandercock's claim that public sector land development is bound to founder sooner or later in a capitalist society (Sandercock, 1978b: 73–74).[5]

Since a social market in land is an anathema to conservatives, the Land Commission programme was amongst the earliest to be reviewed by the Fraser government in 1975. 'The commonwealth government in 1976–77 cut the level of commonwealth support to the minimum obligation under the terms of the respective financial agreements' (Troy, 1978: 143). Similarly, the first move of the South Australian Liberal government in 1979 was to strip the SALC of its development and co-ordination functions. Next, under a new Act (the Urban Land Trust Act, 1981), its marketing function was curtailed and transferred to a private real estate agency. Now the South Australia Urban Land Trust manages the 'broadacres' land bank of some 3,850 hectares and disposes of property upon request (South Australian Urban Land Trust, 1982). Although Urban Land Councils continue to operate in Labor-held states (NSW, and Victoria and South Australia since late-1982), the federal government finally severed all involvement in the land market when the Government

---

[5] Even before the conservative state government, which was elected to office in 1979, began to emasculate the land commission it faced cash flow difficulties. These can be traced to several processes at work in the wider economy and in the regional land market. Firstly, because of the early antagonism towards the programme in most of the other states, the SALC received as much as 50 per cent of the total federal allocation for urban land acquisition between 1973–74 and 1976–77 (table 10.1). Then, having purchased extensively near the top of the market through 1973–76 and committed itself to an ambitious development programme, the SALC was confronted by a credit squeeze in 1976 which, amongst other things, caused a collapse in demand for home sites. Any possibility of a recovery in demand towards the end of the decade was forestalled by rising interest rates, which left the SALC with a serious cash-flow problem and mounting holding charges. By 1981–82 the debt (including interest) owing on Commonwealth loans had grown to $A89 million. At this point the federal government agreed to restructure the renamed Urban Land Trust's liability, and settle for a $A36 million lump sum repayment in lieu of the debt ($A25 million in 1981–82, followed by $A5.5 million in successive years thereafter).

Review of Commonwealth Functions, which reported in May, 1981, recommended that Canberra's leasehold system of land tenure be abolished. Accordingly, all funding for any new servicing of residential land by the National Capital Development Commission was suspended in the 1981–82 budget and approximately 2,600 serviced blocks that were in the pipeline were turned over to the private sector for release (Raison, 1982: 210).

The denouement: urban policy is pushed backstage

By 1972 in the United States the Nixon administration had more or less fulfilled election promises to phase out many of Johnson's Great Society welfare programmes and rationalize urban funding. The rhetoric of 'new federalism' was accompanied by a devolution of fiscal responsibility to lower levels of government, and the replacement of an increasingly unwieldy system of categorical grants by revenue-sharing formula, but *no discernable* improvement in the level of explicit funding for the cities (table 10.2). Along with the principle of decentralization went a greater reliance upon 'block' funding, which returned some of the prerogative for determining the use of federal monies to the states. Despite the enactment in 1973–74 of two important programmes for urban populations, the Comprehensive Employment and Training Act (CETA), and the Community Development Block Grant (CDBG), for a time they failed to accurately reflect the needs of distressed cities in the US. With federal governments operating record postwar budget deficits, and inflationary pressures building up within a stagnant economy, the problem of municipal fiscal stress became more and more accute in the central cities during the mid-1970s. In 1975 the US Congress passed two counter-cyclical aid bills – one for emergency public service jobs in city government, the other for additional public housing – and eventually a 'New York City Seasonal Financing Act' authorizing federal loans of up to $A2.3 billion a year until 1978 (Caraley, 1976: 21). In 1976, the Ford Administration changed the formula for the distribution of the CDBG so that it took account of unemployment, the age of the housing stock, low rates of income and population growth, and employment loss in manufacturing and retailing. But by the mid-seventies, behind the facade of urban policy and the purpose-built programmes for the cities, the storm clouds of slow growth and a tax revolt were beginning to gather.

Urban programmes in Australia are given the red light

It does not take long to report the demise of urban policy in Australia under the Fraser government. Apart from an ideological aversion to the

Table 10.2 The federal urban budget, 1967–79 ($US million)

	Total federal outlay	Total urban outlay	Urban outlay as percentage of total federal outlay	Urban outlays deflated by consumer price index	Urban outlays deflated by urban price index
1967	158,414	3,334	2.1	3,334	3,334
1968	175,635	5,103	2.9	4,897	4,747
1969	186,062	9,570	5.1	8,716	8,552
1970	197,885	13,297	6.7	11,433	11,543
1971	200,771	15,893	7.9	13.102	12,921
1972	231,876	22,844	9.9	18,231	17,060
1973	249,796	29,660	11.9	22,284	19,135
1974	268,665	28,287	10.5	19,152	15,909
1975	324,601	31,473	9.7	19,524	17,360
1976	373,535	38,744	11.0	21,347	19,304
1977	411,800	42,793	10.4	23,578	19,224
1978	463,800	52,928	11.5	27,395	21,437
1979	504,000	53,656	10.6	26,085	19,597

Source: Goldsmith and Derian (1979: table 2)

type of government intervention contemplated by Labor's urban and regional programme, Fraser's 'new federalism' ran counter to the nascent regionalism, whilst the espousal of supply-side economics left no room for the massive appropriations required for area improvement, community preservation and fringe landbanking. The admixture of libertarian politics and monetarist policies, which incidently ran well ahead of the neo-conservative backlash in the United States and Britain, pronounced urban and regional policy irrelevant. Immediately after the election of the Fraser government a single Department of Environment, Housing and Community Development (EHCD) was created in place of the Departments of Urban and Regional Development, Tourism and Recreation, Environment and the relevant sections of Housing and Construction. 'In real terms spending in 1977–78 in a broadly defined urban sector (included transport) was 32 per cent below the levels of 1975–76' (Lloyd and Troy, 1981: 253). Then, in November 1978, the department of EHCD was abolished and its functions farmed out to other ministries. This sealed the fate of a six-year administrative experiment which had as its goal the development of national urban and regional policy. Finally, the last vestige of DURD's urban concerns disappeared in 1981 with the abolition of the Regional Development Division within the Department of National Development and Energy. The remnants of a federal housing programme suffered the same fate with the removal of housing functions from the Department of Transport and Construction in 1981. The Fraser government's actions in relation to urban policy are consistent with its belief that 'small government is good for big business' and that urban and housing matters should properly rest with the states. The 'catch' is that in the process of divesting itself of these functions the Commonwealth simultaneously reduced the level of funding to the states that responsibility for programmes in welfare housing, land development, urban transit, or sewerage reticulation assumes.

Reviving private investment in US cities

By the late 1970s there was a noticeable drift in US urban policy towards programmes that sought to have a catalytic affect on private investment, ideally in distressed urban areas. Foremost amongst the innovations in urban policy under Carter was the Urban Development Action Grant (UDAG), which was designed to provide federal assistance on a competitive basis for use in specific economic development projects. 'The underlying premise of the public–private partnership in the UDAG program is that public sector "gap" financing can make economic opportunities in distressed older cities competitive with those in the suburbs' (Myers, 1982: 99). By August 1981, HUD had made 1,136 awards to economic development projects in 629 distressed cities under the UDAG programme. These projects which absorbed 2.1 billion UDAG dollars generated an estimated $US12.7 billion of private investment and an additional 298,000 permanent jobs in ailing cities (Myers, 1982: 99).

One of the ironies that attended the formulation of Carter's national urban policy in 1978 (President's Urban and Regional Group, 1978) was that almost no new funds were appropriated to bring into fruition the much-heralded 'partnership' between levels of government, community groups in the cities, and more particularly the corporate sector (table 10.2). A further dilution of urban policy was recommended by the President's Commission for a National Agenda for the Eighties. Indeed the panel report on *Urban America in the eighties* (1980) anticipated the more blatant concessions to private capital made by the incoming Reagan administration. It recommended that the federal government abandon 20 years of 'spatially sensitive urban policies' (President's Commission for a National Agenda for the Eighties, 1980: 98), and switch to a 'go-with-the-flow' approach to funding. This would entail a greater measure of federal assistance to areas attracting firms and jobs, and less for the distressed areas (i.e. 'people-to-jobs' in place of a 'job-to-people' strategy). Glickman (1981) and Goldsmith and Jacobs (1982) concur that in this, and in their dismissal of 'urban impact analysis',[6] the President's Commission revealed a callous disregard for the social costs of 'footloose' capital and thoughtless government allocation.

US policy goes 'anti-urban'

At the beginning of the 1980s the whole tenor of federal policy under the Reagan administration was more openly 'anti-urban'. This was due in part to the fact that urban programmes provided the greatest scope for instituting the cost-saving measures promised by the Republicans during the 1981 presidential campaign. According to the US Conference of Mayors, two-thirds of the $US34.1 billion worth of proposed cuts submitted to Congress for approval in 1982 were to come from urban and housing programmes, even though aid to state and local governments represents only 14 per cent of the federal budget (Lewis, 1982: 13). The Economic Development Administration and the public service jobs provided under the Comprehensive Employment and Training Act (CETA) have been dissolved; capital grants for urban mass transit and the UDAG programme have been cut by one-third; the assisted housing programme was pared by 48 per cent; and operating grants for urban mass transit are to be

---

[6] The case for Urban Impact Analysis rested on three main claims: (a) that the government sector may well determine the path of growth and decline in the total urban system; (b) that departments other than those with an explicit urban mandate (HUD) may produce effects of greater consequence for cities; (c) that even the side-effects of 'urban' programmes have not always been fully anticipated (Clark, 1980).

phased out by 1985. It was doubly disheartening for the US Conference of Mayors to learn, therefore, that these cuts were in line with the recommendations of a draft document prepared by HUD staff for presentation to Congress as part of a biennial review of urban policy. In essence, the review concluded that federal aid to cities contributed more to local problems than to their solutions: 'the report said Government help had contributed to urban decline and transformed local officials "from bold leaders of self-reliant cities to wily stalkers of Federal aid" (and that) . . . even those cities with the worst fiscal problems could muddle through without that aid' (*New York Times Weekly Review*, 1982: 4).

Concessions to private capital have been taken further than ever before by the Reagan administration in its efforts to revitalize the American economy and restore profits. The schedule for depreciating industrial plant and equipment has been narrowed from 25 to 10 years as an incentive to new investment and construction. Pollution controls, regulations intended to improve car safety and strengthen consumer protection have been relaxed by the federal administration. Apart from these measures, 'Reagan's only positive (albeit rather lukewarm) proposal for new urban economic development' (Harrison, 1982: 423) remains the enterprise zone. The latest version of the Urban Jobs and Enterprise Zone Bill jointly sponsored by Congressmen Kemp and Garcia would make the more distressed areas of central cities attractive to private investors by eliminating capital gains taxes normally applying to new investment. Half of all company earnings (and interest income on loans to zone enterprises) would be exempted from taxation. Employers would receive tax credits for each eligible (basically low-wage, unskilled, or non-white) resident they engaged. Also, the possibility of suspending environmental health, safety, minimum wage, zoning and building code regulations has been canvassed. The likeness to conditions applying within the 'world-market-factories'/'free production zones' scattered throughout Latin America and South-east Asia is unmistakable. The idea of the Kemp-Garcia Bill, upon which Reagan and his aides seem to have based all their hopes for declining cities, is to bring the 'success' of the 'free production zones' to the South Bronx and neighbourhoods like it; in short, 'to create low-wage districts in which business will be able to extract higher profits than it could otherwise' (Glickman, 1981: 511).

Already a number of critiques of the 'enterprise zone' have been presented indicating why these 'urban sweatshops' are not (Harrison, 1982; Glickman, 1981: 510–11; Goldsmith, 1982; Le Gates and Wilmoth, 1981; Mier, 1982), and never will be, a 'quick-fix' for the intractable problems found in declining cities:

They cannot combat structural unemployment or underemployment, and they ignore other social and economic problems of our cities: insufficient private and public investment, inadequate educational opportunities, concentrations of the elderly and of people who have never experienced work, a deteriorating physical environment. These problems cannot be solved by substituting 'free enterprise' for government. (Mier, 1982: 14)

Turning the clock back?

The bankruptcy of urban policy in Britain, the United States and Australia is palpable. The Fraser government has treated housing and urban and regional policy derisively, whilst in Britain Peter Hall reports that some planners are also arguing that 'the Thatcher Government has not really got an urban policy' (Australian Urban Studies, 1982: 10). The disengagement of the state from the urban arena represents a retreat backwards and an abrogation of the analysis that gave rise to urban policy in the first place. The declaration of an 'open season' for the private sector will generate greater social costs and add to the hardship caused by restructuring. The problems *of* and *in* the declining cities in advanced capitalist societies, if nothing else, will get worse. In spite of the mixed success of spatial policies during the last two decades there will be a continuing need for the judicious use of 'targeted' aid for urban areas, especially those under greatest stress as a result of private disinvestment (i.e. the 'pull-out' of capital). As Glickman (1981: 492–3) says there has been a conceptual gap in the argument over 'place' policies (e.g. block grants to communities) and 'people' policies (e.g. income transfers to the poor): 'they are often juxtaposed as alternatives rather than observed rightly as complements.'

11
What Next, Then?

The end of full employment

All my life I thought that this was a good society and that our system was the best possible system mankind had devised. Now I'm not so sure. So many people are being thrown out of work that there must be something radically wrong with this system. That's what I'm starting to think. Certainly, work as I've known it all my life is fast disappearing, but what will replace it? I have no answer to that question. I don't think anyone has.

(Redundant production planner with 24 years service with International Harvester, Geelong, Victoria, reported in *Age*, 19 October 1982)

At an economic summit meeting of major industrial nations in London in May 1977, President Valèry Giscard d'Estaing of France expressed the view that unemployment, and especially youth unemployment, constitutes 'a basic challenge to our whole economic system' (Chamberlain, 1980: 15). This final chapter evaluates the socialist vision as it is taking shape in cities of the command economies to see if, in fact, state socialism copes with scarcity more justly than the welfare state. Radicals who have given up on the welfare state contend that only a socialist system can guarantee a fair division of society's accumulated wealth. Conversely, the socialist transformation is out of the question for the vast majority of commentators who, nevertheless, admit to being both greatly perplexed and pessimistic about the future of work in the advanced capitalist economies. There is a growing fear that even if a cyclical upturn in international trade is given a nudge by governments reflating their economies, the net result will still not make an appreciable impact upon structural unemployment in the older industrialized economies. One of the more sobering aspects of the OECD forecast of unemployment levels within the 24 member countries is that it has been progressively revised upwards to 35 million by 1985 (Merritt, 1982: 16).

This raises the more general question about the socialist approach to the allocation and distribution of national wealth. For the most part I will attempt to evaluate how scrupulously egalitarian principles have been upheld in allocation, and to assess the degree of social progress achieved under communism. Notionally, of course, communism is an end-state which can only be reached by passing through successive phases of socialist purification. When investigators, some of whom admittedly have ideological axes to grind, try to capture something of the socialist praxis there is a tendency for Marxists to explain away the defects in either of two main ways (see Peet, 1980). We are told that any judgement of socialism is premature since the Soviet Union, for example, has only had 60 or 70 years to rid itself of the detritus of the CMP; or alternatively, that the socialist experiment has been corrupted by deviationism. In a reply to Peet, Fuchs and Demko (1980: 286) dismiss both of these apologies for communism on the grounds that more rapid societal transformation occurred in the case of the modernization of Japan, and that 'maintenance of a double standard, under which capitalism is judged by its realities and socialism by its ideals, is ethically and intellectually unacceptable.'

Urban and regional outcomes under state socialism

'Command' economies: the state as mastermind

The basic building blocks of a socialist system are the collective ownership of the means of production and central planning of the economy. In principle, social priorities or needs take the place of the market mechanism in allocation. The surplus is appropriated by the state on behalf of the people and redistributed according to norms established by central planning committees. Hence the Soviet government, for instance, through the State Economic Planning Commission (GOSSPLAN) and its other agencies, allocates new investment and manpower to priority sectors and regions. It also sets production targets, intervenes in the biological and social reproduction of labour, and determines the pattern of occupational stratification by setting wage differentials and bestowing privileges on those loyal to the state. Lenin envisaged a remoulding of Soviet society – a new pattern of settlement for mankind – such that in time the divisions produced by capitalism between regions, town and country, and along class lines within cities, would disappear. However, bitter experience has shown that command of the economy and state ownership of the means of production do not render all problems and tensions soluble. Soviet authorities have since reformulated Marxist-Leninist theory. Similarly, other satellite states and communist countries have replaced the Stalinist model of 'command' with models that incorporate limited market relations – Titoist, Sîk, Maoist, Castro-Guevarist (Breth and Ward, 1982:

57–70). This allows for a good deal more pragmatism than the state cares to admit. In the Soviet Union, behind the façade of collectivistic rhetoric, moonlighting is widespread and there is a flourishing 'second' economy (Dyker, 1981: 63–5). In Hungary and Czechoslovakia workers frequently use state equipment, materials and time to produce goods privately that the state itself appears incapable of producing (Smiley, 1983; 18). In China, official endorsement is again being given to private entrepreneurs who are expanding employment opportunities in the service, handicrafts and petty-trading sectors. In the CCP Central Committee and State Council decisions of November 1981, individual business people were guaranteed the right to have two 'helpers and five apprentices' (in White, 1982: 618). This move will help to absorb idle labour in the cities and go part way towards meeting the demand for more varied consumer goods and services.

Uneven urban and regional development under socialist conditions

Focusing upon the space economy of communist countries quickly dispels any belief that uneven development is somehow unique to the capitalist mode of production. Certainly in the Soviet Union and eastern Europe concern for growth, productivity and efficiency has overridden principles of equalization in socialist development planning (Fuchs and Demko, 1980: 314–17; Sawers, 1978: 359). As a result, inequalities and uneven spatial development exist over and above those inherited from the pre-socialist mode of production. In view of the fact that in Hungary, for example, over 60 per cent of the total fixed assets have been established since 1945: 'At a minimum, the socialist nations *must* be held to account for the inequalities created by their conscious location of productive capacity and infrastructure' (Fuchs and Demko, 1980: 286).

The contrast between the Russian and Chinese economic strategies following the Great Leap Forward in China (1958) illustrates the considerable scope that exists for differing paths to communism. As under capitalist conditions, the cumulative impact of divergent principles and priorities is visible in the landscape in the form of regional imbalances. The level of urbanization in the two countries is the most telling measure of their respective achievements in urban and regional planning, given that they profess to share the same long-term Marxist goal, which is to eliminate the contradiction between town and countryside (Sawer, 1978; Wertheim, 1977). At the time of their revolutions both were peasant economies with over 85 per cent of the population living in the countryside. By 1979, however, 61.8 per cent of the USSR's 262 million persons was urbanized, compared with 13.2 per cent of China's population of 971 million (White, 1982: 615). What is more, there has been a marked concentration of the Soviet population within big cities at the expense of medium-sized and small cities. In 1959 there were only three Soviet cities with more than one million persons. By 1976 the number had risen to 14, amounting to 18.9 per cent of the Soviet Union's urban population (Houston, 1979). Moscow's population increased from 6 million in 1959 to 7.5 million in 1975. So expedience has overtaken ideals in Soviet spatial policy despite the lip service that is paid to lofty principles like the 'equalization of spatial proportions', or 'autonomy for the primary organs of Soviet power' (ostensibly the local soviet). Massive urbanization has taken place and the Soviet cities form a 'hierarchy of discontent' (Wilsher and Righter, 1975) due to the interference of state ministries and enterprises in urban government and planning.

There is no question that in the Soviet Union, 'spatial policy has been increasingly subordinated to industrial growth' (Sawers, 1978: 360). In the USSR and much of eastern Europe economic planning has remained highly centralized, technocratic and doctrinaire. New investment has been capital intensive, has concentrated on heavy industry and infrastructure, and favoured 'territorial production complexes'. The distortion of the Soviet space economy has arisen, in spite of state powers to regulate the location of industry and control of migration of labour (Houston, 1979), because 'Soviet cities exist, in the overwhelming majority of cases, to meet the needs of Soviet industry' (Wilsher and Righter, 1975: 198). Typically, investment decisions with sectoral and locational ramifications flow down hierarchically from the GOSSPLAN through its industry ministry to the local soviets (figure 11.1). Soviet theoreticians now have a sophisticated appreciation of the advantages of economies of agglomeration in production and these considerations have generally outweighed concern for the

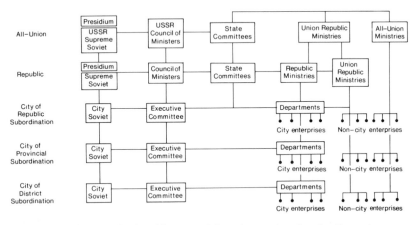

Figure 11.1 The organizational framework for urban and regional policy and development in the Soviet Union
Source: Taubman, 1973: 12

negative social costs associated with big city growth – industrial pollution, environmental despoilation, congestion and extended commuting times, and poor hygiene (see French and Hamilton, 1979: Wilsher and Righter, 1975). Soviet economists have calculated that the productivity of labour in cities over one million persons is 38 per cent higher than in cities between 100,000 and 200,000, while the return on capital is twice as high (Huzinec, 1978: 143). Consequently, a disproportionate share of investment capital continues to flow to republican and oblast centres west of the Urals. In 1971–73, the three main construction ministries allocated over half of their investment capital to projects in large cities in the Soviet republics and only 16.6 per cent to small and medium-sized towns. The central ministries circumvent controls on new building by allocating capital to the expansion and/or reconstruction of existing plant and equipment: 'Reconstruction often exceeds several-fold the production capacity of the existing plant and the cost of rebuilding and re-equipping can be greater than building a new factory' (Andrusz, 1979: 167). Over a four-year period, 1972–75, 3.4 million square metres of new factory space was added to Moscow's stock. As well as this, the development of light industry and the service sector has not been contained in most large Soviet cities (Houston, 1979: 39–40). Because consumer-orientated production like food processing and clothing is exempted from the ban on new industrial construction, twelve industrial estates with over 200 plants were built in the Moscow region between 1967 and 1971. The same inattention to new growth applies to the tertiary and quarternary sectors. Moscow's science-related employment rose from 12.4 per cent to 17.6 per cent during the decade 1960–70.

Now, rather than admitting to their failure to achieve balanced spatial proportions, Soviet planners are in the process of rationalizing planning theory so it more closely matches the Soviet reality (Bater, 1977; French and Hamilton, 1979: 55–6). Acceptance by the Soviets of the economic advantages of industrial concentration finds expression in the following resolution of the Institute of the International Workers Movement of the Soviet Academy of Sciences which was adopted in 1969 (in French and Hamilton, 1979: 56): 'The elimination of differences between town and country, the increase in labour productivity and in the effectiveness of social production, the rise in the cultural and educational level of the population, and the all-round development of the individual – all these things are closely associated with urbanization.' Thus effort that was formerly channelled into establishing the optimum size for cities under socialist conditions has been redirected towards developing new socio-spatial forms that minimize the social costs of urban over-concentration. In the case of Moscow, for instance, this involves decentralizing industry to satellite towns or specialized suburban zones, decreasing residential densities in the old inner core through planned redistribution of the population and by greatly strengthening the transport network within the urban region (see Hamilton, 1976).

By way of contrast, the Chinese have managed to forestall the massive urbanization experienced in the USSR by deliberately breaking with the Soviet model of economic development in 1958 (Wertheim, 1977: 165). Although their urban and regional strategy has been characterized by a measure of improvisation seldom found elsewhere (Schenk, 1974), they have not veered from two key principles that were adopted as part of the Great Leap Forward in 1958. 'Walking on two legs' forms the centrepiece of the revised Chinese development strategy. By the late 1950s the Chinese had come to appreciate the inefficiency and long-term strategic risks inherent in a sluggish agricultural sector and an impoverished peasantry. They saw an immediate need to alleviate the conditions that had forced over 20 million peasants from the land during three years of crop failures between 1959 and 1961. The strategy for 'walking on two legs', as implied, stresses the complementarity of agricultural and industry: 'agriculture as the base, industry as the leading sector' (Kirkby, 1974). The mass mobilization of the peasantry turned labour into human capital by reclaiming land for agriculture, undertaking reafforestation, and by building irrigation and water control systems and dams for the generation of hydro-electricity. Also, industrial development was adapted 'in its rhythm and internal proportions' to the products of agriculture and excess labour available on the communes (Buchanan, 1970). Although the 'backyard' blast furnaces proved to be a dismal failure, many rural communes successfully established their own agricultural, fertilizer works and farm equipment workshops (see Sawers, 1978: 345–481.). 'Walking on two legs' was also supposed to attack the three great divisions in Chinese society – between worker and peasant, city and countryside, and mental and manual work (Thompson, 1974). What started as a campaign to transfer some 'jumped-up' city cadres to the countryside for periods of reorientation became the basis for a much broader programme of return migration. It was expanded in 1962 to include all secondary school students who had failed to gain admission to university. Then during the Cultural Revolution, which dated from 1968, it became rustication proper (*hsia fang*), with over 12 million young people returning to the countryside during the years between 1968 and 1975. In the post-Mao era efforts are being made to appease the transplanted urban youth by segregating them on their own collective farms and paying them twice the ordinary wage. Otherwise, rustication is to be gradually phased out despite the daunting prospect of growing numbers of school-leavers without work in the cities.

The second organizational principle involved replacing the 'tyranny of the line', or the hierarchical approach to economic planning preferred by the Soviet Union, with a more decentralized ('area') power structure (figure 11.2). Greater autonomy is granted to the cities, provinces and

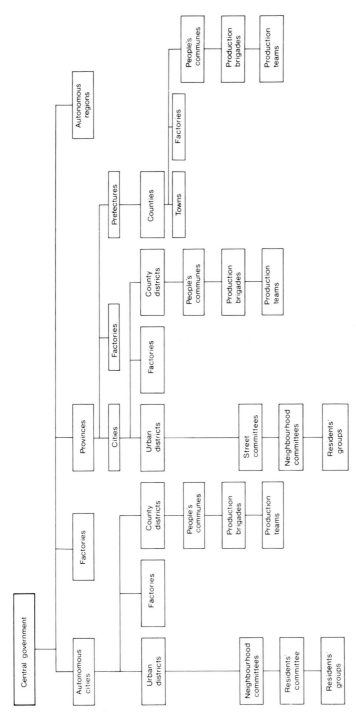

Figure 11.2 The organizational framework for urban and regional policy and development in the People's Republic of China
Source: Jeffrey, 1977: 118

factories than in the Soviet Union and self-reliance in decision-making is permitted within the guidelines set by the national CCP planning committee (Jeffrey, 1977).[1] For example, provisional production targets in agriculture, industry, and family planning are set by the central ministries on the basis of their assessment of the previous year's results and the pending requirements for each commodity and region. These targets are then evaluated at the local committee level and passed back through the administrative channels for final review (figure 11.2). This power-sharing, which is enshrined in the slogan 'from the top down, from the bottom up', also carried over into the cities with the establishment of the primary organs of proletarian power at the neighbourhood and street level. By 1960, 80 per cent of the urban population in China was communalized. In those urban communes that have survived the transition from Maoism, the residents Committees are mainly concerned with routine matters like housing allocation and conditions, the issuing of ration coupons, family planning policy, tree planting and the care of plant stock, and the running of nurseries and clinics. In addition, some neighbourhood committees have set up their own workshops in an effort to increase local self-sufficiency and create work, especially for women. Many of these neighbourhood workshops, or urban collectives, started modestly by recovering and processing waste materials from nearby industrial plants (including discarded metals and chemicals, grease from yarn, fertilizer from tobacco waste, coal from slag heaps). Now over 500 neighbourhood workshops in Beijing, for example, manufacture products ranging from semi-conductor diodes and vehicle accessories to clothing and footwear, or else provide repair and catering services.

The urban collective as an enterprise provides an object lesson: with certainly not much more than five per cent of the total fixed assets in Chinese industry, they employ about one quarter of all workers and account for over 20 per cent of the gross industrial output (table 11.1). The disparity between the performance of the two sectors – the state enterprises and the urban collectives – coupled with the level of urban unemployment (13.2 per cent in 1979 according to official estimates, White, 1982: 615), has led to a review of the present employment system which well-nigh guarantees lifetime employment. Job security for employees of the state enterprises is such that this form of employment is dubbed the 'iron-rice bowl'. Because 'the multitude of unemployed will soon be too heavy a burden on the state and society' (spokesman for the State Economic Commission quoted in Walker, 1982: 6), China is to revert to the contract labour system that operated before the Cultural Revolution in

---

[1] The idea of People's Democracy was taken much further during the Cultural Revolution when Revolutionary Committees forcibly replaced organizational structures based on managerial and technical direction, with 'democratic' power-sharing.

Table 11.1   Chinese industrial structure: state and urban collective sectors

	Workforce (1979) (million)	Number of industrial enterprises (1978)	Proportion of gross industrial output (1980) (b yuan)	Average earnings (1980) (yuan)
State	31.09	84,000	395.1	803
Urban collective	13.28	264,000	102.6	624
Total	44.37	348,000	497.7	

Source: White (1982: 617, table 4)

the mid-1960s. The intention is to reduce overmanning in the state enter-prises by permitting factory managers to lay off workers surplus to their needs, reduce the retiring age, and compulsorily increase the period of maternity leave (Walker, 1982: 6).

Inequalities in the socialist system of earnings and rewards

While the evidence for 'the persistence and self-reproduction of a new system of social inequalities under state socialism' (Szelenyi, 1982: 126) is all but conclusive, it is also generally accepted that the income distribution in the majority of communist countries is more egalitarian than in capita-list societies with a similar per capita GNP. For example, whereas the top 20 per cent of wage earners in Hungary and Czechoslovakia received 36.2 per cent and 34.4 per cent of all incomes in the mid-1960s, the figure for the top quintile in comparable capitalist economies approached or exceeded 50 per cent (Szelenyi, 1982: 124). However, the reduction of income dif-ferentials has not proceeded at the same pace in the various Communist countries. While the socialist transformation in Hungary reduced the manual/non-manual wage gap by 300 per cent between 1938 and 1950, wage differentials actually widened in the Soviet Union between the early 1930s and the late 1950s under Stalin. It was not until Khrushchev's ascent to power that an appreciable drop was recorded in the degree of wage inequality. As a result of a substantial improvement in the earnings of low-placed workers, which went hand-in-hand with the restraint of top incomes, the decile ratio declined by some 38–45 per cent between 1956 and 1968 (McAuley, 1977: 224). Related work by Yanowitch (1977: 23–5) confirms that the ratio between incomes paid to the top and bottom ten per cent of wage earners (the decile ratio) in the Soviet Union fell from 8.1 in 1956 to 4.1 in 1975.

On theoretical grounds, at least, 'The absence of incomes from capital and entrepreneurship, controlled wage scales, full employment and a relatively well developed system of social benefits make it practically inevitable that there should be less income inequality in the socialist countries' (Ferge, 1979: 168–70). But closer inspection of the Soviet system of income distribution reveals that it is firmly grounded in a meritocratic conception of socialism; that is, from each according to his/her ability, to each according to his/her labour. In practice, therefore, the main collective gains from the socialist transformation are the elimination of private ownership of the means of production, and hence of exploitation, and the disapproval of undue accumulation and the transfer of wealth. Meritocracy, which is widely practised by socialist governments, not only determines the official approach to earnings differentials and inequality, it also affects the terms and conditions on which income-support and a range of non-cash services are available. In the USSR, for instance, major cash benefits like old-age pensions, disability pensions and sick pay, and maternity benefits, all require prior employment as a condition of entitlement. In view of this, it should be said that since its 'abolition' by decree in 1932–33 the only unemployment in the Soviet Union is frictional, arising from the movement of workers between jobs. The price of full employment in the Soviet Union is overmanning and busy-work, and inefficiency and low productivity in industry (Dyker, 1981). 'The Soviet approach to income-maintenance, then, has been based on a desire to encourage high levels of labourforce participation and to reinforce the work incentives built into the wage and salary system' (McAuley, 1981: 200). While these cash benefits are amongst the most neutral in a distributive sense, the same cannot be said for a range of other social benefits which one would normally expect to be distributed according to need under socialist conditions:

> fringe benefits are legitimated by a meritocratic ideology which ensures that those with higher qualifications and higher positions in the social hierarchy will get more. Those who are higher in the social hierarchy are thus likely to have higher incomes, better access to the best state owned housing, and better chances of spending their summer vacation in state subsidized vacation homes; they are more likely to be treated free by the better medical doctors, and more likely to have access to private rooms in free state hospitals; their children are more likely to be admitted to universities;[2] they are more likely to be driven to work in state owned cars, and to be allowed to shop in tax free hard currency stores, etc. (Szelenyi, 1982: 125)

---

[2] A set of studies of intergenerational mobility in the Polish cities of Lodz, Szezecin and Koszalin attests to the strength of the transmission of occupational status between generations in a socialist state: approximately half of the sons of the intelligensia maintain their fathers' occupational status (Janicka, 1978).

A more covert array of benefits also flow to the uppermost echelons of communist society in eastern Europe and the Soviet Union. Matthews (1975: 14) estimates that half a million Soviets belonging to the political, military, academic, sporting and artistic elite receive entitlements that greatly increase their real income, and 'widen the income hiatus between the elite and everyone else'. These off-the-record emoluments include personal salary loadings, the 'thirteenth month' bonus, the 'Kremlin ration', and price concessions on goods and services. One is led to the conclusion that 'It is, of course, old hat that privilege and corruption mock the pretensions of Europe's communist societies, especially that of the Soviet Union, to bring genuinely egalitarian reforms' (Smiley, 1983: 18). Moreover, the creation of a classless society appears to have faded from the socialist agenda in most communist states. Polish workers, for example, are conscious of lingering class boundaries (Malanowski, 1978); and it seems that the economic reforms inspired by Liberman in the late 1960s and the 1970s, with their stress on incentives and labour efficiency, will do nothing to blur them.

Unequal housing and services provision within socialist cities

In principle, the powers vested in the state and local soviets in the command economies should provide their urban managers with the opportunities to engineer the equitable outcomes that have so clearly eluded their counterparts in freer urban economies. An examination of outcomes shows that collective ownership of land does in fact minimize much of the regressive redistribution endemic to capitalist land markets (Bater, 1980). Speculation in land is all but eliminated, while the benefits of public investment in urban infrastructure are returned to the community. Minimum standards of provision are determined by the state which sets norms in relation to housing space allowances and rent levels (Matthews, 1979: 108–11), and access to collective goods and services. By the 1970s, after a sustained drive to make up colossal housing shortages which was all the more impressive because of the war damage and the need to replace substandard accommodation, the Soviet Union had sufficient housing stock to guarantee the minimum sanitary norm of 9m^2 per capita to all households (table 11.2). Most housing bureaux in the socialist countries charge nominal rents for public housing which means that housing costs only form a small part of the budget of the average urban household. Similarly, in the private rental sector, which in the USSR accommodates from 5 to 10 per cent of urban households (Matthews, 1979: 110), rent levels are regulated and subject to heavy tax. Otherwise, the only kind of 'rent' in the Soviet Union which is legal and long-term takes the form of repayments on state mortgages advanced to households buying flats in co-operatively owned apartments.

Table 11.2 Adequacy of Soviet housing supply, 1940–75

| | *Actual housing stock as percentage of need* | | | |
| | *Total* | | *Urban* | |
	Minimum[a]	*Rational*[b]	*Minimum*[a]	*Rational*[b]
1940	55	33	66	39
1950	60	35	75	44
1960	72	45	94	56
1970	95	56	111	65
1975	n.a.	n.a.	120	71

[a] Minimum need based on a norm of 10.1 m² per person
[b] Rational need based on a norm of 17.2 m² per person
Source: McAuley (1981: 227, table 8.9)

Most socialist governments have also made a concerted effort to increase the availability and lift the quality of those collective services that are critical to the reproduction of labour-power. For example, in 1940 there were 7.9 physicians per 10,000 persons in the USSR; by 1976 this had risen to 33.5 (at the beginning of the 1970s the equivalent ratios for the UK and USA were 15.7 and 21 respectively). Likewise, between 1950 and 1975 the numbers of children enrolled in urban pre-school childcare facilities rose from 1.38 million to 8.98 million in the Soviet Union (McAuley, 1981: 224–6). Educational and medical services are built into the fabric of Soviet cities at the level of the *mikrorayon*, or 'micro-district', which is a reasonably self-contained suburban estate housing about 8,000–12,000 residents. And even though there is evidence suggesting that service provision often falls well below the prescribed 'norms' in many *mikrorayon*, it has introduced another element of standardization into the socialist city. Indeed, the Soviet preoccupation with labour is reflected in the reasonably uniform provision of school, crèche and medical services, but poor provision of retail services in Moscow (table 11.3). Hamilton (1976: 28) explains that 'shopping centres' as we know them are not found in the *mikrorayon*:

> Retail outlets occupy ground floors of housing blocks on major streets, or kiosks near transport nodes, and supply the bare needs in groceries, medicines, household goods, newspapers and laundering. Usually one *Univermag*, but few other stores · selling consumer durables, are located in each district. Theatres are rare, cinema provision below average, parks and recreation spaces limited. Higher education facilities are also deficient beyond 'factory-floor' training in skills. For all these services, residents must go to central or older, inner Moscow (table 11.3).

Table 11.3 Key indicators of service and amenity provision by zones of Moscow, 1970 (per thousand persons)

	Students at all levels	Library books and journals	Hospital beds	Cinema seats	Retail turnover (thousand rubles)	Population per hectare recreational space
Central area	315	162,000	11	23	3,875	606
Inner ring	260	39,200	12	8	1,621	
Outer ring	170	8,580	11	10	891	221

Source: Hamilton (1976: 28, table 7)

While credit must be given for these broadly based improvements in living conditions within socialist cities, it does not negate the fact that in most of eastern Europe, and certainly in the Soviet Union, 'social inequalities *after housing* are greater than before housing' (Szelenyi 1977: 67). Paradoxically, biases and rigidities built into housing allocation and service provision consistently produce outcomes resembling those found in capitalist cities. How does this come about? A greater part of the 'who gets what where?' question is decided by the intersection of the *priority* principle with the reward structure inherent in the communist system of planning and management. The priority principle is more than just a general strategic orientation: if a dislocation threatens, resources are simply physically shifted from non-priority to priority sectors and locations (Dyker, 1981: 46). The operation of the priority principle leads to inefficiencies in the allocation of urban land and generates unwarranted social costs. Firstly, the absence of a pricing mechanism means that there is no real pressure upon senior ministries to develop valuable inner area land. Because central ministries frequently hold the equivalent of monopoly rights over premium core area sites, lower priority users are forced to leap-frog to the edge of socialist cities to procure development sites. This adds unnecessarily to the already excessive travel times endured by commuters in the biggest cities of the Soviet Union and eastern Europe. In Moscow, where the problem is admittedly at its worst, average travel times have steadily deteriorated from 37 minutes in the mid 1960s to over an hour (Hamilton, 1976: 30–1). For the three million residents and commuters inhabiting the 48 towns in the outer region of the metropolis, the official 'norm' of 40 minutes in cities over 500,000 is now meaningless. Secondly, many of the largest state enterprises in the command economies have not only planned for rudimentary housing and low-cost services, but to make matters worse they often fail to meet supply targets and deadlines (Taubman, 1973). This leaves urban Soviets with heating, water and sewerage systems that are woefully inadequate.

The priority principle also cuts across the allocation of housing because top-dog ministries like Industry and Transport and some state enterprises control as much as 60 per cent of the total funding for housing construction (Bater, 1977). Although their housing stock is transferred to local authorities to manage once it is built, they reserve the right to select the tenants. And because official encouragement has been given to the preferential treatment of meritorious workers since the 1930s, state enterprises have been able to use better quality new housing as an incentive to attract skilled labour or managerial personnel without breaching government regulations. Therefore, this system sees to it that 'people in leading organizations get better accommodation in more attractive locations' (Matthews, 1979: 107). With rents set at modest levels irrespective of income, this represents a housing subsidy to the privileged class. This contradiction in socialist housing allocation was first exposed by Szelenyi and Konrad (Szelenyi, 1972). In the late 1950s the Hungarian government embarked on a building programme with the intention of providing state housing at heavily subsidized rentals to the families of low-paid workers. In Szelenyi's words,

> the original aim of rent subsidies was to close those gaps to some extent which had opened in incomes in the interests of providing incentives for productivity. If, however, those flats systematically came into the possession of those enjoying higher incomes, the effect of the subsidy was the very opposite, differences in standards of living were widened and not narrowed. *Rent subsidies thus turned into wage supplements increasing the differences between low and high incomes.* (Szelenyi, 1972: 274)

There is now ample documentation of housing inequality in socialist cities. A nationwide survey of Russian housing undertaken in 1967 established that while there was sufficient stock to guarantee the urban population $10m^2$ per person, only 27 per cent of households had access to more than $9m^2$ per capita. This implies that the elite enjoy substantially more generous shares of housing space than the urban proletariat. Several housing surveys carried out in Soviet cities in the late sixties and reported in Yanowitch (1977: 40–2) established that the managerial and technical personnel employed by industrial plants are consistently allocated the superior housing; that is, separate apartments as opposed to communal apartments, dormitory accommodation, or a pre-revolution cottage (table 11.4). Data presented in an appendix accompanying Szelenyi's 1977 paper add to the generality of these findings:

> There are no systematic, nationally representative data as far as I know concerning the correction of social status or income with housing allocation, but all data from Hungary, Poland and

Table 11.4 Housing distribution in two Soviet industrial centres: (a) Urals Chemical Machine-building Works; (b) Bogoslovskiy Aluminium Works (percentage)

Occupational Group		Private rent	Hostel dormitory	SC flat	Communal flat (good quality)	Poor quality flat	Pre-revolution cottage
Intelligensia	(a)	2	6	64	9	14	7
Workers	(a)	11	3	38	17	21	7
Intelligensia	(b)	8	3	81	5	4	8
Workers	(b)	8	2	54	14	8	17

Source: Matthews (1979: 115, table 5.2)

Czechoslovakia . . . indicate that the better qualified and consequently higher income groups have better access to State owned housing, the less qualified and lower income groups will more probably depend on the market, they will own their own homes. (Szelenyi, 1977: 83)

Co-operative housing is actually weakening this latter pattern referred to by Szelenyi, especially in the cities. As standards of living rise in the socialist economy co-operative housing ventures are increasing in popularity among the middle and upper income earners. From 1965 to 1973 about one tenth of the total housing constructed in Soviet cities, or 63.5 million m², was of this type. In Moscow, the proportion during the decade 1966–75 was over 15 per cent, reflecting both the greater delays in obtaining public flats and the greater prosperity of Muscovites.[3] Because co-operative housing is privately financed it tends to stand out as a result of the greater care and attention given to communal facilities such as lifts, corridors, staircases, and the surrounding property (French and Hamilton, 1979: 98). Although access to subsidized rental accommodation must represent a considerable disincentive, the co-operative home unit has long-term advantages, if only as a means of partially preserving capital. While it is not yet really clear whether these blocks of co-operatively owned home units are systematically located on the more desirable sites, or whether they represent the beginnings of social segregation in socialist urban space, Matthews (1979: 111) believes that, 'As time goes by, such blocks must tend to develop a distinct social colouring of their own.'

Finally, on the strength of the regularities detected in housing allocation, Szelenyi is prepared to frame a more general proposition about the distributive capacity of the two main social systems: '*while under capitalism*

[3] About 600,000 Muscovites now live in privately owned flats or are buying co-operatively.

the market creates the basic inequalities and the administrative allocation of welfare modifies them slightly, under socialism the major inequalities are created by administrative allocation, and the market can be used to reduce inequalities' (from an unpublished manuscript in Stretton, 1981: 118) [Stretton's emphasis]. Perverse as it may seem, there are a number of structural obstacles peculiar to state socialism that prevent the realization of a more egalitarian social order. By erecting a reward structure of their own making in place of capitalist mechanisms, the socialist states have watered down the benefits promised by the collective ownership of property and limitations upon the inheritance of wealth. Also, the application of the priority principle in Soviet economic development has produced uneven urban and regional development that is no less problematic than that found under capitalism.

Distributional justice in the context of structural change

Try as the apologists for communism might to explain away the short-comings of state socialism (Peet, 1980), the communist model has very little appeal to the majority of voters in Britain, the US and Australia. Apart from the repugnance of totalitarianism, claims about the immunity of the socialist system to economic crisis are beginning to ring hollow (Drewnowski, 1982): the economies of Poland, Czechoslovakia, and Hungary are ailing; and unemployment, much of it hidden, is not un-known in the socialist economy. While the Chinese officially acknow-ledge that urban unemployment is about 12 per cent (White, 1982: 623), *under*employment in the Soviet Union and the satellite states of eastern Europe is 'probably realistically gauged at ten per cent' (Smiley, 1983: 18).

The radical socialist alternative for societies like Britain, the US and Australia is also unrealistic in other respects. Where property rights and individual ownership are woven into the very fabric of society, the advocacy of forfeiture implicit in the notion of collective ownership is not going to win popular support. Remember the Bermondsey by-election in February, 1983? While there were extenuating circumstances, it is note-worthy that the radical Left lost a safe working class seat for Labour which the party had held for over 60 years – with a swing of 44 per cent. Whether or not the working class has been corrupted by the property owning ethic, the fact remains that some four-fifths of the population are not about to accede to the overthrow of a system that by their judgement serves them perfectly well, simply as a means of improving the status of the fifth of the population that is underprivileged. In light of this, the call by Marxist intellectuals for the overthrow of capitalism in the advanced industrial societies is tantamount to a 'cop-out', since it cannot deliver what it promises and in the meantime does nothing to alleviate material hardship or combat alienation. Worse still, because the impact has been more immediate, all the radical critique of the welfare state (Gough, 1979) has done is arm the neo-conservative forces advocating the dismantling of social welfare structures and at a time when 12 to 15 per cent of the workforce is dispossessed of regular employment (Szelenyi, 1981b: 4). It is my belief that the social democratic model developed by the 'social market' economies of Western Europe offers the hope of an altogether higher sense of collective morality than that which currently prevails in Australia, Britain and the United States. We will review the main features of the social democratic model and then conclude by proposing an agenda for the benign transformation of that form of state capitalism found in the UK, the United States and Australia.

Table 11.5 Public welfare expenditure in selected OECD countries[a]

	Early 1960s	Mid 1970s	Elasticity of welfare expenditure with respect to GDP
Australia	9.6	12.8	1.33
United Kingdom	12.6	16.7	1.33
United States	10.3	15.7	1.52
Austria	19.6	23.0	1.17
Belgium	18.6	23.2	1.25
Denmark	14.2	23.4	1.65
Finland	14.0	21.0	1.50
France	17.0	20.9	1.13
Germany	16.5	20.6	1.25
Netherlands	14.2	29.1	2.04
Norway	11.7	20.0	1.72
Sweden	13.6	21.9	1.61
Japan	7.0	8.9	1.28

[a] Expenditure on health, education and income-maintenance services as a percentage of gross domestic product
Source: OECD, 1978

Social democracies of Western Europe

The social democracies of Scandinavia, West Germany, Benelux, Austria and Switzerland out-performed Britain, the US and Australia during the 1960s and 1970s (figure 11.3), even while strengthening the machinery of state intervention and increasing their public expenditure on social welfare (table 11.5). Kuttner's (1981: 34) analysis of the French, West German, Swedish, Japanese, US and British economies gives a good indication that

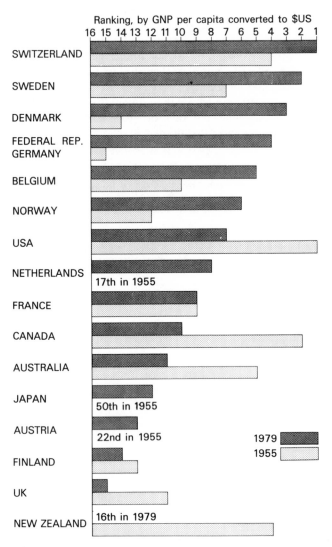

Figure 11.3 Changes in the ranking of selected countries between 1955 and 1979, measured by GNP per capita in US dollars
Source: Australian Industry Development Association, 1982

'the better economic performers among western countries include the more egalitarian ones'. Uniformly high wages and an enormous public sector have not prevented the Swedish economy, for example, achieving the second highest per capita GNP in the world (figure 11.3). Income in Sweden is more highly equalized than in many of the communist economies (Castles, 1978; Stephens, 1979). Indeed, the Swedish Confederation of Trade Unions (LO) is famous for its 'solidaristic' wage policy which strives to narrow wage differentials between groups of employees. Alternatively, the German basic pension system is sufficiently generous to make most retired people independent of supplementary means-tested aid – in Britain one in three pensioners are placed in this situation. Nevertheless, what the German and Swedish experience has shown is that a scaled-up social welfare programme combined with economic growth is still not sufficient to produce a truly egalitarian society. In Sweden the disparity in wealth still finds the top 2.3 per cent of households owning 30.4 per cent of all private resources. Likewise, the top 1.7 per cent of German households own 32 per cent of all wealth in that country (Kuttner, 1981: 40).

The President of the German Construction Workers' Union, Georg Leber, is credited with producing the first blueprint for asset-sharing in industry. Since 1964, 'equity or asset or investment-sharing has moved from being simply an intriguing speculation of dreamers to quite specific legislative proposals that have figured prominently in national elections' (Chamberlain, 1980: 140). The Swedish labour movement has also tackled this general issue of control of resources by: pursuing a centralized collective bargaining system; securing a pension scheme funded by payroll tax; and pressing for the establishment of an investment reserve fund for which contributing companies receive tax concessions (Sandercock, 1982: 26–7). In 1976 the Swedish LO adopted the 'Meidner proposal' for asset-sharing which calls for the diversion of a fixed proportion of company profits into employee investment funds (Meidner, 1978) – the idea being that the unions would increase their share of the equity capital in the firm bit by bit and eventually control the deployment of investment capital. In this alternative to the nationalization of key industries, after 50 or 60 years the Meidner plan foresees Swedish workers controlling most of the strategic capital formation in industry and presumably their own destinies. The Dutch and the Danes have already submitted asset-sharing bills to parliament which were defeated at the time (1974), but are not dead, according to Chamberlain (1980: 142). Equity participation represents one of the few ways open to making capital more accountable to both the state and labour. Although not a complete answer to 'deindustrialization' in the advanced industrial economies, it will at least enable employees to intercept part of the economic surplus that at present is concentrated in the hands of a wealthy minority of stockholders.

'Deindustrialization' and the adaptability of the state

It is the readiness to try something new in the wake of technological change and labour-shedding that distinguishes the governments of western Europe from those of Britain, the US and Australia. As unemployment levels throughout western Europe indicate (table 5.4), the social democracies have not,[4] and will not escape the restructuring of capital that is underway at present. But because they have central planning machinery, manpower policies, and adequate income-support programmes in place, they are better equipped to spread the social and economic costs of dislocation more equitably than governments in the United Kingdom, the US, or Australia. Also,

> there is more and more discussion in Europe on the need for 'structural' adjustments to solve the problem of unemployment – meaning what to do about declining industries, regions of poverty, and neglected segments of the population. Since these are problems that cannot be solved quickly, there is correspondingly a growing belief that Europe's unemployment is a long-term problem, requiring fundamental institutional changes, even if no one can produce the specifications for them yet. (Chamberlain, 1980): 18)

And in Japan, where governments have not felt the same need to barricade themselves in ideologically as those headed by Thatcher, Reagan and Fraser, some opinion has it that:

> Capitalism has served mankind well now for several centuries. But there is a growing feeling in the world that the system must be modified to meet the new needs and changing priorities of society. This doesn't necessarily mean the world will go communist or to the extreme left. But there will have to be some modification in the future. (President of Ishikawajima-Harima Heavy Industries of Japan, quoted in Chamberlain, 1980: 36)

By contrast, at a government level in Britain, the US and Australia at the moment there is an unwillingness to admit that we are no longer simply dealing with the unconnected problems of inflation, unemployment, declining regions and cities, underutilized industrial capacity, and 'fiscal crisis' in the public sector, *but with the malfunctioning of a system.* While conservative governments keep up the pretence that the current unemployment is more cyclical than structural, the economies of Britain,

---

[4] In the five years to 1978 the EEC lost three million jobs in manufacturing industry (Merritt, 1982: 173).

the US and Australia will fall further behind in the industrial marketplace. There is an urgent need for these economies to discard their austerity measures and break with monetarist economic policy and map out a long-term strategy for structural change. This must involve much more than just another bout of Keynesian pump-priming, or a combination of more protection for and the selective streamlining of inefficient industries. Part of the challenge facing the state is to anticipate, rather than engaging in a delayed reaction to the restructuring of capital. At the very least, the state should be endeavouring to channel structural change in socially desirable directions. Here we are not alone in assuming that the economic conditions that lie ahead under advanced, or possibly, late capitalism will demand *more* rather than less state intervention: 'One widely-shared conviction is that in the future governments will necessarily play a more active economic role, presumably directing corporate activities more definitively than is now the case' (Chamberlain, 1980: 36). How should the state respond to the crisis of capitalism? In a text of this sort the onus is not really to draw up a blueprint, but to point to some of the reforms and adjustments that are necessary if the state is to come to grips with the inevitability of restructuring, and in the process achieve a morally defensible social order.

Towards qualitatively new forms of state intervention

If capital is to be made to serve the interests of society as a whole within the advanced capitalist economies then the state will need to: (a) engage in some form of indicative planning and co-ordination; (b) dispense with the adversarial system of market relations; (c) install proper manpower policies; (d) transfer an equitable share of the economic surplus and national wealth to those persons denied the opportunity to participate in its creation; (e) regain the initiative in urban and regional development. Because the conditions and relations between capital, governments and labour vary so markedly in the UK, the United States, and Australia, the proposals below have been drafted primarily with the Australian scene in mind. It should also be said that the type of social transformation that these reforms presage could be exceedingly painful for vested interests on both sides of the class divide. To complicate the task further, experience in western Europe shows that political expediency operates far too often to prejudice the success of some of the reforms proposed. Nevertheless, whatever the temporary difficulties and setbacks, there would appear to be few realistic alternatives in the long-run to what we are proposing. By this account, the throwback in the mid-seventies to monetarism and libertarian values will be judged an aberration in the tortuous but inexorable passage from capitalism to a benign form of democratic socialism.

National economic planning

The cultivation of clichéd views about capitalism versus socialism remains one of the most disabling cankers of economic and political life in Britain, the US and Australia. It is the innate conservatism of these property-owning democracies based upon outmoded and simplistic dichotomies of this kind that has forestalled the setting in place of an indicative plan for national economic development (though a short-lived attempt was made by the Conservatives in Britain during the mid-1960s with a National Economic Development Council). The postwar record of governments, more so in Australia and the US than in Britain, is one of *ad hoc*, reactive, incrementalist policy-making. Yet, ironically, the modern corporation is a tightly structured organization that co-ordinates all facets of its activity and leaves nothing to chance – that is, the whims of the private market (Galbraith, 1967). To compound the irony, it is not only social democracies like Sweden and West Germany that owe their postwar prosperity to national economic planning (indeed America made it a condition of Marshall Plan assistance!), but also avowedly 'free enterprise' states like Gaullist France, Japan, and Singapore.

By allocating capital to high-priority sectors and locations in accordance with national economic development goals, Japan, West Germany, and Gaullist France maintained significantly higher rates of economic growth throughout the sixties and seventies than Britain or even the United States. In Japan, the Ministry of International Trade and Industry (MITI) uses 'administrative guidance' to bring about structural adjustment within the Japanese economy. An important element in several of these frameworks is access to investment capital outside the private banking sector. In France, where most of the banks are nationalized, credit allocation serves national planning objectives. Alternatively, in some countries socialized savings constitute an important source of new capital. Sweden uses its social security savings accumulated on behalf of future pensioners in this way. In Singapore the Central Provident Fund[5] has played a vital part in the island state's economic growth miracle.

Negotiating a truce between capital and labour

The future of effective indicative planning will remain in the balance so long as Australia persists with an adversarial system of industrial relations.

[5] Essentially it is a retirement insurance scheme to which employers and their workers are required to contribute by law in the ratio of 20.5 per cent: 16 per cent; thus 37 per cent of Singapore's payroll bill is compulsorily saved. Not only has the Central Provident Fund underwritten the major part of the government's capital works programme and lent mortgage finance to workers wishing to purchase housing from the Housing and Development Board, but it is now in the position to invest over $US6,000 million outside Singapore.

Faults lie with both sides. In Australia, management seldom takes employees into its confidence when it is planning production or new investment, let alone making provision for representation on the board. Thus at the same time as it is threatening to halt the production of steel in Australia, BHP can clamly announce that it has outlaid $US2,400 million to purchase the mining conglomerate, Utah International. For its part, organized labour now possesses monopolistic powers that are every bit as formidable as the corporations, especially when they are exercised in strategic sectors of the economy. The alienation and cynicism felt by much of the Australian workforce is reflected in the level of industrial disputes: in 1974 6.29 million days were lost because of strikes and in 1981, 4.19 million days; but in 1982, with the recession biting, this level fell to 1.83 million days. Compare this combative atmosphere with West Germany, Norway and Austria where trade union and employer representatives directly participate in the process of income and prices determination via specialized technical and contact committees (Chamberlain, 1980: 169–82). Moreover, in order to secure their interests in economic stabilization, governments furnish the forecasts of expected performance which are taken as an agreed basis for negotiating non-flationary wage settlements. This is considered to be an essential prelude by the trade union movement to greater worker participation and eventual industrial democracy.

Manpower planning and job creation (or rationing)

The end of full employment as we have known it in the advanced capitalist economies necessitates a radical rethinking of the work ethos. The social changes that this will force may well be as profound as those that occurred with industrial urbanization in the mid-nineteenth century. To begin with, the increasingly inappropriate, if not false, division between productive and non-productive work must be abolished. It is this misguided notion that has encouraged monetarists to argue, in the face of the long-run structural shift to a services-based economy, for sizeable cuts in public sector employment. In the process of demystifying work, early retirement, job-sharing, a shorter working week, and even 'opting out' will gain much wider community acceptance. Instead of ostracizing those who would prefer not to work at any one time we should be grateful that they are prepared to make way for those jobless who so dearly wish to work. On the other hand, it would be unwise to view the 'domestic' economy or 'informalization' as long-term alternatives for more than the resourceful minority. To the mass of permanently dispossessed workers they will be looked upon as improbable solutions to the job crisis.

Clearly all governments are going to have to combat structural unemployment on several fronts. Because the conservative regimes in Britain, the United States and Australia have not taken 'de-industrialization' seriously, the commitment so far to manpower planning, retraining and job creation programmes has been half-hearted. The direct and calculable expense of unemployment is only just beginning to dawn upon their treasuries; as yet the 'opportunity costs' of 'lost' demand, ill-health, and the added pressures upon public housing have scarcely figured in the debate (Merritt, 1982: 150–4). There is a need to look beyond once-off, short-term labour absorbing community projects and capital works such as the construction of public housing and transport infrastructure. In Australia, government should be insisting on the *addition of value* by processing more locally sourced materials like wood chip, liquified gas, and alumina.[6]

Before governments have to resort to the rationing of jobs there are a number of avenues still open for absorbing more labour. Firstly, contrary to present policy in Britain, the US and Australia, personal services in medicine, education, recreation and leisure can be expanded. Secondly, unemployment benefits should be used as a wage subsidy for employers who are prepared to make a net increase in the size of their labour-force. Thirdly, in 1977 the Danish government drew up two lists, one of high-priority capital projects, the other of job creation needs. 'Where items matched they went right ahead, and now, more than $US4 billion later, the Danish authorities are convinced that they have not only saved vital jobs, but whole industries such as shipbuilding' (Merritt, 1982: 196). Fourthly, Japanese industry heads off loss of self-esteem, damage to health, and social stress by guaranteeing loyal workers employment for life. This practice has been extended to Australia by Mitsubishi, which took over the Chrysler car plant in Adelaide in the late 1970s: over-manning has been exchanged by the company for harmonious industrial relations.

In Singapore a forward-looking government is making a determined effort to ride the wave of structural change by consciously acceding to high wage settlements. This strategy, which permitted a 20 per cent increase in wage bills during each of the three years 1980–82, aims to phase out labour-intensive industries and encourage the expansion of a mix of high technology and 'sunrise' industries requiring more skilled man-power. Now that this transition has been set in train, wage increases are to be pegged to productivity and 600,000 workers, representing about half the total workforce, will receive vocational and technical retraining

[6] As a case in point, instead of setting up an aluminium fabrication and semi-fabrication industry in Australia, Comalco has just spent $A100 million securing access to the Japanese market. The agreement, which includes a 30 year contract to supply aluminium to Showa Aluminium Industries of Japan, may be a sound strategic decision for Comalco as a primary producer but it effectively means that Australia forfeits the right to develop a significant processing and fabrication industry of its own.

(Richardson, 1982: 13). The Secretary-general of Singapore's Trade Union Congress, in lending the labour movement's full support to the scheme (dissent is outlawed) declared: 'We must not waste time as new technology will penetrate our economy at a very rapid pace. Automation, computerization and robotization will be extensively used and those who remain poorly educated or unskilled will be left out on a limb in this process because the demand for unskilled and semi-skilled workers will decrease' (in Richardson, 1982: 13). Such realism is novel compared with the fallback position of protectionism, which has been widely advocated within the labour movement in Britain, the United States and Australia. The Industries Assistance Commission (1977–78) has established quite conclusively, for Australia at least, that protection does not preserve jobs in the long-term. Their tabulations indicate that the most highly protected group of industries in Australia experienced the greatest falls in employment between 1972/73 and 1975/76, more through technological change than increased imports.

Revamping redistribution

One of the things that becomes clear from Brown and Madge's (1982) profile of Britain's welfare state is that it is 'in no meaningful way compensating for economic and industrial change'. Unemployment benefits were originally conceived as a short-term measure to tide migratory, or temporarily displaced workers and their families over between jobs. The jobless, and especially unemployed youth, now face the prospect of prolonged and indefinite periods without work. The effect of the present reward structure is to heap the costs of structural change almost entirely upon those who are locked out of the workplace. With progressively fewer workers directly engaged in manufacturing, and maybe even in office functions, there will be irresistable pressure to redistribute more generously the surplus generated by industrial technology. The assumption is that Australia is sufficiently well-endowed with resources to support all members of society with status and dignity. Though a redistribution of productive capacity is taking place at present between countries (Shihata, 1982), it is conceivable that in the immediate future automation will cancel out the advantages of low-wage regions in all but a few product areas. If investment in new technology is based upon a system of asset-sharing in industry, then workers in manufacturing are capable of generating enough wealth to support members of the community dependent upon a social wage – in much the same way that a miniscule agricultural workforce is now capable of feeding and clothing the non-farm population in the advanced capitalist economies. The case for increased redistribution between full-time workers and the workless is placed in a better perspective when it is realized that in Australia in the last 15 years, for every 100 workers, the number of people receiving social allowances of some kind has doubled from 20 to 40.

A guaranteed minimum income for workers for whom there is no work may well be the price the community has to pay for political and social stability. In Australia, Professor Russell Mathews, director of the Centre for Research in Federal Financial Relations at the Australian National University, has proposed that the costs of such a programme could be defrayed firstly by breaking down the concentration of private wealth with a capital gains tax and the reinstatement of death duties and, secondly, by completely overhauling the taxation system (including the array of subsidies for homeowners).

Regaining the initiative in urban and regional development

A long-term goal of a national development plan would be the smoothing out, within reason, of the gross regional imbalances that arise if capital is given *carte blanche* by the state to invest and disinvest where it will. In Australia, at a minimum, this would require the establishment of a policy unit by federal government charged with mapping out the broad contours of a balanced space economy, taking into account the existing distribution of natural and human resources. Then, as a matter of some urgency, governmental assistance would be provided, consistent with national planning objectives, to local and regional capitals that are being forced to close down their operations or regroup in response to the worldwide appropriation of space by transnational corporations. Foreign investment would also be supervised much more closely and, if need be, subjected to controls and sanctions of various kinds (cf. the Norwegian government's enlightened custody of its North Sea oil reserves). Also, the co-ordination of resource allocation and the setting of priorities in Australian urban and regional development would help to counteract the perennial distortion to the national space economy that results from internecine rivalry, not only between the states but between capital cities as well.

Secondly, a regional planning framework for Australia 'may be the best way of ensuring wide community involvement in economic planning issues' (Sandercock, 1982: 31). This could be accomplished by extending some of the Whitlam government's initiatives, such as the regional councils for social development, so long as the tendency to overcentralization was avoided.

Thirdly, all governments are going to have to grapple more conscientiously with the looming problem of regional disaffection and greviance within countries and cities. Many local social movements may or may not have a class/racial/gender dimension; nevertheless, with the global reshuffling of industrial capital the reality of the 'throwaway' region or community is upon us. Because of the constraints that operate it is wrong to assume, as many labour economists seem to, that workers discarded by capital are free to move to areas that offer better prospects: housing may be impossible to sell; the person may be one of several workers in the household; the redundant worker may have few or inappropriate skills; school leavers without work depend upon their parents for sustenance. Those people immobilized by circumstance, and jobless for long periods, cannot be expected to put up indefinitely with impoverished, nondescript and desolate residential environments. One would have thought that, if for no other reason than their own peace of mind, the political and economic powerbrokers would be working to dissipate the sense of despair, alienation, and mounting hostility felt by the victims of industrial change. When workers spent most of their working life in a factory, down the mine, or on the land, they were less concerned about living spaces bereft of amenities. One of the real challenges ahead of advanced capitalist societies, and not just their urban and social planners, is to create the conditions and opportunities that will give as much meaning as possible to the daily lives of people out of work within cities.

Concluding prognosis

It has been intimated above that real headway in the search for solutions to problems found in capitalist cities and regions will not be made unless governments adopt a broadly based strategy that addresses structural change in its entirety. There is a body of opinion which holds that such an approach would help in the long-run to prevent the formation of the conditions that the urban aid programmes of the 1960s and 1970s were supposed to cure. While that remains a moot point, there is no doubt that there will be a continuing need for the routine management of cities and the strategic planning of urban development.

A few final observations based upon the Australian urban scene may help to convince the sceptics. Firstly, despite the change in tempo now that the long boom of the fifties and sixties is behind us, property capital will continue to redevelop and refurbish undercapitalized segments of the built environment. The need to monitor and regulate urban property development will not diminish. Secondly, there is good reason for believing that the imminent scarcity of motoring fuel may force some fairly significant structural adjustments in the organization of cities. For example, part-sufficiency in petroleum is in doubt beyond 1990 in both the United Kingdom and Australia. The outermost zones of Australian cities that were purpose-built around the private automobile definitely lack the structural adaptability of the inner area; or for that matter, of the compact British city with its well developed public transport system. The strong government support that is now being given at the state level in Australia to urban consolidation (Archer, 1980; Bunker and Orchard, 1982; Reid, 1981) reflects the growing concern that poor, jobless households will be stranded by fuel shortages on the outskirts of Australia's largest cities.

The ageing of the Australian population, with the added presence of a permanent pool of unemployed workers, will in time necessitate a thorough revision of government policies in relation to collective consumption, especially public housing and urban redevelopment. As the demand for housing assistance creeps upward, the Commonwealth may have to consider broadening the grants to the states so that in turn those local government councils that are willing can also supply housing services (as they do in Britain). This raises the third and final question about the state's future role in reproducing the labour-force and the most efficacious use of collective facilities. The notion of education for *life without work* will not only change the nature of schooling, but it must force educational planners radically to alter the place of school facilities within the Australian urban setting. As well as becoming a genuine hub of community life in the cities, educational infrastructure and resources will have to be freely accessible to students and non-students, and workers and non-workers alike.

Bibliography

Aaron, H. J. 1972: *Shelter and subsidies* (Brookings Institute).
Abel-Smith, B. and Townsend, P. 1965: *The poor and the poorest*. Occasional Papers on Social Administration, No. 17 (Bell).
Abu Lughod, J. L. 1969: Testing the theory of social area analysis: the ecology of Cairo, Egypt. *American Sociological Review* **34**, 189–212.
Adams, B. 1973: Furnished lettings in stress areas. In Donnison, D. and Eversley, D. (eds), 354–82.
Adams, J. S. 1969: Directional bias in intraurban migration. *Economic Geography* **45**, 303–23.
Aitken, H. G. J. (ed.), 1959: *The state and economic growth* (Social Science Research Council).
Akin, J. S. and Auten, G. E. 1976: City schools and suburban schools: a fiscal comparison. *Land Economics* **52**, 4, 452–66.
Albaum, M. and Davies, S. 1973: *Geography and contemporary issues: studies of relevant problems* (Wiley).
Alcaly, R. and Mermelstein, D. (eds), 1977: *The fiscal crisis of American cities* (Random House).
Alexander, I. 1981: Post-war metropolitan planning: goals and realities. In Troy, P. N. (ed.), 145–71.
Alexander, I. 1982: Office suburbanization: A new era? In Cardew, R. V. *et al.*, (eds), 55–75.
Allport, C. 1983: Women and suburban housing: post-war planning in Sydney, 1943–61. In Social Process and the City: *Urban Studies Yearbook* 1, 64–87.
Alonso, W. 1964: *Location and land use: toward a general theory of land rent* (Harvard University Press).
Ambrose, P. and Colenutt, B. 1975: *The property machine* (Penguin).
Amedeo, D. and Golledge, R. G. 1975: *An introduction to scientific reasoning in geography* (Wiley).
Anderson, M. 1967: *The federal bulldozer* (McGraw-Hill).
Anderson, P. and Blackburn, R. 1965: *Towards socialism* (Fontana).
Anderson, R. J. and Crocker, T. D. 1971: Air pollution and residential property values. *Urban Studies* **8**, 3, 171–180.
Anderson, T. R. and Egeland, T. A. 1961: Spatial aspects of social area analysis. *American Sociological Review* **26**, 392–8.

Andreski, S. 1972: *Social sciences as sorcery* (André Deutsch).

Andrusz, G. 1979: Some key issues in Soviet urban development. *International Journal of Urban and Regional Research* **3**, 157–79.

Anell, L. 1981: *Recession, the western economies and the changing world order* (Frances Pinter).

Archer, R. W. 1973: Land speculation and scattered development; failures in the urban-fringe land market. *Urban Studies* **10**, 367–72.

Archer, R. W. 1974: The rising price of land for new housing. *The Developer* **11**, 4, 207–15.

Archer, R. W. (ed.), 1980: *Planning for urban consolidation* (Planning Research Centre, University of Sydney).

Arthur, J. and Shaw, W. H. (eds) 1978: *Justice and economic distribution* (Prentice-Hall).

Ashford, D. E. (ed.), 1980: *National resources and urban policy* (Methuen).

Aspinall, P. J. 1982: The internal structure of the housebuilding industry in nineteenth-century cities. In Johnson, J. H. and Pooley, C. G. (eds), 75–106.

Atkinson, A. B. 1972: *Unequal shares. Wealth in Britain* (Allen Lane).

Aungles, S. and Szelenyi, I. 1979: Structural conflicts between the state, local government and monopoly capital – the case of Whyalla in South Australia. *Australian and New Zealand Journal of Sociology* **15**, 1, 24–35.

Australian Bureau of Statistics, 1978: *Household Expenditure Survey*, 1975–76. Bulletin 4. Expenditure and Income by Regions.

Australian Bureau of Statistics, 1981a: *Weekly Earnings of Employees (Distribution) Australia, August 1980*. No. 6310.0.

Australian Bureau of Statistics, 1981b: *Survey of Housing Occupancy and Costs, Australia, August 1980*. No. 8724.0.

Australian Institute of Urban Studies, 1973: *Inner suburban – outer suburban. A comparison of costs*. Australian Institute of Urban Studies Publication No. 42.

Australian Urban Studies, 1982: Enterprise zones – Peter Hall pleads "not guilty". **10**, 3, 10.

Babcock, R. F. 1966: *The zoning game: municipal practices and policies* (University of Wisconsin).

Babcock, R. F. 1980: The spatial impact of land-use and environmental controls. In Solomon, A. P. (ed.), 264–287.

Babcock, R. F. and Bosselman, F. P. 1973: *Exclusionary zoning. Land use regulation and housing in the 1970s* (Praeger Publishers).

Bacharach, S. B., Reader, J. and Rolleston, G. 1980: Autonomy and dependence: the maze of local government revenues. In Ashford, D. E. (ed.), 45–72.

Badcock, B. A. 1973: The residential structure of metropolitan Sydney. *Australian Geographical Studies* **11**, 1, 1–27.

Badcock, B. A. 1977: Educational achievement and participation rates in Sydney. *Australian Geographer* **13**, 5, 325–31.

Badcock, B. A. 1982: Removing the spatial bias from state housing provision in Australian cities. *Political Geography Quarterly* **1**, 195–215.

Badcock, B. A. and Urlich-Cloher, D. U. 1979: *Low-rent boarding and lodging accommodation* (South Australian Government Printer).

Badcock, B. A. and Urlich-Cloher, D. U. 1980: The contribution of housing displacement to the decline of the boarding and lodging population in Adelaide, 1947–77. *Institute of British Geographers, Transactions* NS **5**, 2, 151–69.

Badcock, B. A. and Urlich-Cloher, D. U. 1981: Neighbourhood change in inner Adelaide, 1966–76. *Urban Studies* **18**, 41–55.

Bagehot, W. 1888: *Lombard Street* (Kegan Paul).

Bahl, R. (ed.), 1978: *The fiscal outlook for cities* (Syracuse University Press).

Bahl, R. (ed.), 1981: *Urban government finance. Emerging trends.* Vol. 20, Urban Affairs Annual Reviews (Sage Publications).

Bahl, R., Jump, B. and Schroeder, L. 1978: The outlook for city fiscal performance in declining regions. In Bahl, R. (ed.).

Balchin, P. N. 1979: *Housing improvement and social inequality* (Saxon House).

Baldock, C. and Cass, B. (eds) 1983: *Women: social policy and the state in Australia* (George Allen and Unwin).

Ball, M. J. 1973: Recent empirical work on the determinants of relative house prices. *Urban Studies* **10**, 213–33.

Ball, M. J. 1981a: The development of capitalism in housing provision. *International Journal of Urban and Regional Research* **5**, 2, 145–77.

Ball, M. J. 1981b: Review of Scott: *The urban land nexus and the state. Environment and Planning* A, **13**, 11, 1454–5.

Ball, M. J. 1982: The speculative housebuilding industry. *Proceedings of the Bartlett Summer School* (1981), **3**, 31–51.

Bannister, H. and Ogborn, K. 1978: Rising petrol prices, residential markets and employment markets in urban areas. Unpublished paper presented to 3rd Annual Meeting of the Science Association (Australia and NZ), Monash.

Banting, K. G. 1979: *Poverty, politics and policy. Britain in the 1960s* (Macmillan Press).

Baran, P. A. and Sweezy, P. M. 1966: *Monopoly capital. An essay on the American economic and social order* (Monthly Review Press).

Barras, R. 1979: The development cycle in the City of London. *Centre for Environmental Studies.* Research Series 36.

Bassett, K. and Short, J. R. 1978: Housing improvement in the inner city: a case study of changes before and after the 1974 Housing Act. *Urban Studies* **15**, 333–42.

Bassett, K. and Short, J. 1980: *Housing and residential structure. Alternative approaches* (Routledge and Kegan Paul).

Bater, J. H. 1977: Soviet town planning: theory and practice in the 1970s. *Progress in Human Geography* **1**, 177–207.

Bater, J. H. 1980: *The Soviet city: ideal and reality* (Edward Arnold).

Beauchamp, T. L. 1980: Distributive justice and the difference principle. In Blocker, H. G. and Smith, E. H. (eds), 132–61.

Bederman, S. H. and Adams, J. S. 1974: Job accessibility and under-employment. *Annals, Association of American Geographers* 64, 378–86.

Bell, C. 1977: On housing classes. *Australian and New Zealand Journal of Sociology* 13, 36–40.

Bell, C. and Encel, S. (eds) 1978: *Inside the whale. Ten personal accounts of social research* (Pergamon).

Bell, C. and Newby, H. 1976: Community, communion, class and community action: the social sources of the new urban politics. In Herbert, D. T. and Johnston, R. J. (eds), 189–208.

Bell, D. 1972: Labor in the post-industrial society. *Dissent. The world of the blue collar worker*, Winter. 163–89.

Bell, D. 1974: *The coming of post-industrial society* (Heinemann).

Benevolo, L. 1971: *The origins of modern town planning* (MIT Press).

Bennett, R. J. 1980: *The geography of public finance. Welfare under fiscal federalism and local government finance* (Methuen).

Bennett, R. J. 1982a: The financial health of local authorities in England and Wales: resource and expenditure position 1974/75–1980/81. *Environment and Planning* A, 14, 8, 997–1022.

Bennett, R. J. 1982b: The financial health of local authorities in England and Wales: role of the rate support grant, 1974/75–1980/81. *Environment and Planning* A, 14, 10, 1283–1305.

Bentick, B. L. 1973: *Report of the working party on the stabilisation of land prices* (Government of South Australia).

Bernstein, R. 1976: *The restructuring of social and political theory* (Blackwell).

Berry, B. J. L. 1964: Cities as systems within systems of cities. *Regional Science Association Papers* 13, 147–65.

Berry, B. J. L. 1965: Internal structure of the city. *Law and Contemporary Problems* 3, 111–19.

Berry, B. J. L. (ed.), 1971: Comparative factorial ecology. *Economic Geography* 47 (Supplement).

Berry, B. J. L. and Horton, F. E. (eds), 1970: *Geographic perspectives on urban systems* (Prentice-Hall).

Berry, B. J. L. and Kasarda, J. D. 1977: *Contemporary urban ecology* (Macmillan).

Berry, B. J. L. and Rees, P. H. 1969: The factorial ecology of Calcutta. *American Journal of Sociology* 74, 445–92.

Berry, B. J. L. and Smith, K. B. (eds), 1972: *City classification handbook* (Wiley).

Berry, M. 1977: The forgotten tenant. *Australian and NZ Journal of Sociology* 13, 53–9.

Berry, M. 1982: The political economy of Australian urbanization. Unpublished manuscript, Royal Melbourne Institute of Technology.

Berthoud, R. C. 1976: *The disadvantage of inequality* (MacDonald and Janes).

Berthoud, R. C., Brown, J. C. and Cooper, S. 1981: *Poverty and the development of anti-poverty policy in the United Kingdom* (Heinemann Educational).

Best, G. 1971: *Mid-Victorian Britain 1851–1875* (Weidenfeld and Nicolson).

Best, M. H. 1982: The political economy of socially irrational products. *Cambridge Journal of Economics* **6**, 53–64.

Birch, A. 1964: *Representative and responsible government* (George Allen and Unwin).

Birch, A. and MacMillan, D. S. 1962: *The Sydney scene, 1788–1960* (Melbourne University Press).

Black, J. 1977: *Public inconvenience. Access and travel in seven Sydney suburbs* (Urban Research Unit, Australian National University).

Black, J. T. 1980a: The changing economic role of central cities and suburbs. In Solomon, A. P. (ed.), 80–125.

Black, J. T. 1980b: Private-market housing renovations in central cities: an Urban Land Institute Survey. In Laska, S. B. and Spain, S. (eds), 3–12.

Blackburn, R. (ed.) 1972: *Ideology in social science* (Fontana).

Blackburn, R. M. and Mann, M. 1979: *The working class in the labour market* (Macmillan).

Block, F. 1977: The ruling class does not rule: notes on the Marxist theory of the state. *Socialist Revolution* **7**, 3, 6–28.

Blocker, H. G. and Smith, E. H. (eds), 1980: *John Rawls' theory of social justice* (Ohio University Press).

Bluestone, B. and Harrison, B. 1980: *Capital and communities: the causes and consequences of private disinvestment* (Progressive Alliance).

Boast, T. 1980: Urban resources, the American capital market, and federal programs. In Ashford, D. E. (ed.), 73–94.

Boddy, M. J. 1976: The structure of mortgage finance: building societies and the British social formation. *Institute of British Geographers, Transactions*, NS **1**, 1, 58–71.

Boddy, M. J. 1981: The property sector in late capitalism: the case of Britain. In Dear, M. and Scott, A. (eds), 267–85.

Boreham, P. and Dow, G. (eds) 1980: *Work and inequality* (Macmillan).

Bosanquet, N. and Townsend, P. 1980: *Labour and equality. A Fabian study of labour in power, 1974–79* (Heinemann).

Bourne, L. S. 1981: *The geography of housing* (Edward Arnold).

Bow Group. 1978: *Saving our cities: freeing enterprise in the inner areas* (Bow Group Publications).

Braddock, G. R. and Archbold, D. A. 1970: *The elements of economic analysis* (McGraw-Hill).

Bramley, G. 1979: The inner city labour market. In Jones, C. (ed.), 63–91.

Braverman, H. 1974: *Labor and monopoly capital: the degradation of work in the twentieth century* (Monthly Review Press).

Brennan, T. 1973: *New community. Problems and policies* (Angus and Robertson).

Breth, R. and Ward, I. 1982: *Socialism. The options* (Hargreen Publishing Company).

Briggs, A. 1968: *Victorian cities* (Pelican).

Broadbent, T. A. 1977: *Planning and profit in the urban economy* (Methuen).

Broom, L. and Jones, F. L. 1969: Father-to-son mobility: Australia in comparative perspective. *American Journal of Sociology* **74**, 333–42.

Brown, L. A. and Longbrake, D. B. 1970: Migration flows in intra-urban space: place utility considerations. *Annals, Association of American Geographers* **60**, 368–84.

Brown, L. A. and Moore, E. G. 1970: The intra-urban migration process: a perspective. *Geografiska Annaler* **52B**, 1–13.

Brown, M. and Madge, N. 1982: Which way for the welfare state? *New Society* **61**, 1025, 52–4.

Brownstein, R. and Easton, N. 1983: *Reagan's ruling class: portraits of the President's top 100 officials* (Pantheon Books).

Bruce-Briggs, B. 1974: Gasoline prices and the suburban way of life. *Public Interest* **34**, 131–6.

Bruegel, I. 1975: The Marxist theory of rent and the contemporary city: a critique of Harvey. In *Political Economy of Housing Workshop*, 34–6.

Bryson, L. and Thompson, F. 1972: *An Australian newtown. Life and leadership in a new housing suburb* (Penguin).

Buchanan, K. 1970: *The transformation of the Chinese earth* (Bell).

Bull, P. J. 1978: The spatial components of intra-urban manufacturing change: suburbanization in Clydeside, 1958–68. *Institute of British Geographers, Transactions*, NS **3**, 1, 91–100.

Bunker, R. and Orchard, L. 1982: *Urban consolidation and Adelaide* Australian Institute of Urban Studies Project 64. (Australian Institute of Urban Studies).

Burchell, R. W. and Listokin, D. 1981: Design standards in developing areas: allowing reduced cost housing while maintaining adequate community development standards. In Sternlieb, G. and Hughes, J. W. 359–417.

Burgess, E. W. 1925: The growth of the city. In Park, R. E., *et al.*, (eds), chapter 2.

Burgess, E. W. (ed.) 1926: *The urban community* (University of Chicago Press).

Burke, T. (ed.), 1978: *Housing problems and housing policy* (Centre for Urban Studies, Swinburne College of Technology).

Burnley, I. H. (ed.), 1974: *Urbanization in Australia. The post-war experience* (Cambridge University Press).

Butlin, N. G. 1959: Colonial socialism in Australia, 1860–1900. In Aitken, H. G. J. (ed.).

Butlin, N. G. 1964: *Investment in Australian economic development, 1861–1900* (Cambridge University Press).

Butlin, N. G., Barnard, A. and Pincus, J. J. 1982: *Public and private choice in twentieth-century Australia* (George Allen and Unwin).

Buttimer, A. 1976: Grasping the dynamism of lifeworld. *Annals, Association of American Geographers* **66**, 277–92.

Buttimer, A. and Seamon, D. 1980: *The human experience of space and place* (Croom Helm).

Byrne, D. 1982: Class and the local state. *International Journal of Urban and Regional Research*, **6**, 1, 61–82.

Cameron, G. C. (ed.) 1980: *The future of the British conurbations* (Longman).

Cameron, G. C. 1980: The economies of the conurbations. In Cameron, G. C. (ed.), 54–71.

Cannadine, D. 1980: Urban development in England and America in the nineteenth century: some comparison and contrasts. *Economic History Review, Second Series* **33**, 3, 309–25.

Cannon, M. M. 1975: *Life in the cities* (Nelson).

Cannon, M. M. 1976: *The land boomers* (Nelson).

Caraley, D. 1976: Congressional politics and urban aid. *Political Science Quarterly* **91**, 1, 19–45.

Cardew, R. V. 1970: Flats: a study of occupants and locations. Ian Buchan Fell Research Project on Housing.

Cardew, R. V. 1977: House lot speculation is consumer led. *Royal Australian Planning Institute Journal* **15**, 85–6.

Cardew, R. V., Langdale, J. V. and Rich, D. C. (eds) 1982: *Why cities change. Urban development and economic change in Sydney* (George Allen and Unwin).

Carmina, M. 1975: Public participation – an Australian dimension. *The Planner*, **61**, 6, 232–4.

Carmody, T., Derody, B., Ironmonger, D. and Sheehan, P. 1979: *Fluctuations in dwelling construction in South Australia*. Institute of Applied Economic and Social Research. Technical Paper No 13.

Caro, R. A. 1974: *The power broker. Robert Moses and the fall of New York* (Alfred A. Knopf).

Carrick, J. L. 1978: Local government and the New Federalism policy. In Mathews, R. (ed.).

Carter, R. A. 1978: Polarisation in housing access. In Burke, T. (ed.), 51–64.

Casetti, E. 1969: Alternate urban population density models: an analytical comparison of their validity range. *Studies in Regional Science*, 105–16.

Cass, B. and Pedler, K. 1981: Where are they hiding the unemployed? Social Welfare Research Centre, University of New South Wales.

Castells, M. 1977a: *The urban question. A Marxist approach* (Edward Arnold).

Castells, M. 1977b: Towards a political urban sociology. In Harloe, M. (ed.), 61–78.

Castells, M. 1978: *City, class and power* (Macmillan).

Castells, M. 1980: Cities and regions beyond the crisis: invitation to a debate. *International Journal of Urban and Regional Research* **4**, 1, 127–9.

Castles, F. 1978: *The social democratic image of society: a study of the achievements and origins of Scandinavian social democracy in comparative perspective* (Routledge and Kegan Paul).

Catanese, A. J. 1971: Home and workplace separation in four urban regions. *Journal of the American Institute of Planners* **37**, 331–7.

Catley, R. and McFarlane, B. 1974: *From Tweedledum to Tweedledee. The new labor government in Australia. A critique of its social model* (Australia and New Zealand Book Company).

Central Statistical Office, 1980: *Social trends, 1980* (HMSO).

Central Statistical Office, 1981a: The distribution of income in the United Kingdom, 1978/79. *Economic Trends* No. 327, 82–7.

Central Statistical Office, 1981b: The effects of taxes and benefits on household income, 1979. *Economic Trends* No. 328, 104–17.

Centre for Urban Research and Action, 1977: *The displaced* (CURA).

Centre for Urban Research and Action, 1979; *Landlords and lodgers* (CURA).

Chamberlain, N. W. 1980: *Forces of change in Western Europe* (McGraw-Hill).

Chapman, S. D. 1972: *The cotton industry in industrial revolution* (Macmillan).

Checkland, S. G. 1964: The British industrial city as history: the Glasgow case. *Urban Studies* **1**, 1, 34–54.

Checkoway, B. 1980: Large builders, federal housing programmes and post-war suburbanization. *International Journal of Urban and Regional Research* **4**, 1, 21–45.

Cheshire, P. C. 1981: Inner areas as spatial labour markets: a rejoinder. *Urban Studies* **18**, 2, 227–30.

Chisholm, M. 1971: In search of a basis for location theory: microeconomics or welfare economics. *Progress in Geography* **3**, 111–33.

Christian, C. M. 1975: Emerging patterns of industrial activity within large metropolitan areas and their impact on the central city workforce. In Gappert, G. and Rose, H. M. (eds) 213–46.

City of Sydney, 1980: *1980 City of Sydney strategic plan* (Council of the City of Sydney).

Clark, G. L. 1980: Urban Impact Analysis: a new tool for monitoring the geographical effects of federal policies. *Professional Geographer* **32**, 1, 82–5.

Clark, G. L. and Dear, M. 1981: The state in capitalism and the capitalist state. In Dear, M. and Scott, A. J. (eds) 45–62.

Clarke, S. and Ginsburg, N. 1975: The political economy of housing. In *Political Economy of Housing Workshop*, 3–33.

Clawson, M. 1962: Urban sprawl and speculation in suburban land. *Land Economics* **38**, 99–111.

Clawson, M. 1971: *Suburban land conversion in the United States.* (Johns Hopkins Press).

Cleary, E. J. 1965: *The building society movement* (Elek Books).
Cleaver, H. 1979: *Reading capital politically* (Harvester Press).
Cleland, E. A., Stimpson, R. J., and Goldsworthy, A. J. 1977: *Suburban health care behaviour in Adelaide*. Monograph Series No. 2. (Centre for Applied Social and Survey Research, Flinders University).
Cockburn, C. 1977: *The local state* (Pluto Press).
Cohen, R. B. 1977: Multinational corporations, international finance, and the sunbelt. In Perry, D. C. and Watkins, A. J. (eds), 211–26.
Cohen, R. B. 1981: The new international division of labor, multinational corporations and urban hierarchy. In Dear, M. and Scott, A. J. (eds), 287–315.
Commission of the European Communities, 1979: *The European Economic Community and changes in the international division of labour* (Directorate-General for Development).
Committee of Inquiry into Housing Costs, 1978: *The Cost of Housing* vols I–III (Australian Government Publishing Service).
Commission of Inquiry into Land Tenures, 1976: *Final Report* (Else-Mitchell) (Australian Government Publishing Service).
Commission of Inquiry into Poverty, 1975: *Poverty in Australia. First main report* vol. 2 (Australian Government Publishing Service).
Commonwealth Bureau of Roads, 1975: *Report on roads in Australia* (Australian Government Publishing Service).
Community Development Project, 1976: *Whatever happened to council housing?* (Community Development Project).
Community Development Project, 1977: *Gilding the ghetto. The state and the poverty experiments* (CDP Inter-Project Editorial Team).
Congressional Budget Office, 1978: *Federal housing policy: current programs and recurring issues*. Background paper (US Congress).
Connell, R. W. 1977: *Ruling class, ruling culture. Studies of conflict, power and hegemony in Australian life* (Cambridge University Press).
Connell, R. W. and Irving, T. H. 1980: *Class structure in Australian history* (Longman Cheshire).
Connell, R. W., Ashenden, D. J., Kessler, S. and Dowsett, G. W. 1982: *Making the difference. Schools, families and social division* (George Allen and Unwin).
Counter Information Services, 1973a: *The recurrent crisis of London*.
Counter Information Services, 1973b: *Your money and your life*. Anti-Report No. 7.
Couper, M. and Brindley, T. 1975: Housing classes and housing values. *Sociological Review* NS **23**, 563–76.
Cowling, K. 1982: *Monopoly capitalism* (Wiley).
Cox, K. R. 1973: *Conflict, power and politics in the city: a geographic view* (McGraw-Hill).
Cox, K. R. 1981: Capitalism and conflict around the communal living space. In Dear, M. and Scott, A. J. (eds), 431–56.

Crecine, J. P., Davis, O. A. and Jackson, J. E. 1967: Urban property markets: some empirical results and their implications for municipal zoning. *Journal of Law and Economics* **10**, 79–99.

Crick, B. (ed.) 1981: *Unemployment* (Methuen).

Cross, M. 1982: For sale: Europe's biggest vacant lot. *New Scientist* **94**, 1309, 710–13.

Crouch, G. 1979: Financial Institutions and the Ownership of Australian Corporations. Research Monograph No. 12. Transnational Corporations Research Project, University of Sydney.

Crouch, G. and Wheelwright, T. 1982: *Australia: a client state* (Pelican).

Cullen, A. C. and Hardaker, R. T. 1975: The role of finance companies in development. *The Developer* **13**, 3, 38–42.

Cullingworth, J. B. 1979: *Essays on housing policy* (George Allen and Unwin).

Dahl, R. 1963: *Modern political analysis* (Prentice-Hall).

Daly, M. T. 1968: Residential location decisions: Newcastle, New South Wales. *Australian and NZ Journal of Sociology* **4**, 18–35.

Daly, M. T. 1982a: *Sydney boom Sydney bust. The city and its property market 1850–1981* (George Allen and Unwin).

Daly, M. T. 1982b: Finance, the capital market and Sydney's development. In Cardew, R. V. *et al.* (eds), 43–53.

Danielson, M. N. 1976: *The politics of exclusion* (Columbia University Press).

Davies, B. P. 1968: *Social needs and resources in local services* (Michael Joseph).

Davis, G. A. and Donaldson, D. F. 1975: *Blacks in the United States. A geographic perspective* (Houghton Mifflin).

Davison, G. 1970: Public utilities and the expansion of Melbourne in the 1880s. *Australian Economic History Review* **10**, 2, 169–89.

Deakin, N. 1977: Inner area problems: positive discrimination revisited. *Greater London Intelligence Journal* **37**, 4–8.

Deakin, N. and Ungerson, C. 1977: *Leaving London. Planned mobility and the inner city* (Heinemann).

Dear, M. 1977: Locational factors in the demand for mental health care. *Economic Geography* **53**, 223–40.

Dear, M. and Clark, G. L. 1981: Dimensions of local state autonomy. *Environment and Planning* A **13**, 10, 1277–94.

Dear, M., Fincher, R. and Currie, L. 1977: Measuring the external effects of public programs. *Environment and Planning* A **9**, 134–47.

Dear, M., Taylor, M. S. and Hall, G. B. 1980: External effects of mental health facilities. *Annals, Association of American Geographers* **70**, 3, 342–52.

Dear, M. and Scott, A. J. (eds) 1981: *Urbanization and urban planning in capitalism and society* (Methuen).

Department of the Environment, 1974: *Land*. Cmnd 5730. (HMSO).

Department of the Environment, 1975: *Community land – Circular 1* (HMSO).

Department of the Environment, 1976: *Housing action areas. A detailed examination of declaration reports.* Improvement Research Note 2–76 (HMSO).

Department of the Environment, 1977: *Housing policy, technical volume,* Part I (HMSO).

Department of the Environment, 1978a: *Inner urban areas act, 1978* (HMSO).

Department of the Environment, 1978b: *General improvement areas,* 1969–76. Improvement Research Note 3–77 (HMSO).

Department of Urban and Regional Development, 1974a: *Urban land: problems and policies* (Australian Government Publishing Service).

Department of Urban and Regional Development, 1974b: *Urban and regional development* 1973–74. *Second annual report* (Australian Government Publishing Service).

De Vise, P. 1973: *Misused and misplaced hospitals and doctors: a location analysis of the urban health care crisis.* Commission on College Geography, Resource Paper 22 (Association of American Geographers).

Diamond, D. B. 1980a: Income and residential location: Muth revisited. *Urban Studies* **17**, 1–12.

Diamond, D. B. 1980b: The relationship between amenities and urban land prices. *Land Economics* **56**, 1, 21–32.

Dogan, M. and Rokkan, S. (eds), 1969: *Quantitative ecological analysis in the social sciences* (MIT Press).

Donald, D. D. 1981: Medical services. In Troy, P. N. (ed.), 63–84.

Donaldson, B. and Johnston, R. J. 1973: Intraurban sectoral mental maps: further evidence from an extended methodology. *Geographical Analysis* **5**, 45–54.

Donnison, D. 1974: Policies for priority areas. *Journal of Social Policy* **3**, 127–35.

Donnison, D. 1976: An approach to social policy (Supplement to *Australian Journal of Social Issues* **11**, 1).

Donnison, D. and Eversley, D. (eds) 1973: *London: urban patterns, problems, and policies* (Heinemann).

Donnison, D. with Soto, P. 1980: *The good city. A study of urban development and policy in Britain* (Heinemann).

Drewett, R. 1973a: The developers: decision processes. In Hall, P. *et al.*, 163–93.

Drewett, R. 1973b: Land values and the suburban land market. In Hall, P. *et al.*, 195–244.

Drewnowski, J. (ed.) 1982: *Crisis in the East European economy* (Croom Helm).

Duncan, J. and Ley, D. 1982: Structural Marxism and human geography: a critical assessment. *Annals, Association of American Geographers* **72**, 1, 30–58.

Duncan, S. S. 1981: Housing policy, the methodology of levels, and urban research: the case of Castells. *International Journal of Urban and Regional Research* **5**, 2, 231–52.

Dunleavy, P. 1978: Protest and quiescence in urban politics: a critique of some pluralist and structuralist myths. *International Journal of Urban and Regional Research* **1**, 2, 193–218.

Dunleavy, P. 1980a: *Urban political analysis: the politics of collective consumption* (Macmillan).

Dunleavy, P. 1980b: Social and political theory and the issues in central-local relations. In Jones, G. W. (ed.) 116–36.

Dunleavy, P. 1981: *The politics of mass housing in Britain, 1945–1975* (Clarendon Press).

Dyker, D. 1981: Planning and the worker. In Schapiro, L. and Godson, J. (eds) 39–75.

Dyos, H. J. 1955: Railways and housing in Victorian London. *Journal of Transport History* **2**, 1/2, 11–21; 90–100.

Dyos, H. J. 1961: *Victorian suburb. A study of the growth of Camberwell* (Leicester University Press).

Dyos, H. J. (ed.) 1968a: *The study of urban history* (Edward Arnold).

Dyos, H. J. 1968b: The slum observed. *New Society* **11**, 279, 151–4.

Dyos, H. J. 1968c: The speculative builders and developers of Victorian London. *Victorian Studies* **11**, 641–90.

Dyos, H. J. and Wolff, M. (eds), 1973: *The Victorian City – images and realities* (Routledge and Kegan Paul).

Eberts, R. W. and Gronberg, J. J. 1981: Jurisdictional homogeneity and the Tiebout hypothesis. *Journal of Urban Economics* **10**, 2, 227–39.

Economist, 1979: Survey of personal finance. Vol. 270, 7073, 24 March, 78.

Economist, 1981: Footsore, weary and workless. Vol. 279, 7188, 6–12 June, 34.

Edel, M. 1976: Marx's theory of rent: urban applications. In *Political economy of housing workshop*.

Edel, M. 1981: Capitalism, accumulation and the explanation of urban phenomena. In Dear, M. and Scott, A. J. (eds), 19–45.

Edel, M. 1982: Home ownership and working class unity. *International Journal of Urban and Regional Research* **6**, 2, 205–21.

Edel, M. and Sclar, E. 1975: The distribution of real estate value changes: metropolitan Boston, 1870–1970. *Journal of Urban Economics* **2**, 4, 366–87.

Edwards, J. and Batley, R. 1978: *The politics of positive discrimination. An evaluation of the urban programme 1967–77* (Tavistock).

Edwards, R. C. 1979: *Contested terrain. The transformation of the workplace in the twentieth century* (Basic Books).

Edwards, R. C., Reich, M. and Gordon, D. M. 1975: *Labor market segmentation* (Heath).

Elkin, S. L. 1974: *Politics and land use planning. The London experience* (Cambridge University Press).

Elkin, S. L. 1980: Cities without power: the transformation of American urban regimes. In Ashford, D. E. (ed.). 265–94.

Elliott, B. and McCrone, D. 1981: Power and protest in the city. In Harloe, M. (ed.), 63–79.

Elman, R. 1966: *The poorhouse state: the American way of life on public assistance* (Pantheon Books).

Emmet, D. and MacIntyre, A. (eds) 1970: *Sociological theory and philosophical analysis* (Macmillan).

Encel, S. 1980: The bureaucratic ascendancy. In Parkin, A., *et al.*, (eds), 314–25.

English, J. 1979: Access and deprivation in local authority housing. In Jones, C. (ed.), 113–35.

Erikson, R. 1970: *The spatial behaviour of hospital patients*. Department of Geography Research Paper 125, (University of Chicago).

Evans, A. W. 1973: *The economics of residential location* (Macmillan).

Evans, A. W. 1980: Poverty and the conurbations. In Cameron, G. C. (ed.), 189–207.

Evans, G. and Reeves, J. (eds) 1980: *Labor essays* (Drummond).

Evans, G. and Reeves, J. (eds) 1982: *Socialist principles and parliamentary government* (Drummond).

Eversley, D. E. C. 1972: Old cities, falling populations and static incomes. *GLC Quarterly Bulletin,* **18**, 5–17.

Eversley, D. E. C. 1973: *The planner in society: the changing role of a profession* (Faber).

Eyles, J. 1979: Area-based policies for the inner city: context, problems, and prospects. In Herbert, D. T. and Smith, D. M. (eds), 244–60.

Faia, M. A. 1981: Selection by certification: a neglected variable in stratification research. *American Journal of Sociology* **86**, 5, 1093–111.

Fainstein, S. S. and Fainstein, N. I. 1979: National policy and urban development. *Social Problems* **26**, 125–46.

Fales, R. L. and Moses, L. N. 1972: Land-use theory and the spatial structure of the nineteenth-century city. *Regional Science Association papers* **28**, 49–80.

Feagin, J. R. 1982: Urban real estate speculation in the United States: implications for social science and urban planning. *International Journal of Urban and Regional Research* **6**, 1: 35–59.

Feldman, A. S. and Tilly, C. 1960: The interaction of social and physical space. *American Sociological Review* **25**, 877–89.

Ferge, Z. 1979: *A society in the making. Hungarian social and societal policy 1945–75* (M. E. Sharpe).

Field, F., Meacher, M. and Pond, C. 1977: *To him who hath: a study of taxation and poverty* (Penguin).

Fincher, R. 1981: Local implementation strategies in the urban built environment. *Environment and Planning* A **13**, 1233–52.

Forrest, R., Lloyd, J., Rogers, N. and Williams, P. 1979: The inner city: in search of the problem. *Geoforum* **10**, 109–16.

Foster, C. D., Jackman, R. A. and Perlman, M. 1980: *Local government finance in a unitary state* (George Allen and Unwin).

Foster, J. 1968: Nineteenth-century towns – a class dimension. In Dyos, J. H. (ed.), 281–300.

Foster, J. 1974: *Class struggle and the industrial revolution* (Weidenfeld and Nicolson).

Freestone, R. G. 1974: Location and allocation: a geographic study of the provision of some urban services in Sydney. Unpublished BSc Hons thesis, University of New South Wales.

French, R. A. and Hamilton, F. E. I., (eds) 1979: *The socialist city. Spatial structure and urban policy* (John Wiley).

Fried, J. P. 1972: *Housing crisis USA* (Penguin).

Friedland, R. 1980: Corporate power and urban growth: the case of urban renewal. *Politics and Society* **10**, 2, 203–24.

Fröbel, F., Heinrichs, J. and Kreye, O., 1980: *The new international division of labour* (Cambridge University Press).

Fuchs, R. J. and Demko, G. J. 1979: Geographic inequality under socialism. *Annals, Association of American Geographers* **69**, 2, 304–18.

Fuchs, R. J. and Demko, G. J. 1980: Comment in reply. *Annals, Association of American Geographers* **70**, 2, 286–7.

Fuchs, V. R. 1968: *The service economy* (National Bureau of Economic Research).

Gagliani, G. 1981: How many working classes? *American Journal of Sociology* **87**, 2, 259–85.

Galbraith, J. K. 1967: *The new industrial state* (Hamilton).

Gappert, G. and Rose, H. M. (eds), 1975: *The social economy of cities*. Urban Affairs Annual Review, vol. 9, (Sage Publications).

Garlick, F. 1978: Consumer issues in housing finance. In Committee of Inquiry into Housing Costs, vol. 2, 117–74.

Garn, H. A. and Ledebur, L. C. 1980: The economic performance and prospects of cities. In Solomon, A. P. (ed.) 204–57.

Gatrell, V. A. C. 1977: Labour, power and the size of firms in Lancashire cotton in the second quarter of the nineteenth century. *Economic History Review* **30**, 1, 95–125.

Gerathy, G. 1972: Sydney municipality in the 1880s. *Journal of the Royal Australian Historical Society* **58**, Pt 1, 23–54.

Gershuny, J. 1978: *After industrial society: the emerging self-service economy* (Macmillan).

Gibbings, M. J. 1973: *Housing preferences in the Brisbane area* Australian Institute of Urban Studies Monograph.

Giddens, A. 1973: *The class structure of the advanced societies* (Hutchinson).

Giddens, A. 1979: *Central problems in social theory* (Macmillan).

Gifford, B. R. 1978: New York City and cosmopolitan Liberalism. *Political Science Quarterly* **93**, 4, 559–84.

Gillard, Q. 1981: The effect of environmental amenities on house values: the example of a view lot. *Professional Geographer* **33**, 2, 216–20.

Glaab, C. H. and Brown, A. T. 1967: *A history of urban America* (Collier-Macmillan).

Glass, R. (ed.), 1964: *London: aspects of change* (MacGibbon and Kee).

Glickman, N. J. 1981: Emerging urban policies in a slow-growth economy: conservative initiatives and progressive responses in the US. *International Journal of Urban and Regional Research* **5**, 4, 492–528.

Glynn, S. 1970: *Urbanisation in Australian History, 1788–1900* (Nelson).

Goheen, P. 1970: *Victorian Toronto, 1850–1900.* Department of Geography Research Paper No. 127 (University of Chicago).

Gold, D. A., Lo, Y. H. and Wright, E. O., 1975: Recent developments in Marxist theories of the capitalist state, Parts 1 and 2. *Monthly Review* **27**, 5/6, 29–43; 36–51.

Goldsmith, M. 1980: *Politics, planning and the city* (Hutchinson).

Goldsmith, W. N. 1982: Enterprise zones: if they work we're in trouble. *International Journal of Urban and Regional Research* **6**, 3, 435–43.

Goldsmith, W. N. and Derian, M. J. 1979: Is there an urban policy? *Journal of Regional Science* **19**, 93–108.

Goldsmith, W. N. and Jacobs, H. M. 1982: The improbability of urban policy. The case of the United States. *Journal of the American Planning Association* **48**, 1, 53–66.

Goldthorpe, J. H., Lockwood, D., Bechhofer, F. and Platt, J., 1969: *The affluent worker: industrial attitudes and behaviour* (Cambridge University Press).

Golledge, R. G. 1981: Misconceptions, misinterpretations, and misrepresentations of behavioural approaches in human geography. *Environment and Planning* A **13**, 1325–44.

Golledge, R. G., Brown, L. A. and Williamson, F. 1972: Behavioural approaches in geography: an overview. *Australian Geographer* **12**, 59–79.

Goodway, D. 1982: *London chartism, 1838–1848* (Cambridge University Press).

Gordon, D. M. 1977: Capitalism and the roots of urban crisis. In Alcaly, R. and Mermelstein, D. (eds).

Gordon, D. M. 1978: Capitalist development and the history of American cities. In Tabb, W. K. and Sawers, L. (eds), 25–63.

Gorham, W. and Glazer, N. (eds) 1976: *The urban predicament* (Urban Institute, Washington, DC).

Gottliebsen, R. 1976: The great crash of '75. *National Times* 19–24 January, 21–25.

Gough, I. 1979: *The political economy of the welfare state* (Macmillan).

Gould, P. 1979: Geography 1975–1977: the Augean period. *Annals, Association of American Geographers* **69**, 139–51.

Gouldner, A. 1980: *The two Marxisms* (Seabury).

Gramlich, E. M. 1976: The New York fiscal crisis: what happened and what is to be done? *American Economic Review* **66**, 415–29.

Gray, F. 1975: Non-explanation in urban geography. *Area* **7**, 228–35.

Gray, F. 1976: Selection and allocation in council housing. *Institute of British Geographers, Transactions* NS **1**, 1, 34–46.

Gray, F. 1979: Consumption: council house management. In Merrett, S., 196–232.

Gray, F. and Boddy, M. 1979: The origins and use of theory in urban geography: household mobility and filtering theory. *Geoforum* **10**, 117–127.

Greater London Council, 1980: *Housing strategy appraisal 1981–83* (Housing Strategy Office).

Greater London Council, 1981: *The Greater London house condition survey. Review and studies series: No. 7* (Housing Strategy Office).

Greene, K. V., Neenan, W. B., and Scott, C. D. 1974: *Fiscal interactions in a metropolitan area* (D. C. Heath).

Gregory, D. 1978: *Ideology, science and human geography* (Hutchinson).

Gregory, D. 1982: A realist construction of the social. *Transactions, Institute of British Geographers* NS **7**, 2, 254–56.

Grether, D. M. and Mieszkowski, P. 1974: Determinants of real estate values. *Journal of Urban Economics* **1**, 127–46.

Grether, D. M. and Mieszkowski, P. 1980: The effects of nonresidential land uses on the price of adjacent housing: some estimates of proximity effects. *Journal of Urban Economics* **8**, 1–15.

Groenewegen, P. D. 1976: *The taxable capacity of local government in New South Wales*. (Centre for Research on Federal Financial Relations, Australian National University).

Groenewegen, P. D. 1982: Reflections on 'Razor gangs', Thatcherism and Reaganomics: a critical evaluation on the contemporary sport of public sector bashing. *Journal of Australian Political Economy* **12/13**, 4–19.

Guest, A. M. 1972: Urban history, population densities, and higher status residential location. *Economic Geography* **48**, 375–387.

Habakkuk, H. J. 1962: Fluctuations in house-building in Britain and the United States in the nineteenth century. *Journal of Economic History* **22**, 2, 198–230.

Habermas, J. 1976: *Legitimation crisis* (Heinemann Educational).

Haddon, R. F. 1970: A minority in a welfare state society: location of West Indians in the London housing market. *New Atlantis* **1**, 80–133.

Haig, R. M. 1926: Towards an understanding of the metropolis: II. The assignment of activities to areas in urban regions. *Quarterly Journal of Economics* **40**, 402–34.

Hall, P. (ed.) 1965: *Land values* (Sweet and Maxwell).

Hall, P. 1966: *Von Thünen's isolated state* trans. C. M. Wartenburg (Pergamon).

Hall, P., Gracey, H., Drewett, R. and Thomas, R. 1973: *The containment of urban England* (George Allen and Unwin).

Hall, P. G. 1962: *The industries of England* (Hutchinson).

Halligan, J. and Paris, C. (eds) 1983: *Australian urban politics: critical perspectives* (Longman Cheshire).

Halmos, P. (ed.) 1972: Hungarian sociological studies. *Sociological Review Monograph No. 17*.

Halsey, A. H., Heath, A. F. and Ridge, J. M. 1980: *Origins and destinations* (Oxford University Press).

Hamilton, F. E. I. 1976: *The Moscow city region* (Oxford University Press).

Hamnett, C. 1973: Improvement grants as an indicator of gentrification in inner London. *Area* **5**, 252–61.

Hamnett, C. and Williams, P. R. 1980: Social change in London. A study of gentrification. *Urban Affairs Quarterly* **15**, 4, 469–87.

Hanford, B. 1980: An anatomy of Balmain. *National Times*, 10–16 February, 1980, 29–32.

Hardman, M. and Manning, P. 1974: *Green bans. The story of an Australian phenomenon* (Australian Conservation Foundation).

Harloe, M. (ed.) 1975: Urban change and conflict. Centre for Environmental Studies Conference Paper 14.

Harloe, M. (ed.) 1977: *Captive cities: studies in the political economy of cities and regions* (Wiley).

Harloe, M. (ed.) 1981a: *New perspectives in urban change and conflict* (Heinemann Educational).

Harloe, M. 1981b: Notes on comparative urban research. In Dear, M. and Scott, A. C. (eds) 179–95.

Harloe, M., Issacharoff, R. and Minns, R. 1974: *The organisation of housing* (Heinemann).

Harloe, M. and Lebas, E. (eds) 1981: *City, class and capital. New developments in the political economy of cities and regions* (Edward Arnold).

Harman, E. J. 1983: Capitalism, patriarchy and the city. In Baldock, C. and Cass, B. (eds).

Harré, R. 1970: *The principles of scientific thinking* (Macmillan).

Harrington, M. 1962: *The other America. Poverty in the United States* (Penguin).

Harris, N. 1980: De-industrialisation. *International Socialism* **2**, 7, 72–81.

Harris, N. 1981: Crisis and the core of the world system. *International Socialism* **2**, 10: 24–50.

Harrison, B. 1982: The politics and economics of the urban enterprise zone proposal: a critique. *International Journal of Urban and Regional Research* **6**, 3, 422–8.

Harrison, J. F. C. 1979: *Early Victorian Britain, 1832–51* (Fontana).

Harrison, P. 1983: *Inside the inner city. Life under the cutting edge* (Pelican).

Hart, D. 1976: *Strategic planning in London: the rise and fall of the primary road network* (Pergamon Press).

Hartman, C. 1979: Comment on 'Neighborhood revitalization and displacement: a review of the evidence'. *Journal of the American Planning Association* **45**, 4, 488–91.

Harvey, D. W. 1969: *Explanation in geography* (Edward Arnold).

Harvey, D. W. 1971: Revolutionary and counter-revolutionary theory in geography and the problem of ghetto formation (Mimeo).

Harvey, D. W. 1973: *Social justice and the city* (Edward Arnold).

Harvey, D. W. 1974: Class-monopoly rent, finance capital and the urban revolution. *Regional Studies* **8**, 239–55.

Harvey, D. W. 1975: The political economy of urbanization in advanced capitalist societies: the case of the United States. In Gappert, G. and Rose, H. M. (eds), 119–62.

Harvey, D. W. 1977: Government policies, financial institutions and neighbourhood change in US cities. In Harloe, M. (ed.), 123–40.

Harvey, D. W. 1978: The urban process under capitalism: a framework for analysis *International Journal of Urban and Regional Research* **2**, 1, 101–31.

Harvey, D. W. 1982: *The limits to capital* (Basil Blackwell).

Harvey, R. and Clark, W. A. 1965: The nature and economics of urban sprawl. *Land Economics* **41**, 1–19.

Hauser, P. M. and Schnore, L. F. (eds) 1965: *The study of urbanization* (Wiley).

Hawke, R. 1975: Trade unions and urban affairs. *Community* **11**, 405.

Hawley, A. H. 1951: Metropolitan population and municipal government expenditures in central cities. *Journal of Social Issues* **7**, 1 and 2, 100–08.

Hawthorn, G. 1976: *Enlightenment and despair: a history of sociology* (Cambridge University Press).

Heilbroner, R. L. 1980: *The worldly philosophers* 5th ed. (Simon and Schuster).

Hempel, C. G. 1965: *Aspects of scientific explanation* (Free Press).

Hepworth, N. P. 1978: The finance of local government, 4th ed (George Allen and Unwin).

Herbert, D. T. 1967: Social area analysis: a British study. *Urban Studies* **4**, 41–59.

Herbert, D. T. and Johnston, R. J. (ed) 1976: *Social areas in cities. Spatial perspectives on problems and policies*, vol. II (Wiley).

Herbert, D. T. and Johnston, R. J. (eds) 1979: *Geography and urban environment: progress in research and applications* (Wiley).

Herbert, D. T. and Smith, D. M. (eds) 1979: *Social problems and the city. Geographical perspectives* (Oxford University Press).

Hickie, D. 1983: Goodbye to the quarter-acre dream. *National Times*, 16–22 January 1983, 21–2.

Hickie, D. McCarthy, P. and Wilkinson, M. 1980: The battle for Sydney. *National Times*, 10–16 August, 30–33.

Highway Research Board, 1969: *Moving behavior and residential choice. A national survey* (National Cooperative Highway Research Program Report 81).

Hill, F. J. and McRae, D. (eds) 1978: *Australian urban trends and indicators: a national perspective* (Department of Environment, Housing and Community Development).

Hill, R. C. 1974: Separate and unequal: governmental inequality in the metropolis. *American Political Science Review* **68**, 4, 1557–68.

Hillman, J. 1980: The shrinking pool of private-rented housing. *New Society* 3 July, 17–18.

Hillman, M. with Henderson, I. and Whalley, A. 1973: *Personal mobility and transport policy* Broadsheet 542 (Political and Economic Planning).

Hindess, B. and Hirst, P. 1978: *Mode of production and social formation* (Humanities Press).

Hirsch, F. 1977: *Social limits to growth* (Routledge and Kegan Paul).

Hirsch, J. 1981: The apparatus of the State, the reproduction of capital and urban conflicts. In Dear, M. and Scott, A. J. (eds), 593–607.

HMSO 1965: *Report of the committee on housing in Greater London.* Cmnd 2605, 3, (Milner Holland).

HMSO 1967: *Children and their primary schools.* Report of the Central Advisory Council for Education (Plowden).

HMSO 1977: *Policy for the inner cities.* Cmnd 6845 6, 1977.

HMSO 1980: *The government's expenditure plans 1980–81 to 1983–84.* Cmnd 7841.

Hobsbawm, E. J. (ed) 1968: *Labouring men* (Weidenfeld and Nicolson).

Hobsbawm, E. J. 1968: The labour aristocracy in nineteenth-century Britain. In Hobsbawm, E. J. (ed.), 272–315.

Hoch, I. 1969: The three-dimensional city: contained urban space. In Perloff, H. S. (ed.), 75–135.

Holloway, J. and Picciotto, S. (eds) 1978: *State and capital: a Marxist debate* (Edward Arnold).

Holmans, A. E. 1978: Housing tenure in England and Wales: the present situation and recent trends. *Social Trends* **9** (HMSO).

Holtermann, S. 1975: Areas of urban deprivation in Great Britain: an analysis of 1971 census data. *Social Trends* **6**, 33–47 (HMSO).

Home Office 1968: *Urban programme circular No. 1, 1968.*

Horne, D. 1981: *Winner takes all?* (Penguin).

Horton, F. E. and Reynolds, D. R. 1971: Effects of urban spatial structure on individual behaviour. *Economic Geography* **47**, 36–48.

Houston, C. J. 1979: Administrative control of migration to Moscow, 1959–75. *Canadian Geographer* **23**, 1, 32–44.

Hoyt, H. 1939: *The structure and growth of residential neighbourhoods in American cities* (Federal Housing Administration).

Hughes, B. 1980: *Exit full employment* (Angus and Robertson).

Hughes, G. A. 1979: Housing income and subsidies. *Fiscal Studies* **1**, 1, 20–38.

Hughes, J. W. (ed.) 1974: *New dimensions of urban planning: growth controls* (Center for Urban Policy Research).

Hurd, R. M. 1903: *Principles of city land values* (The Record and Guide).

Huzinec, G. A. 1978: The impact of industrial decision-making upon the Soviet urban hierarchy. *Urban Studies* **15**, 139–48.

Hyman, G. and Markowski, S. 1980: Speculation and inflation in the market for house-building land in England and Wales. *Environment and Planning* A **12**, 1119–30.

Illich, I. D. 1976: *Deschooling society* (Pelican).

Industries Assistance Commission, 1977–78: *Annual report 1977–78* (Australian Government Printing Service).

Institute of Applied Economic and Social Research, 1981: *Survey of applications for housing finance: Victoria, March 1980*.

Jackman, R. 1979: London's needs grant. *Centre for Environmental Studies Review* **51**, 28–34.

Jacobs, J. 1961: *Death and life of great American cities* (Venture).

James, F. J. 1980: The revitalization of older urban housing and neighbourhoods. In Solomon, A. P. (ed.), 130–60.

Jamrozik, A. and Leeds, M. 1981: Employment benefits: private or public welfare? University of New South Wales Social Welfare Research Centre.

Janicka, K. 1978: Intergenerational mobility in cities. In Slomczynski, K. and Krauze, T. (eds), 81–101.

Janson, C-G. 1969: Some problems of ecological factor analysis. In Dogan, M. and Rokkan, S. (eds), 301–41.

Jeffrey, N. 1977: Administrative/political structure for planning. In Jeffrey, N. and Caldwell, M. (eds), 117–26.

Jeffrey, N. and Caldwell, M. (eds) 1977: Planning and urbanism in China. *Progress in Planning* **8**, Part 2.

Jessop, R. 1977: Recent theories of the capitalist state. *Cambridge Journal of Economics* **1**, 353–74.

Johnson, J. H. and Pooley, C. G. (eds) 1982: *The structure of nineteenth century cities* (Croom Helm).

Johnston, R. J. 1966: The location of high status residential areas. *Geografiska Annaler* **48B**, 23–35.

Johnston, R. J. 1969: Processes of change in the high status residential areas of Christchurch, 1951–1964. *New Zealand Geographer* **25**, 1–15.

Johnston, R. J. 1970: On spatial patterns in the residential structure of cities. *Canadian Geographer* **14**, 361–7.

Johnston, R. J. 1971: *Urban residential patterns. An introductory review* (Bell).

Johnston, R. J. 1973: Spatial patterns in suburban evaluations. *Environment and Planning* **5**, 385–95.

Johnston, R. J. 1979: *Political, electoral and spatial systems. An essay in political geography* (Clarendon Press).

Johnston, R. J. 1980: On the nature of explanation in human geography. *Transactions, Institute of British Geographers* NS **5**, 402–12.

Johnstone, Q. 1976: Government control of urban land development in Australia: the record of the Whitlam government. Unpublished report (shortened version published in *Tulane Law Review* 1977, **51**, 3, 547–610).

Jones, C. (ed.) 1979: *Urban deprivation and inner city* (Croom Helm).

Jones, C. and Stevenson, J. (eds) 1982: *Yearbook of social policy in Britain 1980–1981* (Routledge and Kegan Paul).

Jones, E. and Eyles, J. 1977: *An introduction to social geography* (Oxford University Press).

Jones, G. W. (ed.) 1980: *New approaches to the study of central-local government relationships* (Gower, for Social Sciences Research Council).

Jones, K., Brown, J. and Bradshaw, J. 1978: *Issues in social policy* (Routledge and Kegan Paul).

Jones, M. A. 1980: *The Australian welfare state* (George Allen and Unwin).

Jones, M. A. 1981: *Local government and the people* (Hargreen Publishing Company).

Joyce, P. 1980: *Work, society and politics: the factory north of England in the second half of the nineteenth century* (Harvester).

Jud, G. D. and Watts, J. M. 1981: Schools and housing values. *Land Economics* **57**, 3, 459–70.

Karn, V. A. 1976: Priorities for local authority mortgage lending, a case study of Birmingham. Centre for Urban and Regional Studies Research Memorandum 52.

Karn, V. A. 1979: Low income owner-occupation in the inner city. In Jones, C. (ed.), 160–90.

Kearny, I. F. 1975: The involvement of finance companies in real estate lending. *The Developer* **13**, 3, 13–18.

Keat, R. and Urry, J. 1975: *Social theory as science* (Routledge and Kegan Paul).

Keeble, D. 1981: De-industrialisation means unemployment. *Geographical Magazine* **53**, 458–64.

Kellett, J. R. 1969: *The impact of railways on Victorian cities* (Routledge and Kegan Paul).

Kellner, P. 1980: Wanted: a touch of class war. *New Statesman* **100**, 2595, 5.

Kelly, J. 1982: Useful work and useless toil. *Marxism Today* **26**, 8, 12–17.

Kelly, M. J. 1970: Eight acres; estate sub-division and the building process. Paddington, 1875 to 1890. *Australian Economic History Review* **10**, 2, 155–68.

Kelly, M. P. 1980: *White-collar proletariat* (Routledge and Kegan Paul).

Kemeny, J. 1978a: Home-ownership and finance capital. *Journal of Australian Political Economy* **3**, 89–100.

Kemeny, J. 1978b: Australia's privatized cities: detached house ownership and urban exploitation. In Burke, T. (ed.), 39–50.

Kemeny, J. 1980: Home ownership and privatization. *International Journal of Urban and Regional Research* **4**, 372–88.

Kemeny, J. 1981: *The myth of home ownership* (Routledge and Kegan Paul).

Kendig, H. 1979: *New life for old suburbs* (George Allen and Unwin).

Kendig, H. 1981: *Buying and renting: household moves in Adelaide* AIUS Publication No. 91 (Australian Institute of Urban Studies).

Kennett, S. 1980: *Local government fiscal problems: A context for inner areas* (Social Science Research Council).

Kilmartin, L. and Thorns, D. C. 1978: *Cities unlimited. The sociology of urban development in Australia and New Zealand* (George Allen and Unwin).

King, L. J. 1969: *Statistical analysis in geography* (Prentice-Hall).

King, L. J. 1976: Alternatives to a positive economic geography. *Annals, Association of American Geographers* **66**, 293–308.

King, L. J. 1979: Areal associations and regressions. *Annals, Association of American Geographers* **69**, 124–8.

King, L. J. and Golledge, R. G. 1978: *Cities, space and behavior* (Prentice-Hall).

King, R. (ed.) 1971: *Perception of residential quality. Sydney case studies.* Ian Buchan Tell Research Project on Housing, Sydney.

King, R. 1980: *Interest rates, energy and house prices. Some aspects of the Melbourne housing market, 1966–1980* (Centre for Environmental Studies).

Kirby, M. W. 1981: *The decline of British economic power since 1870* (George Allen and Unwin).

Kirk, G. 1980: *Urban planning in a capitalist society* (Croom Helm).

Kirkby, R. 1974: China's strategy for development. *Architectural Design* **49**, 3, 139–43.

Kirst, M. W. 1982: The state's role in education policy innovation. *Policy Studies Review* **1**, 2, 298–308.

Kirwan, R. 1980a: *The inner city in the United States* (Social Science Research Council).

Kirwan, R. 1980b: The fiscal context. In Cameron, G. C. (ed.), 72–100.

Korporaal, G. 1983: America dumping Milton Friedman's monetarism. *Australian Financial Review* **5581**, 24 February 1983, 6–7.

Krefetz, S. P. 1979: Low – and moderate – income housing in the suburbs: the Massachusetts "Anti-snob zoning" law experience. *Policy Studies Journal* **8**, 288–99.

Kuttner, B. 1981: Growth with equity. *Working Papers Magazine* **8**, 5, 32–43.

Lall, S. and Streeten, P. 1977: *Foreign investments, transnationals and developing countries* (Macmillan Press).

Lamarche, F. 1976: Property development and the economic foundations of the urban question. In Pickvance, C. G. (ed.), 85–118.

Lambert, J. R. and Filkin, C. 1971: Race relations research: some issues of approach and application. *Race* **12**, 329–35.

Lambert, J., Paris, C. and Blackaby, B. 1978: *Housing policy and the state: allocation, access and control* (MacMillan).

Lampard, E. E. 1973: The urbanizing world. In Dyos, H. J. and Wolff, M. (eds) Vol. 1, 3–57.

Lane, J. E. 1977: Some possible implications of rising petroleum fuel prices for road transport. *Third Australian Transport Research Forum, Papers.*

Laska, S. B. and Spain, D. (eds) 1980: *Back to the city. Issues in neighbourhood renovation* (Pergamon).

Law, J. 1975: Spatial variations of rates and services within Adelaide's Local Government Areas. Unpublished BA Hons thesis, University of Adelaide.

Lawless, P. 1979: *Urban deprivation and government initiative* (Faber and Faber).

Lawrence, R. J. 1972: Social welfare and urban growth. In Parker, R. S. and Troy, P. N. (eds), 100–28.

Le Gates, R. and Wilmoth, D. 1981: More sweatshops are not the answer. *In These Times*, 11–17 March, 5.

Le Grand, J. 1982: *The strategy of equality. Redistribution and the social services* (George Allen and Unwin).

Lebas, E. 1982: Urban and Regional Sociology in Advanced Industrial Societies: a decade of Marxist and critical perspectives. *Current Sociology* **31**, 1.

Lee, C. H. 1981: Regional growth and structural change in Victorian Britain. *Economic History Review* **34**, 3, 438–52.

Lee, R. 1976: Surprise and counter-production in radical geography. *Area* **8**, 11–14.

Lees, L. 1973: Metropolitan types – London and Paris compared. In Dyos, H. J. and Wolff, M. (eds), 413–28.

Leonard, S. 1982: Urban managerialism: a period of transition? *Progress in Human Geography* **6**, 2, 190–215.

Leven, C. L., Little, J. T., Nourse, H. O. and Read, R. B. 1976: *Neighbourhood change: lessons in the dynamics of urban decay* (Praeger).

Leven, M. R. and Abend, N. A. 1971: *Bureaucrats in collision: case studies in area transportation planning* (MIT Press).

Lever, W. F. 1981: *Employment change in British conurbations 1952–1973* (Department of Social and Economic Research, University of Glasgow).

Levy, F., Meltsner, A. and Wildavsky, A. 1974: *Urban outcomes* (University of California Press).

Lewis, J. 1983: The Tories and the creation of poverty. *Guardian Weekly* **128**, 7, 10.

Lewis, J. P. 1965: *Building cycles and Britain's growth* (Macmillan).

Lewis, S. 1982: Urban policy on the cheap. *Planning* **97**, 6, 12–18.

Ley, D. 1977: Social geography and the taken-for-granted world. *Transactions, Institute of British Geographers* NS **2**, 498–512.

Ley, D. and Samuels, M. S. (eds) 1978: *Humanistic geography. Prospects and problems* (Croom Helm).

Li, M. M. and Brown, J. H. 1980: Micro-neighbourhood externalities and hedonic housing prices. *Land Economics* **56**, 2, 125–41.

Lindberg, L. N., Alford, R., Crouch, C. and Offe, C. 1975: *Stress and contradiction in modern capitalism* (Lexington Books).

Lineberry, R. L. 1977: *Equality and urban policy. The distribution of municipal public services* (Sage Publications).

Lineberry, R. L. and Sharkansky, I. 1974: *Urban politics and public policy* (Harper and Row).

Linge, G. J. R. 1979a: *Industrial awakening: a geography of Australian manufacturing 1788 to 1890* (ANU Press).

Linge, G. J. R. 1979b: Australian manufacturing in recession: a review of the spatial implications. *Environment and Planning* A **11**, 1405–30.

Lipsey, A. G. and Lancaster, K. 1956: The general theory of the second best. *Review of Economic Studies* **24**, 218–20.

Lloyd, C. J. and Troy, P. N. 1981: *Innovation and reaction. The life and death of the federal Department of Urban and Regional Development* (George Allen and Unwin).

Lloyd, P. E. and Mason, C. M. 1978: Manufacturing industry in the inner city: a case study of Greater Manchester. *Institute of British Geographers, Transactions,* NS **3**, 1, 66–90.

Logan, M. I., Maher, C. A., McKay, J. and Humphreys, J. S. 1975: *Urban and regional Australia. Analysis and policy issues* (Sorrett).

Logan, M. I., Whitelaw, J. S. and McKay, J. 1981: *Urbanization. The Australian experience* (Shillington House).

Logan, T. 1981: *Urban and regional planning in Victoria* (Shillington House).

Logan, T. and Ogilvy, E. 1981: The statutory planning framework. In Troy, P. N. (ed.), 172–94.

Logan, W. S. 1982: Gentrification in inner Melbourne: problems of analysis. *Australian Geographical Studies* **20**, 65–95.

Lojkine, J. 1976: Contribution to a Marxist theory of capitalist urbanization. In Pickvance, C. G. (ed.), 119–46.

Lojkine, J. 1977: *Le Marxisme l'etat et la questione urbanie* (PUF).

Long, B. (ed.) 1982: The state budget 1982 and community services in western Sydney. Western Sydney's Regional Information and Research Service Discussion Paper No. 7.

Lowry, I. S. 1980: The dismal future of central cities. In Solomon, A. P. (ed.), 161–203.

Lubenow, W. C. 1971: *The politics of government growth. Early Victorian attitudes toward state intervention,* 1833–1848 (David and Charles).

Lydall, H. 1968: *The structure of earnings* (Oxford University Press).

Lydall, H. F. and Lansing, J. B. 1959: A comparison of the distribution of personal income and wealth in the United States and Great Britain. *American Economic Review* **49**, 43–67.

McAuley, A. 1977: The distribution of earnings and incomes in the Soviet Union. *Soviet Studies* **29**, 2, 214–37.

McAuley, A. 1981: Welfare and social security. In Schapiro, L. and Godson, J. (eds), 194–230.

McCarty, J. W. 1970: Australian capital cities in the nineteenth century. *Australian Economic History Review* **10**, 2, 107–37.

McEachern, D. 1980: *A class against itself. Power and the nationalisation of the British steel industry* (Cambridge University Press).

McGregor, A. 1979: Area externalities and urban unemployment. In Jones, C. (ed.), 92–112.

McLellan, D. 1979: *Marxism after Marx* (Harper and Row).

Maddocks, D. 1978: Exploring the housing attitudes of future home buyers in four Australian cities. In Committee of Inquiry into Housing Costs 30–46.

Maher, C. A. 1979: The changing role of the inner city: the example of Inner Melbourne. *Australian Geographer* **14**, 112–22.

Malanowski, J. 1978: Relations between classes and perception of social class distance. In Slomczynski, K. and Krauze, T. (eds), 125–40.

Mandel, E. 1975: *Late capitalism* (New Left Books).

Manning, I. 1973: *Municipal finance and income distribution in Sydney* (Urban Research Unit, Australian National University).

Manning, I. 1978: *The journey to work* (George Allen and Unwin).

Marcuse, H. 1964: *One-dimensional man* (Routledge and Kegan Paul).

Marcuse, P. 1981: The targeted crisis: on the ideology of the urban fiscal crisis and its uses. *International Journal of Urban and Regional Research* **5**, 3, 330–55.

Margolis, J. 1968: The demand for urban public services. In Perloff, H. S. and Wingo, L. (eds), 527–66.

Mark, J. H. 1980: A preference approach to measuring the impact of environmental externalities. *Land Economics* **56**, 1, 103–16.

Marx, K. 1967: *Capital: a critique of political economy*, 3 vols Engels, F. (ed), (International Press).

Marx, K. and Engels, F. 1967: *The communist manifesto* (Progress Publishers).

Massey, D. 1978: Regionalism: some current issues. *Capital and Class* **6**, 106–25.

Massey, D., Barras, R. and Broadbent, T. A. 1973: Labour must take over land. *Socialist Commentary*, July 1973.

Massey, D. and Catalano, A. 1978: *Capital and land: landownership by capital in Great Britain* (Edward Arnold).

Massey, D. and Meagan, R. 1982: *The anatomy of job loss: the how, where and when of employment decline* (Methuen).

Massey, D., Minns, R., Morrison, W. I. and Whitbread, M. 1976: A strategy for urban and regional research. *Regional Studies* **10**, 381–7.

Mathews, R. 1967: *Public investment in Australia. A study of Australian public authority investment and development* (F. W. Cheshire).

Mathews, R. 1980: *Australian federalism 1979* (Centre for Research on Federal Financial Relations).

Mathews, R. 1982: A shambles where once was a system. *Age* 3 February 1982, 13.

Mathews, R. (ed.) 1978: *Local government in transition: responsibilities, management and financing* (Centre for Research on Federal Financial Relations, Australian National University).

Matthews, M. 1975: Top incomes in the USSR: towards a definition of the Soviet elite. *Survey* **21**, 3, 1–27.

Matthews, M. 1979: Social dimensions in Soviet urban housing. In French, R. A. and Hamilton, F. E. I. (eds), 105–19.

Meacher, M. 1980: Wealth. In Bosanquet, N. and Townsend, P. (eds), 121–34.

Meade, J. 1964: *Efficiency, equality and the ownership of property* (George Allen and Unwin).

Meade, J. 1978: *The structure and reform of direct taxation* (Institute for Fiscal Studies).

Meidner, R. 1978: *Employee investment funds: an approach to collective capital formation* (George Allen and Unwin).

Mellor, J. R. 1977: *Urban sociology in an urbanized society* (Routledge and Kegan Paul).

Melbourne Metropolitan Board of Works, 1981: *Melbourne housing study. Interim report 1981.*

Menchik, M. 1972: Residential environmental preferences and choice: empirically validating preference measures. *Environment and Planning* **4**, 445–58.

Mendelsohn, R. 1979: *The condition of the people. Social welfare in Australia 1900–1975* (George Allen and Unwin).

Mercer, D. C. and Powell, J. M. 1972: Phenomenology and related non-positivistic viewpoints in the social sciences. *Monash Publications in Geography* **1**.

Merrett, S. 1979: *State housing in Britain* (Routledge and Kegan Paul).

Merritt, G. 1982: *World out of work* (Collins).

Métin, A. 1901: *Le socialisme sans doctrines: la question agraire et la question, ouvriere en Australie et Nouvelle-Zelande* (Alcan).

Michelson, W. 1977: *Enviornmental choice, human behaviour and residential satisfaction* (Oxford University Press).

Mier, R. 1982: Enterprise zones: a long shot. *Planning* **48**, 4, 10–14.

Mieszkowski, P. and Oakland, W. H. (eds) 1979: *Fiscal federalism and grants-in-aid* (The Urban Institute: Washington).

Mieszkowski, P. and Straszheim, M. (eds) 1979: *Current issues in urban economics* (Johns Hopkins University Press).

Miliband, R. 1969: *The state in capitalist society* (Weidenfeld and Nicolson).

Miliband, R. 1972: *Parliamentary socialism* 2nd edition (Merlin Press).

Milligan, V. and McAllister, M. 1982: *Housing and local government. An evaluation of the Waverley community housing officer project.* SWRC Reports and Proceedings No. 18, (Social Welfare Research Centre, University of New South Wales).

Mills, E. S. 1967: An aggregative model of resource allocation in a metropolitan area. *American Economic Review* **57**, 197–210.

Mills, E. S. 1969: The value of land. In Perloff, H. S. (ed.), 231–56.

Mills, E. S. 1970: Urban density functions. *Urban Studies* **7**, 5–20.

Mills, E. S. 1972a: *Urban economics* (Scott, Foresman).

Mills, E. S. 1972b: *Studies in the structure of the urban economy* (Johns Hopkins Press for Resources for the Future Inc.).

Mills, E. S. and MacKinnon, J. 1973: Notes on the new urban economics. *Bell Journal of Economics and Management Science* **4**, 593–601.

Mills, S. 1981: Cautious, nitpicking approach to poor. *Age* 13 November, 13.

Mincer, J. 1974: *Schooling, experience and earnings* (National Bureau of Economic Research).

Mingione, E. 1981: *Social conflict and the city* (Basil Blackwell).

Minns, R. 1981: The select band which owns British industry. *New Statesman* **102**, 2628, 2.

Mohl, R. A. and Betten, N. 1972: The failure of industrial city planning: Gary, Indiana, 1906–1910. *Journal, American Institute of Planners* **38**, 4, 203–14.

Mollenkopf, J. H. 1978: The postwar politics of urban development. In Tabb, W. K. and Sawer, L. (eds), 117–52.

Mollenkopf, J. H. 1981: Neighbourhood political development and the politics of urban growth: Boston and San Francisco, 1958–78. *International Journal of Urban and Regional Research* **5**, 1, 15–39.

Moorhouse, H. F. 1978: The Marxist theory of the labour aristocracy. *Social History* **3**, 1, 61–82.

Morris, J. 1978: Regional disparities in access to community health facilities in Melbourne: a cause for alarm? Australian Road Research Board, Discussion Note 304.

Moser, C. A. and Scott, W. 1961: *British towns: a statistical study of their social and economic differences* (Oliver and Boyd).

Muller, P. O. 1981: *Contemporary suburban America* (Prentice-Hall).

Mullins, P. 1981: Theoretical perspectives on Australian urbanization: 1. Material components in the reproduction of Australian labour power. *Australian and New Zealand Journal of Sociology* **17**, 1. 65–75.

Mullins, P. 1982: The 'middle-class' and the inner city. *Journal of Australian Political Economy* **11**, 44–58.

Mumford, L. 1961: *The city in history* (Penguin).

Mundey, J. 1981: *Green bans and beyond* (Angus and Robertson).

Murdie, R. A. 1969: *The factorial ecology of metropolitan Toronto, 1951–1961: an essay on the social geography of the city*. Department of Geography Research Paper No. 116 (University of Chicago).

Murie, A. 1974: *Household movement and housing choice*. Occasional Paper No. 28, Centre for Urban and Regional Studies, University of Birmingham.

Murie, A. 1982: Council housing under review. In Jones, C. and Stevenson, J. (eds), 154–71.

Murie, A., Niner, P. and Watson, C. 1976: *Housing policy and the housing system* (George Allen and Unwin).

Murphy, D. G. 1976: The introduction of land commissions and the future of the urban land development industry. *Developer* **14**, 2/3, 53–6.

Muth, R. F. 1968: Urban residential land and housing markets. In Perloff, H. S. and Wingo, L. (eds), 285–333.

Muth, R. F. 1969: *Cities and housing. The spatial pattern of urban residential land use* (University of Chicago Press).

Myers, P. 1982: UDAG and the urban environment. *Journal of the American Planning Association* **48**, 1, 99–109.

Nabarro, R. 1980: Inner city partnerships. An assessment of the first programmes. *Town Planning Review* **51**, 1, 25–38.

Nardinelli, C. 1980: Child labour and the Factory Acts. *Journal of Economic History* **40**, 4, 739–55.

Nathan, R. P. and Adams, C. 1976: Understanding central city hardship. *Political Science Quarterly* **91**, 1, 47–62.

Nathan, R. P. and Dommel, P. R. 1979: The cities. In *Setting National Priorities: the 1978 Budget* (Brookings Institution, Washington, DC).

National Academy of Sciences, Committee on Geography, 1973: *Geographical perspectives and urban problems* (National Academy of Sciences).

National Economic Development Office, 1977: *BMRB housing consumer survey 1975* (HMSO).

National Times, 1980: The National Times annual real estate survey, 18–24 May, 30–6.

Neenan, W. B. 1970: Suburban-central city exploitation thesis: one city's fate. *National Tax Journal* **23**, 119–29.

Neutze, M. 1972: The cost of housing. *Economic Record* **48**, 537–73.

Neutze, M. 1977: *Urban development in Australia* (George Allen and Unwin).

Neutze, M. 1978a: *Australian Urban Policy* (George Allen and Unwin).

Neutze, M. 1978b: Urban land. In Scott, P. (ed.), 72–87.

Neutze, M. 1981: Housing. In Troy, P. N. (ed.), 104–22.

New South Wales Planning and Environment Commission, 1978: *Social Indicators*. Research Study no. 4.

Newman, I. and Mayo, M. 1981: Docklands. *International Journal of Urban and Regional Research* **5**, 4, 529–45.

Newsweek, 1982: The decaying of America. **50**, 5, 28–34.

New York Times Weekly Review, 1982a: Ill wind for urban aid. 27 June–3 July, 4.

New York Times Weekly Review, 1982b: What? Penalizing the poor? 20–6 July, 6.

Nicholson, J. L. 1974: Distribution and redistribution of income in the UK. In Wedderburn, D. (ed.), 71–92.

Niner, P. and Watson, C. J. 1979: Housing in British cities. In Herbert, D. T. and Johnston, R. J. (eds), 319–51.

Nittim, Z. 1980: The coalition of resident action groups. In Roe, J. (ed.), 231–47.

Nourse, H. O. 1968: *Regional economics. A study in the economic structure, stability, and growth of regions* (McGraw-Hill).

Oakland, W. H. 1979: Central cities: fiscal plight and prospects for reform. In Mieszkowski, P. and Straszheim, M. (eds), 322–58.

Oates, W. E. 1969: The effects of property taxes and local public spending on property values: an empirical study of tax capitalization and the Tiebout hypothesis. *Journal of Political Economy* **77**, 6, 957–71.

Observer, 1981: Liverpool wary of smoothie. 9 August, 7.

O'Connor, J. 1973: *The fiscal crisis of the state* (St Martin's Press).

O'Connor, J. 1974: *The corporations and the state* (Harper and Row).

O'Connor, J. 1981a: The meaning of crisis. *International Journal of Urban and Regional Research* **5**, 3, 302–29.

O'Connor, J. 1981b: Accumulation crisis: the problem and its setting. *Contemporary Crises* **2**, 109–25.

Odland, J. 1978: The conditions for multi-centre cities. *Economic Geography* **54**, 234–44.

OECD, 1973 and 1982: *Labour force statistics, 1960–71; 1969–80* (OECD Economic Statistics and National Accounts Division).

OECD, 1976: *Public expenditure on income maintenance programmes.* OECD Studies in Resource Allocation No. 3.

OECD, 1977: *Measuring social well-being* OECD Social Indicator Programme Series, No. 3.

OECD, 1978: *Public expenditure trends* Studies in Resource Allocation.

OECD, 1980: *The tax/benefit position of selected income groups in OECD member countries, 1974–1979.*

OECD, 1981: *Measuring local government expenditure needs: the Copenhagen workshop.*

OECD, 1982: *Economic Outlook* (OECD Secretariat).

Offe, C. 1975: The theory of the capitalist state and the problem of policy formation. In Lindberg, L. *et al.* (eds), 125–44.

Ogawa, H. and Fujita, M. 1980: Equilibrium land use patterns in a nonmonocentric city. *Journal of Regional Science* **20**, 455–75.

Ogden, K. W. 1980: Some thoughts on the effects of Australian urban transport on structural economic change. *Environment and Planning* A **12**, 409–25.

O'Higgins, M. 1980: The distributive effects of public expenditure and taxation: an agnostic view of the CSO analysis. In Sandford, C., *et al.* (eds), 28–46.

Olives, J. 1976: The struggle against urban renewal in the 'Cité d'Aliarte' (Paris). In Pickvance, C. G. (ed.), 174–97.

Ollman, B. 1971: *Alienation: Marx's conception of man in capitalist society* (Cambridge University Press).

Olson, S. H. 1979: Baltimore imitates the spider. *Annals, Association of American Geographers* **69**, 4, 555–74.

Open University, 1972: *Social geography* (Open University Press).

Open University, 1976: *Occupational structure and placement* (Open University Press).

Pahl, R. E. 1975: *Whose city? And further essays on urban society* (Penguin).

Pahl, R. E. 1977: Managers, technical experts and the state: forms of mediation, manipulation and dominance in urban and regional development. In Harloe, M. (ed.), 49–60.

Pahl, R. E. 1979: Socio-political factors in resource allocation. In Herbert, D. and Smith, D. (eds), 33–46.

Papageorgiou, G. J. 1978: Spatial externalities, Part I and II. *Annals, Association of American Geographers* **68**, 465–92.

Papageorgiou, G. J. (ed.) 1976: *Essays in mathematical land use theory* (Lexington, DC Heath).

Papageorgiou, G. J. and Casetti, E. 1971: Spatial equilibrium residential land values in a multicentric setting. *Journal of Regional Science* **11**, 385–9.

Paris, C. and Blackaby, B. 1979: *Not much improvement* (Macmillan).

Park, R. E. 1926: The urban community as a spatial pattern and moral order. In Burgess, E. W. (ed.).

Park, R. E., Burgess, E. W. and McKenzie (eds.) 1925: *The city* (University of Chicago Press).

Parker, R. S. and Troy, P. N. (eds) 1972: *The politics of urban growth* (Australian National University Press).

Parkes, D. 1971: A classical social area analysis: Newcastle, N.S.W. and some comparisons. *Australian Geographer* **11**, 555–78.

Parkin, A. 1982: *Governing the cities. The Australian experience in perspective* (Macmillan).

Parkin, A. 1983: The states and the cities: a comparative perspective. In Halligan, J. and Paris, C. (eds).

Parkin, A., Summers, J. and Woodward, D. (eds) 1980: *Government, politics and power in Australia* 2nd ed (Longman Cheshire).

Parsons, T. (ed.) 1968: *Theory of social and economic organization* (Free Press).

Paterson, J. 1974: *Melbourne metropolitan residential land study (John Paterson Urban Systems)*.

Paterson, J. 1975a: Home owning, home renting and income redistribution. *Australian Quarterly* **47**, 4, 28–36.

Paterson, J. 1975b: Social and economic implications of housing and planning standards. In Priorities Review Staff, 373–434.

Payne, M. 1981: A preferred approach to development and financing of residential land releases in western Sydney. Unpublished Report to the Western Sydney Regional Organisation of Councils.

Peach, C. (ed.) 1975: *Urban social segregation* (Longman).

Peet, J. R. 1969: The spatial expansion of commercial agriculture in the nineteenth century: a von Thünen interpretation. *Economic Geography* **45**, 283–301.

Peet, R. (ed.) 1977a: *Radical geography: alternative viewpoints on contemporary social issues* (Methuen).

Peet, R. 1977b: The development of radical geography in the United States. *Progress in Human Geography* **1**, 64–87.

Peet, R. 1980: On 'Geographic inequality under socialism'. *Annals, Association of American Geographers* **70**, 2, 280–6.

Peet, R. and Slater, D. 1980: Reply to the Soviet Review of *Radical Geography*. *Soviet Geography: Review and Translation* **21**, 541–4.

Pennance, F. C. and Gray, H. 1968: *Choice in housing* (Institute of Economic Affairs, London).

Perin, C. 1977: *Everything in its place. Social order and land use in America* (Princeton University Press).

Perlgut, D. 1982: Local government finance and Commonwealth revenue-sharing in western Sydney. Unpublished Report to the Western Sydney Regional Organisation of Councils.

Perloff, H. S. (ed.) 1969: *The quality of the urban environment. Essays on 'new resources' in an urban age* (Resources for the Future).

Perloff, H. S. and Wingo, L. (eds) 1968: *Issues in urban economics* (Resouces for the Future).

Perry, D. C. and Watkins, A. J. 1981: Contemporary dimensions of uneven urban development in the USA. In Harloe, M. and Lebas, E. (eds), 115–42.

Perry, D. C. and Watkins, A. J. (eds) 1977: *The rise of the sunbelt cities* vol. 14, Urban Affairs Annual Reviews (Sage Publications).

Peters, J. 1981: Interstates: nearing the end of the road. *Planning* **47**, 12, 12–5.

Peterson, G. E. 1974: *The influence of zoning regulations on land and housing prices* (Urban Institute, Washington DC).

Peterson, G. E. 1976: Finance. In Gorham, W. and Glazer, N. (eds).

Petras, J. and Gundle, S. 1982: A critique of structuralist state theorizing. *Contemporary Crises* **6**, 2, 161–82.

Piachaud, D. 1980: Social security. In Bosanquet, N. and Townsend, P. (eds), 171–86.

Pickvance, C. G. (ed.) 1976: *Urban sociology: critical essays* (Tavistock).

Pickvance, C. G. 1976: On the study of urban social movements. In Pickvance, C. G. (ed.), 198–218.

Pimlott, C. 1981: The North East: back to the 1930s? In Crick, B. (ed.), 51–63.

Pinch, S. 1979: Territorial justice in the city: a case study of the social services for the elderly in Greater London. In Herbert, D. T. and Smith, D. M. (eds), 201–23.

Pinker, R. 1979: *The idea of welfare* (Heinemann).

Podder, N. 1978: *The economic circumstances of the poor* Commission of Inquiry into Poverty (Australian Government Publishing Service).

Political Economy of Housing Workshop, 1975: *Political economy and the housing question* (Conference of Socialist Economists).

Political Economy of Housing Workshop, 1976: *Housing and class in Britain* (Conference of Socialist Economists).

Pollins, H. 1964: Transport lines and social divisions. In Glass, R. (ed.), 29–61.

Pond, C. 1980a: Low pay. In Bosanquet, N. and Townsend, P. (eds), 85–107.

Pond, C. 1980b: Tax expenditures and fiscal welfare. In Sandford, C. *et al.* (eds), 47–64.

Popper, K. R. 1959: *The logic of scientific discovery* (Hutchinson).

Poulantzas, N. 1973: *Political power and social classes* (New Left Books).

Poulantzas, N. 1976a: The capitalist state: a reply to Miliband and Laclan. *New Left Review* **95**, 63–83.

Poulantzas, N. 1976b: *Classes in contemporary capitalism* (New Left Books).

Poulsen, M. F. 1976: Restricted lateral movement: an initial test of the locational attachments hypothesis. *Environment and Planning A* **8**, 289–98.

Prais, S. J. 1976: *The evolution of giant firms in Britain* (Cambridge University Press).

Pred, A. R. 1966: *The spatial dynamics of US urban-industrial growth, 1800–1914: Interpretive and theoretical essays* (MIT Press).

President's Commission for a National Agenda for the Eighties, 1980: *Urban America in the eighties* (US Government Printing Office).

President's Urban and Regional Group, 1978: *A new partnership to conserve America's communities: a national urban policy* (US Government Printing Office).

Priorities Review Staff, 1975: *Report on housing* (Australian Government Publishing Service).

Procter, I. 1982: Some political economies of urbanization and suggestions for a research framework. *International Journal of Urban and Regional Research* **6**, 1, 83–95.

Rachells, J. 1978: What people deserve. In Arthur, J. and Shaw, W. H. (eds), 150–63.

Radford, W. C. and Wilkes, R. E. 1975: *School leavers in Australia 1971–1972* (Australian Council of Education Research).

Rainwater, L. 1975: *Behind ghetto walls. Black families in a federal slum* (Penguin).

Raison, D. V. 1982: Land tenure in the Australian capital territory. Planning and leasehold changes in Canberra. *Valuer* **27**, 2, 209–10.

Ratcliff, R. U. 1949: *Urban land economics* (McGraw-Hill).

Ravetz, A. 1980: *Remaking cities. Contradictions of the recent urban environment* (Croom Helm).

Rawls, J. 1971: *A theory of justice* (Belknap Press of Harvard University).

Redford, A. 1964: *Labour migration in England, 1800–1850* (Manchester University Press).

Reece, B. F. 1975: The income tax incentive to owner occupation in Australia. *Economic Record* **51**, 134, 218–31.

Reeder, D. A. 1968: A theatre of suburbs: some patterns of development in West London, 1810–1911. In Dyos, H. J. (ed.), 253–72.

Rees, J. 1981: Urban water and sewerage services. In Troy, P. N. (ed.), 85–103.

Rees, P. H. 1970: Concepts of social space: toward an urban social geography. In Berry, B. J. L. and Horton, F. E. (eds), 306–94.

Rees, P. H. 1971: Factorial ecology: an extended definition survey, and critique of the field. *Economic Geography* **47** (Supplement) 220–30.

Reich, C. A. 1972: *The greening of America* (Penguin).

Reid, A. 1978: Politics and economics in the formation of the British working class: a response to H. F. Moorhouse. *Social History* **3**, 3, 347–61.

Reid, G. L. and Robertson, D. J. 1965: *Fringe benefits, labour costs and social security* (George Allen and Unwin).

Reid, H. M. (ed.) 1981: *Urban consolidation for Sydney* (Planning Research Centre, University of Sydney).

Rein, M. 1976: *Social science and public policy* (Penguin).

Reischauer, R. 1981: The economy and the federal budget in the 1980s: implications for the state and local sector. In Bahl, R. (ed.), 13–38.

Reisman, D. 1977: *Richard Titmuss: welfare and society* (Heinemann).

Reschovsky, A. 1979: Residential choice and the local public sector: an alternative test of the 'Tiebout' hypothesis. *Journal of Urban Economics* **6**, 4, 501–20.

Reuter, F. 1973: Externalities in urban property markets: an empirical test of the zoning ordinance of Pittsburgh. *Journal of Law and Economics*, **11**.

Rex, J. 1981: *Social conflict* (Longman).

Rex, J. and Moore, R. 1967: *Race, community and conflict* (Oxford University Press).

Rhodes, R. A. W. 1981: *Control and power in central-local government relations* (Gower, for Social Science Research Council).

Rich, P. C. 1982: Structural and spatial change in manufacturing. In Cardew, R. V., *et al.* (eds), 95–114.

Rich, R. C. 1979: Neglected issues in the study of urban service distribution: a research agenda. *Urban Studies* **16**, 143–56.

Richardson, H. W. 1969: *Regional economics. Location theory, urban structure and regional change* (Praeger).

Richardson, H. W. 1973: A comment on some uses of mathematical models in urban economics. *Urban Studies* **10**, 259–70.

Richardson, H. W. 1977: *The new urban economics: and alternatives* (Pion).

Richardson, H. W., Vipond, M. J. and Furbey, R. A 1974: Dynamic tests of Hoyt's spatial model. *Town Planning Review* **45**, 401–14.

Richardson, M. 1982: Singapore's road to jobs for all. *Age* 20 October, 13.

Ridker, R. G. and Henning, J. A. 1967: The determinants of residential property values with specific reference to air pollution. *Review of Economics and Statistics* **49**, 246–57.

Roberts, J. T. 1976: *General improvement areas* (Saxon House).

Robinson, J. 1972: The second crisis of economic theory. *American Economic Association Papers and Proceedings*.

Robinson, R. V. F. 1980: Housing tax-expenditures, subsidies and the distribution of income. University of Sussex Working Paper.

Robson, B. T. 1969: *Urban analysis. A study of city structure with special reference to Sunderland* (Cambridge University Press).

Robson, B. T. 1973a: *Urban growth: an approach* (Methuen).

Robson, B. T. 1973b: Forward. *Social Patterns in Cities*. Institute of British Geographers Special Publication No. 5, vii–ix.

Roddewig, R. J. 1978: *Green bans. The birth of Australian environmental politics* (Allanheld and Osmun).

Rodger, R. 1982: Rents and ground rents: housing and the land market in nineteenth-century Britain. In Johnson, J. H. and Pooley, C. G. (eds), 39–74.

Rodgers, H. B. 1960: The Lancashire cotton industry in 1840: a case study. *Institute of British Geographers, Transactions and Papers* **28**, 135–53.

Roe, J. (ed.) 1980: *Twentieth century Sydney. Studies in urban and social history* (Hale and Iremonger).

Roebuck, J. 1979: *Urban development in nineteenth century London, Lambeth, Battersea and Wandsworth, 1883–1888.* (Chichester Press).

Romanos, M. C. 1977: Household location in a linear multi-center metropolitan area. *Regional Science and Urban Economics* **7**, 233–50.

Rose, D. 1981: Accumulation versus reproduction in the inner city: *The Recurrent Crisis of London* revisited. In Dear, M. and Scott, A. J. (eds), 339–82.

Rose, R. 1980: *Do parties make a difference?* (Macmillan).

Rose, R. and Page, E. G. (eds) 1982: *Fiscal stress in cities* (Cambridge University Press).

Rosen, G. 1973: Disease, debility and death. In Dyos, H. J. and Wolff, M. (eds) vol. 2, 625–67.

Rostow, W. W. 1977: Regional change in the fifth Kondratieff upswing. In Perry, D. C. and Watkins, A. J. (eds), 83–104.

Roweis, S. T. 1981: Urban planning in early and late capitalist societies: outline of a theoretical perspective. In Dear, M. and Scott, A. J. (eds), 159–78.

Rowles, G. D. 1978: *The prisoners of space? Exploring the geographical experience of older people* (Westview Press).

Rowley, D. 1981: Suburb of broken homes and poverty. *Australian* 14–15 November 1981, 21.

Rubinstein, W. O. 1977: The Victorian middle classes: wealth, occupation and geography. *Economic History Review* **30**, 4, 602–23.

Runciman, W. G. 1966: *Relative deprivation and social justice* (Routledge and Kegan Paul).

Ryan, A. 1981: John Rawls and his theory of justice. *New Society* **55**, 228–30.

Sampson, A. 1981: *The money lenders. Bankers in a dangerous world* (Hodder and Stoughton).

Sandercock, L. 1975: *Cities for sale. Property, politics and urban planning in Australia* (Melbourne University Press).

Sandercock, L. 1978a: Citizen participation: the new conservatism. In Troy, P. N. (ed.), 117–32.

Sandercock, L. 1978b: A socialist city in a capitalist society? Property ownership and urban reform in Australia. *Journal of Australian Political Economy* **3**, 66–79.

Sandercock, L. 1979: *The land racket. The real costs of property speculation* (Silverfish).

Sandercock, L. 1982: Democratic socialism and the challenge of social democracy. In Evans, G. and Reeves, J. (eds), 16–34.

Sanford, C. 1980: Taxation and social policy: an overview. In Sandford, C., *et al.* (eds) 1–12.

Sandford, C., Pond, C. and Walker, R. (eds) 1980: *Taxation and social policy* (Heinemann Educational).

Saunders, D. A. L. 1967: Three factors behind the form of Melbourne's nineteenth century suburbs. In Troy, P. N. (ed.), 1–17.

Saunders, P. 1978: Domestic property and social class. *International Journal of Urban and Regional Research* **2**, 2, 233–51.

Saunders, P. 1979: *Urban politics. A sociological interpretation* (Penguin).

Saunders, P. 1981a: *Social theory and the urban question* (Hutchinson).

Saunders, P. 1981b: Community power, urban managerialism and the 'Local State'. In Harloe, M. (ed.), 27–79.

Sawer, G. 1973: *Australian government today* (Melbourne University Press).

Sawers, L. 1978: Cities and countryside in the Soviet Union and China. In Tabb, W. K. and Sawers, L. (eds), 338–64.

Sayer, R. A. 1976: A critique of urban modelling: from regional science to urban and regional political economy. *Progress in Planning* **6**, 3.

Sayer, R. A. 1979: Philosophical bases on the critique of urban modelling: a reply to Wilson. *Environment and Planning A* **11**, 1055–67.

Schaar, J. H. 1980: Equality of opportunity and the just society. In Blocker, H. G. and Smith, E. H. (eds) 162–84.

Schaefer, F. K. 1953: Exceptionalism in geography: a methodological examination. *Annals, Association of American Geographers* **43**, 226–49.

Schaeffer, K. H. and Sclar, E. 1975: *Access for all. Transportation and urban growth* (Penguin).

Schaffer, R. L. 1973: *Income flows in urban poverty areas* (Lexington Books).

Schapiro, L. and Godson, J. (eds) 1981: *The Soviet worker* (Macmillan Press).

Schenk, H. 1974: Concepts behind urban and regional planning in China. *Tidschrift voor Economische en Sociale Geografie* **65**, 5, 381–8.

Schmid, A. 1968: *Converting land from rural to urban use* (Johns Hopkins University Press).

Schneider, J. B. and Symons, J. G. 1971: *Regional health facility system planning: an access opportunity approach* Discussion Paper No. 48 (Regional Science Research Institute).

Schnore, L. F. 1963: The socio-economic status of cities and suburbs. *American Sociological Review* **28**, 76–88.

Schnore, L. F. 1966: Measuring city-suburban status differences. *Urban Affairs Quarterly* **1**, 95–108.

Schultz, A. 1970: Concept and theory formation in the social sciences. In Emmet, D. and MacIntyre, A. (eds).

Scott, A. J. 1976: Land and land rent: an interpretative review of the French literature. *Progress in Geography* **9**, 101–46.

Scott, A. J. 1980: *The urban land nexus and the state* (Pion).

Scott, J. 1979: *Corporations, classes and capitalism* (Hutchinson).

Scott, P. (ed.) 1978: *Australian cities and public policy* (Georgian House).

Seabrook, J. 1982: *Unemployment* (Quartet Books).

Shannon, G. W. and Dever, G. E. A. 1974: *The geography of health care* (McGraw-Hill).

Sheehan, P. J. 1980: *Crisis in abundance* (Penguin).

Shefter, M. 1980: National-local interaction and the New York City fiscal crisis. In Ashford, D. E. (ed.), 185–213.

Shepard, J. W. and Jenkins, M. A. 1972: Decentralizing high school administration in Detroit: an evaluation of alternative strategies of political control. *Economic Geography* **48**, 1, 95–106.

Sheppard, E. S. 1980: Ideology of spatial choice. *Papers, Regional Science Association* **45**, 197–221.

Shevky, E. and Bell, W. 1955: *Social area analysis. Theory, illustrative application and computational procedures* (Stanford University Press).

Shevky, E. and Williams, M. 1949: *The social areas of Los Angeles: analysis and typology* (University of California Press).

Shihata, I. F. I. 1982: *The other face of OPEC: financial assistance to the Third World* (Longman).

Short, J. R. 1978: Residential mobility. *Progress in Human Geography* **2**, 419–47.

Short, J. R. 1982: Urban policy and British cities. *Journal of the American Planning Association* **48**, 1, 39–52.

Short, J. R. and Bassett, K. 1978: Housing action areas: an evaluation. *Area* **10**, 2, 153–7.

Showler, B. and Sinfield, A. 1980: *The workless state* (Martin Robertson).

Simmie, J. M. and Hale, D. J. 1978: The distributional effects of owner-ship and control of land use in Oxford. *Urban Studies* **15**, 9–21.

Simon, N. W. H. 1977: The relative level of changes in earnings in London and Great Britain. *Regional Studies* **11**, 87–98.

Simpson, M. A. and Lloyd, T. H. 1977: *Middle class housing in Britain* (David and Charles).

Simpson, R. 1978: Big cities pile up their debts. *New Society* **48**, 839, 270.

Skocpol, T. 1980: Political response to capitalist crisis: neo-Marxist theories of the state and the case of the New Deal. *Politics and Society* **10** 2, 155–201.

Slater, D. 1975: The poverty of modern geographical enquiry. *Pacific Viewpoint* **16**, 159–76.

Sloane, M. 1968: The 1968 Housing Act: best yet, but is it enough? *Civil Rights Digest* **1**, 1–8.

Slomczynski, K. and Krauze, T. (eds) 1978: *Class structure and social mobility in Poland* (M. E. Sharpe).

Smiley, X. 1983: Hungary tries 'socialist capitalism'. *National Times*, 30 January–5 February, 18–19. Reprinted from *The New Republic*.

Smith, C. J. 1976: Distance and the location of community mental health facilities. *Economic Geography* **52**, 181–91.

Smith, C. M. 1972: *Curiosities of London life* 1st edn 1853. New Impression (Frank Cass).

Smith, D. M. 1973: *The geography of social well-being in the United States* (McGraw-Hill).

Smith, D. M. 1974: Who gets what where and how: a welfare focus for human geography. *Geography* **59**, 289–97.

Smith, D. M. 1977: *Human geography: a welfare approach* (Edward Arnold).

Smith, D. M. 1979: *Where the grass is greener. Living in an unequal world* (Penguin).

Smith, J. W. 1981: Principles of a grant distribution system. In OECD, 251–80.

Smith, N. 1979a: Geography, science and post-positivist modes of explanation. *Progress in Human Geography* **3**, 3, 356–83.

Smith, N. 1979b: Gentrification and capital: practice and ideology in Society Hill. *Antipode* **2**, 3, 24–35.

Smith, N. 1982: Gentrification and uneven development. *Economic Geography* **58**, 2, 139–55.

Smith, W. F. 1964: *Filtering and neighbourhood change*. Centre for Real Estate and Urban Economics, Research Report No. 24 (University of California).

Snell, B. 1974: *American ground transport: a proposal for restructuring the automobile, truck, bus and rail industries* (US Government Printing Office).

Soja, E. W. 1980: The socio-spatial dialectic. *Annals, Association of American Geographers* **70**, 2, 207–25.

Solomon, A. P. (ed.) 1980: *The prospective city. Economic, population, energy and environmental developments* (MIT Press).

Sonquist, J. A. and Morgan, J. N. 1970: *The detection of interaction effects* Survey Research Center, Institute for Social Research (University of Michigan).

South Australian Urban Land Trust, 1982: *Annual report* (South Australia Government Printer).

Stanback, T. M. and Knight, R. V. 1976: *Suburbanization and the city* (Allanheld, Osmun).

Stedman Jones, G. 1971: *Outcast London. A study in the relationship between classes in Victorian society* (Clarendon Press).

Stegman, M. A. 1969: Accessibility models and residential location. *Journal of the American Institute of Planners* **35**, 22–9.

Stegman, M. A. 1972: *Housing investment in the inner city: The dynamics of decline* (MIT Press).

Stephens, J. D. 1979: *The transition from capitalism to socialism* (Macmillan).

Sternlieb, G. and Hughes, J. W. 1980: *America's housing: prospects and problems* (Center for Urban Policy Research).

Stewart, A., Prandy, K. and Blackburn, R. M. 1980: *Social stratification and occupations* (Macmillan Press).

Stewart, M. 1972: *The city: problems of planning* (Penguin).

Stilwell, F. 1980: *Economic crisis, cities and regions* (Pergamon).

Stilwell, F. 1982: Towards an alternative economic strategy. *Journal of Australian Political Economy* **12/13**, 40–59.

Stilwell, F. and Hardwick, J. 1973: Social inequality in Australian cities *Australian Quarterly*, **45**, 4, 18–36.

Stone, K. 1974: The origins of job structures in the steel industry. *Review of Radical Political Economics* **6**, 2, 113–73.

Stone, M. E. 1978: Housing, mortgage lending, and the contradictions of capitalism. In Tabb, W. K. and Sawers, L. (eds), 179–208.

Stretton, H. 1970: *Ideas for Australian cities* (Georgian House).

Stretton, H. 1974: *Housing and government: 1974 Boyer lectures.* (Australian Broadcasting Commission).

Stretton, H. 1976: *Capitalism, socialism and the environment* (Cambridge University Press).

Stretton, H. 1978a: *Urban planning in rich and poor countries* (Oxford University Press).

Stretton, H. 1978b: Capital mistakes. In Bell, C. and Encel, S. (eds), 76–92.

Stretton, H. 1979: The Australian war on the poor. *New Society* **50**, 893, 368–70.

Stretton, H. 1981: Intellectuals and inequalities under state socialism. *International Journal of Urban and Regional Research* **5**, 1, 117–21.

Struyk, R. J. and James, F. J. 1975: *Intrametropolitan industrial location* (Heath and Co.).

Stull, W. J. 1975: Community environment, zoning, and the market value of single family homes. *Journal of Law and Economics* **18**, 535–57.

Sumka, H. J. 1979: Neighborhood revitalization and displacement. A review of the evidence. *Journal of the American Planning Association* **45**, 4, 480–7.

Sutcliffe, A. 1982: The growth of public intervention in the British urban environment during the nineteenth century: a structural approach. In Johnson, J. H. and Pooley, C. G. (eds), 107–24.

Suttles, G. D. 1972: *The social construction of communities* (University of Chicago Press).

Sweetzer, F. L. 1969: Ecological factors in metropolitan zones and sectors. In Dogan, M. and Rokkan, S. (eds), 413–56.

Sydney Morning Herald, 1972: Why the door is closed to Government housing. 24 July, 8.

Szelenyi, I. 1972: Housing system and social structure. In Halmos, P. (ed.), 274–92.

Szelenyi, I. 1977: Social inequalities in state socialist redistributive economies. *International Journal of Comparative Sociology* **19**, 1–2, 63–87.

Szelenyi, I. 1978: Ecological change and residential mix in Adelaide. In Urlich-Cloher, D. U. and Badcock, B. A. (eds), 15–18.

Szelenyi, I. 1981a: The relative autonomy of the state or state mode of production? In Dear, M. and Scott, A. J. (eds), 565–92.

Szelenyi, I. 1981b: Structural changes of and alternatives to capitalist development in the contemporary urban and regional system. *International Journal of Urban and Regional Research* **5**, 1, 1–14.

Szelenyi, I. 1982: Inequalities and social policy under state socialism. *International Journal of Urban and Regional Research* **6**, 1, 121–7.

Taaffe, E. J. 1979: Geography of the sixties in the Chicago area. *Annals, Association of American Geographers* **69**, 133–8.

Tabb, W. K. and Sawers, L. (eds) 1978: *Marxism and the metropolis. New perspectives in urban political economy* (Oxford University Press).

Tarn, J. N. 1966: The Peabody Donation Fund: the role of a housing society in the nineteenth century. *Victorian Studies* **10**, 1, 7–38.

Taubman, W. 1973: *Governing Soviet cities* (Praeger).

Taussig, M. K. 1973: *Alternative measures of the distribution of economic welfare* (Princeton University).

Tawney, R. H. 1952: *Equality* Revised edition (George Allen and Unwin).

Taylor, M. J. and Thrift, N. J. 1981: Spatial variations in Australian enterprise: the case of large firms headquartered in Melbourne and Sydney. *Environment and Planning A* **13**, 137–46.

Taylor, P. J. 1979: 'Difficult-to-let', 'difficult-to-live-in', and sometimes 'difficult-to-get-out-of': an essay on the provision of council housing with special reference to Killingworth. *Environment and Planning. A* **11**, 1305–20.

Taylor, S. 1981: De-industrialisation and unemployment in the West Midlands. In Crick, B. (ed.), 64–73.

Teitelbaum, F. 1982: The relative responsiveness of state and federal aid to distressed cities. *Policy Studies Review* **2**, 1, 309–21.

Thomas, B. 1972: *Migration and urban development; a reappraisal of British and American long cycles* (Methuen).

Thompson, E. P. 1968: *The making of the English working class* Revised edn (Penguin).

Thompson, E. P. 1978: *The poverty of theory and other essays* (Merlin Press).

Thompson, F. M. L. 1963: *English landed society in the nineteenth century* (Routledge and Kegan Paul).

Thompson, F. M. L. 1981: Social control in Victorian Britain. *Economic History Review* **34**, 2, 189–208.

Thompson, R. 1974: Containing the city. *Architectural Design* **49**, 3, 150–3.

Thurow, L. C. 1980: *The zero-sum society. Distribution and the possibilities for economic change* (Basic Books).

Tiebout, C. M. 1956: A pure theory of local expenditure. *Journal of Political Economy* **64**, 5, 416–24.

Timms, D. W. G. 1971: *The urban mosaic: towards a theory of residential differentiation* (Cambridge University Press).

Titmuss, R. M. 1958: *Essays on 'The welfare state'* (George Allen and Unwin).

Titmuss, R. M. 1962: *Income distribution and social change: a study in criticism* (George Allen and Unwin).

Titmuss, R. M. 1976: *Commitment to welfare* Second edition (George Allen and Unwin).

Tobin, G. A. (ed.) 1979: *The changing structure of the city. What happened to the urban crisis.* Urban Affairs Annual Reviews, 16.

Tomer, J. 1980: The mounting evidence on mortgage redlining *Urban Affairs Quarterly* **15**, 4, 488–501.

Touraine, A. 1971: *The post-industrial society* (Random House).

Townsend, A. R. 1982: Recession and the regions in Great Britain, 1976–1980: analyses of redundancy data. *Environment and Planning* A **14**, 10, 1389–1404.

Townsend, P. 1973: Everyone his own home – inequality in housing and the creation of a national service. *Royal Institute of British Architects Journal* **80**, 1, 30–42.

Townsend, P. 1979: *Poverty in the United Kingdom. A survey of household resources and standards of living* (Allen Lane).

Townsend, P. 1980: Social planning and the treasury. In Bosanquet, N. and Townsend, P. (eds), 3–23.

Troy, P. N. 1978: *A fair price. The land commission program 1972–1977* (Hale and Iremonger).

Troy, P. N. (ed.) 1967: *Urban redevelopment in Australia* (Urban Research Unit, Australian National University).

Troy, P. N. (ed.) 1978: *Federal power in Australia's cities* (Hale and Iremonger).

Troy, P. N. (ed.) 1981: *Equity in the city* (George Allen and Unwin).

UNCTAD, 1975: *International subcontracting arrangements in electronics between developed market-economy countries and developing countries* TD/B/C 2/144.

Urlich-Cloher, D. U. and Badcock, B. A. 1978: *Proceedings of RGS symposium on residential mix in Adelaide* (Royal Geographical Society of Australasia).

Urry, J. 1981: Localities, regions and social class. *International Journal of Urban and Regional Research* **5**, 4, 455–74.

US Advisory Commission on Intergovernmental Relations, 1978: *Intergovernmental Perspective* **4**, 1.

US Bureau of Census, 1975: *1972 Census of governments: local governments in metropolitan areas* (US Government Printing Office).

US Bureau of Census, 1978: *Statistical abstract of the United States* (US Government Printing Office).

US Congress, 1978: *Federal housing policy: current programs and recurring issues*. Background Paper (Congressional Budget Office).

US Office of Management and Budget, 1980: *Budget of the United States: fiscal year, 1981* (US Government Printing Office).

Van den Berg, A. 1980: Critical theory: is there still hope? *American Journal of Sociology* **86**, 3, 449–78.

Vaughan, R. J. 1980: The impact of federal policies on urban economic development. In Solomon, A. P. (ed.), 348–98.

Vinson, T. and Homel, R. 1976: *Indicators of community well-being* (Australian Government Publishing Service).

Vipond, J. 1980: The impact of higher unemployment on areas within Sydney. *Journal of Industrial Relations* **22**, 326–41.

Wagner, C. 1977: Sydney's Glebe project: an essay in urban rehabilitation. *Royal Australian Planning Institute Journal* **15**, 1, 2–24.

Waite, L. J. 1980: Working wives and the family life cycle. *American Journal of Sociology* **86**, 2, 272–294.

Walker, R. A. 1981: A theory of suburbanization: capitalism and the construction of urban space in the United States. In Dear, M. and Scott, A. J. (eds), 383–430.

Walker, R. A. and Heiman, M. K. 1981: Quiet revolution for whom? *Annals, Association of American Geographers* **71**, 1, 67–83.

Walker, S. 1979: Inequalities in education and educational services. *Australian Geographical Studies* **17**, 2, 175–92.

Walker, T. 1982: Peking revamping urban workforce. *Age*, 30 December, 6.

Wallace, I. 1978: Towards a humanized conception of economic geography. In Ley, D. and Samuels, M. S. (eds), 91–108.

Ward, D. 1964: A comparative historical geography of streetcar suburbs in Boston, Massachusetts and Leeds, England: 1850–1920. *Annals, Association of American Geographers* **54**, 477–89.

Ward, D. 1971: *Cities and immigrants* (Oxford University Press).

Ward, D. 1980: Environs and neighbours in the 'Two Nations': residential differentiation in mid-nineteenth century Leeds. *Journal of Historical Geography* **6**, 2, 133–62.

Warner, S. B. 1962: *Streetcar suburbs: the process of growth in Boston, 1870–1900* (MIT Press).

Warner, S. B. 1972: *The urban wilderness* (Harper and Row).

Wastell, R. J. 1980: Speculation in residential land: Adelaide, 1969–79. Unpublished BA Hons thesis, University of Adelaide.

Weber, A. F. 1899: *The growth of cities in the nineteenth century* (Macmillan).

Webster, D. 1980: Housing. In Bosanquet, N. and Townsend, P. (eds), 244–63.

Wedderburn, D. (ed.) 1974: *Poverty, inequality and class structure* (Cambridge University Press).

Wertheim, W. F. 1977: The integration of town and countryside in China. In Jeffrey, N. and Caldwell, M. (eds), 163–70.

Wheare, K. C. 1968: *Federal government*, 4th edn (Oxford University Press).

Wheaton, W. C. 1977: Income and urban residence: an analysis of consumer demand for location. *American Economic Review* **67**, 620–31.

Wheaton, W. C. 1979: Monocentric models of urban land use: contributions and criticisms. In Mieszkowski, P. and Straszheim, M. (eds), 107–129.

White, G. 1982: Urban employment and labour allocation policies in post-Mao China. *World Development* **10**, 8, 613–32.

Whitehead, C. 1980: Fiscal aspects of housing. In Sandford, C., *et al.*, (eds), 84–114.

Wilcox, D. with Richards, D. 1977: *London. The heartless city* (Thames).

Wildavsky, A. 1979: *Speaking truth to power. The art and craft of policy analysis* (Little Brown and Co.).

Wilenski, P. 1980: Reform and its implementation: the Whitlam years in retrospect. In Evans, G. and Reeves, J. (eds), 40–63.

Williams, M. 1982: White Liverpool loses patience. *New Society* **61**, 1032, 333–6.

Williams, P. R. 1976: The role of institutions in the inner London housing market: the case of Islington. *Institute of British Geographers, Transactions* NS **1**, 1, 72–81.

Williams, P. R. 1978: Building societies and the inner city. *Institute of British Geographers, Transactions* NS **3**, 1, 23–34.

Williams, P. R. 1982: Restructuring urban managerialism: towards a political economy of urban allocation. *Environment and Planning* A **14**, 95–105.

Williamson, J. G. 1980: Earnings inequality in nineteenth-century Britain. *Journal of Economic History* **40**, 3, 457–175.

Williamson, W. and Byrne, D. S. 1979: Educational disadvantage in an urban setting. In Herbert, D. T. and Smith, D. M. (eds), 186–200.

Wilsher, P. and Righter, R. 1975: *The exploding cities* (Quadrangle).

Wilson, D. 1981: State makes loss on land. *Age* 16 November, 5.

Wilson, J. Q. 1967: *Urban renewal: the record and the controversy* (MIT Press).

Wilson, M. 1982: Developers' damages on Woolloomooloo plan: Govt and city face $50m claims. *Sydney Morning Herald,* 13 May, 1.

Windshuttle, K. 1979: *Unemployment. A social and political analysis of the economic crisis in Australia* (Penguin).

Wingo, L. 1961: *Transportation and urban land* (Resources for the Future).

Wohl, A. S. 1977: *The eternal slum* (Edward Arnold).

Wolch, J. R. and Gabriel, S. A. 1981: Local land-development policies and urban housing values. *Environment and Planning* A **13**, 1253–76.

Wolfe, A. 1977: *The limits of legitimacy: political contradictions of contemporary capitalism* (Free Press).

Women's Bureau, 1981: *Facts on women at work in Australia 1980* Department of Employment and Youth Affairs (Australian Government Publishing Service).

Wright, D. 1978: *Understanding intergovernmental relations* (Duxbury Press).

Wynhausen, E. 1982: Bedlam on Wall Street. *National Times* 29 August–4 September, 12.

Yanowitch, M. 1977: *Social and economic inequality in the Soviet Union. Six studies* (Martin Robertson).

Yeates, M. 1972: The congruence between housing space, social space, and community space, and some experiments concerning its implications. *Environment and Planning* **4**, 395–414.

Yelling, J. A. 1981: The selection of sites for slum clearance in London, 1875–1888. *Journal of Historical Geography* **7**, 2, 155–65.

Young, E. 1981: Socio-economic changes and the 'downzoning' of residential areas in the inner suburbs of Adelaide, 1966–76. Unpublished BA Hons thesis University of Adelaide.

Young, K. 1980: Implementing an urban strategy: the case of public housing in metropolitan London. In Ashford, D. (ed.), 239–63.

Young, K. and Kramer, J. 1978: *Strategy and conflict in metropolitan housing. Suburbia versus the Greater London Council, 1965–75* (Heinemann).

Young, M. 1958: *The rise of the meritocracy 1870–2033. An essay on education and equality* (Thames and Hudson).

Young, M. and Willmott, P. 1975: *The symmetrical family. A study of work and leisure in the London region* (Penguin).

Zweig, F. 1961: *The worker in an affluent society* (Heinemann).

Zweig, F. 1976: *The new acquisitive society* (Barry Rose Publications).

Index